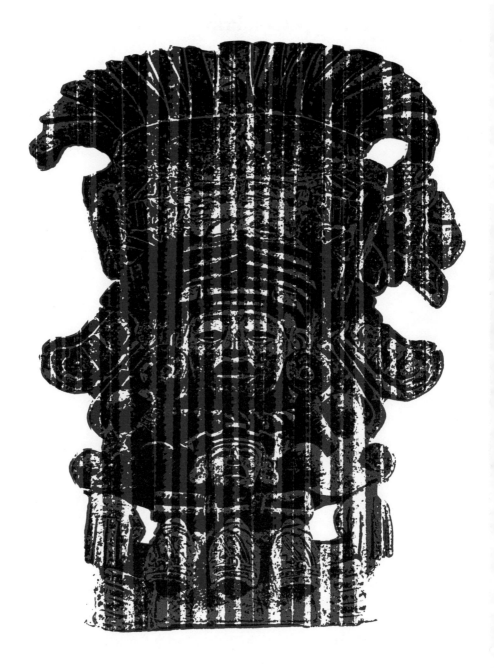

The Zapotecs: Princes, Priests, and Peasants

THE CIVILIZATION OF THE AMERICAN INDIAN SERIES

THE
ZAPOTECS
PRINCES,
PRIESTS,
and PEASANTS

By Joseph W. Whitecotton

UNIVERSITY OF OKLAHOMA PRESS : NORMAN

Library of Congress Cataloging in Publication Data

Whitecotton, Joseph W   1937–
    The Zapotecs.

    Bibliography: p.
    Includes index.
    1. Zapotec Indians. I. Title.
F1221.Z3W48   970'.004'97   76–62508
ISBN 0–8061–1374–X

To Gordon and Lisa

Preface

THIS BOOK traces the social and cultural history of an indigenous New World people who have continuously inhabited the state of Oaxaca in southern Mexico from 1500 B.C. until the present. The Zapotec-speaking inhabitants of this state cover a considerable percentage of its area, occupy diverse habitats, and have somewhat different histories. The Valley Zapotecs, who occupy the fertile basin in the center of the state, who are the best known of the various Zapotecs, and who are associated with the core region of Oaxacan history, are the primary subject of this account. The Northern Zapotecs, the Southern Zapotecs, and the Isthmus Zapotecs also are discussed, primarily for purposes of comparison, although limitations of space and knowledge have by necessity relegated them to a secondary role here.

While this book traces the history of a specific people and culture, it is also an anthropological history, a term I have borrowed from Robert T. Anderson. Anthropological history, in my conception of it, attempts to integrate the divers anthropological subdisciplines of archeology, linguistics, ethnohistory, ethnology, and social anthropology. It also seeks to explore the common ground between the particular history of a specific culture and those processes which cut across a broader spectrum of human societies and cultures.

Thus, this book reflects not only my concern with the Zapotecs, but also my concern with anthropology, both of which began in 1957. Since that year, although I have continued to study the Zapotecs, I also have done research on the Spanish-Americans of New Mexico and on the peoples and cultures of Italy. The themes explored in this book also reflect the cross-cultural anthropological interests which I have developed in my study of these other two cultures: the rise and nature of state societies, the nature of peasant societies, and the meaning and context of ethnicity in complex societies. In discussing these topics, I have attempted to present anthropological concepts in a language removed from the technical, and frequently unnecessary, jargon which pervades the monographs and journals written by and directed to professional anthropologists. The only exception is the Appendix; it is intended primarily for the specialist.

In 1957 there were but a handful of scholars interested in the Zapotecs. Since 1965 there has been a tremendous growth of scholarly activity. Knowledge and publications have accumulated so rapidly that it is difficult for one person to cope with this expanding field, with publications pouring off the press at a remarkable rate and many others projected or in progress as well.

The research on which this book is based was completed in January 1974 and the manuscript on which it is based was submitted in June of that year. Therefore, I have used only those materials which were available at that time. Some of the unpublished manuscripts cited in the notes have now appeared in print.

In the course of my study of the Zapotecs I have incurred many obligations. My longest standing debt is to John Paddock, now Director of the Institute of Oaxaca Studies, whose knowledge of Oaxacan anthropology is unsurpassed. He not only expanded my already budding interest in Oaxaca during my student days at Mexico City College in 1959–60, but also has served as a source of inspiration for me since then. A remarkable scholar, Paddock has almost single-handedly managed to cultivate a whole generation of Oaxacan anthropologists; much of what is now known about Oaxaca is the fruit of his efforts. Through the years he has graciously answered my many inquiries and has helped me keep informed of recent developments. My debt to him is great indeed.

I also must acknowledge Julian H. Steward and Oscar Lewis, both now deceased, who directed my graduate program at the University of Illinois and who contributed significantly to many of the ideas contained in this book. In 1968 Julian Steward supervised my doctoral dissertation, "The Valley of Oaxaca at Spanish Contact," and presented me with visions of anthropology as a cross-cultural science freed from the burden of a particularistic descriptive tradition which treated all cultures as unique entities. His *Theory of Culture Change* stands as a seminal work of anthropological theory.

Oscar Lewis taught me mostly about peasants. His books on peasants and city dwellers (*Life in A Mexican Village, Pedro Martínez, Five Families, The Children of Sánchez,* and *La Vida*) have forever changed anthropological conceptions of poverty.

Joseph Casagrande, Demitri Shimkin, Douglas Butterworth, and Carl Deal of the University of Illinois and J. Ignacio Rubio Mañé of the Archivo General de la Nación, Mexico, were also most helpful to me during an earlier period of research on Oaxaca. Funds from the Department of Anthropology at the University of Illinois and from the Faculty Research Program at Lawrence University in Appleton, Wisconsin, permitted me to pursue research in Mexico.

Many individuals have been most helpful to me during the time that this book has been in preparation. Ralph L. Beals, Ignacio Bernal, Richard E. Blanton, Beverly Chiñas, Scott Cook, Martin Diskin, Theodore E. Downing, Kent V. Flannery, James A. Neely, Carl W. O'Nell, Arthur J. Rubel, Henry Selby, and Ronald Waterbury responded to specific inquiries and provided useful information on their own work in Oaxaca. Richard E. Blanton, John K. Chance, Beverly Chiñas, Scott Cook, Philip Dennis, Theodore E. Downing, Carl O'Nell, and John Paddock generously shared with me their unpublished manuscripts.

Richard E. Blanton, Kent V. Flannery, Ronald Spores, and Charles R. Wicke read portions of various versions of the manuscript and made helpful suggestions for improvement. Jimmy C. Diecker, my advanced graduate student at the University of Oklahoma, spent months reading various versions of the complete manuscript and saved me from many errors of fact and interpretation; this work has been improved because of his tireless efforts on my behalf. It is with eager anticipation that I await the results of his own work on a village in New Mexico which should prove to be the most thorough study of a Spanish-American community to date.

Several individuals helped in the preparation of the illustrations. Terry Prewitt drew all of the maps and some additional drawings; Sarah Whitecotton and Carol Smith also contributed some drawings; Kay Parker, Ronald Spores, Bruce Bylan, and Beverly Chiñas kindly permitted me to use some of their photographs. The Peabody Museum of Harvard University and the Department of Anthropology of the National Museum of Natural History, Smithsonian Institution, Washington, D.C., provided me with photographs of Zapotec ceramic sculptures. The specific contributions of these individuals and institutions are acknowledged in the captions to the plates and figures. All other photographs are my own.

Robert Fields, Jr., and Roberta Pailes contributed their expertise in photographic processing to many a difficult problem. Carolyn Emery typed and retyped the final manuscript and coped successfully with my incessant deletions, additions, and last-minute changes.

The University of Oklahoma granted me a sabbatical leave of absence from my duties in the Department of Anthropology during the spring semester of 1974. Without this released time it is doubtful that I could have finished this book.

Of course, none of the above individuals or institutions necessarily endorse, are responsible for, or agree with the final outcome; I alone assume this responsibility.

JOSEPH W. WHITECOTTON
Norman, Oklahoma

Contents

Illustrations

Maps

Tables

The Zapotecs: Princes, Priests, and Peasants

1
Oaxaca and the Zapotecs

THE INDIGENOUS PEOPLES of Oaxaca, a state in southern Mexico some two hundred kilometers below the sprawling metropolis of Mexico City, have contributed significantly to Mexican and New World history. In pre-Spanish times Oaxaca was the locale of the distinctive Zapotec and Mixtec cultures, equal in complexity to the better-known Aztecs and Mayas. As in central Mexico and Yucatan-Guatemala, complex state societies have long been part of the Oaxacan scene. In fact, archeological evidence indicates that Oaxaca had one of the earliest fully developed civilizations. The site of Monte Albán, metropolis of the Zapotecs, was the cultural rival of other great Meso-american centers of the Classic stage (ca. A.D. 100–900), and exerted influences throughout southern Mexico. Teotihuacán in the Valley of Mexico, Cholula in the state of Puebla, and the Classic Maya sites of Tikal, Uaxactún, Copán, and Palenque are no more significant in the history of complex society than is Zapotec Monte Albán in the state of Oaxaca.

The post-Classic stage (ca. A.D. 900–1519), to which the Toltec and Aztec cultures of central Mexico belong, also is well represented in Oaxaca. Among the most important post-Classic peoples were the Oaxacan Mixtecs, who influenced developments throughout Meso-america. The Mixtecs not only were innovators but also in part were responsible for preserving the values of the "civilized" Classic tradi-tion. By influencing the essentially "barbarian" Toltec and Aztec groups of central Mexico, they preserved the Classic heritage in much the same way that the Etruscans and Greeks represented the "civi-lized" traditions of the Mediterranean Basin to the upstart Romans.

After the Spanish conquest of Oaxaca in 1521, part of the state was included in the vast estates of Hernán Cortés, the conqueror of Mexico. Cortés apparently chose this region because of its dense population and potential wealth. A thriving but short-lived silk industry developed in the state during the sixteenth century. During the seventeenth and eighteenth centuries and part of the nineteenth, Oaxaca was the major producer of cochineal, used for the production of a dye that was the rage of Europe. Oaxaca also was a province of the Dominican friars, who, accompanying the Spanish colonists and conquistadors, brought with them a religious fervor dedicated to eradicating "idolatry" and "barbarism" among the Indians; they concentrated early on the peoples of Oaxaca.

While the conquest of Oaxaca was relatively peaceful in comparison with the conquest of central Mexico, the Zapotecs and Mixtecs ultimately were stripped of their native elites, their priesthoods, and their religious and political traditions; this process was slower than that in central Mexico and differed from it in details, but eventually most of the Zapotecs and Mixtecs also were reduced to a subject peasantry concentrated in rural communities, where they served as a repository of labor, goods, and souls for the crown, the nobility, and the clergy.

During the later periods of Spanish control, and increasingly during the nineteenth century, Mexico became a classic land of haciendas, extensive estates designed to support a new nobility based on the exploitation of the peasant, who became a debt peon. Especially in the northern, central, and western states, Indian peasants lost control of their communities and most—or all—of their land. Oaxaca, however, generally remained oriented to intensive peasant agriculture, and, while there were some agrarian reformers (*agraristas*) there also, the Mexican Revolution, which was intended to break up the large landed estates, had less effect in Oaxaca than elsewhere. As a result, Oaxaca has remained an area composed of a large Indian peasantry concentrated in medium-sized towns and villages, somewhat isolated from the larger political society, and generally conservative. Thus, it is still one of the most "Indian" states in Mexico, comparable in this regard to its neighboring state of Chiapas.

But, although Oaxaca was a politically and economically marginal area of Mexico after the country became independent, it contributed two major political figures to Mexican history. The first, Benito Juárez, was born of Zapotec parents in a remote village and emerged from this humble beginning to become president of Mexico in the 1850's. Imbued with the liberal spirit of the Enlightenment, he fought

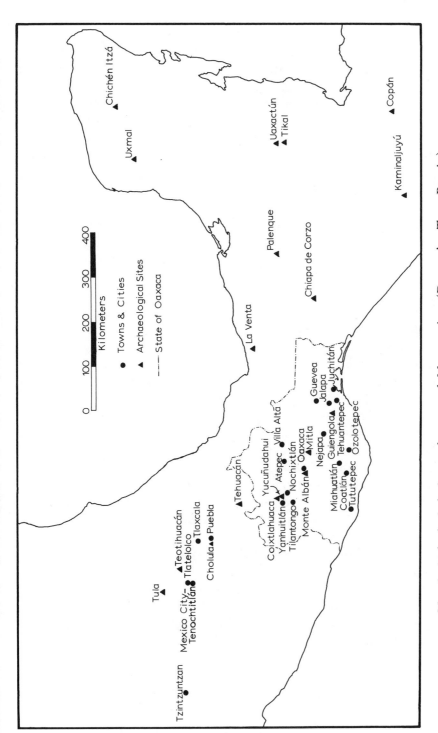

Map 1. Archeological sites and towns of Mesoamerica. (Drawn by Terry Prewitt)

for constitutional government, attacked the privileges of the Church and the army, and opposed the restoration of a monarchy under the French-imposed Maximilian. After many years of struggle, he finally overthrew the conservatives, and Mexico was invigorated with a new program, called La Reforma, which was a series of laws designed to transfer political powers from an exclusive elite to a democratic republic of Mexican citizens.

A second Oaxacan, who claimed to be part Mixtec, helped destroy Juárez' plans. He was Porfirio Díaz, who learned his caudillo politics in the chaotic Isthmus of Tehuantepec; he became president of Mexico in 1876 and ruled until 1910. Díaz had supported Juárez and the liberals in the War of the Reform (1858–61), but he shortly turned to different policies. During his regime he surrounded himself with an exclusive elite of intellectuals and large landowners and promoted coercive political oppression. While Mexico prospered under Díaz as a land of favored elites, as a land of the poor and oppressed it had no equal. Díaz ultimately was overthrown in the bloody Mexican Revolution that began in 1910.

Juárez and Díaz, then, were "Indians" who became presidents of their country. However, the term *Indian* in Mexican society has connotations quite different from those it has in North American society. Except in a few atypical areas, reservations were not significant in Mexican history. Tribal affiliation in North America, as denoted by tribal rolls and tribal councils, has no parallel in the core areas of Mexico; in those areas *Indian* is a generic term which has applied, since colonial times, primarily to social status, sometimes to use of an indigenous language, but seldom to physical characteristics.[1]

During Spanish colonial times, Indians were defined primarily with reference to a peasant community, often called the *república de los indios*. As such, they became part of the Spanish estate system, which had long distinguished between nobles, clergymen, and peasants. While race was important in the official rhetoric of Spanish colonial society, it tended to be more a social and cultural than a biological phenomenon. For example, Indians who had been nobles in pre-Conquest times remained so under the Spanish system once they accepted Christianity, and they became rapidly acculturated to Spanish life-styles. If an individual could acquire the wealth, contacts, and cultural traits necessary to occupy a different position in the social order, admittedly difficult in the rigid Spanish system, he could acquire a document to make his biological origin coincide with his new social position.

Thus, to be Indian was, and has continued to be, largely a social and cultural phenomenon, synonomous with peasant and with the particular relationship to land and community which that term implies. Contemporary Mexican society, like the Spanish colonial society which preceded it, still places great emphasis on the "gentleman complex." Individuals who work the land for subsistence, who work with their hands and who display primary allegiance to their small community, are low in the social order. For example, it is reported that rural inhabitants who live very near the modern city of Guadalajara, who speak only Spanish, and who clearly are of mixed origin are referred to as Indians; they reside in a tightly knit community and practice subsistence agriculture and pottery making.[2]

In a sense, then, this appellation is largely derogatory; to be called *muy indio* in Mexican Spanish implies that one is deferent, is probably illiterate, and displays little knowledge of the world outside his small community. And, while the revolutionary intellectuals of the twentieth century have aimed their programs toward incorporating the Indian into the mainstream of Mexican society, they have worshiped primarily at the shrine of the great Indian tradition of pre-Spanish times. The modern Indian, with his little tradition and peasant heritage, has been incorporated only slowly into the mainstream of Mexican society.

Patterns of dress and behavior likewise have been used to identify an Indian in modern Mexico. In certain regions, such as Oaxaca, specific communities display distinctive clothing styles, behavioral characteristics, and craft specializations. These traits often are thought to be typical of particular Indian groups. However, they tend to be most typical of communities or regions, not of any particular group or linguistic affiliation. Also, since local populations have been subject to various acculturative influences throughout history, these cultures represent complex fusions of pre-Spanish, Spanish colonial, and modern Mexican cultural traits—a fusion which almost always defies separation into constituent elements.

Another criterion for defining an Indian in modern Mexico is the retention of an indigenous language. Indigenous languages still are spoken by a sizable percentage of the Mexican population. Although bilingualism is widespread, children in many parts of rural Mexico still continue to learn an Indian language before Spanish. While Spanish is used everywhere as the official language of Mexico, in many areas an indigenous tongue remains the language of the home and of the pueblo.

Table 1. States in the Republic of Mexico with the
Largest Numbers of Speakers of Indigenous Languages.*

	State	Indian Speakers	Monolingual
		1950	
1.	*Oaxaca*	586,853	212,520
2.	Puebla	297,490	118,971
3.	Yucatán	279,380	43,523
4.	Veracruz	252,739	87,318
5.	Chiapas	198,087	104,244
6.	México	183,051	39,207
7.	Hidalgo	179,629	60,401
8.	Guerrero	124,693	59,241
9.	San Luis Potosí	89,096	28,972
10.	Michoacán	51,273	12,106
11.	Campeche	32,816	5,351
12.	Sonora	25,058	1,892
		1970	
1.	*Oaxaca*	677,347	206,323
2.	Veracruz	360,309	89,623
3.	Yucatán	357,270	56,570
4.	Puebla	346,140	94,194
5.	Chiapas	287,836	147,720
6.	Hidalgo	201,368	77,868
7.	México	200,729	20,683
8.	Guerrero	160,182	85,091
9.	San Luis Potosí	113,898	25,953
10.	Distrito Federal†	68,660	1,447
11.	Michoacán	62,851	12,326
12.	Campeche	55,031	5,920

* Citation in Chapter 1, Note 7.
† Distrito Federal in 1950 had 18,812 speakers of indigenous languages with only 170 monolinguals.

Table 2. Speakers of Indigenous Languages in the State of Oaxaca (1970).*

	Total			Bilingual (with Spanish)			Monolingual		
	Total	Male	Female	Total	Male	Female	Total	Male	Female
1. Amuzgo	1,973	1,029	944	1,255	700	555	718	329	389
2. Chatino	11,608	5,672	5,936	5,958	3,321	2,637	5,650	2,351	3,299
3. Chinantec	52,313	25,985	26,328	38,605	21,115	17,488	13,710	4,870	8,840
4. Cuicatec	9,695	4,825	4,870	8,526	4,458	4,068	1,169	367	802
5. Huave	7,250	3,690	3,560	4,509	2,575	1,934	2,741	1,115	1,626
6. Mazatec	93,376	45,508	47,868	41,437	23,995	17,442	51,939	21,513	30,426
7. Mixe	51,636	25,501	26,135	31,728	17,246	14,482	19,908	8,255	11,653
8. Mixtec	168,725	84,171	84,554	118,147	64,341	53,806	50,578	19,830	30,748
9. Popoloca	1,642	795	847	1,564	769	795	78	26	52
10. Zapotec	246,138	122,755	123,383	197,638	108,991	93,647	48,500	18,764	29,736
11. Zoque	5,352	2,646	2,706	4,390	2,190	2,200	962	456	506

*Population 5 years or older; Ixcatec, Chocho and Trique are not included   monolingual, are unspecified as to language in the census. Source in Chapter 1,
in the census. Some 10,268 speakers of Indian languages, of whom 6,756 were   note 7.

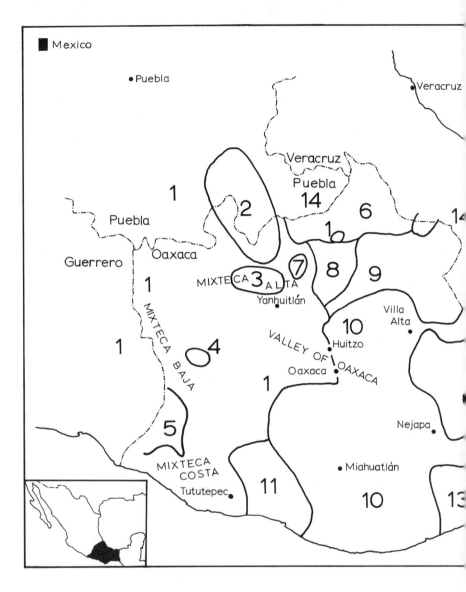

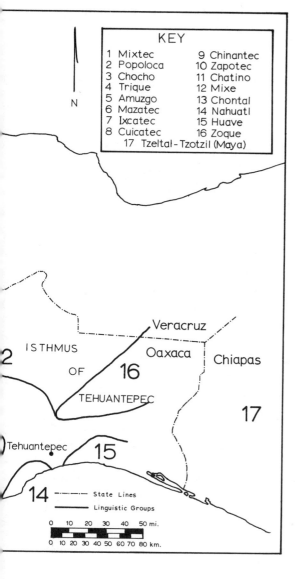

KEY
1 Mixtec   9 Chinantec
2 Popoloca   10 Zapotec
3 Chocho   11 Chatino
4 Trique   12 Mixe
5 Amuzgo   13 Chontal
6 Mazatec   14 Nahuatl
7 Ixcatec   15 Huave
8 Cuicatec   16 Zoque
        17 Tzeltal-Tzotzil (Maya)

N

Veracruz

ISTHMUS   Oaxaca   Chiapas

OF   16

TEHUANTEPEC

17

Tehuantepec   15

14   ———— State Lines
        ———— Linguistic Groups

0   10   20   30   40   50 mi.
0 10 20 30 40 50 60 70 80 km.

Map 2. Regions and Linguistic groups of southern Mexico. (Drawn by Terry Prewitt)

In 1970 Oaxaca had a total population of 2,015,424; approximately 34 per cent—677,347—spoke at least one indigenous language, the highest number in any state in Mexico. Of these indigenous language speakers, 206,323 were monolingual, 246,138 (approximately 36 per cent) spoke Zapotec, and 168,725 (approximately 25 per cent) spoke Mixtec. There were 50,578 monolingual Mixtec speakers and 48,500 monolingual Zapotec speakers.[3]

Zapotec and Mixtec are related languages and belong within a larger grouping called Otomanguean, a phylum which includes five branches: Otomian, Mixtecan, Chinantecan, Manguean, and Zapotecan.[4] The Otomian branch includes such languages as Otomí, Mazahua, Matlatzinca, Pame, and Ocuilteca, all of which are spoken in the states of Mexico and Hidalgo. The Mixtecan branch contains Mixtec, Popoloca, Ixcatec, Chocho, Mazatec, Trique, Cuicatec, and Amuzgo. Mixtec is spoken in the highland region of western Oaxaca called the Mixteca Alta, in a lowland region bordering on the states of Puebla and Guerrero called the Mixteca Baja, and in the coastal region in the southwestern part of the state called the Mixteca Costa. This distribution corresponds closely to known Mixtec distribution in pre-Spanish and Colonial times, except that Mixtec-speaking elites were distributed throughout a wide area of southern Mexico.

Popoloca is spoken in the southwestern part of the state of Puebla as well as a portion of the northwestern part of Oaxaca. Ixcatec and Chocho speakers exist as enclaves in the Mixtec-speaking territory of the Mixteca Alta, while Trique speakers, located in the states of Guerrero and Oaxaca, are surrounded by Mixtecs of the Mixteca Baja and Costa. Mazatec speakers occupy the extreme northwest section of Oaxaca, while the Cuicatec speakers border them on the south. Chinantec, the sole language within the Chinantecan branch, is spoken to the east of Cuicatec.

Within the Mixtecan branch, Popoloca, Ixcatec, and Chocho form one family, Mazatec and Amuzgo form second and third families, and Mixtec, Trique, and Cuicatec make up a fourth.

Manguean consists of Chiapanec and Mangue, languages spoken in Central America. Zapotecan includes the Zapotec languages as well as Chatino, which is spoken in a southwestern part of the state of Oaxaca bordering on the Pacific Ocean.[5]

While linguists differ over the details of the exact placement of these languages within a larger classification, their studies do show that the Otomanguean languages have links with other languages in Mesoamerica and belong to a very ancient stratum of Mesoamerican languages. Based on studies of the distribution of these languages, their internal and external relationships, and on glottochronological calculations, it has been posited that from 7000 to 5000 B.C. Mesoamerica consisted of an uninterrupted belt of related dialects. By about 4000 B.C. the Mesoamerican languages had begun to differentiate into Otomanguean, a more northerly Uto-Aztecan (which includes languages spoken in northern Mexico and the southwestern United States as well as Nahuatl—the language of the Aztecs), and Mayan to the south. Between 4000 and 1500 B.C., because of migrations and the isolation of various groups, the Otomanguean languages began to diverge from one another. The Manguean languages probably split off first, followed by the Otomian languages. The divergence between Mixtecan and Zapotecan probably occurred next;[6] many scholars have posited that it occurred somewhere in the region of northwestern Oaxaca or southwestern Puebla. The Zapotecs may not have reached their present locations in Oaxaca before 1500 B.C.[7]

The Zapotec or Zapotecan languages, like the Otomian and Mixtecan languages of Otomanguean, are tone languages. In Zapotec, the meaning of a word frequently is determined by voice pitch. These tones, as in the Chinese languages, are absolutely essential to distinguish among certain words and thus are technically called tonemes. The Zapotecan languages differ, however, in the number of tonemes they employ: in some there are four tones—high, low, rising, and falling; and others have but three tones—high, low, and rising.[8]

Generally, Zapotecan has a staccato and musical character, very liquid and sonorous, features which prompted the French traveler Brasseur de Bourbourg to characterize Zapotec as the Italian of the Americas. The utilization of tones and the presence of long and short, nasalized, and rearticulated vowel sounds, along with a soft, liquid r and a frequently used glottal stop, undoubtedly influenced this depiction. Zapotec also contains a series of contrasting pairs of strong and weak (fortis and lenis) consonants.

Syntactically, Zapotecan has a number of interesting features. Verbs are modified by the addition of prefixes and suffixes which become fused with the verb stem to indicate voice (passive or active), tense (present, past, or future), and mood (indicative, imperative, or conditional). Tense in Zapotec displays very fine shades of meaning between actions that were completed in the past, actions that are occurring or have occurred regardless of present or past, and actions that will occur. In addition, two special tenses are used for customs or conditions which are neither past nor present and for those indefinite actions which do not refer to specific persons or actions in either the past, present, or future.

Adjectives are of the verb type and in general follow the same conjugations as the verbs. Nouns and pronouns are changed depending on the person speaking; whether the object is human, animal, inanimate, or sacred; and the specific relationship (such as intimate or distant, inclusive or exclusive) to the person, animal, or object addressed or referred to. While most languages employ juxtaposition in some form, Zapotec differs from many in that elements are combined in various positions without modification.

While Zapotec has received many loan words from Spanish, structurally it has remained quite conservative. In the other direction, Zapotec has had an important influence on the Spanish of the region, especially on pitch, tense structure, and the use of plurals. Oaxacan Spanish in particular tends to have a "sing-song" quality, to exhibit a modified Spanish tense structure, and to drop plurals as endings on nouns. Nouns in Zapotec do not have different singular or plural endings; number is indicated by the preceding word or prefix.[9]

Zapotec never has been written to any great extent, although popular songs and poems often are composed in Zapotec. There is a group of scholars and intellectuals in Oaxaca who pride themselves on their knowledge of the subtleties of Zapotec; some from Juchitán in the Isthmus of Tehuantepec have become nationally famous for their poetry.[10]

Although Zapotec is a viable language, it remains primarily a situational language spoken mostly in the home and the village. But Spanish also is used in every village, and also as the language of discourse among those from different villages or regions, as the *lingua franca* of trade, and as the official language of the Mexican Republic. As a result, Zapotec has tended to fragment into linguistic entities which do not necessarily correspond with cultural entities. For example, Laura Nader has pointed out that most Zapotecs share more culturally with their non-Zapotec-speaking neighbors than they do with other Zapotecs.[11] To many Zapotec speakers, pueblo or regional affiliations are much more important than is the commonality of speaking Zapotec. In short, Zapotec is used in specific social contexts; speaking Zapotec, then, does not constitute an overriding or unidimensional attribute denoting a distinctive cultural pattern.

Today, also, although Zapotec may have been a single language in the remote past, one cannot speak of a single Zapotec language, but instead must speak of numerous Zapotec languages, as different from one another as are the various Romance languages. Some authors, for example, distinguish six Zapotec languages: Valley Zapotec (spoken in the Valley of Oaxaca), Isthmus or Tehuano Zapotec (spoken on the Isthmus of Tehuantepec), Serrano Zapotec (spoken in the district of Ixtlán in the Sierra de Juárez), Nexitzo or Rincón Zapotec (spoken in the Villa Alta district), Villalteco (from Yalálag in the Villa Alta district), and Southern or Miahuatlán Zapotec (spoken in the Sierra de Miahuatlán).[12] Others distinguish nine Zapotec languages, adding an additional language in the northern mountain district of Choapan (Bixanas) and dividing the southern unit into three distinct languages (Lachiregi, Yohueche, and Loxicha).[13] It also appears that of these various languages, the Northern Zapotec languages (Serrano, Nexitzo, Villalteco, and Bixanas) are more closely related to one another than to the Valley, Isthmus, and Southern languages, which form another group. Thus, the Zapotecs occupy a considerable proportion of the state of Oaxaca; the major groups also occupy distinct habitats, a factor partly explaining the cultural differences among them.

Oaxaca is primarily mountainous; the Mesa del Sur, the wide eastern section of the southern Mexican highlands, lies within its boundaries. Intermontane basins within this region, however, have constituted the major population centers. The largest of these, the Valley of Oaxaca, located almost in the center of the state, has been and continues to be one of the most densely inhabited regions of Mesoamerica. The Valley also has been the province of the Valley Zapotecs, the builders of Monte Albán, throughout pre-Spanish, Colonial, and modern times and has been the setting for major social and cultural developments in Oaxaca. While Mixtec and Aztec speakers have been present in the Valley, Zapotecs have always constituted the majority of the indigenous population there.

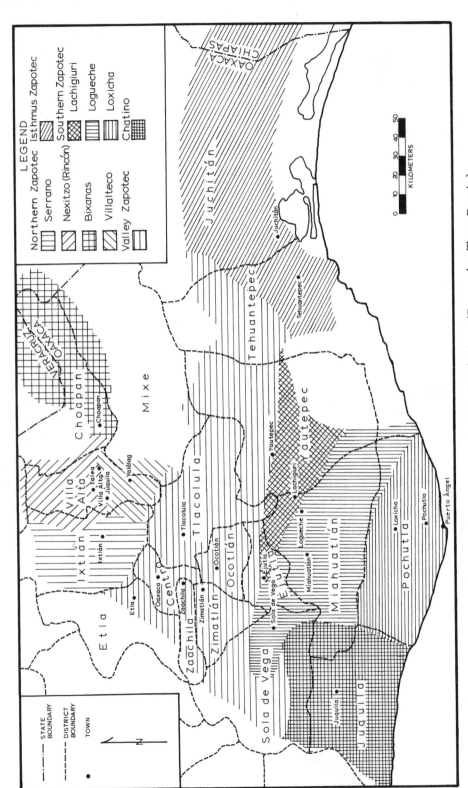

Map 3. The Zapotec languages and their distribution. (Drawn by Terry Prewitt)

An area of the Valley of Oaxaca, showing the contrast between the valley floor and the mountains.

A fertile basin, almost totally surrounded by mountains, the Valley of Oaxaca is some ninety-five kilometers long, twenty-five kilometers wide, and about fifteen hundred meters above sea level. Hydrographically, this intermontane cavity is the basin of the River Atoyac, which flows from north to south. The Atoyac has a tributary, the Río Salado or Tlacolula, which branches generally southeast from the Atoyac near the city of Oaxaca de Juárez, the capital of the state.

The Valley has the general shape of a Y and consists of three smaller basins, all of which converge at the city of Oaxaca. These three Valley arms are Etla (to the northwest), Tlacolula (to the southeast), and Zaachila-Zimatlán (to the south). Bounded on the north by the Sierra Madre Oriental and on the southeast by the mountains of Tlacolula, the southern boundary of this Zapotec region is less clearly defined, although the terminus is generally put near Ayoquesco.

Of all the Zapotec regions, the Valley of Oaxaca has the greatest agricultural potential and productivity, which explains why it was there that the Zapotecs achieved their highest level of cultural development and why that area has figured so prominently in the history of the state. There are a number of environmental aspects that help to account for the agricultural potential of the Valley and that explain why it is particularly suited for the cultivation of maize—that mainstay of the peasant Indian population of Mesoamerica since early pre-Spanish times.[14]

The Valley of Oaxaca has seven hundred square kilometers of relatively flat land—a larger area than is found anywhere in the Mexican highland region south of the Valley of Puebla. The higher valleys to the north of the Valley of Oaxaca, such as Tamazulalan, Yanhuitlán, and Nochixtlán in the Mixteca Alta, have been subject to and have suffered from extensive soil erosion. In these higher valleys, generally two thousand meters in elevation or higher, the vegetative cover was oak-pine forest, and its clearing has destroyed the soil. But in the Valley of Oaxaca, with its gentle slopes and scrub vegetation, land clearing has never appreciably increased erosion. The oak-pine forest zone surrounding the Valley has been rarely cleared for agriculture throughout its history.

Temperatures on the Valley floor also are well suited to the year-round growing of primitive maize. The Valley lies in a temperate zone and the mean annual temperature hovers at twenty degrees

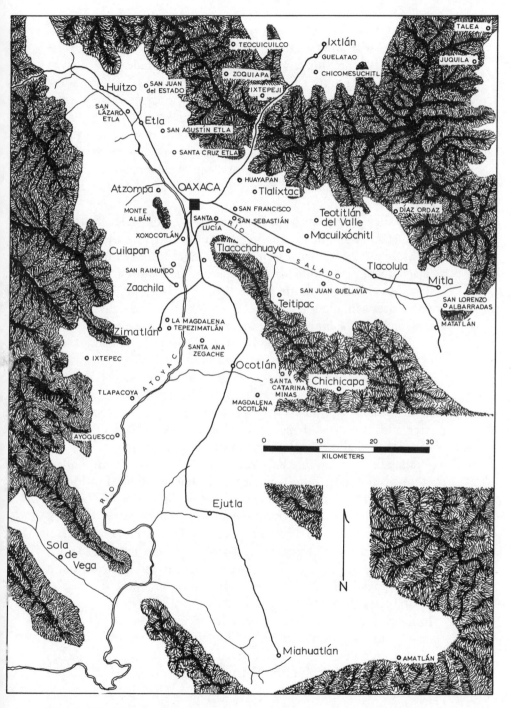

Map 4. The Valley of Oaxaca and its environs. (Drawn by Terry Prewitt)

Centigrade—the annual range is six degrees Centigrade, while the daily range is approximately fifteen degrees Centigrade. In any given year there is but a slight chance of frost, and in some areas, such as the main Atoyac floodplain south of the city of Oaxaca, frosts rarely occur.

At altitudes above two thousand meters, these conditions change markedly. Summer temperatures can drop so low that the cultivation of maize is inhibited. Frost-resistant strains of maize were developed in later periods of pre-Spanish history, but their absence in earliest times helps to explain the choice of the Valley as a key area for intensive cultivation.

The Valley is not uniform. Elevations vary from 1,420 meters to 1,740 meters. Rainfall (occurring predominantly in the summer months, while the winter season is dry) ranges from 490 millimeters at Tlacolula to 740 millimeters at Ocotlán in the southern wing of the Valley. Most Valley soils are of the Brown Soils group, but in drier areas, as near Mitla in the Valley of Tlacolula, they tend toward Gray Desert Soils. In the higher alluvium areas of the Valley, as in parts of the valley of Etla, are found the finest-grained soils with the greatest water retention, thus the most productive.

In other areas, the depth of the water table is more important than soil texture in determining agricultural productivity. Along the floodplain of the Atoyac, water is within three meters of the surface, but in higher alluvium areas it may be as deep as ten meters. Where the water table is shallow, well irrigation can be practiced.

Availability of water has been of crucial importance in the Valley, for the soils are low in humus and nutrient concentrations. In addition to rainfall and well irrigation, canal irrigation also is possible in some areas, as it is in Etla, where the River Atoyac makes a deep channel. In other areas the river channel is shallower and has flooded frequently in past times, depositing a layer of sand detrimental to agriculture on the bottomland. In some areas of the Valley, streams and rivers are mostly dry but become raging torrents, more destructive than useful, in the rainy season.

In those areas of the Valley where dry farming (*temporal*) can be coupled with small-scale irrigation, the cultivation of two or more annual crops is possible. However, canal irrigation on a large scale has been largely impractical in the Valley because springs are small and surface flows inadequate.

The habitat of the Valley Zapotecs can be distinguished clearly from those of their neighbors to the north, south, and southeast. The various Zapotecs who live to the north occupy an area of high mountains dissected by hundreds of small torrential streams, creating a land of precipitous slopes and sharp ridges. This cool mountain region varies greatly in its productive capacity and is characterized by wide diversity among locales. While the mountains have not barred contact between the Zapotecs of the Ixtlán and Villa Alta districts with the Valley Zapotecs (nor with their neighboring Mixe and Chinantec speakers), the Zapotecs of Choapan have sought more contacts with the peoples of Veracruz.

However, this highland region always has been historically somewhat peripheral to the Valley. In pre-Spanish times it displayed little of the cultural complexity of the Valley; in Colonial times it was an outpost secured only by creation of a Spanish settlement at San Ildefonso de Villa Alta after a bitter battle between the Spanish and the local inhabitants. It also was the scene of one of the most serious Indian rebellions in Oaxacan colonial history. It therefore is not surprising that the liberal Benito Juárez, who was to become one of Mexico's leading reformists, was born in the village of Guelatao in the sierra in the district of Ixtlán.

The Isthmus of Tehuantepec is another distinct geographical habitat of the Zapotecs. This flat, extensive region borders on the Pacific, and its Zapotec-speaking inhabitants are concentrated primarily in the Tehuantepec and Juchitán districts. The isthmus is also occupied by Huave, Chontal, and Mixe speakers and by Zoque speakers of the Mayan family of languages.

In this area of low, rolling plains with a humid tropical climate, the Zapotecs of the isthmus appear particularly proud and independent. Well known for their elaborate ceremonial dress, isthmus women have particularly been noted for their independence and worldly manner, characteristics that have prompted the myth that Isthmus Zapotec society is a "matriarchy." However, in a recent study of isthmus society, Beverly Chiñas has shown that this myth is exaggerated and otherwise incorrect.[15] Extensive trade is of particular importance in the economy of the Isthmus Zapotecs. Women are heavily involved in this trade, and this involvement partly explains their seemingly worldly and independent manner.

The isthmus is a region of marked geographical and historical contrasts. It contains jungles and arid brush, oases of green orchards and cornfields, and lagoons and port towns, and it has attracted oil magnates, canal and railway construction schemes, and sailors and itinerants from many parts of the world. All these were accompanied by a turbulent political history.[16]

The Southern Zapotecs (the Lachiregi, Yohueche, and Loxicha) have historically inhabited the Oaxacan districts of Ejutla, Sola de Vega, Miahuatlán, Pochutla, and Yautepec. This region includes the Sierra de Miahuatlán, a mountain system which runs almost parallel to the Pacific until it terminates at the Isthmus of Tehuantepec and contains high mountains (the highest point is El Cerro de Pluma, 2,120 meters above sea level) as well as a relatively fertile coastal plain along the Pacific. The Zapotecs today inhabit the highest parts of this mountain system, from Miahuatlán to the coastal area very near the towns of Pochutla and Puerto Ángel. These Southern Zapotecs probably have the smallest population of all the Zapotec groups; they are also the least known.[17]

2
The Growth of the Zapotec Great Tradition

MIXTECS AND ZAPOTECS have both called themselves the Cloud People—in Mixtec proper, *Ñusabi*; in Zapotec, *Ben 'Zaa*—indicating that the two have a common origin. *Mixtecatl*, the Nahuatl word used by the Aztecs to refer to the Mixtecs (from which their modern name was derived) also means Cloud People; *Tsapotecatl*, the Nahuatl word from which Zapotec was derived, may represent a phonetic instead of a semantic translation of the Zapotec. It means people of the *zapote*; the *zapote* is a tree found in abundance in the Zapotec area. However, the Zapotecs probably never referred to themselves by this term.[1]

There are a number of Mixtec and Zapotec origin legends. According to one, the Mixtecs descended from a divine couple, who themselves came from a tree. This legend seems to refer specifically to Mixtec-speaking overlords who conquered the non-Mixtec-speaking (but not necessarily non-Mixtecan) inhabitants of the Mixteca Alta, perhaps in the seventh century after Christ. Some accounts claim that the original inhabitants of the Mixteca Alta came from the earth and not from trees.[2]

Some Zapotec origin legends, which were first transcribed shortly after the Spanish Conquest, claim that the Zapotecs were the original inhabitants of the Valley of Oaxaca and were born from rocks or were the descendants of wild animals such as pumas and ocelots. Another legend places their origin to the north; it states that the Zapotecs settled in Oaxaca before the founding of the Toltec empire in central Mexico and that they came from Chicomostoc, or Seven Caves, which also was the legendary homeland of the Nahua tribes of the Valley of Mexico. Some post-Conquest Mixtec legends also attribute their origins to the Seven Caves. These later legends probably are the result of Aztec influence on Mixtecs and Zapotecs in later pre-Spanish times.[3]

Guide	VALLEY OF OAXACA				
	STAGES	Monte Albán	Zaachila-Etla Regions	Eastern	Ethnohistorical Periods and Groups
1521		Ⅴ	HUITZO ZAACHILA YAGUL MITLA TOMB TOMBS TOMB30 MURALS (contents)		Aztecs–Mixtecs–Zapotecs
1350	Postclassic				Mixtecs & Zapotecs CUILAPAN & TEHUANTEPEC HEGEMONIES
		Ⅳ		YAGUL PALACES MITLA PALACES	Zapotec Princedoms ZAACHILA HEGEMONY–TETLAMIXTECA (?)
1100					Zapotec Princedoms
900				LAMBITYECO	MITLA THEOCRACY–ZAACHILA HEGEMONY
750	Classic	ⅢB			"Classic" Zapotecs –
650		TRANSITION ⅢA-ⅢB			
		ⅢA		MITLA SOUTH GROUP	Monte Albán Empire
200		TRANSITION Ⅱ-ⅢA			
AD	Terminal (PROTOCLASSIC)	Ⅱ		DAINZÚ CABALLITO BLANCO	Zapotec Regional Centers & States
BC 100				YAGUL	
	Late	I	C B A		
400					
500	Middle			Rosario	
	Formative	Unoccupied		Guadalupe	Zapotecs
850				San José	
1150	Early				
				Tierras Largas	
1450					
	Archaic			MITLA CAVES	Oaxacan Branch of Otomanguean
8000					

Most authorities agree, however, that these legends are products of various factors, subject to distortion, and almost impossible to interpret in direct historical terms. Also, since assignment of archeological remains to ethnic or linguistic groups is beset with difficulties, it is difficult to ascertain exactly when Zapotecs first can definitely be identified in the Valley of Oaxaca. Most scholars agree that the inhabitants

OTHER AREAS OF MESOAMERICA			Guide
_owland Maya Olmec Region	Mixteca Alta-Baja-Costa	Central Mexico	1521

Pre-Spanish sequences in the Valley of Oaxaca and Mesoamerica. (Drawn by Terry Prewitt.)

of the area in the time of Monte Albán III (beginning about A.D. 200) were Zapotecs. Since many traits characteristic of this culture also are found in earlier times, perhaps as early as 1400 B.C., other scholars argue that if the Monte Albán III inhabitants of the Valley were Zapotecs, so were the earlier peoples.[4]

The prehistory of the Valley of Oaxaca traditionally has been di-

vided into five periods, called Monte Albán I (ca. 400–100 B.C.), II
(ca. 100 B.C.–A.D. 200), III (ca. A.D. 200–900), IV (ca. 900–1350), and V
(ca. 1350–1521).[5] These periods have been defined on the basis of
ceramics found in the rubble of structures constructed during the
various Monte Albán periods and at more than three hundred sur-
veyed sites in the Valley of Oaxaca.[6] As archeological knowledge of
the Valley has increased, greater refinements have been made, and
the periods have been subdivided: Monte Albán I into three sub-phases
(A, B, and C), and Monte Albán III into two sub-phases (A and B).
While logic dictates that there are transitions between all of the major
Monte Albán periods, some scholars single out two transitions that
seem to have been of particular importance, designating them Transition II–IIIA, and Transition IIIA–IIIB.[7]

Earlier periods also have been added before the Monte Albán sequence: Tierras Largas (ca. 1450–1150 B.C.), San José (ca. 1150–850
B.C.), Guadalupe (ca. 850–500 B.C.), and Rosario (ca. 500–400 B.C.).
These earlier phases are designated largely on the basis of ceramic
complexes which can be correlated with other regions, settlement patterns, subsistence techniques, excavations of houses, storage pits and
burials, and inferred social patterns.[8]

The periods or phases in the Valley of Oaxaca have been correlated
with major developmental stages—called the Formative, the Classic,
and the post-Classic—which are manifested throughout Mesoamerica.
While some authors treat both regional periods and general stages as
chronological entities, stages are defined in this work on the basis
of the climax or culmination of inferred sociopolitical patterns and
not on the presence of specific artifact types, traits, or crossdating.[9]
Thus, the various stages will not have the same chronological profile
everywhere in Mesoamerica. For example, the Classic stage seems to
have begun earlier in the Valley of Mexico and in the Valley of
Oaxaca than in the Maya Petén, whereas it probably lasted longer in
the Valley of Oaxaca and the Maya Petén than it did in the Valley of
Mexico.

Tierras Largas, San José, Guadalupe, Rosario, and Monte Albán
I and II are here assigned to the Formative stage, a time in which
Mesoamerican peoples became fully sedentary, residing in towns and
villages and practicing agriculture. The Formative stage generally
is divided into Early, Middle, and Late. Some authors prefer to clas-

sify Monte Albán II as Classic or to indicate that it is near the threshold of the Classic, as Terminal Formative or proto-Classic.

In Monte Albán III the sociocultural features characteristic of the Classic societies of Mesoamerica reach their culmination. Both Monte Albán IIIA and IIIB in the Valley of Oaxaca represent periods in which a specific, complex social and political organization, the theocratic state, became pervasive. The presence of this form of state organization certainly had its roots in the Formative and may have been achieved through conquest; it may be inferred from the nature of the population centers, writing, monumental architecture, and the iconography of the art, all of which emphasize hieratic matters and the worship of gods of agriculture and fertility. For this reason, it has often been argued that the major leaders of the Classic states were priests.

Monte Albán IV and V are of the post-Classic or Militaristic stage. This was a stage in Mesoamerican cultural history when settlements were ruled by military leaders, when warfare became extremely important, and when expansive conquest states based on the exaction of tribute became prevalent. While such phenomena were in evidence in late Formative and, to some extent, in Classic states, in the post-Classic they reached a pervasiveness unknown in earlier times—a pervasiveness reflected by the breakdown of distinctive regional art styles and the emergence throughout Mesoamerica of new styles with their associated cults of war and human sacrifice.[10]

CIVILIZATION AND THE STATE

The term *civilization* is limited as a concept for anthropological purposes, for, while it can be used to distinguish gross differences of scale between societies or cultures, its connotations are vague and value-laden. Traditionally, it was thought that wherever civilizations were found, they would exhibit a common set of regularities. Writing, social stratification, a state polity, monumental architecture, complex art styles, and cities, among other features, all were posited as synonomous with civilization and thought to be mutually interdependent traits; that is, the presence of one necessarily implied the presence of all.

However, this concept was an oversimplification. Cultures exhibiting some but not all of these traits were found. The Incas of Peru lacked writing, the Yorubas of West Africa lacked writing and monumental architecture, and the Mayas of the Guatemalan Petén lacked cities—depending on how one defines this last term. The definition of a city, or urbanity, considered synonomous with civilization in the classic sense of the word, has presented great difficulties.[11]

Some of the problems with the concept of civilization can be overcome by shifting to a conceptual order of a different nature, for civilization implies more than a congeries of cultural traits. It also suggests the formation of complex social units, especially the differentiation of society into stratified entities (based on unequal access to key resources) and the centralization of power in a single group. In short, civilization denotes the coming of the state.

Thus, while the core features of a civilization may lie in what Robert Redfield has called the "Great Tradition"—that is, the "sacred" or "classical" tradition of an intellectual class of literati—the organizational forms which produce this core lie elsewhere. The state must be present before literati can be trained, before architects and artists can be directed by the literati, and before armies can be organized for conquest.

Increasingly, scholars seek to explore the nexus between this aggregation of cultural traits, civilization, and this particular kind of social organization, the state—a nexus that is complex. For example, it may be stated that civilization implies the presence of the state, but the state may be present without civilization. Literati do not necessarily follow the formation of coercive power (although elites do), nor do cities (although centers bearing a special relationship to elites do), nor does a specific religion or complex art style (although most elites legitimate their power through religious ideology and its artistic expression).

On one level, cultural variations that develop in state societies, some of which may be called civilizations, are alternate expressions of power and its particular configuration within a specific society. On another level, such variations have their roots somewhere in the adaptation of the little tradition of a folk to the Great Tradition of an elite. Elites also borrow heavily from, or emulate the patterns of, other elites.

A civilization may or may not be more inclusive than a state, for the term *state* also may imply a unit of various dimensions. Greek civilization included many independent states and achieved integration only very late in its history Byzantine civilization was politically unified almost from the beginning. The sharing of a Great Tradition may facilitate the unification of a people into a single political entity, although it is not a sufficient cause for development of a larger political unity. The centralization of a number of smaller states or groups into a single entity is more likely to bring about the crystallization of the Great Tradition of a civilization.[12]

THE FORMATION OF THE STATE IN THE VALLEY OF OAXACA

For years, archeological knowledge of the Valley of Oaxaca effectively began with Monte Albán I, dating from approximately 400 B.C. In other areas of Mesoamerica, however, archeologists had revealed a much longer sequence, and their recent work in the Valley of Oaxaca now has outlined a long sequence of cultural development beginning as early as 8000 B.C. and continuing into Monte Albán times.

Evidence of an early food-collecting, incipient cultivation culture (ca. 8000–1500 B.C.) is known from a series of caves and rock shelters, located near Mitla, in a transition zone from piedmont to mountains. There the native inhabitants collected acorns, piñon nuts, mesquite beans, prickly pear and organ cactus fruits, wild onion bulbs, hackberries, magueys, and other wild plants and hunted deer, cottontail rabbits, and mud turtles. Incipient cultivation, comparable to that found in other areas of Mesoamerica, also is in evidence toward the latter part of this period—small black beans and squash seeds can be found in the refuse. Experiments with maize also probably were carried out.

The inhabitants of this region apparently camped seasonally in the caves and formed seminomadic bands which moved from area to area during various parts of the year. The upper piedmont area of the Valley was of major importance in this early quest for food, primarily because it contained the widest variety of edible wild plants in the region.[13]

Between about 1500 B.C. and 1000 B.C. farming became fully de-

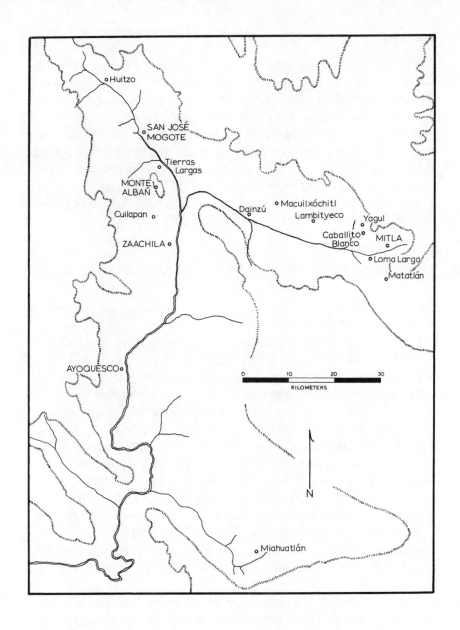

Map 5. Archeological sites of the Valley of Oaxaca. (Drawn by Terry Prewitt)

veloped in the Valley; this period corresponds to the Early Formative Tierras Largas and San José phases.

The Early Formative, although represented by at least twenty-two sites in the Valley, is best known from the sites of Tierras Largas and San José Mogote, both located north of the present city of Oaxaca. Early Formative sites mainly are in areas of high alluvium, especially where the water table was near the surface. For this reason more sites are found in the Etla and the central part of the Valley of Oaxaca (around Zaachila), while in areas like the Tlacolula valley, where the water table is low, they are sparse.

Most Early Formative sites are associated with areas where pot or well irrigation could be practiced. Well or pot irrigation consists of digging sometimes as many as ten shallow wells in the cornfield and then pouring water, drawn from the wells with a large pot, around the corn plants. No large labor force or centralized direction is required for this type of irrigation; it can be performed by individuals of a single household.[14]

This kind of agriculture can support nucleated sedentary villages. For example, at Tierras Largas, by 1300 B.C., a hamlet of some eight to ten households existed; it still contained about eight to ten households about 900 B.C. Households are estimated to have consisted of from two to four persons; houses were of wattle and daub construction, some six to seven meters long by four to five meters wide.[15]

By 1300 B.C. San José Mogote was a village of perhaps fifteen to thirty households; in the San José and Guadalupe phases it grew to a settlement of perhaps several hundred households, containing a population of at least 1,500 inhabitants by Middle Formative Guadalupe times. In the late San José or Guadalupe phases San José Mogote probably represented a center from which surpluses from surrounding hamlets (perhaps as many as from twelve to twenty and including Tierras Largas) were controlled and redistributed by high-ranking lineages.[16] At San José Mogote artifacts have been found over a large area as the site grew from ten to forty hectares in these two phases. In addition to storage pits, hearths, and household implements, the artifacts have included fragments of figurines, decorated pottery, black and white mica fragments, small polished mirrors of magnetite, and imported marine shells.

Houses were constructed of wattle-and-daub walls (plastered with mud and whitewashed), and they sometimes had stone foundations; they were separated from one another by courts and patios. Excavation of these houses has led to inferences about social patterns. The location of tools on the floors suggested that houses were divided into men's and women's work areas. Tools used by women in Mesoamerican culture, such as grinding stones, maize huskers, and cooking pots, were found to the right as one entered the door; flint chipping areas with cores, scrapers, knives, burins, and drills—presumably men's tools—were found on the left.

Houses at San José Mogote also displayed differences in the amount of presumed luxury items they contained, such as magnetite, *Spondylus* and pearl oyster shell—perhaps used for ornaments—and imported ceramics.[17] The distribution of these traits within the site implies the presence of status differentiation in the society.

In addition, these traits demonstrate that the inhabitants of San José Mogote had contacts with other regional groups in Mesoamerica. For example, marine pearl oyster comes not from the Valley of Oaxaca but from the Pacific coast, while pearly mussels come from the Gulf coast; one mollusk found at San José Mogote apparently comes from the Chiapas-Guatemala coast.

Small magnetite mirrors from Oaxaca are also found in deposits of the "Olmec" culture of the southern Gulf coast of Mesoamerica, although large concave mirrors of local ilmenite also are found in the Olmec zones. Olmec culture at that time showed evidence of well-developed ceremonial activity and social differentiation, including complex art styles, temple-pyramids, stelae and altars with carved inscriptions, and monumental stone heads. Jade carving and glyphic inscriptions are found in the Olmec area in the Middle Formative, corresponding to the Guadalupe phase in the Valley.

Ceremonial zones also are found at San José Mogote. Excavations of the Early Formative at San José Mogote revealed a recessed circular area which had been plastered and painted red. In the late San José or early Guadalupe phase, an artificial platform with stone terrace walls was constructed with a north-south orientation.

Evidence of ceremonialism and artifacts displaying a general resemblance to those of the Olmec culture have led some scholars to postulate its close affinity with the Valley of Oaxaca. Some have suggested that the Valley was invaded by the Olmecs and that it formed

part of an Olmec "empire." Others have suggested that religious pilgrims were sent out from the Olmec area to proselytize among the
inhabitants of the Valley as well as much of central Mesoamerica.
Many of the traits on which such hypotheses are based are found in
Monte Albán I and earlier times.[18]

But as Kent V. Flannery has pointed out, "classic" manifestations
of the Olmec culture correspond not with these later developments
but with the Guadalupe phase in the Valley. His interpretation of
the evidence is that contacts between the Valley of Oaxaca and the
Olmec region generated exchanges of luxury goods and patterns
which enhanced the prestige of the emerging Valley elites as well as
the elites of the Olmec area.[19] Exchanges between elites serve to reinforce and widen the gulf between the local elite and commoners, for
it puts them in possession of items and knowledge not available to
the mass of the population.

There is increased evidence of social differentiation, the centralization of political power, and ceremonial activity by Monte Albán I
times. The Valley population expanded significantly; for example,
Monte Albán I materials are found at more than forty locations, and
Monte Albán II materials are found at more than sixty sites.[20]

A number of environmental zones were exploited in those times.
Along with the dry farming and pot irrigation of earlier periods,
small-scale canal irrigation coupled with hillside fallowing systems
appeared. Canal irrigation was generally practiced outside the high
alluvium on perennial streams, generally located in the piedmont
zone, where the most water was available. Settlements in both this
zone and the pot-irrigated high alluvium supplemented water control farming and, with fallowing on the lower piedmont, produced
a kind of "infield-outfield" system.[21]

Some settlements attained considerable prominence. For example,
San José Mogote grew to more than 250 hectares by Monte Albán II
times and became internally differentiated into ceremonial and secular
precincts, cemetery areas, and zones reflecting craft specialization.
Monte Albán was first colonized in the Early Monte Albán I period
and expanded to cover an area of more than four square kilometers
by the beginning of Monte Albán II.[22] In the eastern arm of the
Valley, the site of Dainzú displays considerable complexity as an elite
center.[23] In the southern arm of the Valley, Ayoquesco seems to have

been particularly important. Other, smaller sites in the Valley also display differentiation into various zones.

Densely populated, and displaying regional centers of power and cult, the Valley seems to have been fragmented during Monte Albán I and II times into a number of independent states. These perhaps were allied in various ways through intermarriage, exchange, and trade, although they seem to have maintained political independence. The number of states in those times is not known now, but it is clear · that the state as a sociopolitical form had arrived in the Valley of Oaxaca.

What factors were responsible for generating the state in this region? Increased differentiation of the society plus "massed power,"[24] much in evidence, are not unique to developments in the Valley but represent a cross-cultural regularity found in a wide variety of early cultures such as those of central Mexico, the Hwang-Ho Valley in China, Egypt, coastal Peru, early Mesopotamia, and the Indus Valley. These cultures all represent what have been called "pristine civilizations."

Generally, anthropologists are not content to explain each of these cultures in its own unique terms, but instead seek explanations that have broad applicability. Some have argued, for example, that intensive agriculture—which they feel is a precondition for the development of the state—could only have been carried on in these semiarid and arid regions with large-scale canal irrigation works and that the construction, control, and maintenance of such irrigation systems necessitated a centralized authority, that is, the state.[25]

This "hydraulic theory" of the formation of the state, while it has been productive as a hypothesis to be tested, needs considerable modification. First, while irrigation agriculture in the Valley of Oaxaca undoubtedly facilitated a more effective exploitation of the environment, it is not clear that irrigation there required an extensive political bureaucracy to coordinate it. Instead, the Valley inhabitants seem to have depended on a variety of techniques other than large-scale canal irrigation, such as well-pot and small, largely localized, canal irrigation coupled with a fallowing system.

The type of irrigation agriculture developed thus seems to be strongly influenced by the peculiarities of the local environment. In the Tehuacán Valley of Puebla, where a long Mesoamerican sequence has been established, large-scale canal irrigation was practiced. Unlike the Valley of Oaxaca, pot irrigation was not practical because of the depth of the water table. Also, prolific springs made large-scale canal irrigation much more feasible in the Tehuacán Valley.

Second, most investigators now agree that where large-scale canal irrigation was practiced, it appeared after, not before, increased social differentiation and political centralization; thus, it may be a result of them instead of a cause.[26]

The assumptions that underlie the hydraulic hypothesis also have been questioned. For some time anthropologists have proposed that the invention of agriculture increased productivity to the point that a surplus was accumulated, thus freeing part of the population to pursue other endeavors. With newly found leisure, they turned to other specialized matters such as religion and crafts. This specialization in time led to social differentiation, the development of writing and law, and advances in political organization. Agriculture also implied sedentary living, population increase, and nucleated settlements.

It is now known, however, that agriculture does not require sedentary life, nor does sedentary life imply nucleated settlements, nor do nucleated settlements require agriculture or sedentary life. Moreover, we have learned that even hunting and gathering societies, if located in favorable environments, can produce some surplus and that the food quest for them does not require as much time as previously had been thought. But hunters and gatherers, like agriculturalists who practice extensive cultivation (slash-and-burn or swidden agriculture), generally do not produce the surplus of which they are capable. The problem then becomes one of explaining the organization of labor that generates increased productivity, or what causes "people to work more, or more people to work."[27]

Thus, the causal chain is no longer linear; that is, increased productivity, population growth, surpluses, social differentiation, nucleated settlements, and sedentary life may not necessarily cause the state, but equally they may be caused by the increased centralization of power. The relationship among these factors constitutes a "feedback" process, one wherein a number of factors influence one another. It is probable that there are no prime movers that can be found to explain the origin of the state. Instead, explanations must be sought in terms of several related, but not necessarily identical, factors acting on one another.[28]

While the exact processes that give rise to a massing of power are numerous, the mechanisms for the legitimation of power display greater regularity. Power must be legitimized through an ideological system in which certain individuals possess, or are imputed to possess, special abilities or crucial answers to specific problems. In early agricultural societies these individuals are religious practitioners who work their "magic" on life-crisis situations. They may receive their power for various reasons: because they are particularly close to the lineal ancestors of the group or to the gods, or because of "spirit" possession.

It is not surprising, then, that the earliest examples of monumental architecture in connection with temple-idol cults, complex art styles, and "writing" (evidence for increased social differentiation and the massing of power) are found in conjunction with ceremonial centers. In all of the "pristine civilizations" sacred centers are set apart from the majority of the population, are dedicated to gods of sustenance and fertility, and are presided over by an elite which possesses a special relationship to these gods.[29]

MONTE ALBAN AND THE ZAPOTEC GREAT TRADITION

Monte Albán contains the most impressive, and the best studied, ceremonial zone in the Valley of Oaxaca. Located on a series of ridges about 400 meters above the Valley floor and 1,540 meters above sea level, Monte Albán is slightly southwest of the present city of Oaxaca near the confluence of the three valley branches which form the Valley of Oaxaca.

The central and defensible location of this site in the Valley was probably a factor that attracted its earliest settlers; it was unoccupied, however, until Monte Albán I times. Its setting, literally on top of a mountain, suggests a strategic defensive location. An apparently defensive wall, roughly two and one-half kilometers in length, was built along the north, northwest, and west edges of the site in late Monte Albán I or II times.[30] This feature probably attests to competition between various states in the Valley—a competition that could have forced some of the population to seek a defensive and strategic location.

The hill of Monte Albán, looking north.

It also is possible, although present knowledge permits only speculation, that Monte Albán could not have been settled without the technological and political advances which came about in the Valley during Monte Albán I times. An irrigation system, constructed at Monte
Albán in period I, supplied water to bottomlands east of the site and
permitted intensive cultivation of this area.[31]

The name of Monte Albán has been shrouded in mystery, as are
its origins. Generations of scholars have performed linguistic gymnas-
tics in an attempt to derive its name from a Zapotec word. Wilfrido
Cruz, for example, has argued that Monte Albán is an Hispanicized
version of the Zapotec word *danibaan*, meaning "sacred mountain or
hill."[32]

A more probable interpretation is that Monte Albán was named by
the Spanish conquerer of the Valley, Francisco de Orozco, who previously had served in Italy.[33] There are many such places in the
Italian peninsula, including settlements in the Alban hills near Rome,
Monte Albano in Tuscany, and a number of other settlements with
that name throughout Italy. Although it is not known exactly what
Monte Albán looked like when Orozco saw it (although undoubtedly
it was in ruins), its character does display a close resemblance to the
hill towns of Italy.

The hill of Monte Albán proper (for the site in various stages also
includes the neighboring hills of Monte Albán Chico, El Gallo, and
Atzompa) contains the major ceremonial zone. This zone, called
the Grand Plaza, was begun in period I, and its architectural remains,
such as the Building of the Danzantes, show considerable complexity.

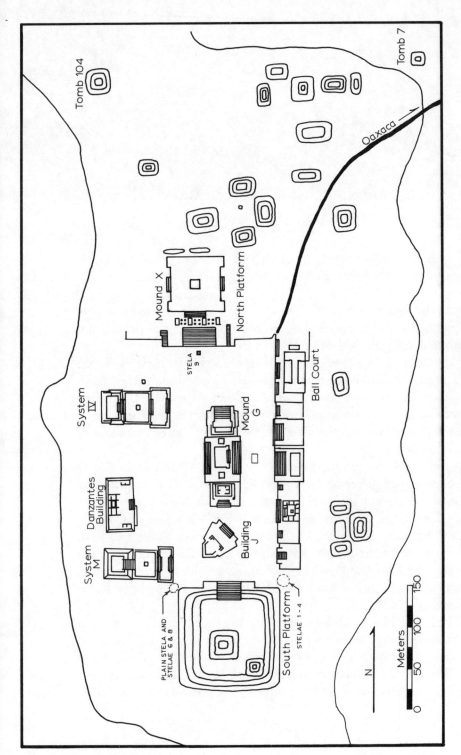

Map 6. Grand Plaza of Monte Albán. (Drawn by Terry Prewitt)

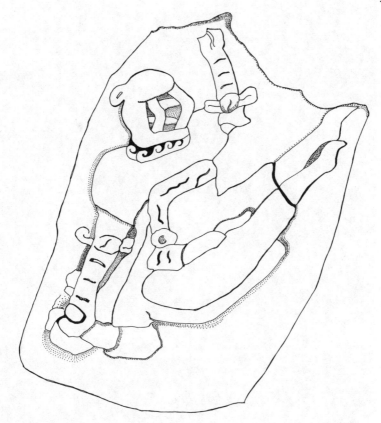

Dainzú stone carving of a ball player holding a ball in his right hand. (Drawn by Sarah Whitecotton after Ignacio Bernal, "The Ball Players of Dainzú," *Archeology*, Vol. 21, No. 2 [1968].)

The structure of the Building of the Danzantes suggests that it was probably a temple-pyramid. Constructed of stones sealed with mud mortar, and resting on deep foundations, it consists of a pyramidal platform of huge, irregular stones, set in rows and displaying bas-relief sculptures of nudes in grotesque positions who have what appear to be mutilated genital organs.

The Building of the Danzantes was so named because it was thought that carvings associated with it depicted individuals engaged in ritual dances; others have argued that they represent individuals with de-

Danzantes from Monte Albán, in Monte Albán I style, reused in the construction of Building J. (Courtesy Kay Parker.)

Grand Plaza of Monte Albán, looking north; Building J is in the foreground. (Courtesy Kay Parker.)

formities who, in ancient Mesoamerica, were thought to possess special powers; still others suggest that they represent slain and mutilated captives, a suggestion that now seems most plausible.[34] *Danzante*-style carvings are found in both periods I and II at Monte Albán. Stones apparently carved in a similar style have been found at the site of Dainzú in the Tlacolula arm of the Valley; these stones, which may date from Monte Albán II times, depict ball players—a theme common in the Formative stage of Mesoamerican cultural history.[35]

Additional traits suggest the elite character of Monte Albán. Toward the end of period I, stelae were erected displaying calendrical glyphs or dates, glyphs also found carved on the *danzante* slabs. These glyphs indicate a form of writing. Most of them undoubtedly deal with calendrical matters, probably representing the ritual calendar of 260 days (the *tonalpohualli*, as it was called in Nahuatl), although the 365-day calendar, which was geared to the agricultural

cycle, also may be represented. Some eleven calendrical glyphs are known from Monte Albán I times.

Other finds reflect the presence of status differences within the society. Burials contain offerings of pottery, which include effigy vessels of animals, birds, and gods, along with figurines and incised pottery. All are technically well made. Some ten male gods have been identified from Monte Albán I along with figurines of naked females. Men are depicted wearing cloaks, breechclouts, and bracelets, with headgear including helmets, hats, and scarves. Face and body painting, tattooing, the wearing of masks, and false beards also are represented.[36]

With Monte Albán II, the ultimate plan of the ceremonial-administrative zone becomes clearer. In that period the zone was leveled and paved to accommodate a central precinct which ultimately became 750 meters long by 300 meters wide. Construction of the plaza must have required considerable organization of labor, for deep concavities were filled and rock outcrops were leveled, although some of those outcrops were used as nuclei for the stone constructions on the north and south sides of the plaza.

The temple-pyramid continued as the most characteristic architectural form in Monte Albán II. Although the pyramids of Monte

Albán never reached the lofty heights of those of Teotihuacán and Cholula in central Mexico, they followed a similar conception, consisting of a platform with a temple on their summit. At Monte Albán the sloping planes of the pyramids were made by plastering over small stone steps. The temples on the summits usually contained two rooms constructed of adobe walls set on the stone base and covered by a thatched roof.

Monte Albán II also exhibits a new structural form. This structure, Building J, has a pentagonal construction resembling the point of an arrow.[37] It is presumed by some to have been an astronomical observatory because of its strange shape and orientation. Building J also displays stone slabs carved with glyphs, many in the style of the *danzante* slabs. A new form also appears there—inverted figures with accompanying glyphs. Alfonso Caso suggested that these carvings depicted the conquest of towns by Monte Albán, since they contain representations of individuals in an inverted position; the conquered often are portrayed upside-down in other Mesoamerican glyphic systems. Accompanying these figures are place glyphs, some of which have now been identified by Joyce Marcus as indicating the town conquered, and calendrical glyphs indicating the date of the event.[38]

A number of new traits appeared in Monte Albán II. The modeled pottery of Monte Albán I disappeared and was replaced by more impersonal geometric forms. The *xicalcoliuhqui* symbolic and decorative motif, a stepped-fret design, also appeared, as did flower and human bone motifs. The trefoil ornament as a terminal element, a distinguishing characteristic of later Zapotec art, was introduced in this period.

With figurines and other decorated or sculptured pottery, in addition to the stone sculpture, representations of some fifteen deities, known in later periods, now can be identified. Also in period II, females appear clothed and there are at least two female deities. Male attire becomes more elegant and sumptuous: there now are elaborate headdresses with chinstraps, plumes, topknots, and ribbons. One of the most spectacular pieces associated with Monte Albán culture also comes from this period—a beautiful jade mask of the bat god found as an offering below the floor of the Grand Plaza. This god is composed of twenty-five pieces of jade, carefully made to fit together, with eyes and teeth of shell. Three pendants of slate hang from it.

Figure depicting conquest—stone carving, Building J, Monte Albán. (Drawn by
Sarah Whitecotton after Alfonso Caso, "Calendario y escritura de las antiguas
culturas de Monte Albán," in Miguel Othón de Mendizábal, *Obras completas*,
Vol. 1 [México, 1946].)

It has been suggested that Monte Albán II was not an indigenous
development but was introduced by a group of conquerors perhaps
from Chiapas or the Guatemalan Highlands, for the new traits are
of an upper-class or aristocratic nature.[39] But such an interpretation
now seems less likely. First, Monte Albán II displays variation
throughout the Valley of Oaxaca. Second, while these traits indeed
may have been characteristic of elites in other areas, there is no necessary reason to adopt an "invasion theory" to account for them. As

Jade mask representing a bat, from Monte Albán II. (Museo Nacional de Antropología, Mexico City; By Tenth Muse, Inc.)

already noted, exchange and the emulation of other elites simply enhances the prestige of both. Perhaps more than anything else, the presence of new elite traits in period II expresses the widening gulf between elites and commoners.

After Monte Albán II times, the site grew to enormous proportions, consisting of an urban complex of from five to six square kilometers. All the surrounding hills (including El Gallo, Atzompa, and Monte Albán Chico) ultimately were occupied. The plaza also was enlarged and apparently served as the administrative and religious center for the whole complex.[40]

It is also in Monte Albán III that a tradition became crystallized which can be referred to as "Classic Zapotec." Traits typical of this culture continued in the Valley until the time of Spanish contact, a continuity of some fourteen hundred years. Further, Spanish documents permit the determination that this tradition belonged to the Zapotec-speaking people of the Valley.

Monte Albán III does not appear suddenly, but is preceded by a transition known from Monte Albán and from Loma Larga near Mitla (Transition II–IIIA). This transition is defined by the persistence of Monte Albán II traits plus traits displaying strong influences from Teotihuacán in the Valley of Mexico. Teotihuacán influence on Monte Albán elite culture is noticeable throughout Monte Albán IIIA (ca. A.D. 200–650) and, as with Monte Albán II traits, is confined almost exclusively to characteristics that would be associated with upper classes or elites. Such influences may be seen in ceremonial pottery, architecture, sculpture, and mural painting.

It is most unlikely that Monte Albán became part of a Teotihuacán "empire." Practically all of Mesoamerica was influenced by Teotihuacán during this period. Some centers, such as Kaminaljuyú in highland Guatemala, display massive Teotihuacán intrusions, perhaps indicating that local elites there were undermined. Much more characteristic, however, are strong Teotihuacán influences—not intrusions—as found in the lowland Maya Petén and at Monte Albán.

These influences probably indicate that elite groups throughout Mesoamerica were in contact, through trade and perhaps even intermarriage, with the elite at Teotihuacán and found that emulation of the metropolis accorded them considerable prestige and status. In fact, recent finds at Teotihuacán indicate that perhaps there was a Zapotec

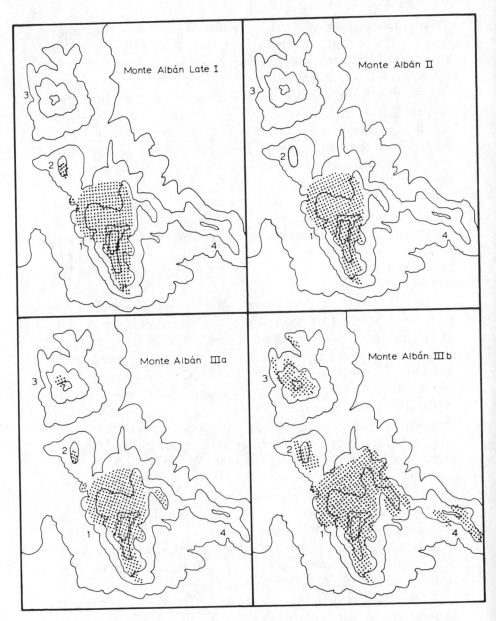

Map 7. Urban growth of Monte Albán. Estimated site limits at various periods: 1, Monte Albán; 2, El Gallo; 3, Atzompa; 4, Monte Albán Chico. (Drawn by Terry Prewitt, data courtesy of Richard E. Blanton)

barrio or section in the city, suggesting not only that contact was intimate, but also that influences went both ways.[41] In summary, as with all Great Traditions, the Zapotec one was not forged exclusively in the local environment, but was also the result of influences from other Great Traditions in its orbit.

Teotihuacán was destroyed about A.D. 650, and its impact on Monte Albán culture ceased at that time. Monte Albán IIIB (ca. A.D. 650–900) represents the climax of classic Zapotec culture; its style is distinctive and displays an art style florescence which reaches a baroque flamboyancy. Few outside influences are identifiable in the elite culture of this period. Instead, the Monte Albán elite appear to have established themselves as the literati *par excellence* of the Valley and its environs, including the sierra region, the Southern Zapotec region, the Isthmus of Tehuantepec, parts of the Pacific coast, and into the Mixteca Alta.[42]

MATERIAL CULTURE OF MONTE ALBAN

Urns, usually called funerary urns because they are most frequently found in tombs and with burials, are characteristic of Zapotec culture. These urns or ceramic sculptures—for they are made of a hard-baked, fine-grained light grey clay—display a basic form that was established in Monte Albán I times: a cylindrical vessel with a figure on the front and with the rear of the vessel generally open to the top. No contents have been found in the vessels.[43]

Ranging in size from about seven centimeters to as much as one and one-half meters, they persist from Monte Albán I until the end of period IV. By Monte Albán III, after a transition displaying Teotihuacán stylistic influences, they became extremely elaborate, and figures or deities on the front came to dominate their structure. In most of the Classic Zapotec urns, attention is focused on the upper part of the body, and the torso and limbs are diminished in proportion to the face, whether masked or plain; glyphs and symbols of identification also are made prominent. In IIIA and increasingly in IIIB these symbolic elements, which most frequently are found in the headdress, became much more elaborate and dominant, while the human figure was less important and retained a smaller proportion in relation to the whole.

Zapotec urn of the god Cocijo, Monte Albán IIIB; provenance, Zimatlán. (By permission of the Department of Anthropology, National Museum of Natural History, Smithsonian Institution; catalog no. 198,427.)

Zapotec urn, Monte Albán IIIA; exact Mexican provenance unknown. (By permission of the Department of Anthropology, National Museum of Natural History, Smithsonian Institution; catalog no. 273,401.)

The characteristic Zapotec depiction on these urns is of a seated figure with crossed legs and hands placed on the knees; the details of the hands and feet generally are quite crude, while other aspects of the urns, such as facial features (which at times seem to be realistic portraitures), masks, and symbolic elements, are carefully detailed.

In Monte Albán IIIA the urns were mostly hand modeled, but by IIIB most of their elements were stamped out in molds. Although sometimes left plain, they commonly were painted in various combinations of red (the color that has survived best), white, black, yellow, and green.

After extensive study of the elements and glyphs on the fronts of the urns,[44] many deities have been identified and their major characteristics defined. The particular relationship between the figure depicted and the deity that is associated with it is not known: perhaps some represent priests of a particular cult; perhaps some were simply depictions of the major deities; perhaps others identify particular important personages, since individuals in Zapotec culture were named after the calendrical sign under which they were born, and the deities who governed this sign constituted an individual's alter ego; and perhaps also they identify the lineage of an important personage, for lineages often trace their origins to specific deities or deified ancestors.

As would be expected, there is a predominance of deities associated with fertility and agriculture. The most prominent is Cocijo, god of lightning and rain; his representations extend from period I through period IV and are found more than any other. Pitao Cozobi, the god of maize or abundant sustenance, also is much in evidence, as are a number of associated deities which form the so-called "Maize Complex." Included in this complex are representations of the bat and monkey. For most of the deities, both male and female representations are found; they are distinguished by costumes. Males generally wear breechclouts and sometimes capes, while females are represented wearing skirts and *huipiles*. Female hair styles also are frequently and vividly represented.

Deities not strictly associated with Zapotec culture are also depicted. Quetzalcoatl, the feathered serpent, and the butterfly god, both characteristic of Teotihuacán culture, are in evidence. There also are representations of Tlaloc, the Teotihuacán rain god, as distinct from the

Zapotec urn with a female figure displaying the regional coiffure of Yalálag. Monte Albán IIIA; provenance Tlacochahuaya. (By permission of the Peabody Museum, Harvard University; catalog no. 47,114.)

Zapotec Cocijo.[45] Xipe Totec, a deity associated with spring in Nahuatl culture, also is prevalent, as is Xiuhtecuhtli, the god of fire, although in Oaxaca, unlike central Mexico, he is depicted as a young man instead of an old man until Monte Albán IIIA. Of the forty-four primary categories of urns that have been postulated, many cannot be correlated with known deities and instead are defined only on the basis of stylistic elements. Archeologists have assigned such names to these as the God with a Mask of the Serpent, the God 11 Death, the Goddess whose Headdress is Composed of a Large Plume, and the Goddess with the Beaded Turban.

In addition to providing insights into Zapotec religion, the urns and similar ceramic sculptures provide glimpses of more mundane aspects of Zapotec life. Acrobats, jugglers, ball players, merchants, priests, warriors, musicians, soothsayers, farmers, and porters all are depicted. Features of dress and costume, including nose ornaments, ear plugs, medallions and jewelry, hair styles, and headdresses, are realistically portrayed. Animals—such as bullfrogs, squirrels, dogs, ducks, deer, wolves, opossums, and jaguars—and humans, young and old, are represented in varying poses. There are men with small or large paunches, cleft palates, cataract-infested eyes, exaggerated nipples, and sunken cheeks, displaying toothless grins and dental mutilations. Little boys as well as busty matrons with double chins and broad hips were modeled in clay. Temples and other buildings also are depicted.[46]

Aspects of social organization also can be inferred from the urns. For example, after the urns of Cocijo, the greatest number belong to a category called "Companions," or "acompañantes," which usually are found, from three to seven in number, on the floors of tombs and typically are arranged in a semicircle around a central, larger deity or personage.

It has been suggested that these urns represent either effigies of the devotees of a religious cult or an entourage accompanying an important personage on his journey through the afterlife. It seems probable, from evidence at Monte Albán, that many individuals (perhaps slaves) were sacrificed upon the death of an important personage and were buried with him.[47]

The companion urns associated with each large urn generally are identical even though, depending on the specific tomb, they represent men and women of all ages, dressed in various degrees of sumptuous ornament. It previously had been thought that the companions provided evidence for polygyny, for the larger figure was a male while the companions, which were female, represented the wives of an important personage. But the reverse arrangement subsequently has been found: a large female urn accompanied by a number of smaller male ones.[48]

Stylistic elements on the urns also have provided archeologists with a relative chronology of Monte Albán culture. Most important in this regard is the so-called Glyph C, found on a considerable percentage of the urns and persisting from Monte Albán I until Monte Albán IV. Thought to represent a stylized jaguar, intimately associated with Cocijo, its changing styles permit assignment of the urns to the various Monte Albán periods.

Of equal importance in this regard, however, are other ceramics, which have provided the major diagnostic features of the Monte Albán sequence.[49] In period IIIA the most characteristic type is a polished grey ware, molded into vessels with engraved or incised decoration, which continues, in part, from period II. Beginning with Transition II–IIIA, however, Teotihuacán influence is significant. In IIIA are found globular or spouted jars, vases with cylindrical supports, conical bowls, bowls with rounded bases, *tecomates*, and reclining dog effigies, all like those of Teotihuacán. Some of these ceramics are in Thin Orange, an almost eggshell-thin ware that is typical of Teotihuacán ceremonial pottery. The *florero*, a characteristic Teotihuacán form, also is present, although vessel lids, so typical of Teotihuacán, are rare. Of the Teotihuacán forms, most are made of local clay and have become modified by local tradition to the extent that they probably are copies of those of the central Mexican metropolis. Some typical Monte Albán II forms, such as vessels with "spider feet," continued into period IIIA.

In Transition IIIA–IIIB, the Teotihuacán influence began to diminish, and by Monte Albán IIIB times it had subsided. Periods IIIB and IV are almost indistinguishable ceramically at Monte Albán except that craftsmanship seems to have deteriorated, some new shapes slowly began to appear, and some pan-Mesoamerican trade wares, such as Plumbate and Fine Orange, are found in Monte Albán IV. For this reason, periods IIIB and IV often are lumped together in discussions of ceramics.

Ceramics of Monte Albán III-IV: *a, b, c, d*, and *e*—Monte Albán IIIA; *g, h, i*, and *j*—Monte Albán IIIB-IV. (Drawn by Terry Prewitt after Alfonso Caso and Ignacio Bernal, "Ceramics of Oaxaca," in *Handbook of Middle American Indians*, ed. Robert Wauchope and Gordon R. Willey.)

The most characteristic forms of ware in IIIB and IV are a conical bowl of grey ware, incense burners of coarse grey ware with conical or hemispherical bodies, "tiger claw" vases in grey and yellow ware, and the *"florero-olla"* of polished grey ware. This last type represents a fusion of the Teotihuacán *florero* and the Zapotec *olla* and is found in jars containing tubular spouts, open spouts, and jars with three handles (sometimes with a cover). The most characteristic is a small jar with a spherical body, a flat bottom, and an open neck.

Human ceramic figurines, some representing gods, others warriors, and some made into whistles, are found in abundance throughout Monte Albán III and IV. In general, these do not resemble, even in period IIIA, Teotihuacán figurines.

While metal was not worked until Monte Albán IV times— metallurgy was most characteristic of post-Classic Mesoamerica—jade and other hard stones were worked there from earliest times.[50] In Monte Albán I they were used almost exclusively for ornaments such as earplugs and necklaces. By Monte Albán II, however, jade figurines appeared which represent males, females, and anthropomorphic figures and which depict both the head and the full figure form. In Monte Albán III, ear ornaments of *tecali*; mosaics with plaques of jade or green stone, quartz, obsidian, *tecali*, and mica; and shell ornaments are found along with figurines of hard stone, some very crudely carved. As with ceramics, these carvings show Teotihuacán influence in IIIA, an influence which subsided in IIIB.

Some of the hard stone pieces, after what has been interpreted as degeneration in craftsmanship in Teotihuacán times, display a revival in Monte Albán IIIB, and some of the crudeness disappears. Some of these IIIB pieces, such as a jade offering from the Temple of the Jaguar, display definite Maya influence and are so close to the Maya style that they must have been imported. Most, however, are carved in the Classic Zapotec style.

Tombs evolved from little more than a stone box in Monte Albán I to elaborately decorated structures, some of cruciform construction, containing niches and sculptured entryways, in period IIIA. Most of the funerary urns, with accompanying items of ceramic and stone, have been found in these tombs.

Some of the tombs of Monte Albán, such as Tombs 72, 103, 104, 105, and 112, contain elaborate mural paintings. Tomb 72 probably is

Mural painting, Tomb 105, Monte Albán. (Drawn by Carol Smith after Alfonso Caso, *Exploraciones en Oaxaca* [México, 1938].)

earlier than IIIA, 105 and 112 date from Monte Albán IIIA, while Tombs 103 and 104 belong to Transition IIIA–IIIB.

The subject matter of the murals seems to be hieratic and symbolic, depicting complex representations of deities or priests with associated glyphs. Multiple colors, such as white, two varieties of red, yellow ochre, green turquoise, blue, and black decorate the walls and form the figures and glyphs. The tomb paintings of Monte Albán IIIA show a resemblance to the frescoes of Teotihuacán, although the style is clearly Zapotec. Those of period IIIB show much less resemblance to Teotihuacán and become smaller and less elaborate. Overall, throughout the long Monte Albán sequence, elaborate tombs are much more in evidence from the Valley of Oaxaca than from any other area in Mesoamerica.[51]

The stone sculpture of Monte Albán, represented in periods I and II by the *danzantes* and the reliefs on Building J, is found in more abundance and in many more contexts in later periods. Stelae, found in limited numbers in Monte Albán I and II times, increased in importance in Monte Albán III and are found erected at various places in the Grand Plaza. *Lápida* slabs also occur, and the famous Lápida de Bazán, found in the rubble of Temple X, probably dates from Monte Albán IIIA. As do other objects from this period, the Lápida shows strong Teotihuacán elements. It depicts a priest or god known as 8

Lápida de Bazán. Incised in onyx. Now in the Museo Nacional de Antropología, México. (Drawn by Carol Smith after Ignacio Marquina, *Arquitectura prehispánica* [Mexico, 1951].)

Turquoise, who stands to the left of what is believed to be the patron deity of Monte Albán, Jaguar 3 Turquoise. He bears a striking resemblance not only to the figures painted in Tombs 104 and 105 but also to figures who appear in Teotihuacán frescoes.[52]

Numerous stelae, along with carved door jambs and lintels, date from Monte Albán III. Nine stelae, for example, have been found in the area of the south platform. One of these, the so-called Plain Stela, is of particular importance. This bas-relief carving depicts an important personage, sitting on a throne and holding a scepter in his hand, who is believed to be a ruler or *cacique* of Monte Albán at that time. He displays the attributes or insignia of the Old Man God 5F. Accompanying this important personage on the carving are four other individuals who appear to be approaching the throne. It is believed that these personages are *caciques* or ambassadors of other cities in the Oaxacan area and that the glyphs which accompany them identify both the personage and city he represented.[53]

Other stelae from the south platform, such as Stelae 1, 2, 3, 5, 6, and 8, depict individuals with their hands bound behind them who appear to have been taken captive or made prisoner. There are a number of other stone carvings which also date from Monte Albán III times (possibly IIIB). On the north platform, near the *adoratorio* or altar at its northeast angle, three stelae, three door jambs, and one carved lintel were located. An additional stela and two jambs also were found across from, or at the center of, the stairway on the north platform. The stela, Stela 9, now is in place in front of the stairway where it probably was erected. When first discovered, this stela showed vestiges of the red color with which it was painted.

Plain Stela, Monte Albán.
Stone Carving. (Drawn by
Carol Smith after Jorge R.
Acosta, "Exploraciones
arqueológicas en Monte
Albán," *Revista mexicana
de estudios antropologicos,*
Vol. 15 [1958].)

Zapotec stone sculpture, of course, is not restricted to Monte Albán.
In fact, some of the most detailed carvings come from other sites in
the Valley of Oaxaca, such as Zaachila, Cuilapan, Yagul, Lambityeco,
Huitzo, and other places. An important stela which may or may not
be Zapotec is known from Yaguila in the district of Ixtlán in the sierra.

While changes in other aspects of culture occurred quite rapidly,
writing and the calendrical glyphs of Monte Albán display considerable conservatism. The calendar-writing complex seems to have
achieved full development in Monte Albán II times and showed very
little modification throughout its history, although the content undoubtedly changed. However, present knowledge of this writing system is not nearly as extensive as, for example, that of the Classic Maya
glyphic system. One reason for this lack is that Zapotec inscriptions
are not as abundant as those found in the Maya area, even though the
Valley of Oaxaca probably ranks second among the Mesoamerican
regions in the number of carved glyphic monuments in the Classic.
Another reason is that many Zapotec inscriptions are short, and some
are incomplete. While a number of calendrical glyphs can be identified, the exact calendrical system to which they belong is not yet
known. Lack of such knowledge, and of any references such as the
Maya "long count" of time, have thwarted efforts to place Zapotec
calendrical dates into a larger chronological framework which can be
correlated with the Christian calendar. In addition, scholarly interest
in the Zapotec glyphic monuments has lagged far behind the vo-
luminous scholarship devoted to the Maya hieroglyphic system, and
as a result this important Oaxacan writing system remains poorly
understood.[54]

Stela 2 at Monte Albán. (Courtesy Kay Parker.)

Stela 6 at Monte Albán. (Courtesy Kay Parker.)

Most of the Grand Plaza that can be seen today in reconstructed form dates from Monte Albán IIIB, with earlier buildings buried underneath. Except for the *danzantes* and Building J, which date from Monte Albán I and II, and the South Platform, which may date from IIIA, the rest of the central ceremonial-administrative precinct apparently is Monte Albán IIIB.[55]

One distinctive architectural feature which appeared in Monte Albán IIIA is the so-called *talud-tablero*, a feature that combines a sloping wall with a panel. In Monte Albán I and II times the lower walls of pyramids apparently formed a gentle slope to the summit. With the introduction of the *talud-tablero* in IIIA, pyramids contained a decorative panel, generally framed, which interrupts the slope. This trait, widespread in the Mesoamerican Classic stage, traditionally has been associated with Teotihuacán architecture.

Stairways in Monte Albán III also became more elaborate, being set into the structures and, on some of the larger buildings, divided into flights. Most structures were covered with stucco and painted, many in red, as were some of the stelae which accompany them.

Another characteristic feature of Classic Monte Albán architecture consists of the great quadrangular patio surrounded by buildings. Apparently, two types can be distinguished: ceremonial and residential. The ceremonial type invariably has an altar or *adoratorio* in the middle of the patio, a feature lacking in the residential type. The ceremonial patios are flanked with temple-pyramids, while the residential patios contain structures which probably were dwellings for the upper classes. The patios of the elites are structurally similar to the patios of the gods.

A ball court, which originally may have been constructed in Monte Albán II times, took form in period III. The plan of this court is that of an I, and it has the peculiar characteristic of having two niches in opposite diagonal interior angles of the court along with a circular stone set in the center of the floor. As plaster undoubtedly covered what today look like steps or seats, producing smooth side walls, the game probably was watched from surrounding temples. The ball court was called *gueya* in Zapotec; the game played there was called *lachi*.[56]

Little is known about the way *lachi* was played. From sculptures and from accounts of the game among the post-Classic Mayas and

Stela 9 at Monte Albán. (Courtesy Kay Parker.)

Grand Plaza of Monte Albán, looking south from the North Platform; Mound G is in the foreground. (Courtesy Kay Parker.)

Grand Plaza of Monte Albán, east side. (Courtesy Kay Parker.)

Grand Plaza of Monte Albán, west side. (Courtesy Kay Parker.)

Ball Court at Monte Albán. (By Tenth Muse, Inc.)

System M at Monte Albán, with prominent *talud tableros*; *danzante* slabs are at the lower right. (Courtesy Kay Parker.)

Aztecs, it apparently was played with a hard rubber ball. The players passed the ball to one another by bouncing it gently with their hips. A ball player represented in a Zapotec ceramic sculpture wears a yoke around his waist—presumably to give momentum to the ball—and protective kneepads. Ball players also may have worn helmets in the Zapotec area as they did elsewhere in Mesoamerica.

Apparently, a team scored by passing the ball into the opposite team's end zone. Like other Classic ball courts, the Zapotec ones had no rings in the end zones. In many areas, such as central Mexico, rings were added in post-Classic times. However, even in Aztec times, knocking the ball through the ring was a rare feat—perhaps comparable to pitching a perfect game in baseball. Presumably the game was both religious and secular; in Aztec times the spectators placed bets on the outcome of the event.

SOCIAL AND POLITICAL ORGANIZATION OF MONTE ALBAN

In period III times, the settlement of Monte Albán assumed enormous proportions, covering not only Monte Albán proper but also, as has been pointed out, the adjacent hills of El Gallo, Monte Albán Chico, and Atzompa. Based on surface collections and mapping by Richard E. Blanton and his associates, the total site apparently covered five to six square kilometers during period IIIA and encompassed nearly seven and one-half kilometers in period IIIB, its maximum extent.[57]

Although population estimates based on archeological remains are always approximations, it has been estimated that the Monte Albán urban complex contained from 45,000 to 75,000 inhabitants in Monte Albán IIIB times. In comparison, Teotihuacán, probably the largest urban conglomeration in Classic Mesoamerica, is estimated to have had a population of between 125,000 and 200,000 in A.D. 600 and to have covered an area of twenty square kilometers.[58]

The urban complex of Monte Albán, unlike Teotihuacán, apparently had no main axes of streets or avenues; nor does it display, like Tikal in the Maya Petén, overall central planning. Instead, it contained two major ceremonial-administrative districts—one at Atzompa and the other and larger being the Grand Plaza of Monte Albán. Both of these districts appear to have represented high-status elite complexes and seem to have been relatively inaccessible to the majority of the population, for there are few major roads leading directly to them. The remainder of the population resided on terraces—some 2,300 have been mapped—on the hills and hillsides, clustered in residential complexes and linked by roads or streets with smaller civic-ceremonial precincts. While some of the terraces are separated enough to have permitted farming between them, it is presumed that most farming took place in the Valley below.[59]

The lack of a grid pattern and of evidence for overall planning does not suggest that Monte Albán lacked political integration. Such features are not easily adapted to hill or mountain towns.[60] For example, Renaissance town planners had to abandon the hills and seek locations on the plains, or render them on canvas, to construct their carefully proportioned, symmetrical cities. The hill and mountain towns of the Mediterranean world display a maze of winding roads and streets, and precincts and plazas are geared more to the terrain than to accessible central locations.

However, the distribution of the population of Monte Albán does suggest a number of socioeconomic features. Clearly, the population was spatially divided into various social classes, the most prestigious and powerful located near the major administrative-religious precincts of Monte Albán and Atzompa. The less prestigious, in varying degrees of luxury, resided in clustered neighborhoods. Although terraces—areas leveled to accommodate structures—ranged in size from ten by five meters to three hundred by one hundred meters (not including the large terrace of the Grand Plaza) and contain from one small structure to dozens of buildings, many complexes seem to be structural replications of others; their major differences apparently are ones of scale and in the quantities of luxury items possessed. It may be assumed, as is so in many preindustrial societies and in the societies of the modern Latin world, that Zapotec society was elite-oriented. Many aspired, to the extent possible and even if on a small scale, to emulate the lofty elite of the Grand Plaza. Such values promote the perpetuation of elites.[61]

Blanton tentatively has suggested, since work on the urban complex of Monte Albán is still in the preliminary stages, that corporate groups or lineages may have resided on the residential terraces surrounding each civic-ceremonial cluster. Also, the "commemorative" buildings flanking the Grand Plaza perhaps represented the various lineages found at Monte Albán.[62] It is also possible that the stelae erected in association with these commemorative buildings may contain the markings or insignia of the various lineages.

In certain respects, Monte Albán may have resembled ancient cities in other parts of the world. For example, each of the various hills that composed ancient Rome was the province, in earlier times, of a particular "tribe" or gens; the dominant gens controlled the Palatine, flanked by the Forum, which became the social, administrative, religious, and economic center of the city. At later dates, various Roman rulers, such as Julius Caesar, Augustus, Nerva, and Trajan, erected their own forums as expressions of their particular rule and power. At present, it is not known to what extent such analogies might be appropriate to Monte Albán.

Unlike the central precinct at Teotihuacán, or the Forum of ancient Rome, the Grand Plaza of Monte Albán does not seem to have been a central market place or a place of general public gathering, for, as has been pointed out, its access roads do not seem to have been built for these purposes. Instead, it is postulated that the various smaller terraced civic-religious clusters may have been locations for markets; it also has been suggested that a public market may have been located outside the residential zone north of the main defensive wall.[63]

Also unlike Teotihuacán, it does not appear that Monte Albán was the major center for, nor held a monopoly over, craft production in its region. Few workshops have been found in the Monte Albán urban complex; in fact, it appears that craft production was dispersed throughout the Valley of Oaxaca region, much as it is today, instead of being centralized.[64]

It does appear, however, that Monte Albán was the political center of the Valley in period III; the entire Valley seems to have been united under its political hegemony. This hegemony also may have extended beyond the Valley into the sierra, the Southern Zapotec region, the Valley of Nochixtlán to the north, and the Isthmus of Tehuantepec, all of which show Classic Zapotec manifestations.[65]

While evidence for the extension of Monte Albán political hegemony outside the Valley remains unclear, evidence within the Valley is more substantial. First, in Monte Albán II times a number of regional centers of about equal importance and dominance are prevalent in the Valley. But by period III the regional centers became reduced in size, while Monte Albán underwent a tremendous growth. The number of sites displaying period IIIA materials also is reduced; in the Etla wing of the Valley they drop from about sixty in period II times to about twenty in Monte Albán IIIA.[66]

In period II, Monte Albán appears to have been relatively self-sufficient economically, evidence which would support the hypothesis that the Valley was fragmented into various states. There also is evidence of warfare in this period. In period IIIA the irrigation system at Monte Albán seems to have been abandoned, suggesting that the city had control of the resources of other areas in the Valley. There also seems to have been a cessation of military activity, or at least a decrease in its frequency, in Monte Albán III times.[67]

Study of the stone carvings from the Valley of Oaxaca also confirms the impression that a political synoecism had taken place. During Monte Albán I and II times, styles are strongly regionalized and display independence. But by Monte Albán III times, these local styles have disappeared and a uniform style is prevalent wherever monuments are found throughout the Valley.[68]

Although it seems likely that the Valley was politically unified in the Classic stage, the exact nature of that integration is unclear. The traditional interpretation, which is applied to similar situations in other parts of Mesoamerica, is that these were states or "empires" in which a number of towns or cities were united under the tutelage of rulers who resided in a central metropolis. These rulers are assumed also to have been priests, since great concern is evident in ceremonial and religious matters through the architecture and the art work. It also is assumed that the bond that united these various towns or cities was a religious one—or a common allegiance to serve the gods and their human representatives, the priests. It is primarily for these reasons that the Classic states of Mesoamerica have been called theocratic.[69]

Another view has modified this earlier interpretation. Michael D. Coe has argued, for example, that Classic Mesoamerican societies were not organized solely on a priestly basis, but also contained "secular lords who drew their power from lineage and conquest."[70] This interpretation projects backward in time some of the patterns of post-Classic society which prevailed at the time of Spanish Conquest. William Sanders as well as others also have suggested that the theocratic-militaristic dichotomy used to separate Classic Mesoamerica from its post-Classic manifestations needs qualification.[71]

While none of these scholars would seem to be denying that religion was an important integrative mechanism in Classic Mesoamerican societies, their qualifications serve to warn against the reification of broad typological contrasts. "Secular" influences also were present in the Classic stage, and the states and empires were not integrated exclusively through allegiance to a common theocratic principle. Intermarriage, trade, warfare, conquest, and the subjugation of conquered peoples for the purposes of exacting tribute also were factors promoting social and political synoecism.

In the Valley of Oaxaca, the hegemony of Monte Albán seems to have been achieved through conquest; a unified religion seems to have come after, not before, the synoecism of the Valley states. Once this unification was achieved and peace was restored, perhaps an allegiance to an ethnic-theocratic principle (the Zapotec Great Tradition) did constitute a vehicle which held the society together throughout the Classic stage.

This is not to suggest that the theocratic-militaristic dichotomy should be abandoned and that both Classic and post-Classic societies were organized on the same basis; a warrior-military complex seems much more dominant in post-Classic times than in the Classic. Rather, a careful analysis of the relationship between warfare and religion, and warriors and priests, should be made for both stages and for the periods within these stages. From what is known about preindustrial societies in other parts of the world, the priest-warrior dichotomy is a matter of relative position and emphasis, not the presence or absence of one or the other, and it depends on a multiplicity of factors, both internal and external, acting on particular states. In some societies, for example, a priestly elite may hold the upper hand and be able to subordinate a warrior class to its own interests. In others, the opposite is true. In still others, the two may be combined into a single group. In any society, religion may serve to legitimate warriors, just as warfare may serve to strengthen religious beliefs.

In summary, the Classic stage in the Valley of Oaxaca, as generally in Mesoamerica, contains a number of long and complex periods. Its climax in Monte Albán III perhaps is a case in which priests were dominant and were able to subordinate and control a warrior class, although at one time the priests also may have been warriors. In the post-Classic stage the reverse would seem to hold; warriors subordinated priests and employed them for their own purposes, even though the most prestigious of the warriors also had priestly functions.

The distinction between the Classic and post-Classic stages in Mesoamerica also perhaps suggests the same difference found between the medieval Papal States of Italy and the princely city-states of central Italy (a Guelph-Ghibelline distinction) or between the Byzantine and Spanish-American empires.

In still earlier times in the Old World, the Etruscan states were ruled by a king or prince (*lucumo*) who was also a priest and a warrior. In later Republican times this fusion segmented as priests and warriors diverged into separate structures. But they converged again.

With the achievement of the Pax Romana, after the fall of the Republic, the emperor was warrior as well as *pontifex maximus*. The study of such phenomena certainly would lead to productive insights into ancient Mesoamerican societies and states, insights that could lead to hypotheses testable in a number of state societies.

But regardless of the warrior-priest problem and its applicability to Mesoamerican rulers, there are other unanswered questions concerning the nature of Classic Mesoamerican states and empires, questions whose answers are crucial if these states are to be included in broader analyses of state societies. For example, what was the relationship between the rulers of Monte Albán and the constituent statelets which formed this central Oaxacan empire? Were the rulers of the constituent statelets of the same lineage as those at Monte Albán? Was the empire so tightly centralized that the ruler or rulers of Monte Albán controlled the appointment of constituent statelet rulers? Were there ranking hierarchies or district rulers intermediate between the rulers of the empire and those of the statelets?

To answer such questions, two lines of research are needed. In one, explicit hypotheses should be formulated concerning relationships between sociopolitical forms and archeological remains such as pottery distributions, settlement patterns, and art styles. It would seem that this approach could best be pursued where sociopolitical forms could be ascertained from historical records; hypotheses then could be formulated and tested in a controlled situation, that is, where historical records as well as comparable archeological data are available. If the results of such an approach prove fruitful, then archeologists would have a better indication of the kind of data to gather in areas such as the Valley of Oaxaca to answer the above questions. A second companion line of research would be to undertake coordinated, intensive studies of the inscriptions and monuments carved throughout the Valley and at Monte Albán. Work already accomplished in this area suggests that the Classic Zapotecs may have left more answers than is generally recognized.

3
Cycles of Conquest: Political Relationships in the Valley of Oaxaca During the Post-Classic Stage

ONTE ALBÁN IV, which has been designated as post-Classic, signals the collapse of the empire centered at Monte Albán as well as abandonment of that city. This depopulation probably was a gradual process; while some inhabitants may have lingered on for a time, it appears that after about A.D. 900 the bulk of the Monte Albán urban complex had fallen into ruins.[1]

Building activity ceased in the Grand Plaza during period IV. Only a number of burials are found, and various offerings are found in the temple ruins. These remains continue to reflect the Zapotec tradition.

The reasons for the collapse of Monte Albán in period IV are not clear. John Paddock suggests that the population had expanded to the limits of its agricultural technology and that cultural values had become so focused on "over-elaborated" areas of religion and art that technological innovations in agriculture were choked.[2] As a result, the priestly rulers were unable to cope with technological crises, which may have led to their demise, either through conquest, the rise of militarism, or some similar "revolutionary" movement. Whatever the causes, the period between A.D. 650 and A.D. 1000 was a time of upheaval throughout Mesoamerica. The Classic center of Teotihuacán was abandoned about 650; the great Maya centers of the Petén about 900.

A period V also has been distinguished at Monte Albán, beginning about 1350. Monte Albán still was uninhabited, as it had been in period IV. However, the burials and offerings of period V contained artifacts of a style different from those of period IV. The elaborate polychrome pottery, the detailed bone carvings, and the gold and metal work, such as that found in the famous Tomb 7 by Alfonso Caso, are characteristic of the post-Classic Mixtec cultural tradition.[3]

81

Mixteca-Puebla polychrome pottery in the Valley of Oaxaca: *top*: Monte Albán; *middle*: Zaachila; *bottom*: Yagul. (Drawn by Terry Prewitt after Alfonso Caso, Ignacio Bernal, and Jorge R. Acosta, *La cerámica de Monte Albán*; John Paddock (ed.), *Ancient Oaxaca*.)

In retrospect, Monte Albán was not the ideal site at which to establish a post-Classic sequence in the Valley of Oaxaca; however, earlier investigators could not have known this fact since, as has been noted, the site was essentially uninhabited at that stage. For example, period IV has been found at as many as 130 sites in the Valley; thus, while Monte Albán was abandoned, many other sites were not. It also appears that period IV begins much earlier in some places in the Valley than it does at Monte Albán—perhaps as early as the eighth or ninth century after Christ.[4]

Furthermore, although "Mixtec" traits have been used as the diagnostic for Monte Albán V, they are not as easy to identify as previously had been thought, since Mixtec culture had various regional manifestations, was subject to a variety of influences, and influenced developments in the Valley in various ways. Monte Albán V now appears to be less an ethnic period marked by the replacement or absorption of one ethnic group by another than it was a period of fluctuation and instability involving various ethnic groups, even though these groups tended to converge toward a common cultural tradition. In short, period V is a late manifestation in the Valley and is marked by the appearance of new cultural traits with various antecedents.

Consequently, what seems to be most important in distinguishing the post-Classic is not as much the addition or presence of different cultural traits as what these cultural traits express—a shift in the nature or orientation of the society. Militarism, and its associated features, also becomes pervasive in the Valley, as it does elsewhere in Mesoamerica. Neither a single dominant site, nor a singularly pervasive style, as was typical of the period of the Classic Monte Albán empire, is to be found in this stage. Instead, a number of sites are in evidence which display local expressions of style and elite culture. No single site seems to dominate—in size, complexity, or influence—the entire Valley region.

The fall of Monte Albán created a power vacuum; as a result, the post-Classic stage in the Valley was a time of turmoil, instability, and rapid social and cultural change. The Zapotecs retreated into lordships, princedoms, or city-states which fought against one another and against invading groups from the outside, particularly the Mixtecs and the Aztecs. Attempting to recapture their past glories, the Zapotec nobles instead struggled to maintain their very existence.

There are at least three periods or phases in this struggle after the fall of Monte Albán. First, as Monte Albán had been the religious center of the Classic stage, Mitla now became the Zapotec holy place and center of the priestly cult. As Monte Albán had been the seat of a political synoecism, attempts were now made to unify the Zapotec statelets under a single entity with Zaachila (Teozapotlán) as the political head.[5] The separation of Mitla and Zaachila, one primarily religious, the other primarily political, examplifies the segmentation of the Zapotec Great Tradition into the theocracy of the Classic stage and the militaristic state of the post-Classic and sets the tone for the basic tensions which generated changes in Zapotec culture and society.

A second period begins when the Valley Zapotec elites appear to have been influenced by ideas emanating from the Mixtecs, who were the archetypes of the post-Classic militarists. Some time in the fourteenth century, Mixtec cultural influence turned to conquest as the Mixtecs conquered Zaachila and drove the Zapotec supreme lord into exile at Tehuantepec, where he attempted to retain control of the Valley towns over which he had previously reigned. The Mixtecs then seem to have expanded their political power in the Valley, conquering some towns formerly held by Zaachila and influencing others; even Mitla became infused with Mixtec ideas and may have been conquered for a short period. The Mixtecs then came to dominate the western part of the Valley, with a political seat at Cuilapan.

A third phase seems to begin in the midst of this turmoil, sometime in the fifteenth century, when the Mexicas or Aztecs entered the area, conquering Cuilapan, Zaachila, Mitla, and other places. But their attempts to control the Valley, like those of the Zaachila Zapotecs and the Cuilapan Mixtecs, only brought more shifting alliances, warfare, and struggles between elites to establish and maintain power. The political unification of the Valley of Oaxaca was not to be realized until the Spanish conquest. Thus, as the militaristic atmosphere of the post-Classic produced political fragmentation along various lines, the Zapotec Great Tradition of the Classic was also fractured and never again constituted the standard for the Zapotec-speaking inhabitants of southern Mexico.

DOCUMENTARY SOURCES

For the Classic stage, the sources of information are almost exclusively archeological; for the post-Classic stage, written documentary resources are also available. Some of the best sources of information on ancient Mesoamerica come from Oaxaca in the form of the Mixtec codices, which consist of hieroglyphics or pictographs painted on deer skin and contain historical data on marriage alliances, the conquests of towns, and the genealogies of various lords. These codices also permit the reconstruction of the culture of the Mixtec peoples, for they depict not only lords and their families but also gods, names, places, geographical locations, calendrical dates, plants and animals, houses, temples, weapons, dress, and other items. Similar pictographic writings also are found carved, engraved, incised, or painted on bone, pottery, jewelry, and other objects.

These codices are both pre-Spanish and post-Conquest in origin; the most important ones are probably the following:

1. The *Codex Vindobonensis*, along with codices *Becker I* and *II* in Vienna. The reverse side of the *Vindobonensis* is of pre-Hispanic origin and probably was painted as early as 1357.

2. The *Zouche-Nuttall Codex* in the British Museum. This probably is the earliest of the Mixtec codices and dates from about 1350.

3. The *Codex Colombino* in the National Museum of Mexico. This is a post-Conquest document dealing with the Mixtec lordship of Tututepec on the south coast of Oaxaca and probably dates from about 1541.

4. The *Bodley 2858* and the *Selden I* and *II* codices in the Bodleian Library of Oxford University. The *Bodley* dates from about 1521 and the *Selden II* from about 1555.

5. Several important *lienzos*, all of post-Conquest origin, such as the *Lienzo de Antonio León* in Toronto, the *Map of Teozacoalco* in Austin, and the *Lienzo de Ihuitlán* in the Brooklyn Museum in New York.[6]

Painstaking work by many scholars, but notably by Alfonso Caso, now allows these manuscripts to be read with some certainty. Caso, for example, discovered in 1949 that the *Map of Teozacoalco* could be used as a kind of Rosetta Stone to read earlier manuscripts.[7]

Some documents attributed to the Aztecs of central Mexico also pertain to matters concerning the peoples of the Valley of Oaxaca in the post-Classic stage. Noteworthy among these are the *Matricula de los tributos* and the *Codex Mendocino*, which deal with the tribute lists of the Aztec "empire."[8]

Since pre-Conquest history was still in the memories of the native inhabitants of Mesoamerica during the early Spanish Colonial period, there are many Spanish accounts which deal with aspects of pre-Spanish culture history. These sources have a very diverse character. For example, the *Relaciones Geográficas* compiled toward the end of the sixteenth century by order of Philip II of Spain were to provide a detailed description of the inhabitants and lands of the Indies and were to be used in the preparation of official histories. To get uniform information, López de Velasco, the official royal chronicler-cosmographer, made a questionnaire containing fifty chapters of questions, with topics ranging from the aboriginal form of government to matters of colonial economy. Local crown representatives, called *corregidores*, using members of the Indian nobility as informants, were asked to provide answers to the questions and return the completed material to the viceroy. While most of the documents which resulted from this questionnaire were completed in the 1580's, some of the material to which they refer date from pre-Conquest times.[9]

Use of the *relaciones* on matters of the pre-Spanish period does, of course, have its difficulties. They are often vague and incomplete, and sometimes misleading, for various motives were involved in imparting information. In short, the *relaciones*, like all documentary sources, must be used with caution.

Additional sources of information are the dictionaries and grammars of native languages compiled by Dominican friars. The Dominicans of Oaxaca, like their Franciscan counterparts in central Mexico, paid great attention to the native languages and generally adopted the policy of teaching the Indians Christian dogma in their native tongues instead of attempting to teach them Spanish. Although there are Nahuatl dictionaries by Molina and Olmos,[10] as well as Mixtec works by Fray Francisco de Alvarado and Antonio de los Reyes,[11] the most important works, for purposes here, are the Zapotec dictionary and grammar compiled by Fray Juan de Córdova. Córdova came to the Valley of Oaxaca some twenty years after the Spanish conquest in 1521 and remained until his death. Both his dictionary and his grammar were published in 1578 and represented almost thirty years of labor.

There are some uncertainties concerning Córdova's whereabouts at times, although it appears that he was first assigned to Huitzo, later was sent to Teitipac or Tlacochahuaya, or both, and may have served for a time in Tehuantepec. Taken together, these two works by Córdova comprise an encyclopedic account of Zapotec culture, even though there are problems of interpreting them, especially from a linguistic point of view, since the friar was not a trained linguist. A recent study argues that the Zapotec represented by Córdova is that of the Valley and corresponds most closely to that spoken in Teotitlán del Valle today, although in the sixteenth century Valley Zapotec dialects were not as marked as they are today, and Valley and Isthmus Zapotec also were not distinct.[12]

The *Junta Colombina* dictionary of the Zapotec language is comparable to Córdova's work.[13] Although its author has not been positively identified, it undoubtedly was compiled during the same period and parallels Córdova's work in many respects. Other grammars and materials, such as the *Confesonarios*,[14] also contain Zapotec language material.

Unfortunately, no chronicler of Oaxaca compares with Bernardino de Sahagún or Alonso de Zorita, who left detailed accounts of the native culture and society of the Aztecs.[15] Their nearest counterpart is Fray Francisco de Burgoa, a Dominican friar born in Oaxaca in 1600 and a descendant of the first conquistadores of the province. His two works are dedicated primarily to recording the history of the mission of his order in Oaxaca.[16] His entire life was spent in that region, living among the people, collecting legends and customs, and teaching the Christian doctrine. Burgoa died in 1681 in Zaachila, where he was vicar.

Burgoa's accounts remain the primary chronicles for Oaxacan history during the pre-Spanish as well as the early Colonial period, even though he, like most Spanish chroniclers, frequently failed to differentiate between data he collected and those that were borrowed or copied from other sources. As a result, Burgoa often is inconsistent. His accounts contain constant digressions and citations of Biblical stories and references intermixed with legends and stories concerning pre-Spanish Oaxaca. In addition, the pre-Spanish customs and legends he relates had undergone many years of various influences.

Other chroniclers, such as Torquemada, Antonio de Herrera y Tordesillas, Chimalpahin, Ixtlilxóchitl, Durán, Tezozómoc, and Sahagún,[17] deal briefly with events in the Zapotec country, specifically with the incursions of the Mexicas or Aztecs into Oaxaca. Their coverage of other topics relating to the Zapotecs is very slight. Additional sources consist of Spanish colonial documents from the Archivo General de la Nación, Mexico, and the Archivo General de las Indias in Seville, Spain. They include miscellaneous decrees of the viceregal government of New Spain relating to various aspects of Indian affairs and government, land grants, appointments to office, tribute lists and censuses, records of litigation over ownership of lands pertaining to specific Indian communities and individuals, inquisition proceedings, and confirmations of status.[18]

While these documents, mostly unpublished, deal primarily with events during the Spanish Colonial period, they often contain information that refers to aboriginal conditions or continuities in the Indian society. Thus, it is often possible to make inferential statements about aboriginal society and culture from them. The Spaniards, for example, were extremely interested in the rights and prerogatives of the Indian nobility as well as the native Indian communities and their pre-Conquest political affiliations.

Unfortunately, no pre-Spanish Zapotec codices are known from the Valley of Oaxaca, although a number of sources indicate that they existed at one time.[19] However, there are various extant colonial documents dealing with the genealogies of the Zapotec lords of Zaachila and Tehuantepec, such as the *Lienzo de Guevea* and the *Mapa de Huilotepec*.[20] These documents contain pictographs with Zapotec and Spanish notations. Additional post-Conquest pictographic sources from the sierra Zapotec area include the *Lienzo de Tiltepec*, the *Lienzo de Tabaa*, the *Codex Pérez García*, and the *Lienzo de Analco*.[21] Many codices that were previously thought to be Zapotec, such as the *Codex Sánchez Solís* and the *Codex Baranda*, are now considered to be Mixtec even though they have some content pertaining to Zapotec areas.[22]

THE MIXTECS AND THE CONQUEST
OF THE VALLEY OF OAXACA

The name *Mixtec* has been used to designate a linguistic grouping, an art style, and a social or cultural type. However, it is now clear that the three are not necessarily coterminous. As has been discussed, Mixtecan included a variety of languages in addition to Mixtec proper. While the distribution of these languages can be plotted at the time of Spanish contact and in modern times, it is not always certain which was spoken in a given area in the remote pre-Spanish past. Nor can the proportion of speakers of a given Mixtecan language in a certain place be easily ascertained; a language which today dominates a region may in the pre-Spanish past have been spoken only by a tiny minority of overlords.

While a distinctive art style seems to have been shared by the various Mixtecan speakers, or the Tetlamixteca, as John Paddock prefers to call them,[23] its distribution was not confined only to the regions of Mixtecan speech but also was found in other areas, particularly in Puebla and Tlaxcala, where Nahuatl was spoken at the time of Spanish Conquest. For this reason, this style has been called Mixteca-Puebla.[24]

The most important general features of this style are the codical art and detailed work in several media, such as pottery, bone, precious stone, and metal—particularly gold. The finest pottery in Mesoamerican history, especially a type centered in Cholula and the Mixteca Alta and traded throughout Mesoamerica, also is associated with this style. Polished brown ware, tripod bowls finished with animal feet or stepped ends, globular jars, and goblets were painted black, white, yellow, ochre, pink, red, and orange colors, which on firing acquired a brilliant luster. This ware was decorated with stepped-frets (*xicalco-liuhquis*) and meanders and depicted feather plumes, ritual animals, day glyphs, ceremonial objects, gods, symbols of war, flowers, clouds, and crossed bones in a style like that of the codices.[25]

Two other wares may be associated with this style and have been found particularly at the site of Coixtlahuaca in the Mixteca Alta. One is a grey ware which is very thin and fine and is associated with large pottery jars. Another, and perhaps a basic one, is an unpolished cream ware with a red decoration on a conical or hemispherical bowl.

The red (or sometimes almost black) painted designs are typically geometric and display little variation.[26]

However, the artistic talents of the producers of the Mixteca-Puebla style were not restricted to pottery and codices. They also were the metallurgists *par excellence* of Mesoamerica and undoubtedly taught this craft to the Toltec and Aztec peoples of central Mexico. Gold, silver, and copper, and perhaps also a type of tin, were all worked. While objects made from these metals are associated with burials and were primarily symbols of prestige, many utilitarian objects, such as hoes, axes, spades, adzes, chisels, fishhooks, blowpipes, awls, punches, tweezers, nails, nets, needles, pins, lance heads and arrowheads, also were made of metal.[27] Bones, intricately carved in the style of the codices, and precious stones, such as greenstone, jade, rock crystal, shell, coral, turquoise, obsidian, tecali, and pearl, also were worked. While architecture and sculpture are characteristics not generally associated with the Mixteca-Puebla style, these artists were masters of "the decorative and the precious" and emphasized "highly developed technique and fine craftsmanship."[28]

The Mixteca-Puebla art style traditionally has been associated with the Mixtecs of the Mixteca Alta, as Mixtec culture and society traditionally have been associated with the states of that region. In the Mixteca Alta, an elite group speaking Mixtec proper subjugated the earlier population of the region perhaps as early as the seventh century, from which time there is evidence for the establishment of the first Mixtec dynasty.[29]

The rise of the Mixtec states signals the beginning of the post-Classic in Mesoamerica and the arrival of a particular type of militaristic state based on tribute and conquest. Post-Classic Mixtec society involved a transfer of political power from what were theocratic rulers to secular warlords, although their culture was built on the remnants of the Classic heritage.

It is possible that Mixtecs, or a Tetlamixteca group, constituted part of the Teotihuacán population and retreated to the Mixteca Alta when the city fell. Possibly the Mixtecs also resided at Cholula in Puebla, where the largest pyramid in Mesoamerica was built and where, from about the same time, the finest polychrome pottery occurs. Wherever they had been previously, by the time the Toltecs constructed Tula in the tenth century and developed their militaristic tribute state, the

Mixtecs were well entrenched in the Mixteca Alta and had developed alliances and relationships with the Toltecs, serving as the source of many of their artistic ideas.

Thus, the Mixtecs, as well as the Mixtecan or Tetlamixteca peoples, were intimately associated with the Mixteca-Puebla style, and the Tetlamixteca were perhaps its originators and major craftsmen. However, the presence of artifacts in this style does not, without additional evidence, necessarily imply the presence of Mixtecan or Mixtec speakers, for artifacts can be traded, and styles and techniques borrowed.

Although there was some overall similarity in the Mixteca-Puebla style, the various Tetlamixteca peoples were not politically unified. For example, by the time of the Spanish conquest, a people, or an elite, speaking Mixtec proper, occupied not only the Mixteca Alta, but also the coastal region (Mixteca Costa), where the important "kingdom" of Tututepec flourished. It appears that the Mixteca Alta was organized into a number of autonomous "kingdoms," or lordships, although the Mixteca Costa may have been more politically centralized. In general, Mixtec society was organized around a dispersed community consisting of a head town and a number of subject hamlets ruled by a hereditary lord and stratified into a noble and common class. Community or lordship autonomy was fostered through the worship of a specific patron deity, although there were also, on another level, deities common to Mixtec culture as a whole. Quetzalcoatl, for example, seems to have been worshiped throughout the Mixtec area.[30]

The post-Classic was a time of population expansion in Mesoamerica. It is not clear what caused this growth. In many local regions, the population may have reached the limits of its food supply, and militarism may have constituted one solution to an ecological dilemma. The political vacuum created by the fall of the Classic empires may have generated a search for new bases of political power coupled with a shift in values on the part of elites, which in itself could create a competition for a scarce resource.

At any rate, militarism and the subjugation of peoples for the purposes of exacting tribute, coupled with the sacrifice of victims to the gods, became a prevalent pattern. But while various lordships vied for supremacy over one another, few succeeded in maintaining supremacy for very long.

Eight Deer in the Mixtec codices: *a*, ♂ 8 Deer "Tiger Claw" and ♀ 13 Serpent "Flowered Serpent"—Nuttall 26c; *b*, ♂ 8 Deer "Tiger Claw" captures ♂ 4 Wind "Fire Serpent"—Nuttall 83a–b; *c*, ♂ 8 Deer "Tiger Claw" captures town of Acatepec—Bodley 10–11; *d*, the sacrifice and interment of ♂ 8 Deer—Bodley 14. (Source: Mary Elizabeth Smith, *Picture Writing from Ancient Southern Mexico*, figs. 7b, 15b, 51a, and 75.)

The only evidence there is for an attempted unified "Mixtec" state illustrates this pattern. A famous warrior lord, 8 Deer Tiger Claw of Tilantongo, Tututepec, and various other places, conquered some lordships throughout Oaxaca. 8 Deer, however, met the inevitable warrior's fate—he was defeated and was sacrificed to the gods at Cuilapan in the Valley of Oaxaca.[31]

Rulers of Mixtec princedoms or lordships, as did others in post-Classic Mesoamerica, used various devices to satisfy their expansive tendencies. Alliances and marriages generally were the first step on the road to military conquest. This method apparently is the way the Mixtecs entered the Valley of Oaxaca. According to the *relaciones* of Cuilapan and Teozapotlán (Zaachila), the Mixtecs moved into the Valley about three hundred years before 1581, that is, about 1280. The *relaciones* state that there were two Mixtec-Zapotec marriages. One, apparently the first, took place between a Mixtec woman and a lord of Zaachila about three hundred years before the writing of the *relación* of that town, but the association attracted few Mixtecs. The second marriage occurred between the sister of the wife of the lord of Teozapotlán and a Mixtec nobleman a few years before the coming of the Spaniards. As a result of the latter marriage, the new couple was given Cuilapan and took up residence there; many Mixtecs came there as a result of this marriage.[32]

These Mixtecs came from the region of Almoloyas, which Burgoa places in the Mixteca Alta some seven leagues to the northwest of Yanhuitlán.[33] Alfonso Caso, by carefully correlating Mixtec codices of the pre-Spanish period with Colonial *lienzos* and documents, has related individuals from Cuilapan to those of Yanhuitlán, the center of a lordship to which Almoloyas was subject. He also has been able to relate the nobles in the documents to individuals depicted in the tombs of Zaachila, thus confirming the historical value of the codices.[34]

According to the *relación* of Cuilapan, its site originally was called Sayucu, "at the foot of the hill."[35] Burgoa elaborates: ". . . the main settlement in early times was in a very humid, muddy land, good for cultivation. It was situated at the bottom of a hill, where water from streams could be filtered off. This place was called Sahayuyu [Sayucu]. . . . In this place they [the Mixtecs] were found by the Marqués del Valle [Hernán Cortés]."[36] From this site at Sayucu the

Mixtecs expanded their influence in the Valley of Oaxaca, founding new towns, establishing themselves in Zapotec towns, and subjecting the Zapotec towns to tribute. According to Burgoa, the Mixtecs had expanded

> . . . and surrounded the town of Theozapotlán [Zaachila] with towns which today are the nearby towns of San Raimundo to the north and, across the river to the east, San Pablo. Although built like a castle, the *cabecera* [Zaachila] was unable to resist. He [the Zapotec prince] was forced to flee . . . and withdrew, allowing the Mixtecs to advance and found the town of Xoxocotlán. . . . They went on to found Huayapa, San Francisco, San Sebastián, and Santa Lucía, all of which are to the east of the Ciudad of Antequera. In this way the Mixtecs were taking over when the Marques arrived at the Conquest. . . .[37]

Dating the expansion of the Mixtecs from Cuilapan into other areas of the Valley is difficult, in part because of the turmoil created by Aztec incursions into the region, culminating in the subjugation of Cuilapan. The *relaciones* differ on this date.

For example, the *relación* of Chichicapa states that the Mixtecs were waging war against Zaachila when the news of the Spanish arrived. The *relación* of Teotitlán del Valle notes that the Teotitleños had been subject to the Zapotec lord of Tehuantepec—which occurred after the Mixtecs had taken Zaachila—before being subject to Cuilapan, thus placing the date earlier than the Chichicapa *relación*.[38]

There is abundant evidence that the Mixtecs of Cuilapan had ousted the Zapotec lord from Zaachila and had forced him to seek refuge in Tehuantepec, an area he had previously subjugated. It seems that "the Mixtecs took offence at an insult they felt was directed at the son of an Indian lady who came from the Mixteca to marry into Teozapotlán. This son went to his homeland and from there stirred up war. Eventually these [Mixtecs] engaged in battle with the inhabitants of Teozapotlán, who, realizing the advantage their enemies had, fled to Tehuantepec."[39]

Insulting one's masculinity, one's ethnicity, or one's women was a common native explanation for warfare in post-Classic Mesoamerica. Burgoa provides an additional, more specific reason for the open hostilities between the Mixtecs and the Zapotecs. He states that the lord of Zaachila had engaged the Mixtecs as allies in his conquest of the Mixe and of the Huave of the Isthmus of Tehuantepec. As their reward, the lord of Zaachila gave the Mixtecs only a small piece of land at Mixtequilla. The Mixtecs, insulted by such measly spoils, went to war against their former Zapotec ally.[40] They won the struggle, forcing him to flee.

One pattern of Mixtec expansion in the Valley, then, consisted of displacing the Zapotec ruler and taking over political authority in the town. Eventually, these towns contained both Mixtec and Zapotec inhabitants, who resided in different *barrios*. A number of towns are known to exhibit this kind of arrangement, especially those around Cuilapan. There was a Mixtec *barrio* in Zaachila, according to Burgoa, for he writes that ". . . as I find myself priest of this town of Teozapotlán, I have in it a Mixtec *barrio*." Furthermore; "The Mixtecs still hold the lands and towns they conquered as principal evidence of their deeds. Even within the capital at Theozapotlán in which I am writing, they had a stronghold, and they still occupy it as a *barrio* of this town, not to mention the other places that they founded around it."[41]

Santa Ana (Santa Ana Zegache), near Cuilapan, also had a Mixtec and a Zapotec *barrio* which apparently dated from the time when the Zapotecs and Mixtecs were at war. In this community there was intermarriage between the Mixtecs and the Zapotecs. Burgoa relates that "because its lands were the best ones the Mixtec chiefs had gotten from the King of Teozapotlán [Zaachila] in open battle . . . taking over the lands . . . they did not take the lives of the inhabitants, so that they might profit from the knowledge and experience of the conquered. . . . the survival of both groups . . . has taken place in this town of Santa Ana."[42] The Mixtecs also founded towns in the area of the present-day city of Oaxaca and probably placed officials appointed by the lord of Cuilapan into these new settlements. This pattern also was followed in the relationships between the head town and its *sujetos* (subject towns or villages) on the lordship level among the Mixtecs of the Mixteca Alta. That these new settlements were probably *sujetos* in this sense is suggested by the fact that San Francisco (Nuhuhuyyo in Mixtec) and Xoxocotlán (Nuhuyoho) were still subject to Cuilapan in 1580; Xoxocotlán remained a *sujeto* as late as 1659.[43]

It also appears that Mixtec Cuilapan subjugated towns in the valley of Etla. Burgoa mentions that there were both Mixtecs and Zapotecs in Huitzo (Guaxolotitlán),[44] indicating that there might have been two *barrios*, one Zapotec and one Mixtec. The *relación* of Huitzo also states that its people had wars with Coatlán, Miahuatlán, Chichicapa, and Nejapa and allied themselves with Oaxaca, Cuilapan, and Etla.[45] This may be interpreted to imply that the people of Huitzo were conquered by the Mixtecs and, since they were all allied to Cuilapan, that Huitzo and Etla were Mixtec towns.

Evidence is contradictory on the Cuilapan Mixtec expansion into other areas. The Mixtec-based *relación* of Cuilapan and Burgoa indicate that all of the towns of the Valley of Oaxaca had been subjugated, including the Zapotec towns of Mitla and Teitipac in the Valley branch of Tlacolula.[46] However, the *relaciones* of these towns, which probably display a Zapotec bias, state that they only paid tribute to Zapotec Zaachila and to the Aztecs or Mexicas.[47] The *relación* of Teotitlán del Valle, in the same Valley branch, states that tribute was paid to the Mixtecs of Cuilapan,[48] while the *relación* of Macuilxóchitl, a town near Mitla, states that they had made war against Mitla by order of the prince of Zaachila. This information might imply that Mitla was also under Mixtec subjugation, although it is possible that this was not Cuilapan Mixtec subjugation but perhaps control by the Mixtecs of Tututepec, who also attempted to conquer that area.[49] It might also suggest that Zaachila had turned against Mitla, the theocratic center of Zapotec culture, and was trying to bring it under secular militaristic rule.

The first archeological evidence of Mixteca-Puebla influences in the Valley of Oaxaca came from Monte Albán, where, as has already been noted, period V was originally defined in conjunction with burials. While the seven tombs in which various burials and offerings were found displayed a typical Zapotec architectural style, the contents clearly were not of Zapotec style.

The most spectacular discovery of twentieth-century Mesoamerican archeology was Tomb 7 at Monte Albán. In it were found silver objects with a total weight of 325 grams, including a vessel (the largest silver object known from pre-Columbian Mexico), bracelets, tweezers, plaques, rings, and bells. There were also 121 gold objects with a total weight of 3,598.7 grams, including pectorals, garment ornaments, pendants, rings, necklaces, tweezers, ear ornaments, and other objects. Carved bones, turquoise mosaics, and objects carved

Patio of the Tombs at Zaachila. (By Tenth Muse, Inc.)

of precious stone added to the already rich array of status items. Careful study of the stylistic motifs and workmanship techniques of this "jewelry" showed its clearest analogs to be from Coixtlahuaca and other sites in the Mixteca Alta as well as items depicted in the Mixtec codices of that region.[50]

The tombs at Monte Albán did not contain identical offerings, nor did they display identical cultural characteristics; some, including Tomb 7, were used more than once. In no single tomb was a full association of Mixteca-Puebla traits found, particularly that of a clear association of polychrome and gold. Again, Monte Albán was not a good place to precisely define period V.[51]

At Zaachila, in two tombs excavated in 1962, a more typical Mixteca-Puebla assemblage was found. Tombs 1 and 2 display abundant polychrome pottery, gold objects, carved bones, and turquoise mosaics. Two additional tombs, Tombs 3 and 4, have more recently been found and also display Mixteca-Puebla traits even though they are not identical to those found in Tombs 1 and 2.[52]

Personages depicted on the walls of Tomb 1 have been identified with individuals in the Mixtec codices. For example, two personages named ♂ 9 Flower and ♂ 5 Flower were found represented. While the association of ♂ 9 Flower is not certain, ♂ 5 Flower is the individual mentioned in the *Codex Nuttall* as the great-grandfather of ♂ 6 Water "Colored Strips" from Yanhuitlán. The latter had a daughter who married ♂ 8 Deer "Fire Serpent," possibly the individual buried in Tomb 1.[53] It is also significant that Tomb 1 was located near the highest mound at Zaachila, which was probably the stronghold or "castle" quoted above in Burgoa.

The data from Zaachila suggest that the spectacular contents of Tomb 7 at Monte Albán probably are quite late period V and date from the time when the Mixtecs had already conquered Zaachila,

Lords of Yanhuitlán as depicted in plaster sculptures of Tomb 1, Zaachila: *a*, ♂ 9 Flower; *b*, ♂ 5 Flower. (Source: Mary Elizabeth Smith, *Picture Writing from Ancient Southern Mexico*, figs. 39d and e.)

a   *b*

probably some time in the late fourteenth or the fifteenth century. The other Mixteca-Puebla traits found in various tombs at Monte Albán perhaps represent earlier influences, displaying mixed Zapotec-Mixtec cultural traits. Caso, for example, has published information on two stelae which "suggest certain Mixtec (Mixteca-Puebla) traits incorporated into Zapotec writing."[54] One of these stelae comes from San Jaunito, located at the foot of Monte Albán.

A tomb found at Huitzo, in the extreme northern part of the Valley of Oaxaca, also indicates the presence of Mixteca-Puebla influences in that region. This tomb, decorated with carved door jambs very similar to those found at Tilantongo in the Mixteca Alta, contained, in addition to the bones of many individuals, beads of gold, green stone, and amethyst with polychrome vessels in Mixteca-Puebla style. The tomb has no exact parallels in either the Mixteca Alta or in the Valley of Oaxaca, although some of the polychromes resembled those found in Tomb 30 at Yagul in the valley of Tlacolula. The polychromes have more direct affinities, however, with those of Las Pilitas and Coixtlahuaca in the Mixteca Alta. It has been suggested that this was the tomb of an important family or lineage.[55]

Tomb 1 at Huitzo appears to have been reused many times. Although it cannot be related specifically to the Zapotec tombs, it also is not definitely Mixtec, although the contents are of Mixteca-Puebla style. Nevertheless, Huitzo was at one time Zapotec, and even though it was located on the periphery of the Mixteca Alta, it must be inferred that it was well within the arena of the post-Classic struggle between Zapotec and Mixtec elite groups.

Mixteca-Puebla influence on the Valley of Oaxaca seems to have occurred over a long period of time, dating from perhaps as early as the twelfth century. Furthermore, archeological evidence for Mixteca-Puebla influences in this region is not restricted to Monte Albán, Zaachila, or Huitzo, but also is found in the eastern or Tlacolula arm.

Mitla, a well-preserved ruin in the valley of Tlacolula known for centuries by travelers, while occupied in earlier times, assumes its greatest importance in the post-Classic. Two types of structures are represented there. First, there is a group of temple-pyramids, located south of the river at Mitla, called the South Group, which represents what was probably the ceremonial center of the site at one time. The Adobe Group, north of the river, also is apparently pyramidal.[56]

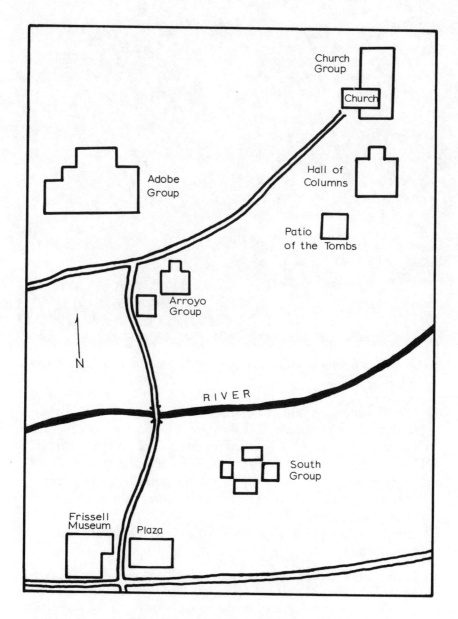

Map 8. Archeological zone of Mitla, Oaxaca. (Drawn by Terry Prewitt after John Paddock (ed.), *Oaxaca in Ancient Mesoamerica*)

Hall of the Columns at Mitla, seen from the Patio of the Tombs. (By Tenth Muse, Inc.)

The remaining groups of buildings at Mitla (the Church Group, the Group of the Columns, and the Arroyo Group) are north of the river and contain palatial structures instead of temple-pyramids. These palatial structures dominate the site as it is seen today, a factor that some interpret as indicating that in the post-Classic stage monuments to the gods were relegated to a secondary role in contrast to dwellings for the living.[57]

These buildings, arranged around patios, have a number of characteristic features:

> In all cases the rectangular patios are bordered on each side by an apartment. The Group of the Columns is on a platform; the others are only slightly raised above the level of the patio. These patios are sometimes connected to one another or, as in the Group of the Columns, are separate. Only in one case is there a small adoratorio in the center. The rooms are long and narrow; when two patios are connected it is by the winding passage from a room to its adjacent patio. The rooms have either one

Patio of the Tombs at Mitla, showing the distinct levels.

Hall of the Columns at Mitla, looking east, showing the greca or stepped-fret designs in the panels. (Courtesy Kay Parker.)

or three doors. In some cases the outside corners of the apartments meet in a right angle, in others there is an empty space between them.[58]

Various tombs, which indicate that the site was used as a burial ground, also have been found. In some, gold beads, copper bells, and polychrome pottery, of apparent Mixteca-Puebla affiliation, have been found. The tombs, however, appear to be of Zapotec construction.[59]

Construction techniques at Mitla seem to have been relatively uniform. Walls consisted of a core of mud and stone covered with plaster or trachite and often were filled with rubble containing sherds of fine grey or polychrome pottery of Mixteca-Puebla affiliation. Stones are well fitted, although of different sizes, and joined with mortar. The Mitla palatial structures, inside and out, were decorated with a mosaic of fitted small stones which form step-fret patterns in various designs. The wall panels in which the stones were fitted were painted red, while the frets were painted white for contrast and emphasis.[60] Although step-fret designs had their beginnings in Monte Albán II,

Interior room of the Hall of the Columns at Mitla, showing the greca designs.

Detail of a greca panel at Mitla, showing the mosaic construction.

Mitla mural painting in Mixteca-Puebla style. (Drawn by Carol Smith after Ignacio Marquina, *Arquitectura prehispánica* [México, 1951].)

in the post-Classic stage they assumed more importance than before in the Valley. They also are found at Zaachila and are frequently encountered in the Mixtec codices.

Monolithic stones of extraordinary size and weight, drawn from a nearby quarry without draft animals and fashioned with only stone tools, are known from Mitla. They were used as columns and lintels in both the palatial structures and the tombs. Mural paintings from the Mitla Church Group are Mixteca-Puebla in style. The nature of the year sign, plus depictions of deities and lords, relate them to Mixteca-Puebla and not Zapotec style.

While the palatial structures at Mitla generally have been assigned to period V and thus identified as "Mixtec," this classification must remain tentative. First, the palaces contain no stratigraphy, and, as a result, it is difficult to assign them to either period IV or period V, although they are almost certainly post-Classic. Second, the stratigraphy elsewhere at Mitla is unclear. For example, the South Group showed a peculiar sequence: First, it revealed Zapotec of Monte Albán IIIA (Burial 1); then Zapotec of period IV (Burial 2). However, the next two sequences are difficult to assess. A tomb (3C) has been identified as Mixteca-Puebla although it contains no polychrome or metal but only stone mosaics and miniature vessels of possible Mixteca-Puebla derivation. Tomb 3C was destroyed, however, and over its ruins was

constructed a pyramidal mound of Zapotec style. The sequence then becomes: III, IV, V, IV(?).[61]

The *relación* of Mitla, and Burgoa, indicate that Mitla was the Zapotec religious center, presided over by a Zapotec high priest, who is likened to a bishop or pope—a common equation in Spanish sources. It also was a burial ground for the highest-ranking Zapotec nobility; second-rank nobles were apparently buried in Teitipac.[62] Burgoa relates further that the palaces of Mitla contained the dwellings of the high priest and his attendants as well as apartments for visiting dignitaries.[63] Mitla also had a *cacique*, a secular lord.[64] Of course, it is not certain to which specific period of Zapotec history these accounts refer, except that it was sometime after the fall of Monte Albán.

Extensive excavations undertaken at Yagul (probably the old Tlacolula) relate to the problems at Mitla.[65] Yagul is built on the south and west slopes of a low hill to the northeast of present-day Tlacolula. On the summit of this hill is a fortress of stone and mud walls which is in most respects identical to a fortress located on a crag some 154 meters above the valley floor a mile or two from Mitla. These fortresses apparently were used as places of refuge during military attacks. On the south slope are the chief ceremonial, commercial, and administrative areas of Yagul. There were located bases for temples (pyramidal mounds), palace structures with patios, a ball court similar to the one at Monte Albán, and some thirty-five tombs. The central precinct measures approximately 140 meters from east to west and 180 meters

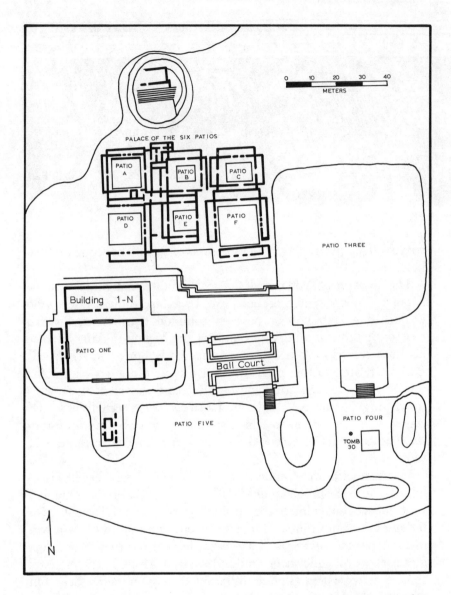

Map 9. Archeological zone of Yagul, Oaxaca. (Drawn by Terry Prewitt after John Paddock (ed.), *Ancient Oaxaca*)

Yagul, looking east from Patio 1; Yagul fort is located near the outcrop in the background.

from north to south. The site also extends for some distance beyond the central precinct and contains what were domestic dwellings.

Near the center of the precinct is a compact group of buildings containing a large palatial structure—the Palace of the Six Patios—which, as its name implies, consists of a number of structures joined by patios. The southeastern part of this group (Patio F) contained the best stratigraphy at the site. Patio F contains five floors and five and one-half meters of superimposed construction.[66] Of the various levels, the later ones, particularly those below floors 1 and 2, con-

Palace of the Six Patios at Yagul. (By Tenth Muse, Inc.)

tained polychrome pottery of Mixteca-Puebla character. The lower
levels contained pottery of Monte Albán III–IV style. Classic Zapotec-
style buildings are found in the lower levels of this complex but have
been replaced by structures in a different style in the three upper levels,
a style that links them to the palaces of Mitla.

Both polychrome and unpolished cream ware of general Mixteca-
Puebla style are found at Yagul, although they seem to occur later
than the grey ware and miniature vessels which also have been linked
to the Tetlamixteca peoples. Necklaces of jade and long copper
needles, of Mixteca-Puebla affiliation, also occur, although there are
no spectacular carved bones or elaborate metal jewelry (although
some jewelry has been found) as were found at Monte Albán or
Zaachila.

Greca mosaics are common in the various tombs at Yagul, as they
are on the facades of the buildings. While some of their architecture
resembles that of earlier Zapotec tombs, one feature has no precedent

Interior room of the Palace of the Six Patios at Yagul. (Courtesy Ronald Spores.)

in Zapotec architecture—the placement of tombs with their facades joined at right angles to one another in a unit of three tombs, as is found in Tomb 30. The only other grouping of this type is known at Coixtlahuaca in the Mixteca Alta.[67]

The processes of cultural development in this area are further revealed at the site of Lambityeco, near Yagul. Excavations at this site have been particularly important, for it is here that Monte Albán IV, as distinct from period IIIB, has been most clearly delineated.[68] At Lambityeco the Zapotec tradition continues, for many traits characteristic of Monte Albán IIIB are found, such as urns of Cocijo, the Zapotec rain god and patron, the *talud-tablero* architectural feature, and other objects associated with Classic Monte Albán culture. All of these, however, show a kind of decadence or deterioration in craftsmanship.

But a difference in emphasis plus the addition of some new traits not found in Monte Albán IIIB define Monte Albán IV at Lambityeco.

Building 1-N at Yagul, showing a greca panel (at left) similar to those of Mitla. (By Tenth Muse, Inc.)

These traits include new pottery types, iconographically novel urns, stone veneer construction, the use of true grecas or stepped-frets on buildings, and, perhaps most important of all, inscriptions on stone and plaster sculptures which display a quite different content from those of Monte Alban III.[69]

Also, a number of plaster sculptures, located on the sides of a stairway, as portraitlike heads on the facades of tombs, and on friezes in the *tableros* of an altar, have been found at Lambityeco. Other sculpture is reported from Monte Albán in Period IIIA and is later found in Tomb 1 at Zaachila. The content of these plaster sculptures is striking. The friezes depict males grasping human femurs, a symbol of valor and bravery associated with battle. The portraitures depict what appear to be husbands and wives, with associated name glyphs, and

Facade of Tomb 30 at Yagul; grecas on either side of the entrance are carved instead of mosaic construction. (By Tenth Muse, Inc.)

are accompanied by information of a more worldly and secular nature. The tombs at Lambityeco are apparently those of secular elite families or lineages, and their facades record matters of lineage, marriage, and perhaps the noteworthy deeds of those interred within instead of the complex religious iconography common at Monte Albán in Classic times.

Stone carvings from the Valley of Oaxaca, such as a *lápida* from a tomb between Cuilapan and Zaachila (along with numerous other examples), also seem to display a content similar to the Lambityeco plaster sculpture, representing matters of lineage, marriage, and conquest associated with secular elite families and, for the first time, children. Earlier tentative assignment of these stone carvings to Monte Albán IV now seems confirmed.[70]

Plaster sculptures
at Lambityeco, Right
Frieze, Mound 195-sub.
Individual on right
holds a human femur.
(Drawn by Terry
Prewitt after Emily
Rabin, "The Lambityeco
Friezes," *Boletín de
estudios oaxaqueños*,
No. 33 [1970].)

However, there is no reason to believe that the plasters from Lambityeco, or the stone slabs elsewhere, are not Zapotec. All are stylistically affiliated with the sculptures of Classic Monte Albán. The glyphs contain bar-dot numerical indicators, as do the Classic Monte Albán inscriptions, instead of the exclusively dot numerals of the post-Classic Mixtec and Aztec cultures. Enormous plaster sculptures of Cocijo are found at Lambityeco, and the portrait sculptures are much like the Classic Zapotec funerary urns. There is no evidence of Monte Albán V, or Mixteca-Puebla influences, at Lambityeco.

Lambityeco seems to have declined sometime during early to middle Monte Albán IV times as the population center of that area shifted to Yagul, a more defensible location. Period IV sites in the valley of Etla also display locations selected for defense.[71] The shift from Lambityeco to Yagul also seems to coincide with the building of the palaces at Yagul and Mitla. This evidence undoubtedly indicates that the palatial architecture of the eastern arm of the Valley of Oaxaca, along with the greca motifs with which it is associated, represents a shift in emphasis in the society toward militaristic or secular elites. Mixteca-Puebla influences also are included in this complex, for the Mitla and Yagul fortresses show mixed Monte Albán IV and V ceramics.

The origins of the somewhat distinctive tradition of the periods IV–V complex at Yagul and Mitla are not yet clear. However, they seem to be tied to general late Classic or early post-Classic trends in Mesoamerica as well as to local traditions. Greca or stepped-fret mo-

tifs, for example, also are associated with palatial complexes in the Yucatán Peninsula, as at Uxmal.[72] Features of this kind also are found in the Mixtec codices.

The Mixteca-Puebla style also seems to have various manifestations . and origins. Some years ago, for example, John Paddock delineated a

Tomb 6 at Lambityeco (partially excavated), showing portraitures in the *tablero* immediately above the tomb. (Courtesy Bruce Bylan.)

regional variant of the Classic which he called the Ñuiñe style, associated with an area historically and ethnographically inhabited by
the Chocho-Popolocas and Mazatecs and centered in the Mixteca Baja
around Huajuapan. The Ñuiñe style seems to have had prominence
in late Classic times between the fall of Teotihuacán and the rise of
Tula. Filling an important gap in Mesoamerican prehistory, this style
not only helps account for some of the origins of the Mixteca-Puebla
style of the post-Classic, as well as its spread into the central valleys
of Mexico, but also broadens the conception of the Mixteca-Puebla
tradition and its relationship to the Valley of Oaxaca.[73] Some of the
post–Monte Albán influences on the Valley could have come from
this Ñuiñe region.

Ronald Spores, who has conducted an extensive study of the
Nochixtlán Valley of the Mixteca Alta, has clarified some of the relationships between this bordering region and the Valley of Oaxaca.[74]
The post-Classic Mixtec occupation of the Mixteca Alta region corresponds to the Natividad Phase in the Nochixtlán Valley (ca. A.D.
1000–ca. 1520) and was the period of its maximum population density.
Sites, however, are not located in defensive settings, nor do they display abundant fortification; evidence seems to indicate that there was
relative tranquility in the region, in contrast to the usual conception
of post-Classic Mixtec states. However, Spores believes that the coastal
kingdom of Tututepec and the Mexicas constituted real threats to the
Nochixtlán Valley Mixtecs, causing them to react to protect themselves with expansive tendencies and increased militarism. Yanhuitlán,
the dominant community in the Valley of Nochixtlán, seems to have
ruled over perhaps twenty-five to thirty settlements at one time, although this control was relatively unstable, since Mixtec princedoms
or kingdoms were very fluid, a characteristic reflected in constant
processes of fission and fusion, fluctuating patterns of marital alliance
and inheritance, conquests and colonization, and rising and declining
populations. This conclusion, based on archeological and ethnohis-
torical sources, indicates that the changing nature of Mixtec alliances
and conflicts with the Zapotecs, and the various types of Mixtec influence on the Valley, were not inconsistent with patterns found in a
typically Mixtec region like Nochixtlán.

Archeological data from Nochixtlán also support the contention
that Mixtec culture was not uniform; neither was its relationship to

Lápida 1, of post-Classic Zapotec style, in the Museo Nacional de Antropología, México. (From Alfonso Caso, *Las estelas zapotecas* [México, 1928].)

Plaster sculpture of Cocijo at Lambityeco. (Courtesy Bruce Bylan.)

the Mixteca-Puebla style. For example, polychromes were not as abundant in archeological deposits in the Nochixtlán area as they were in
Coixtlahuaca, and they seem to have had their origin in Cholula, or
the Puebla region, instead of Nochixtlán. These polychromes from
Nochixtlán do show affinities with those of Monte Albán V in the
Valley of Oaxaca, although there also seem to be crucial differences
between Nochixtlán and the Valley; a red-on-cream or bichrome
ware, very abundant in Nochixtlán, is scarce or absent in period V
sites in the Valley of Oaxaca. In addition, a fine grey ware, often
attributed to "Mixtec" influence on the Valley of Oaxaca, is relatively

scarce in the Nochixtlán Valley. Spores's work indicates, then, that careful studies must be made before specific material items can be identified as Mixteca-Puebla, let alone as "Mixtec."

Another study has attempted to clarify the archeological meaning of "Mixtec." Donald L. Brockington, in excavations at Miahuatlán, south of the Valley of Oaxaca, found polychromes in association with fine grey ware as in the Valley; this ware seemingly was influenced by the previous Zapotec tradition and apparently partly derived from Monte Albán ceramics. Comparing Miahuatlán with the Mixteca Costa, Brockington found that polychromes were associated with bichromes, as in the Nochixtlán Valley and Coixtlahuaca, and not with fine grey ware (although fine grey also has been found at Coixtlahuaca). On this basis, he suggests that the grey wares represent attempts by subordinate groups to emulate the changing stylistic values of their elites.[75] However, this does not necessarily mean that the elites were Mixtecs, as Brockington implies. It instead seems to represent a convergence of elite patterns in post-Classic Mesoamerica around a tradition associated with the Mixteca-Puebla style.

Other Tetlamixteca peoples also may have influenced developments in the Valley region. John Paddock has pointed out that the sixteenth-century *relación* of the Cuicatec town of Tepeucila lists as one of its *sujetos* the town of Tlacolula, called Yagu in Cuicatec.[76] While this *relación* may not specifically refer to the site of Yagul in the Valley of Oaxaca (for there are many places named Tlacolula in Oaxaca), it may indicate that the word Yagu (which was elicited from the Zapotecs of Tlacolula as the name of the site even though it had no specific meaning for them) is not Zapotec but Cuicatec.

In summary, based on the documents and the archeology, the following statements can be made concerning the Mixtecs, the Mixteca-Puebla style, and the Valley of Oaxaca:

1. Archeological data confirm the presence of Mixteca-Puebla influences in the Valley of Oaxaca. No difficulty is presented in dating the beginning of this influence in the twelfth century, or even earlier. The *relaciones* and other sources speak of Zapotec-Mixtec alliances and marriages. Patterns of emulation and cultural exchange between Zapotec and Mixtec elites would be expected.

2. At an apparently later date, the Mixtecs conquered Zaachila, re-

placed the Zapotec prince of that town, founded new towns in the area, and established *barrios* in conquered Zapotec towns. The seat of the Mixtec hegemony was at Cuilapan. The rich finds at Zaachila and Monte Albán may link the western area of the Valley with the Mixtecs of the Mixteca Alta, specifically those in the region of Yanhuitlán.

3. Events in the eastern arm of the Valley are less clear, for the documentary sources are not as good. Since the present state of knowledge does not permit the specification of types of political control or the identification of ethnic group occupations on the basis of archeology alone, only some possible alternatives can be suggested. In deciding among them, it should be emphasized that the archeological evidence now available pertains almost exclusively to the culture of elites, not to that of peasants, and, given the vacuum created by the fall of Monte Albán, rapid stylistic change and local variations and expressions in material remains should be expected. The post-Classic was a time when elite groups were struggling to create a power base for the formation of more enduring political units and, thus, their security. Under such conditions, ideas are easily modified, borrowed, or manipulated.[77]

4. There are definite Mixteca-Puebla influences on the sites of the eastern arm of the Valley, particularly Mitla and Yagul, although Zapotec traditions also are found there. Such information suggests the following:

A. The Mixtecs of Cuilapan may have subjugated some of the princedoms of the eastern part of the Valley. At other times, the Mixtecs and Zapotecs may have been allies, especially against the Mexicas or Aztecs, as noted earlier. But neither of these situations was very stable. Frequent warfare and changing alliances would have produced different periods or phases of influence. Perhaps at one time the emulation of Mixtec nobles by the Zapotecs produced a kind of synthesis of the two cultures in the eastern wing; intermarriage between the two groups also could have produced a similar result. Further, Zapotecs may have thrown off Mixtec influences at times because of their animosity towards them.[78] Many interpretations are possible here, but they all indicate that greater clarity is needed in the conceptualization of periods IV and V and that period V was not exclusively a "Mixtec" period.

B. The documents are not so much contradictory as they are incomplete. It may be that at one time Mitla was allied to a Tetlamixteca group (Tututepec), and that Macuilxóchitl and Tlacolula, allied with Zaachila, fought Mitla, as the documents claim. Later, Tlacolula and Macuilxóchitl may have been conquered by the Mixtecs of Cuilapan or another Tetlamixteca princedom. The period from the fall of Monte Albán to the Spanish Conquest was a long one, and the documents provide only pieces of that complex era.

5. While Ignacio Bernal has found "Mixtec" traits at approximately seventy Valley sites, the "Mixtecs" never were a single group, nor did they unite the Valley under a centralized empire.[79] Instead, the political ecology of the Valley of Oaxaca, much like that found in central and southern Italy during the periods of Etruscan and Greek domination, was one of petty lordships or princedoms vying for supremacy, with shifting alliances between Mixtecs and Zapotecs, and among the Zapotecs, coupled with constant warfare. Local community allegiance seems to have partly replaced, or become dominant over, larger ethnic group loyalties, as various Tetlamixteca lords, such as those of Tututepec, Yanhuitlán, and elsewhere fought with one another over the spoils of war as Zapotec lords allied with them, fought them, or tried to play them against one another.

THE AZTEC CONQUEST OF THE VALLEY OF OAXACA

The Aztecs, or more properly the Mexicas or Tenochcas, were the last wave of "barbarians" or Chichimecs to enter central Mexico after the fall of Teotihuacán. For a time they were mere tribesmen, but soon they were to become the most powerful group in Mesoamerica, and their capital, Tenochtitlán, became one of the most impressive cities in Mesoamerican history.

When the Mexicas entered the Valley of Mexico, they were relegated to a no-man's land, an island in the middle of Lake Texcoco. But they soon learned from their epigonal Toltec neighbors, acquired the symbols of civilization, and reduced their allies in the Triple Alliance to mere puppets. The Mexicas set upon empire building with a vengeance and placed their puppet rulers in most of the major cities of central Mexico, subjugating conquered peoples to the wrath of their ferocious war deity Huitzilopochtli—who had selected the Mexicas as his chosen people and demanded the sacrifice of human flesh and blood in return for his favor.

Mexica society soon left the tribal level. By the middle of the fifteenth century it was highly differentiated into noble and commoner groups (*macehualtin*) and included serfs (*mayeques* or *tlalmaitl*) and slaves. Specialization had reached a new high level, and craftsmen of all varieties were to be found in Tenochtitlán. Warriors, priests, and lesser lords were presided over by an emperor, nearly divine, who dispensed favors to a supporting bureaucracy. Long-distance traders (*pochteca*) were especially favored and were accorded noble status; they brought in the wealth of the empire, blazed new trails through unknown regions, and served as spies preceding military engagements.

The empire of the Mexicas, as do most, displayed both centralizing and decentralizing tendencies. The emperor was the supreme ruler of all Mexicas even though he often dispensed favors to certain nobles, giving them virtual political and economic autonomy. Some cities that were conquered by the Mexica armies had their princes sacrificed and replaced and their temples razed in favor of one dedicated to Huitzilopochtli. In other areas of the Mexica realm, rulers were permitted loose autonomy as long as tribute continued to flow to Tenochtitlán. Intimidated by mock battles in which they were to lose and to witness the sacrifice of some of their best warriors, or by being invited to witness the sacrifice of others, some lordships were spared the full impact of Mexica conquest.[80]

At the end of the reign of Moctezuma II, who met Cortés, the Mexica state consisted of thirty-eight tributary provinces and covered much of central and southern Mexico. But it was less a territorial empire than it was a mixed "bag" of lordships subject to various degrees of Mexica control; some were mere fiscal entities. Some cities and towns within the vast reaches of the Mexica state had not been subjugated at all; this was the status of Tlaxcala, for example, whose people were bitter enemies of the Mexicas and later allies of Hernán Cortés in the conquest of Tenochtitlán.

The Mexicas expanded to the south, primarily to sustain lucrative trade routes, first into the hot country of the Gulf Coast and later into the rich cacao lands of Soconusco on the Pacific. Having subjugated many of the Mixtec states of the Mixteca Alta, they then moved into the Valley of Oaxaca.

Some sources places their first expansion into the Valley as early as the rule of Moctezuma I, the period between 1440 and 1470. Mexica merchants, passing through the area on their return from Tabasco, were slaughtered and robbed of their costly wares by the inhabitants of the city of Guaxacac.[81]

Moctezuma I (Moctezuma Ilhuicamina) sent a punitive expedition into the area and exterminated the inhabitants of the town of Guaxacac, later sending colonists from Mexico to settle the depopulated site and to establish a military garrison. This apparently was ruled by two Mexica officials with the titles of Tlacatectli and Tlacochtectli.[82]

After establishment of the garrison at Guaxacac, Mexica commercial ventures into the Pacific lands of Soconusco were launched, apparently under the rule of Axayacatl, the next Mexica emperor. Some sources report that the expansion into Tehuantepec and the Pacific coastal region was an independent enterprise carried out by the merchants of the cities of Tenochtitlán and Tlatelolco.[83]

The story at this point becomes confused. Apparently, under Ahuitzotl, who ruled the Mexicas after Tizoc, there were insurrections against the Mexicas in the Valley and at Tehuantepec. According to various sources, punitive expeditions were sent against the Oaxacan cities. Mitla was subjugated, or destroyed, according to some accounts, in 1494; Zaachila, capital of the province of Guaxaca (meaning here the Valley of Oaxaca), was subjugated a year later. Sometime later, the Mexicas fought the Zapotecs, who had Mixtec allies, at Tehuantepec.[84]

Regardless of the details and chronology of Mexican expansion, which is far from clear, all sources agree that the Mexicas had managed to subjugate a number of lordships in the Valley of Oaxaca for tribute purposes some years before the Spanish Conquest. The following towns are listed in the *Codex Mendocino* as paying tribute to the Mexicas: Coyolapan (Cuilapan), Etlan (Etla), Guaxacac, Macuilxochic (Macuilxóchitl), Octoan (Ocotlán), Guaxilotitlan (Huitzo), Teticpac (Teitipac), and Tlalcuechahuaya (Tlacochahuaya).[85] The *relaciones* add other valley towns, such as Teotitlán del Valle, Mitla, and Teozapotlán (Zaachila), which are mentioned as going to war against the Mexicas.[86]

Glyphs depicting the Aztec conquest of the Valley of Oaxaca. (Drawn by Sarah Whitecotton after Eduard Seler, "The Wall Paintings of Mitla," *Bureau of American Ethnology*, Bulletin 28 [1904]; original from Codex Telleriano-Remensis.)

These towns, along with others, were grouped by the Mexicas into the province of Coyolapan, although this does not mean that the Mexicas simply took over the towns that were formerly subject to Zaachila or Cuilapan. The province of Coyolapan included peoples who had previously had diverse allegiances. Ocelotepec, Miahuatlán, and Coatlán also were included; these lordships seem not to have been subject to either Zaachila or Cuilapan.[87]

As they had done in other areas, the Mexicas created the province of Coyolapan primarily for tribute or fiscal purposes. In each fiscal province of the empire, agents of the Mexicas supervised the assembly and delivery of tribute. Many sources relate that the seat of the province of Coyolapan was Guaxacac, near the present site of the city of Oaxaca. There the Mexicas had a garrison on the Cerro de Fortín (Acatepec), where soldiers and tribute collectors were stationed.[88] They, like the Spanish who followed them, chose a central location in the Valley for their administrative seat.

The *relación* of Huitzo provides one view of how the Mexica process operated in this region:

> The said town of Guaxilotitlan [Huitzo] and its natives have been subject for many years before the coming of the Spaniards to Moctezuma. ... they paid tribute to him of white cotton blankets, *guaypiles*, which are like shirts ... some loincloths which in Mexican they call *maxtle* ... some copper hoops ... some green birds which in the said language they call *xihuytototl*, and maize. In order to collect this tribute there are three *principales* who are called *calpizques*. One is in Guaxaca, the other in this town, and another in Cuestlahuaca, which is in the province of the Mixteca, to where the *calpizque* of this town sends the maize and the blankets and the rest goes to Mexico to Moctezuma himself.[89]

Additional data concerning what some of the towns paid to the Mexicas are also available. Teitipac gave fowl, hares, rabbits, deer and honey to Moctezuma, and other towns gave military service, feathers, gold dust, cotton mantles, fowl, bundles of chilies, and slaves.[90] The whole province of Coyolapan contributed tribute to the Mexicas as follows: four hundred bundles of richly worked mantles, eight hundred bundles of large mantles, four wooden cribs (two of maize, one of beans, and one of chia), twenty gold disks, the size of an average plate and as thick as one's forefinger, and twenty bags of cochineal.[91]

It appears, then, that in the Valley of Oaxaca the Mexicas primarily were interested in booty and in sustaining an open route to the south. While native lords of the Valley may have been influenced by Nahuatl culture, for many spoke Nahuatl at the time of the Conquest and intermarried with the Mexicas,[92] they were permitted to hold their positions in the native hierarchy. Mexicas always constituted a small minority in this area.

It also appears that the Mexicas had difficulty holding the Valley towns and that their hold over them was tenuous at best. This weakness undoubtedly meant, as the sources indicate, that there were many battles between Zapotecs and the Mexicas, between Mixtecs and the Mexicas, or between other combinations of these groups. One "war" in particular is prominent in the sources—the Battle of Tehuantepec, which probably took place during the last years of the reign of Ahuitzotl (1486–1503) or during the early years of the rule of Moctezuma II (surnamed Xocoyotzin).

In this battle, the supreme lord of the Zapotecs fought the Mexicas at Tehuantepec, some sources say with Mixtec allies (although it is not known whether they refer to the Mixtecs of Cuilapan), and did so much damage to the Mexicas that the Mexica emperor was obliged to consent to a cessation of hostilities and an amnesty. He offered his daughter, Pelaxilla, to the Zapotec lord (Cosihuesa) in marriage. Cosihuesa and Pelaxilla later had a son, Cosijopii, who became lord of Tehuantepec and later allied himself with the Mexicas against the Mixtecs.[93]

It can be said, then, that the nature of Mexica domination over the princedoms of this region was probably typical. The Mexicas were almost everywhere despised: "There was always some city trying to regain its former independence, refusing the tribute and massacring the *calpixqui* [tax collector] and his men. Then a military expedition would have to be sent to restore order and punish the rebels."[94]

The major effect of the Mexica incursions into the Valley of Oaxaca was to continue the standoff between the petty states (whether Mixtec or Zapotec) in the region; had they not come, some lordship or princedom might have achieved domination. Unfortunately, archeological evidence of the degree of Mexica influence has not yet been found or archeological materials in the Valley have not been linked to the incursions of the Mexicas.

THE ZAPOTEC TRIBUTE STATE

It is from this morass of incomplete documentary accounts of Mixtec expansions and of Mexica imperialism that the nature of Zapotec society and the culture of the post-Classic stage must be reconstructed. It seems probable from the above data on wars and transfers of power that in the Valley of Oaxaca the princedom, lordship, or city-state was the major unit of identification for the mass of its inhabitants. This also was true of most of post-Classic Mesoamerica—of the Otomí, the

Pokam-Maya,[95] and even of the Mexicas of Tenochtitlán: "the fundamental unit was the autonomous city [lordship]; it could be allied to others or subjected to another, but nevertheless it remained the essential unit of political structure. The empire was a mosaic of cities."[96]

Such a conception of empire among the peoples of post-Classic Mesoamerica meant that territorial entities were but loosely defined and lordships could be subject to other lordships regardless of their proximity or previous alliances. A town also could be subject simultaneously to two different independent units. This was the case at Ixtepeji, a sierra Zapotec community near the northern boundary of the Valley of Oaxaca. There the inhabitants apparently became confused because they owed tribute to two lords in addition to the local one; they were subject simultaneously to the Zapotecs of Tehuantepec and to the Mixtecs of Tututepec.[97] Such a phenomenon probably happened in more than one case and illustrates the type and manner of larger alliances.

The history which has been reviewed also indicates that sometime after the fall of Monte Albán, many Valley Zapotec lordships recognized Zaachila as the most powerful. The extent of the alliances formulated by the Valley Zapotec princedoms during the time when Zaachila held supremacy can be reconstructed, if only incompletely. The following towns in the Valley of Oaxaca recognized the lord of Zaachila and paid tribute to him: Teitipac, Tlacolula, Mitla, Macuilxóchitl, Teotitlán del Valle, Tlalixtac, and Chichicapa.[98]

However, the amount given varied greatly from town to town. Mitla presented the lord of Zaachila some honey and turkeys and went to work in his fields,[99] Tlacolula gave him military service,[100] Tlalixtac paid in feathers, mantles, and military service,[101] while Teotitlán del Valle gave gold dust, cotton mantles, fowl, bundles of chilies, and slaves.[102] Macuilxóchitl paid nothing more than sending people for war;[103] Teitipac gave fowl, hares, rabbits, deer, and honey.[104]

It can be assumed that the lord of Zaachila held, in addition to the above towns—which except for Chichicapa are all located in the Tlacolula wing of the Valley—others in the valley of Zaachila-Zimatlán, even though the *relaciones* of these towns make no mention of being subject to Zaachila.[105]

The Zapotec-speaking towns of Miahuatlán, Ocelotepec, and Amatlán to the south of the Valley did not acknowledge being subject to Zaachila. All of their *relaciones*, however, stress their local autonomy even though they mention being subject to Moctezuma and paying tribute to his garrison in Guaxacac. This region was something of a frontier area as far as the Valley was concerned. Tututepec, the Mixtec lordship on the Pacific coast, was constantly at war with Zapotec Coatlán and may have conquered it. The four Zapotec towns in this area also were constantly at war with one another.[106]

The princedoms in the valley of Etla also were probably allied with Zaachila. Burgoa contends that Etla recognized the lord of Zaachila.[107] The evidence on Huitzo is incomplete. At some point, Huitzo was allied with Cuilapan against Coatlán, Miahuatlán, and others.[108] It does not necessarily follow, however, that Huitzo was once allied with Zaachila because it was allied with the Cuilapan Mixtecs; since there were many alliances for various purposes, they involved different towns and were mutable. Huitzo, however, was at one time a Zapotec town before the Cuilapan conquest and was probably of such importance that it would be strange were it not allied to Zaachila.

Zaachila also had allied itself with some of the towns in the sierra. The *relación* of Ixtepeji notes that this town was allied with nearby towns such as Zaachila, Cuilapan, Chicomesuchitl, and Teocuicuilco; its people traded with them and married their daughters to the lords of these towns.[109]

While most of the documents stress the strong, independent nature of each of the lordships as well as the ephemeral character of larger alliances, there are two other tendencies found in post-Classic Zapotec society. One seems to relate to the increased militarism of the post-Classic; the other to an ethnic allegiance, based on a theocratic principle, characteristic of the Classic.

There is some evidence that centralization of a Zapotec state at Zaachila had been attempted with the replacement of local lords. For example, in Macuilxóchitl they were governed by a noble appointed by the lord of Zaachila, for "the government which they had was what the lord of the town of Teozapotlán ordered them and by his order they obeyed a noble which he had in this town."[110] Teitipac also was governed at one time in this way, according to its *relación*.[111] It is not known, however, how extensive this pattern was, nor is it known when this attempt occurred.

Other evidence indicates that the new militarism of the post-Classic, with its emphasis on secular kings, warlords, or princes, formed a counterpoint with another principle and that the lord of Zaachila, at least in the beginning, was not totally supreme. Specifically, it has been noted that Burgoa described the town of Mitla as the residence of a kind of Pope or High Priest of the Zapotec nation, a concept undoubtedly referring to a nation in the classic sense of a religious and moral association of city-states, founded on ethnic identity instead of the post-Classic notion of a tribute state based, if necessary, on ethnic plurality and conquest.

Burgoa goes on to relate that the various complexes or palaces at Mitla were reserved for specific personages—one for the high priest, another for the supreme Zapotec lord, and another for the officials and military officers of the supreme lord. He also states that the high priest ruled from a throne covered by a jaguar skin and was hidden from the eyes of the uninitiated; the supreme lord even had to take a lesser seat when in the presence of this high priest.[112]

Michael D. Coe is puzzled by this seeming contradiction in post-Classic society and provides one solution to it: "We know of nothing else like it in the Postclassic, but it conforms rather accurately to the reconstruction of Classic society which has been made by many archaeologists, namely, an organized theocracy presided over by a spiritual power to whom all temporal rulers owed their allegiance. Mitla seems to have been an island in time, a survival of this older kind of social organization into an era in which the priesthood was little more than a mouthpiece for kings who even rewrote the sacred myths for their own ends."[113]

But Burgoa seems to be depicting more than a survival. He seems also to give a composite, seen from Mitla, of the two principles that made up the post-Classic state: the old theocracy and the new militaristic state. Burgoa, a priest, gives the view from Mitla, a priestly center. Unfortunately, a view from Zaachila, the seat of the Zapotec tribute state, is lacking. Warriors often defer to priests on their home grounds, but the reverse also holds.

However, that Zapotec society in the post-Classic displays what seem to be conflicting tendencies or principles should not come as a surprise. Societies, like the men who compose them, are seldom totally consistent. Even though circumstances may bring one or another tendency to the forefront for a period, older ones linger in the crevices of the new order. Societies do not as much undergo transformations, dropping all the trappings of the old order, as they change through new combinations or syntheses of the old and new. In short, they are involutional instead of evolutional in a cumulative sense.[114]

That Zapotec society in the post-Classic also embodied the militaristic state principle is reflected not only in the picture of the tribute state that is reconstructed above, but also in the legends concerning the princes or lords of Zaachila. While these legends are not necessarily to be taken as *specific* historical fact, they nevertheless reflect the *general* nature and character of the post-Classic social order.

One legend maintains that the founder of the military dynasty of the Zapotecs was the last high priest of Mitla, who, sensing the necessity for militarism to protect the Zapotec nation, placed his son, Zaachila I, at Zaachila. Zaachila I led armies against the Chontales, west of the Isthmus of Tehuantepec, and fought the Mixes, who, with their warrior chief Condoy, held out against him. His son, Zaachila II, continued the war against the Mixes, defeated them, and pressed on to Tehuantepec, conquering the native peoples of the region on the way. Zaachila III was ruler when the Mixtecs and Aztecs tried to conquer this Valley princedom. He was succeeded by Cosihuesa,[115] mentioned above, who fought both the Mixtecs and the Aztecs. The date of 1482 or 1487 is given for his accession to the head of this princely dynasty.

During the period of Zaachila III and Cosihuesa, the capital at Zaachila was lost and a dynasty was founded at Tehuantepec. Cosijopii, the son of Cosihuesa and the Aztec princess Pelaxilla (or Coyolicatzin, as she was called in Nahuatl), ruled Tehuantepec at the time of the Spanish Conquest. Cosihuesa and Pelaxilla also had two daughters, Donají and Pinopias, both heroines of Zapotec legendary history.[116]

Some legends maintain that Cosihuesa survived until the Spanish Conquest, was able to reassert political control of Zaachila, and, with the help of Mixtec allies, held off the Mexicas but surrendered peacefully to the Spanish upon their entrance into the Valley of Oaxaca.[117]

That these legends are not total fancy is corroborated by documentary sources, archeology, and linguistic evidence. The *Lienzo de Guevea* clearly links the Zapotec princes of Tehuantepec with those of Zaachila. Next to a place glyph in this document is written the

Zapotec gloss, "Zaachila." The princes, while here given different names from the ones above, are Yobiocoxi Chalachi, Rinicosi, Chaleguesa, Cosiobi, Cosihuesa, and Penobiya. A road with footprints on it separates these from a group of lords above them. This road designates a migration or movement. Then follows the place glyph for Tehuantepec and the names of three lords: Cosiobi, Cosihuesa, and Don Juan Cortés.[118]

The Zapotecs of Jalapa, a mixed settlement of Zapotecs and Mixes on the isthmus, claimed to be descendants of the Zapotecs of Zaachila.[119] Cosihuesa made his son, Cocijopii, the prince of Tehuantepec and made Jalapa a subject of that town. The *relación* of Tehuantepec, along with other sources, permits identification of Don Juan Cortés as Cosijopii.[120]

According to glottochronological reckonings, Isthmus Zapotec displays a separation of a minimum of six and one-half centuries from Mitla Zapotec, which makes the relationship between the Valley and isthmus languages very close indeed.[121] Although the isthmus shows archeological remains resembling those of the Valley of Oaxaca from at least early Classic times, the ruins of Guiengola, where Cosihuesa resisted the

Lower right-hand portion of *Lienzo de Guevea* depicting princes of Zaachila and Tehuantepec. (Drawn by Sarah Whitecotton; glosses by Terry Prewitt. After Eduard Seler, "Das Dorfbuch von Santiago Guevea," in *Gesammelte Abhandlungen zur amerikanischen Sprach und Altersthumskunde*, Vol. 3 [1908]. Copy A now in the Museo Nacional de Antropología, México.)

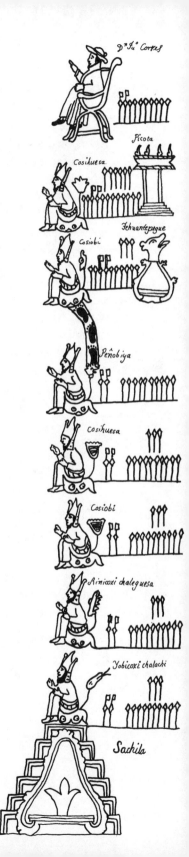

Mexicas, display a distinct Monte Albán IV occupation, an occupation that seems to persist until the Spanish Conquest.[122] This
evidence undoubtedly confirms the close linkage between the Zapotec
rulers of the Valley and those of the Tehuantepec area.

The fact that the Zapotecs of Zaachila did move into the Tehuantepec area, setting up their own rulers and settling the area with
Zapotecs from the Valley of Oaxaca, seems well established. This fact
also indicates that they, too, conceived of an empire based on tribute
and conquest. But, as now seems evident, this empire was not to suc-
ceed; the Zapotec Valley of Oaxaca and its environs instead dissolved
into a number of petty constituents infused with invaders from other
regions. Even the Zapotec holy place, Mitla, could not ward off these
influences. As with the Etruscans and Greeks of the Mediterranean
world, ethnic loyalty soon waned once petty states were pitted against
one another by divisive militants, a situation brought on by expanding
populations, colonization, and competition with others for scarce
resources.

4
Princes, Priests, and Peasants: Patterns of Post-Classic Zapotec Culture and Society

As discussed in Chapter 3, Zapotec culture and society underwent considerable changes after the time Monte Albán was the dominant center in the region. The Zapotec nobility no longer could look to Monte Albán as the source of all ideas. Influenced by the new developments of the post-Classic, they were no longer masters of their own land; other nobles from other areas appeared more lordly and innovative.[1] The Zapotec elite now were influenced by the Great Traditions of these groups.

To an extent, post-Classic elites of Mesoamerica, like nobles in other world areas, shared a similar culture as alliance, intermarriage, and conquest promoted cultural exchange and borrowing. A Great Tradition stemming from the "Toltecs" (more of an epithet connoting "civilized" than a specific people) had a tremendous influence on the nobility throughout Mesoamerica. It became the fashion to emulate the Great Tradition of "Tollan" (more of an idea of a great metropolis-center of civilization than a specific place) and to claim descent from the lords of that place.[2]

To an extent also, the widespread militarism of the post-Classic meant that Mesoamerican societies were similar in structure and organization, even though similar cultures and societies did not promote political integration. Generally, except perhaps for the late Aztec domination of Central Mexico, political units remained small and fragile.

Although the Zapotec elites borrowed Mixtec and Nahuatl ideas, to a degree they remained outside the "Toltec" tradition; there is no evidence, for example, that the Zapotec lords claimed descent from the lords of Tollan, and the old Zapotec deities retained their prominence even though new ones were added to the pantheon. Zapotec society, however, seems to have been a quite typical post-Classic one.

Although Zapotec nobles probably used Nahuatl as a *lingua franca*, as did many other Mesoamerican nobles, most of the inhabitants of the Valley and its environs, the great majority of whom were peasants, remained Zapotec speakers. Mixtec and Nahuatl speakers always were a minority in this region.

SUBSISTENCE, ECONOMY, POPULATION, AND SETTLEMENTS

The subsistence base of the post-Classic Zapotecs, like their Meso-american contemporaries, included maize, grown in a number of varieties, as the primary crop. The maize was either roasted or boiled and was ground into a flour for tortillas or for a biscuit or cake used principally in connection with fiestas. Combined with turkey meat, it made a kind of tamale.[3]

Although maize was universal in the Valley, some towns grew more of it than others; there apparently was an abundance of maize in Zaachila, Teotitlán del Valle, Teitipac, and Huitzo, while Tlaco-lula, Macuilxóchitl, and Mitla generally experienced maize short-ages.[4] In Mitla, "the peasants seldom ate corn as it did not exist [in sufficient quantity]."[5] Such contrasts as these among Valley towns emphasize the productive diversity of the Valley, a factor discussed in Chapter 1.

Beans and squash also were important in the native diet. Beans came in a number of varieties, large ones being planted with maize, small ones in separate fields. Some varieties were boiled and eaten while others were used primarily for their extracted oils. Squash also came in several varieties, both wild and domesticated.[6]

The chili was a common item in the diet,[7] and the tomato also was grown. Maguey, generally grown on less productive lands, had a variety of uses. The stock of the large maguey was roasted and eaten, a syrup was made from the plant, and maguey fiber was used to make clothing for the commoners or peasant class. An alcoholic beverage, *pulque*, also was made from maguey. *Mezcal*, a distilled alcoholic beverage similar to tequila, was not produced in pre-Spanish times.[8]

Cacao trees grew in the Valley region, and the bean was used to make a chocolate drink, sometimes mixed with honey or chili.[9] The cacao bean was distributed widely in Mesoamerica as currency and,

according to the *relación* of Teocuicuilco, was also used for that purpose in the Valley region.[10] Copper axes or counters, found in archeological deposits, also were used as currency in ancient Oaxaca.[11]

Agricultural practices included dry farming and fallowing, canal
irrigation (although there is no evidence that this irrigation was
coordinated by centralized state structures), and the cultivation of
moist bottomlands.[12] The digging stick, perhaps tipped with copper,
was the major agricultural implement.[13]

By A.D. 1000, the agricultural center of the Valley apparently had
shifted from the Etla arm to the Zaachila arm, since expansion in the
Etla region was limited because of the Valley's narrow width there.
Zaachila, however, contained enough valley floor land to permit the
opening of new areas for cultivation, as did the Tlacolula arm, although the scarcity of water resources there prevented growth on a
scale comparable to that in the Zaachila arm. For the first time,
Zaachila seems to have led the Valley in agricultural production, and
the percentage of area cultivated also became greater than that in
Etla, suggesting that the Zaachila arm supported the largest population in the Valley.[14] This phenomenon undoubtedly partly explains
the prominence Zaachila assumed as a political center in the post-
Classic.

The agricultural diet was supplemented by other plants—some domesticated, some wild. The people of Tlacolula, for example, ate the
prickly pear fruit produced by the nopal cactus, and "they also ate
the roots of certain trees and from the damp earth they dug up certain
nuts which served them as nourishment."[15] The inhabitants of other
towns in the eastern arm of the Valley also used such items; they
ate avocados, a native crab apple (*tejocote*), and, in Mitla, guavas. The
Mitleños also ate some wild herbs and nopal prickly pears. Macuilxóchitl residents ate the fruit of the *zapote* as well as *guayaba* (guava)
fruit, which also was eaten in Teotitlán del Valle. The Teotitleños also
ate *aguacates* (avocados). Roots and wild herbs were eaten by the
commoners in Teitipac.[16]

It is interesting to note that the *relaciones* from the western part of
the Valley do not stress the gathering of wild foods as do those from
the Valley wing of Tlacolula, which give them major importance in
the overall subsistence economy. Burgoa mentions, however, that in
Huitzo, in the Etla arm of the Valley, there was an abundance of

"fruitales de la tierra," referring specifically to nopal fruit, *aguacates* and *guayabas*.[17]

Hunting also was important to the diet, especially to the upper classes. Wild rabbits, turkeys, deer, and other animals were hunted in Macuilxóchitl, Teotitlán del Valle, Teitipac, and Mitla.[18] Fewer animals were hunted by the people of Zaachila,[19] but the people of Ixtepec were known as great hunters.[20] The inhabitants of Chichicapa hunted deer and wild mountain pig; pigs also were hunted by the Mitleños, along with doves and mud turtles.[21]

Of the domesticated animals in the Valley of Oaxaca at the time of the Spanish Conquest, the most important food animal was the turkey. Bees, dogs, and cochineal insects also were present. The insect yielded a red dye which was paid to the Mexicas as tribute and became extremely important in the Spanish Colonial period as a cash crop. In part, the process involved in producing the dye included gathering the females of this insect from the cactus plants on which they were raised and then drying them and placing them in small bags.[22]

The productive diversity within the Valley of Oaxaca also stimulated a system of local specialization and trade. Apparently, markets were held within each region of the Valley as well as at interchange points which brought together products and people from the whole Valley area. This market system continued through the Colonial period and survives today among the Valley inhabitants. In pre-Spanish times markets apparently were held every five days in the Valley, a pattern common throughout Mesoamerica at that time.[23]

The people of Teotitlán del Valle were great merchants and traders, as were those of nearby Tlacolula, Mitla, and Tlalixtac.[24] The inhabitants of Teotitlán del Valle were then famous for their weaving, and still are today. The tribute list of the lord of Zaachila specified that the Teotitleños paid tribute in cotton mantles, confirming this long weaving tradition.[25]

Some materials imported from outside the Valley probably were purchased or obtained in a regional market. For example, Macuilxóchitl, Tlacolula, Teitipac, Teotitlán del Valle, and Ixtepec obtained their cotton from Tehuantepec, Jalapa, and Nejapa.[26] Interestingly enough, the Mitleños grew their own cotton, according to the Mitla *relación*;[27] first thought to have been incorrect, this statement has been confirmed by archeological excavations at Mitla.[28]

Although much salt also was imported into the Valley from Tehuantepec, many of the Valley towns, including Teitipac, Mitla,
Tlacolula, Macuilxóchitl, and Teotitlán del Valle, had their own salt
deposits.[29] The towns in the Zaachila-Zimitlán arm of the Valley
probably obtained their salt from Tehuantepec, while those in the
Etla arm may have obtained their salt from the province of Teposco-
lula in the Mixteca Alta. The Etla towns also obtained cotton from
Tehuantepec.[30]

Many other commodities were obtained outside the Valley or
brought to the marketplaces of various Valley towns. The wide variety
of ecological zones in the Oaxacan area meant that a complex symbi-
osis and exchange among the various groups made available a wide
variety of products to the Valley Zapotecs. Metals, precious stones,
animal skins, fish, quetzal feathers, and tropical fruits were included
among the items brought into the Valley. Herbs, plants, roots, and
leaves from various trees were either produced locally or imported
from the outside and were used to cure ailments. Native tobacco, apparently wild, was of some importance, especially to promote physical
strength and for the treatment of ulcers, headaches, fever, and especially asthma, a common ailment in the region today as well.[31]

The size of the population of the Valley of Oaxaca at the time of
Spanish contact is difficult to estimate. Population must be inferred
from both archeological and documentary sources. Most of the documentary sources do not provide accurate counts of the total population but generally include only the heads of tributary families (nobles,
among others, were exempt from the payment of tribute and were not
listed). Not only does the size of a typical family, then, have to be
estimated but also the percentage of exempt individuals in any given
area. In addition, most of the sources date from after the Spanish Conquest, and population losses because of conquest and epidemic disease
must be evaluated.

William Sanders has interpreted Ignacio Bernal's archeological
survey of the Valley, which shows a steady increase in the number
of sites in the region as evidence for an increasing population from
Monte Albán I times until the Spanish Conquest.[32] Based on archeological settlement surveys and the maximum possible corn production
(given the nature of the technology and the varieties of maize in
use), Ann V. T. Kirkby has calculated the maximum possible popu-

lation of the Valley at various points in pre-Spanish times. Between 300 B.C. and A.D. 1, she estimates that the total maximum population of the Valley would have been 64,000; for A.D. 900 she calculates a figure of 121,000 inhabitants.[33] She does not give a calculation of the population at the time of Spanish Conquest.

Woodrow Borah and Sherburne F. Cook have postulated, based on the *Matrícula de los Tributos* (the Mexica tribute list), that the four tributary provinces of Yoaltepec, Tlachquianeco, Coayztlahuaca, and Coyolapan (Cuilapan) had a population of 1,741,721 inhabitants in 1519. On the same basis, the province of Cuilapan would have had approximately 350,000 inhabitants.[34] This estimate, which does not necessarily include all of the Valley of Oaxaca, is higher than Kirby's calculation of the maximum possible contemporary population for the Valley, which she estimated to be 341,000 in 1970.[35]

Another approach is to simply attempt to assess the size of the individual Valley communities and their constituent parts, ignoring an overall figure, since most of the documents give only a community by community count. I estimate that Valley communities (head towns plus their subject hamlets) ranged in size from five thousand to thirteen thousand inhabitants and that the former figure was more typical. The head towns alone probably had populations of from two thousand to eleven thousand, while four thousand inhabitants probably more closely approximated the norm. In many cases the combined population of all the subject hamlets (communities may have had as few as one subject hamlet or as many as twelve) equaled or surpassed that of the head town.[36]

The settlement pattern of the late pre-Spanish community varied throughout the Valley. One type consisted of a nucleated center or town with a number of subject hamlets located some distance from it. There seem to have been two types of centers: one displayed a combined religious, administrative, and commercial precinct, while the other had separate administrative, ceremonial, and commercial areas. The nature of the terrain had a significant effect on the nature of the settlement pattern; some communities, for example, displayed considerable dispersion.[37]

The post-Classic stage in the Valley of Oaxaca seems not to have had a metropolitan center approaching the size or complexity of Monte Albán in the Classic. Instead, the settlement pattern consisted largely of a number of regional or local centers. There appears to have been no settlement that attained the population size or urban character of the Mexica capital of Tenochtitlán in the Valley of Mexico.

LOCAL ZAPOTEC POLITY AND WARFARE

Documents indicate that the local community (a town and its subject hamlets) was the dominant Valley Zapotec political entity, regardless of the nature of the larger system of political integration. Local control was vested in a native lord (Zapotec *coquihalao*; Spanish *cacique* or *señor natural*). Since the powers of these lords generally were restricted to their own town, community, or city-state, perhaps the term *prince* may describe them more accurately.[38]

The prince supervised labor, collected tribute, directed the government and maintenance of the community, administered justice, and supervised warfare. Some sources are vague concerning the general functions of the prince. The *relaciones* of Mitla and Tlacolula contain typical statements. For Mitla: "It is said that in that time they did not have organized government, nor people who had a vote in the government system, but only in the town they had a lord that they called Coqui Galaniza. The latter told them what to do and sent them where he pleased and they had no [other form] of government."[39] And for Tlacolula: "They say that [their form of] government was [the following]: living among them was a native lord of the town, whom they obeyed. This [chieftain] told them what to do, as he wished and thought [best]. He would not [tell them] what his orders were to be [in the future]. [So] they did not know what [they would be commanded] to do in the [future]."[40] Other *relaciones* provide more information on the role of the local prince and the officials under him. In Ixtepec, the inhabitants were governed by a *señor natural* who was assisted by a few officials who resided in the palace. The prince also appointed administrative officials who governed individual hamlets.[41]

The *relación* of Huitzo contains the following:

. . . they say that for their form of government they had an Indian, which was their *señor natural*, who governed them and ordered what they were to do and administered justice in the disputes which they had. He named in each *barrio* and *estancia* an Indian whom they called *tequitato* who is like the magistrates in Spain and who had charge of the Indians of his *barrio* or *estancia*. He collected the tribute and took notice of the crimes they had amongst them and settled the disputes they had amongst them concerning lands as well as other matters.[42]

This statement makes explicit what is implicit in most of the documentation concerning the political organization of the Zapotec lordship or princedom. As in Ixtepec, the prince resided only in the head town while the subject hamlets were governed by *tequitlatos* (Zapotec *colaabachiña*);[43] the princedom thus was politically centralized.

The *relación* of Teocuicuilco provides yet another account of local polity. Although this community was located in the Zapotec sierra, its proximity to the Valley and its similar cultural base indicate that it probably had a system much like that of the Valley towns. It was also probably at one time allied with Zaachila. In Teocuicuilco, the native prince was assisted by an elder kinsman who functioned as an intermediary. All matters of war, demands of the townspeople, and ambassadors from other parts came before this intermediary, who conferred with the prince and served as the mouthpiece for his decisions, desires, and wishes. If the prince wished to issue an order, he did so through this elder, who communicated it to the other nobles. Matters dealing directly with the *macehuales* (the commoners or peasants) were supervised by *tequitlatos*. The absolute power accorded to this prince is further emphasized in that anyone appearing before him was required to remove his shoes and to keep his head bowed throughout any proceedings.[44]

The position of prince carried with it the right to exact tribute and obtain services from the subject population. Most of the *relaciones* indicate that commoners gave tribute to their prince, although few indicate specifically what was given. Commoners gave maize and some cotton mantles to the prince of Ixtepec. The *relación* also states that there was no stipulated quantity of mantles or maize, but that they gave whatever the prince demanded and that no accounts were kept. Other towns paid to their princes such things as gold dust, jewelry or gold, precious stones, feathers, jaguar skins, and cotton clothing as well as fowl, maize, chilies, beans, and animals of the hunt, such as rabbits and deer.[45] Labor also was performed by commoners for the local prince. Labor schedules must have been demanding, for some of the *relaciones* mention that the native inhabitants worked harder in the pre-Spanish period than they did during the Colonial period.[46]

The major part of the work done on public buildings, in the fields of the lords, and in the fields reserved for the support of religious cults and temples was performed through a labor draft. Generally, the Indians were assigned for a certain period of time and then were permitted to return to normal duties. The *relación* of Ixtepeji specifically indicates that this conscription was done in pre-Spanish times. Indians were sent by their Ixtepeji prince to the prince of Tehuantepec, where they worked in his fields for six or seven months or even for a year. The data also suggest that such assignment privileges were not restricted to princes, for Indian laborers also were allotted to other members of the nobility.[47]

The Valley princes also must have been warriors or military leaders, judging from the importance given to matters of military skill and prowess in the chronicles and from legends pertaining to the Zapotecs. There is evidence that military acumen and skill was an important duty in fulfilling the role of prince; the adeptness of the *cacique* as a warrior is mentioned specifically in the *relación* of Teocuicuilco.[48]

There also is considerable evidence that warfare was a constant feature in the lives of the Zapotecs of the Valley. The *relaciones* make continual references to military encounters. Tlacolula, for example, commonly went to war against the Mixes of the sierra and against the town of Mitla.[49] Tlalixtac had frequent war with the Indians of the sierra and the neighboring communities; Chichicapa was at continual war with its neighbors; and Huitzo usually was at war with Teocuicuilco, Coatlán, Miahuatlán, Chichicapa, and Nejapa.[50] It may be inferred from the *relaciones* that these encounters were of a local nature and that decisions regarding war were made by the local princes except in those cases in which a prince was subject to the orders of a larger entity such as Zaachila.

Exaction of tribute and the taking of captives for human sacrifice to the gods figure prominently as the major purposes for warfare in the sources. Furthermore, the local Zapotec princedoms had to defend themselves continuously against aggression by other lords as well as those of Mixtec or Mexica origin. Military victory, however, seems not necessarily to have implied territorial gain, the replacement of conquered elites, nor the resettlement of populations; in most cases tribute and slaves were the major desiderata. The Zapotec abandonment of Zaachila, forced by Mixtec pressure, and Zapotec expansion into the Isthmus of Tehuantepec would seem to constitute an exception to this pattern.

Various tactics were used in warfare. One tactic, mentioned in the *relación* of Teocuicuilco, involved forming companies on an area of high terrain where they would wait for the enemy. Then they would descend upon the advancing opponents and engage them in hand-to-hand combat. Sometimes the march into battle was accompanied by singing to the beat of a wooden drum; idols were also carried to help insure success.

The characteristic instruments of war were the flint-edged, double-edged broadsword and the bow and arrow. Padded cotton armor and shields made of reeds also were used.[51]

DIVISIONS IN ZAPOTEC SOCIETY

Zapotec society was differentiated into hierarchical divisions or groupings based on status, descent, and differential access to economic resources. Class, caste, and other terms have been used to express these distinctions, although the term *estate* seems most appropriate. An estate is a jurally defined division combining aspects of status, wealth, and hereditary position. Three primary estates in Zapotec society were the nobility, the commoners, and the priests. Membership in the noble and common estates was perpetuated by heredity, sumptuary rules, and endogamy. The priestly estate, linked most closely to the nobility, employed varying criteria for membership.

The noble division consisted of two subgroupings or ranks: the *tijacoqui*, the highest ranking, ruling, or princely nobility; and the *tijajoana* or *tijajoanahuini*, those of second rank. These two subgroups were referred to as *caciques* and *principales* in the Spanish documents.[52] Both men and women were accorded rank in Zapotec society, at least in the noble estate. A woman of the highest rank in this estate was called *coquitao xonaxi*, while a noblewoman of second rank was designated *xonaxi xinijoana*.[53]

Commoners were called *tijapeniqueche* in Zapotec society or *macehuales* in the Spanish documents.[54] This latter form is a Hispanicized version of the Nahuatl term for commoners, *macehualtin*.

The division into commoners and nobles was accompanied by sumptuary rules pertaining to kinds of dress and ornamentation, diet, and linguistic habits. The *caciques* and nobles in Huitzo, for example, dressed in brightly woven cotton mantles and loincloths while the common people wore clothing made of maguey fiber. Also, at Huitzo only *caciques* and *principales* were allowed to eat turkeys, deer, hares, and rabbits.[55] In Mitla as well, only nobles consumed rabbits and maize or were allowed to dress in cotton clothing; like their Huitzo counterparts, Mitla commoners had clothing only of maguey.[56] Nobles in Tlalixtac ate maize and turkeys; *macehuales* ate only beans and nopal fruit.[57] A similar phenomenon is reported for Teitipac, although there nobles feasted on rabbits, turkeys, deer, and other animals while commoners consumed only grasses and wild fruits.[58] While these accounts, especially with regard to the consumption of maize, are probably exaggerations—for nearly everywhere commoners must have consumed maize—they do serve to emphasize the strong status distinctions in Zapotec society.

Other *relaciones* pertaining to Zapotec-speaking towns supplement these accounts. Elites in Teocuicuilco wore brightly decorated, woven cotton or feathered mantles and shirts as well as lip plugs, earrings, brightly colored feather headdresses, and gold and precious-stone bead necklaces; the common estate wore plain maguey-fiber clothing devoid of ornamentation. In addition to the food restrictions noted above, in Teocuicuilco commoners could not drink chocolate; its consumption was restricted to the nobility.[59] The *caciques* and *principales* were equipped in battle with different weapons and armor from those of commoners in both Ixtepeji and Ocolotepec,[60] also Zapotec-speaking communities. These phenomena are characteristic of most Mesoamerican societies of the post-Classic.

The estates also were distinguished in language usage. Commoners employed a special set of pronouns when addressing a noble. A special type of verb, which Córdova called reverential, also was employed only by commoners speaking with nobles.[61]

THE NOBILITY: CACIQUES AND PRINCIPALES

The prince or *cacique* (*coquihalao*) in Zapotec society received both his rank and his authority by ascription through direct succession. Rank among the *principales* (*tijajoana*) also was ascribed; however, various positions of authority, such as that of *tequitlato* or intermediary for the prince, seem generally to have been the result of appointment or selection from a group of noblemen. Thus, to a certain degree, positions could be achieved.

Caciques (*tijacoqui*) were endogamous as a rank in their selection of senior wives, since legitimate succession to prince was traced through her as well as her husband. However, *caciques* were exogamous as far as the princedom was concerned, since there appears to have been only one legitimate ruling family per community. Thus, the *cacique* would select his senior wife from the family of the prince of another lordship. Although evidence is not conclusive on this point, it seems probable that primogeniture was the principle that defined succession to the princely position.

Nobles other than the *cacique* held a number of administrative and auxiliary positions. These positions seem to have been primarily the result of appointment, although it is also possible, if not probable, that kinship played a part in determining selection for a specific position. If he was of sufficient age, for example, it seems likely that the firstborn son of the *cacique* would have been appointed to an administrative or military position such as *tequitlato* or lower-ranking military commander or, in exceptional cases, even as prince of a conquered town, for the prince ruled for life. Second or third sons of *caciques* may also have been given positions as *tequitlatos*, as were other members of the nobility.

Both kinship and achievement probably operated in assigning such positions. If a man displayed characteristics considered worthy for a position and he also was eligible for it by heredity, confirmation would be automatic; otherwise, some deviation might be made. However, the documents do not provide the specificity necessary to draw firm conclusions about these matters even though the strongly centralized character of the princedom, as emphasized in the documents, makes it unlikely that the prince would not have controlled the administrative and military positions in the society.

Marriage functioned in a number of ways in Zapotec society; local exogamy among *caciques* strengthened already existing alliances among ruling elites and also served as a mechanism for the creation of new ones. Exogamy functioned also to reinforce the distinction between the *tijacoqui* and the *tijajoana* as well as to secure the status of the *coquihalao* or prince. Local *cacique* exogamy also was characteristic of other Mesoamerican peoples, such as the Mixtecs.[62]

Caciques, as did the rest of the nobility, generally practiced polygyny, as specifically indicated in the *relaciones* of Teocuicuilco, Huitzo, and Tehuantepec and in other sources.[63] In Huitzo, for example, *caciques* married as many as fifteen or twenty women in pre-Spanish times. The lord would appoint a person to negotiate with the parents of the woman whom he wished to marry; apparently she had to be of noble birth, for the offspring of a noble man and a common woman was considered illegitimate in Zapotec society, indicating that noble endogamy was the rule.[64]

If the parents agreed to the marriage, and agreement was contingent on the amount and value of gifts presented, the two individuals were brought together at a stipulated date and both were seated on a *petate* (palm mat). They then drank two vessels of *pulque* which were placed in front of them; then their cloaks were tied together and the marriage ceremony was ended.[65]

Data from other sources indicate that the presentation of gifts for the initiation of a noble marriage was not always a bride price, as the above example suggests, but also was dependent on other considerations, including the relative prestige and status of the individuals involved. For example, a prince might desire to arrange a marriage between his daughter and the son of a highly prestigious prince or, more probably, a very powerful and aggressive one. In this case, as seemingly happened in the marriage between the daughter of the prince of Zaachila and the son of the Mixtec prince of Yanhuitlán, the father would offer a dowry to the male—in this example Cuilapan.

It is not known to what extent community endogamy operated in the selection of additional wives for the *cacique* or in the selection of wives of *principales*. Undoubtedly, this selection was dependent on several factors, such as the size of the lordship, the nature of alliances between lordships, the relative prestige of each, the degree of domination of one over the other, and perhaps the ethnicity of the groups involved.

Marriages also could be dissolved in Zapotec society. For example, women in Huitzo accused of committing adultery were brought before the prince. If found guilty of the offense, they were shamed by being publicly killed and eaten. In other places, such as Ixtepeji, adulteresses were not killed, but were shamed merely by being sent back to the house of their parents.[66]

Córdova gives some other reasons why marriages were dissolved in Zapotec society:

> The first was if there was a mistake in the marriages as when a woman was of high rank and a man below her rank. The second was when a couple did not have any children [sons?] and this was the principal cause. The third was when the combination of their names would be such that it would bring misfortune to them or their children. . . . The fourth was when one of the two, especially the woman, was very lazy. The fifth was when the two were always fighting. . . . The sixth was when the male used the woman too much as a beast of burden without her consent. The seventh was when the woman committed adultery and sometimes when the male did. The eighth was when sometimes a man asked for a woman and had her for a while and she did not suit him, he would leave her and take another, although this was not very common.[67]

The good friar adds in seriousness, although it is humorous today, that "from what I have said you might infer that these Indians did not have matrimony."[68]

THE PRIESTHOOD

Princes or *caciques* had some religious functions and were treated with as much awe and reverential respect as if they were divine; they also frequently performed marriages. However, they were clearly distinct as a group from the priests. The dual division of priest and secular lord is common in post-Classic Mesoamerican societies and represents, as noted in Chapter 3, a combination of the theocratic tradition of the Classic stage and the new secularism of the post-Classic.

Priests were recruited mainly from the nobility and were sons of princes or *principales*, according to the *relación* of Teocuicuilco. They also might be appointed by the *cacique*. Such individuals were raised from childhood in the temples of the deities, learning the ceremonies so they could assume the duties of a priest when he died or completed his term of office. Some priests apparently had a seven-year term of office.[69]

Priests were not allowed to marry or, ordinarily, to drink *pulque*. Violation of such prescriptions evidently was punishable by death. In Teocuicuilco, high priests were accorded special dignity in that nothing vital to the community was undertaken without consulting them. In this sense, they were accorded dignity and respect equal to that due the *cacique*. Princes conferred with the priests concerning auspicious times to wage war, when to marry, whom to marry, and the gravity of illnesses.[70]

Burgoa provides additional information on priests and their recruitment. He distinguishes three types in reference to Mitla: *huipatoo* (*huijatao*), "the great seer"; *cope vitoo*, "guardians of the gods"; and *neza-eche*, "great sacrificers," and the priest pupils or novices.[71]

The function of the high priest (*huijatao*)[72] was, through a process of autosuggestion, to consult with the gods and to transmit their desires to believers. He accomplished this purpose by placing himself in an ecstatic state, after which he had visual and auditory hallucinations, perhaps aided by eating mushrooms. Eduard Seler, who did a great deal of scholarly research on the Zapotecs, believed that the Zapotec priests functioned in a manner similar to priests of central Mexico called Quetzalcoatl.[73] In Tenochtitlán there were two such priests, one for the cult of Tlaloc, the old Classic rain god, and one for Huitzilopochtli, the Mexica patron and state deity associated with war and human sacrifice. Burgoa and other accounts imply that the *huijatao* of Mitla was in fact in charge of the major Zapotec religious cult; this cult probably was related to Cocijo, as there is no evidence that the Zapotecs as a group had a special patron deity that emerged in the post-Classic.

The Zapotec high priests, like their Mexica equivalents, were not appointed to office, according to Burgoa, but transmitted their positions to their sons or nearest relatives. They generally were required to be chaste and to avoid drunkenness. Burgoa, however, states that at certain festivals these priests became intoxicated and had intercourse with the unmarried daughters of princes. If one of these daughters became pregnant, she was confined until the child was born. If the child were a son, he was trained to be the successor of the priest.[74]

The second class of priest, *cope vitoo* (alternatively *copa pitao*), had the function of keeping the sanctuary, the idols, and all that pertained to worship in orderly condition; they also assisted the high priest. It was this body of priests who performed human sacrifices and similar group ceremonials.[75]

The *relación* of Huitzo provides additional data on the *copa pitao*: ". . . and the religious customs which they had were that they made in the heights of a mountain a temple, in which they had some carved stones in the form of a person which they called in their Zapotec language, *bezaloo*, which is to say 'devil'; and they had in watch of these temples some twenty-five individuals as priests, who were called *piçana* in Zapotec, and these had charge of the rites and customs dealing with these [dieties]."[76] The term *piçana* used here seems to be the same as *pizana*, which was employed by Burgoa to refer only to novices or priestly pupils, who were chosen from among the younger sons of *caciques* and other nobles. They were castrated when they were boys.[77]

It seems that the more important priests were recruited exclusively from the nobility, as they were among the Mexicas. As also may have been true of the Mexicas, subsidiary priests may have come from the commoner group in special circumstances.[78]

COMMONERS

Commoners constituted the majority of the inhabitants of the Zapotec princedom or city-state and primarily were agriculturalists or peasants. The word *vecino* (family head of a town) is synonymous with *penigueche* or *benigueche*, the Zapotec lexeme for commoner, according to both Córdova and the Junta Colombina dictionary.[79]

While nobles and priests were exempt from tribute requirements, commoners gave service as well as tribute to the nobles and priests. In fact, the glosses given for the Zapotec words *cani penigueche, cani penilaoqueche, naaqueche* and *copaci* are "vassal," "subject or common people," and "tributary."[80]

Most commoners undoubtedly were tied to the land and were the basic producers of foodstuffs for the society. While nobles and priests resided in sumptuous masonry palaces, commoners inhabited houses of mud and adobe with thatched roofs. The Valley Zapotec peasants, especially those residing in nucleated settlements, probably did not have contiguous strips of land, but instead had dispersed plots in various places on the outskirts of the villages and towns. This situation probably arose by a pattern of cooperative clearing in which land was divided among those taking part in the endeavor.[81] This process, also found in Medieval Europe, promoted nucleated settlement patterns and prevented peasant dispersion, a clear advantage for the elite estate.

However, commoners were not exclusively peasant agriculturalists. Tribute demands by the upper classes fostered specialization. Therefore, a number of occupations were found among the *tijapeniqueche* (commoners). There were day laborers, free servants, weavers, dancers, musicians, sculptors, metal workers, painters, interpreters, diviners, curers, merchants, and peddlers, among others.[82]

Merchants have been included in the Zapotec *macehual* group with some reservations, since among the Mexicas of central Mexico, long distance traders (*pochteca*) belonged to the nobility. The Mexicas, however, before their emergence as a large-scale tribute state or empire, did not have this class; ordinary merchants or peddlers were restricted to the commoner division. Since there is no evidence to indicate that the Zapotecs had entered into long-distance trading with the intensity that the Mixtecs did, they probably did not have a merchant nobility. Merchants rarely are members of the nobility in most preindustrial societies, so the Mexicas were somewhat exceptional in this regard.[83]

It is probable that some commoner specializations constituted full-time occupations, although, as among the modern Zapotecs, many probably carried on agricultural pursuits as well. Some specialists, such as musicians and artisans, also may have been exempt from tribute (in agricultural products and in labor on lands of lords or temples), as they were among the Mexicas.[84] This does not necessarily imply, however, that they did not give "tribute" in the form of the products of their specialized trades.

Marriage among commoners probably was mostly monogamous, although polygyny was permitted if one could support more than one wife.[85] Apparently, marriage occurred quite late in life; some of the *relaciones* indicate that in pre-Spanish times men might not marry until thirty or forty years of age.[86]

Before marriage, a diviner was consulted to see if the two individuals would make good mates.[87] The *relación* of Ixtepeji provides more specific information. A man considering marriage would consult with a woman's parents to determine if she was a virgin and otherwise eligible. If the parents consented, he would take her back to his own house, by force if necessary, and there consummate the marriage. A ceremony at the house of the bride's parents would then be held to consecrate this act; there would be sacrifices and much eating and drinking.[88]

Strong cohesiveness of the local community in political and religious matters might indicate that community endogamy prevailed among *macehuales*. Ronald Spores has argued that the post-Classic Mixtec community was endogamous for similar reasons;[89] he adds that the modern Mixtec community is endogamous, as is the modern Zapotec community, and that this trait is widespread in the Mixteca Alta, which perhaps indicates the antiquity of this pattern, although community endogamy in modern Mexico is certainly as much a function of the nature of Spanish Colonial and modern Mexican economic and political policies as it is a survival of a pre-Spanish trait. However, it does appear that the conditions of the post-Classic might have promoted endogamy among commoners. Further, the same term is applied to both a subdivision of a town and a *sujeto* or *estancia* in ancient Zapotec,[90] which may indicate that spatial separation did not connote social division.

SERFS AND SLAVES

Outside of three-estate system of nobles, priests, and commoners existed two other groups: serfs or tenants (Nahuatl *mayeque* or *tlalmaitl*) and slaves. Among the Mexicas of central Mexico certain individuals were permanent tenants on the patrimonial lands of noblemen. This group existed somewhat outside of the common estate in that they had lost their right to the ward or *calpulli* lands and were exempt from the payment of normal commoner tribute to the rulers of a town or ward; their tribute consisted of labor performed and items paid to the nobleman whose land they worked and to whom they were bound.[91] This situation arose primarily from conquest, as noblemen or warriors distinguished for their service to the Mexica ruler were rewarded with these almost feudal "fiefdoms."

It is doubtful that the general situation among the Valley prince-doms reached the complexity of that found in central Mexico, al-though undoubtedly various nobles had their own fields and workers to support them. Commoners, as they were drafted to work temple lands and lands of the prince, also could have been assigned to work the lands of lesser nobles, as was the situation in central Mexico, with-out becoming bound serfs.

Most of the evidence for the possible existence of a *mayeque* group in the Valley fails to distinguish between commoners assigned to nobles to work their lands and those who may have been bound to them on a hereditary basis. Burgoa informs us that the Prince of Zaachila had many workers in his fields at Etla, a statement that has been taken by some to imply that they were serfs.[92] Many Colonial documents also may provide indirect evidence of *mayeques*, primarily in the Etla and Zaachila wings of the Valley and less in the Tlacolula or eastern branch.[93] It is likely that the serfs were more common in the western part of the Valley, since *mayeques* generally came into being as a result of conquest, with the subsequent usurpation of con-quered lands; as the Mixtecs took over Zapotec towns in the region, they may well have converted some Zapotec commoners into *mayeques* in some cases. Conquered hamlets may also have been given to lesser nobles, in part as rewards for their bravery or service to a prince.

However, the distinction between *mayeque* and commoner is not clear in the surviving sources on the Zapotecs. As has been noted, the Zapotec glosses for "vassal" or "peon" are clearly linked to those for "commoner" or "tributary."[94] Thus, no clear distinction between serf and commoner emerges from the dictionaries.

More positive information is available about slaves in Zapotec so-ciety. Slaves were obtained in war, could be bought or sold, were sacrificed in ceremonies, and were used as domestic servants. A num-ber of *relaciones* attest that slaves were taken in war and used in cere-monies involving human sacrifice; this fact is reported for Teitipac, Huitzo, Ixtepeji, Miahuatlán, and Tehuantepec.[95] The Córdova dictionary gives the following entry: "Man whom they sacrifice as a result of being taken in war or a captive presented to their lord in order to be sacrificed. *Peniyypeniquij, peniye, xoyaa.*"[96] In some cases, the sacrificed individual was eaten; the Zapotec gloss for "a captive when they ate him" was *xoyaaquij.*[97]

Slaves were bought and sold; some were used for servants. The dictionaries of Córdova and the *Junta Colombina* give the following entries: "slave, bought or sold. *Choco, pinijni, xillani.* servant, to be slave. *Nacapinijnia, chocoa.* servant, slave (male). *Pinijni, choco, xillani.* servant, slave (female). *Pinijni gonna, xillanini.*"[98]

The *relación* of Miahuatlán, pertaining to the Southern Zapotecs, provides the fullest account of slavery. It describes a situation similar to that found in the Valley and confirms the above information. Many of the captives who were taken in war were made slaves and were bought and sold in markets. Miahuatlán had a market where slaves were brought from other provinces such as Mexico, Tlaxcala, Tepeaca, and the Mixteca Alta. Each slave was valued in Spanish currency at about one to one and one-half pesos in powdered gold. The *relación* also relates that some slaves were sacrificed by having their hearts cut out with a stone knife; the hearts then were presented to a stone idol. The meat of these individuals was eaten during a fiesta.[99]

It is not known to what extent slavery in the Valley of Oaxaca was comparable in other respects to that found in Mexica society. There, an individual could sell himself into servitude, the only obligation being that he give service to his master. He could continue to keep his own property, marry, and even maintain his own slaves. In cases of this kind, the children of slaves were freemen.

Besides those taken in war and those who sold themselves, there were two other types of slavery in Mexica society. A family, for example, could place itself in hereditary servitude to another. Since the bond was perpetual, children in this group were not free. Also, individuals could be enslaved as punishment for crimes. The severity of the slavery was dependent on the severity of the crime committed; in some cases the person performed services deemed equivalent to the object stolen, if the crime was theft. In others, he could be sold for sacrifice. If slaves misbehaved in Mexica society, they might be collared and sold at market. Apparently if this happened four times, a slave then could be sacrificed.[100]

KINSHIP AND SOCIAL ORGANIZATION

Some anthropologists have argued for the presence of unilineal kinship groupings or egalitarian clans (corporate kin groups in which descent is traced only in one line—through either males or females) among the Zapotecs and have taken the position that the Zapotecs were a democratic tribal confederacy with clan chiefs and a tribal council. Noteworthy among this group was Adolf Bandelier, who, strongly influenced by Lewis Henry Morgan, hypothesized that the societies of ancient Mesoamerica, in their final state of development, were in the stage of "middle barbarism" and had developed a type of organization roughly similar to that of the Iroquois tribal confederacy of North America.[101] However, Bandelier's contentions lacked substantive foundation.

The use of kinship terminologies alone to infer other social phenomena must be approached with caution, since they are subject to various influences; however, the Zapotec terminological system, as revealed in the Córdova and *Junta Colombina* dictionaries, does not support the notion of unilineal kinship groupings. Instead, it seems to conform to Murdock's "Hawaiian Type of Social Organization" (for a listing of Zapotec kin terms and additional discussion, see the Appendix: "Zapotec Kinship Terms—Ancient and Modern"). This analysis indicates that the Zapotec system was bilateral or ambilineal (reckoning descent in both lines) rather than unilineal.[102]

However, it would be difficult to decide on the basis of the kinship terminology alone whether the kinship groupings of Zapotec society were primarily of a lateral nature (such as a kindred or deme) or were lineal (as in an ambilineal ramage). The latter possibility, of course, is not excluded simply because descent, as indicated by the kinship terminology, was reckoned in both lines. Anthropologists have posited for some time that there are at least two possible systems displaying bilaterality: one is the so-called kindred (which is not properly a descent group), and the other is the ramage (which is a lineal descent group but displays characteristics not common to unilineal groups).[103]

In many respects, the Zapotec community probably corresponded to Murdock's *deme*, a term derived from the ancient Greek word for people or citizens, *demos*. The deme, as Murdock uses it, is actually a kindred (a loose bilateral grouping lacking clear boundaries) that has common spatial propinquity. Community endogamy operates to hold this compromise kin group intact.[104] Spores has employed this concept to elucidate the character of the post-Classic Mixtec community, and a similar phenomenon was characteristic of at least one type of the Mexica *calpulli*.[105]

But such a characterization fails to do justice to other features of Zapotec social organization: the strong emphasis on lineality and the estate system. It has been mentioned, for example, that Zapotec society consisted of estates which were partly constituted through lines of descent—descent that could be reckoned in both the male and the female lines. There is evidence to support this contention. For example, Córdova, when referring to the division between rulers and other nobles, uses the term "lineage." The *tijacoqui* are defined as the "lineage of the highest lords," the *tijajoana* are the "lineage of the nobles lower than those of the highest lineage," and the *tijapeniquecha* are the "lineage of commoners or workers." In another place he refers to this principle as the "casta linaje" or "rank, tribe, or caste lineage."[106] While Córdova was not an anthropologist, it appears he could have been referring only to a principle of lineal descent as the criterion defining membership in, or recruitment into, the major social groupings.

Further, Córdova makes it clear that both men and women were assigned to the estates, divisions, or ranks on the basis of this principle. As has been indicated, a prince's successor in theory could come only from the offspring of the prince and his "muger natural" or wife of equal rank.[107] In addition, noble status was acquired only when both parents were of noble rank.

As such, it seems that the Zapotec system corresponded in part to the conical clan, as Paul Kirchhoff has called it,[108] or the ambilineal ramage, as it has been referred to by others.[109] This system also is known in other Mesoamerican societies, such as the Mexica, and is found in its classic form among the chiefdoms of Polynesia.

The ambilineal ramage or conical clan consists of a corporate kinship group which is ambilineal and partly endogamous. The only similarity between a conical clan and a unilineal exogamous clan is that both are based on the principle of descent. The unilineal clan, however, consists of individuals who are related through either the

male or female line, while in the conical clan the nearness of relationship to the common ancestor of the group is of most importance. Kinship in both of these clans, of course, may only be assumed and need
not actually be reckoned among all members of the group.

In the unilineal clan, members are of equal standing—it is egalitarian. In the conical clan, members who are the nearest descendants
of the common ancestor of the clan (who might be a deity or deified
ancestor) are the most important. These individuals control all economic, social, and religious functions; they usually constitute the
nobility or *aristoi*.

Descent generally will be traced ambilineally and not patrilineally
or matrilineally in the conical clan, although it may display a patri-
potestal or patrilineal skewing. A principle such as primogeniture
may be employed to demarcate the line of succession, although others,
such as ultimogeniture, also might be employed. While males generally are the major successors to positions of important office, this feature need not always be the case. The important point is that the line
is chosen which gives a person a more direct descent or closer relationship to the ancestor of the group. These factors explain why
genealogies, especially those of the elite group, are of such importance
in societies of this type; they are the means by which the line of
descent is established. In Mesoamerica the Mixtec codices and the
Zapotec carvings and sculptures of the post-Classic primarily seem
to be concerned with just such issues.

In addition, the conical clan, unlike the unilineal clan, permits clan
endogamy. This must be so, Kirchhoff argues, for otherwise there
would be no mechanisms by which fixed boundaries within the
conical clan could be maintained. Thus, close endogamy, especially
among the nobility, is found to perserve the nearness of descent with
the ancestor.

This model of the conical clan also helps to account for certain other
features of Zapotec society. Córdova indicates that in matters of inheritance and succession the male line was preferred; primogeniture
also was an apparent Zapotec practice.[110] In some cases, in the absence
of a lineal male, lateral relatives from the same ramage or branch were
chosen, thus preserving the supremacy of the branch.[111] While in
pre-Spanish times males seem almost always to have become successors to princes, in Colonial times females sometimes inherited the

position of *cacique*.[112] Apparently, then, the system was not inflexible.

One major characteristic of the conical clan is that it is adaptable to a number of conditions. It is a system which permits features of inequality of power and status, localization, and descent to be modified under changing situations without destroying its basic principles. This system probably had great antiquity in the Zapotec region and, as increased differentiation occurred in society there, it provided a mechanism of legitimation through which a monopoly of economic goods could be maintained by those claiming the closest relationship to the "original" ancestors.

It also was a system in which the highest rank or ramage could promote increasing political centralization. At one time or stage, it may be inferred that positions of power and authority within the conical clan were ascribed almost exclusively on the basis of descent— that is, those closest to the ancestors could occupy the highest chiefly positions, those of second rank the next highest, and so on; this was the case in the Polynesian chiefdoms at a given stage. However, it would require only one move to strengthen the position of those at the top—the highest could claim, on the basis of descent (and, of course, bolstered with actual power), the authority to control all positions or offices in the society as his exclusive domain. This apparently is exactly what happened in Zapotec society; the prince controlled all positions of authority within the noble estate.

Expansionist tendencies also were not inconsistent with the basic premises of the conical clan. Some groups used it more for this purpose than did others: the Mixtecs, for example, following the conquest of a new town, frequently sacrificed the conquered prince and made captives of the lesser nobility. The women, however, would be married into the conquering Mixtec nobility. Expansion then would be achieved when the eldest son inherited the princedom of the father, while the second son inherited that of the mother.[113]

The potentialities of this system were almost infinite. Lineage books or codices could be rewritten, and individuals could rise to power, if they had the prowess to do so, claiming authority from newly favored deities, who were claimed to be their ancestors. This practice certainly was true among the Mexicas, who often rewrote their official histories just as Julius Caesar justified his usurpation of power in ancient Rome by claiming descent from Venus. In a similar vein, other ethnic groups could be conquered and reduced to servitude because they lacked closeness to favored ancestors.

These examples illustrate the many ways in which the basic principles of the conical clan may be used and the manner in which kinship and descent may promote political centralization or coercive power. It should not be expected that Mesoamerican societies or any others, will conform perfectly to "rules" they espouse or to ideal types which social scientists construct. On the other hand, men make an attempt, no matter how devious, to follow rules. They thus can serve as a guide towards processual understanding.

RELIGION AND WORLD VIEW

Zapotec religion consisted of a complex pantheon of deities, interconnected in various ways, who mirrored aspects of human reality. As in most societies, religion functioned not only to bring solidarity to social groups, but also to alleviate the constant crises in the everyday lives of individuals.

The *relaciones* indicate that in the pre-Spanish period each lordship, princedom, community, or city-state ascribed a particularly important role in its pantheon of gods to a local patron deity. Major ceremonies were held in honor of this deity, with whom the individuals of the community felt a particular affinity.[114] It is quite probable that the inhabitants of a particular community, who often took their names from their patron deity, felt that the deity was their ancestor.[115]

In Tlalixtac, the local god was Coquihuani, god of light. To this deity boys and men were sacrificed and quetzal feathers, dogs, and blood were offered by the priests. This ceremony involved excessive drinking of *pulque* and dancing before the idol to the accompaniment of music.[116]

The patron deity of Macuilxóchitl was undoubtedly 5 Flower, implied by both its Zapotec name, Quabelagayo, and its Nahuatl name. Macuilxóchitl was the Mexica god of pleasure. The *relación* of Macuilxóchitl indicates that they worshiped Coquehuilia, lord of the center of the earth, whose calendrical representation may have been 5 Flower. In connection with the worship of 5 Flower there were periods of fasting of from forty to eighty days, during which the celebrant consumed only a kind of native tobacco every four days; he also let blood from his tongue and ears as offerings. During the ceremonial feasts, dancing and intoxication were typical.[117]

Teotitlán del Valle was called Xaquija in Zapotec, after the sun god, also called Copichja, worshiped there. He was associated with the macaw, a solar bird who descended from the heavens to enter his temple. Of apparently great antiquity, the sun god was given great prominence by the inhabitants of Teotitlán del Valle.[118]

Chichicapa recognized a healing god, Pichana Gobeche, as its major deity. However, Pichana Gobeche was a powerful god and had to be appealed to through an intercessor or intermediary, called Pichanto. The latter deity probably was the goddess Huichanatao, also associated with children and with her male counterpart, Pitao Cozaana, "the begetter."[119]

The *relación* of Mitla states that the major gods worshiped there, Xonaxi Quecuya and her husband Coqui Bexelao, were important to all the Zapotec towns in the Valley. According to Spores and Caso, those deities were gods of death and the underworld and also were called Coquechila and Xonaxi Huilia in other towns;[120] such an analysis confirms the importance of these concepts to the Mitleños and the identification of Mitla as the "place of rest," of "death" or the "underworld." Probably these deities were the special patrons of Mitla.

Bezelao (also Pezelao) also was worshiped in the Southern Zapotec town of Ocelotepec, although their particular patron undoubtedly was the intercessor Cozichacozee: "This was the god of war for whom they had much need since they were constantly engaged in warfare. They pictured him as very ferocious, holding bows and arrows in his hands."[121] Cozichacozee, as god of war, also was associated with the sun god, Copichja. The latter, in turn, was a refraction of Pitao Cozanna, "the begetter," also associated with Pezalao. This association probably explains the reference in the *relación* to "Bezalao, who was the devil, the supreme universal god."[122]

In Ocelotepec they worshiped a deified *cacique* called simply Petela. This name undoubtedly is incomplete, for alone it simply means "dog."[123] A calendrical number also must have accompanied this calendrical day name, as was the practice in Zapotec as well as most other Mesoamerican cultures.

At Coatlán, also in the Southern Zapotec area, Benelaba (more probably Pilalapa Caache, 7 Rabbit) and his wife Jonaji Belachina (or Xonaxi Peochina Coyo, 3 Deer) were worshiped. These were deities who had been brought back to Coatlán by one of its *caciques* after a visit to the Mixteca Alta. Interestingly, this *relación* says that the Zapotecs of Coatlán did not perform sacrifices until they learned the practice from this Mixtec-influenced *cacique*. To Benelaba, a god reserved for males, they sacrificed dogs, turkeys, quail, and male slaves captured in war. Similar sacrifices were made to Jonaji Belachina, although she was attended exclusively by women.[124]

The *relación* of the sierra Zapotec town of Teocuicuilco describes the fiesta of its patron deity. The fiesta was held every 260 days (260 days corresponded to the cycle of the ritual calendar). All residents came to the ceremony and brought offerings of quails, brightly colored feathers, and precious green stones which were given to the priests. On the top of a mountain called *qurazee* in Zapotec, the priests offered the sacrifices, letting blood from their tongues and ears, and prayed for the health of the town, good agricultural seasons, and remedies for maladies from which the town suffered. The fiesta began the night before the sacred day and continued until the same hour the next day. Sacrifices always were made at night; only the priests entered the temple where the idol of the god was kept.[125]

The *relación* of the town says that its deity was Coquibezelao, "the principal devil." It might be suspected that the Spaniards found "the principal devil" everywhere and attributed widespread "devil worship" to the Indians. While Teocuicuilco probably worshiped Coquibezelao, their patron deity probably was another god. Nearby, Zoquiapa worshiped Coquenexo, lord of the multiplication, while Atepec revered Quezelao, provider of the seasons, who probably was a refraction of Cocijo, the major Zapotec rain deity.[126]

Zapotec religion, of course, functioned in ways other than to emphasize local solidarity and distinctiveness. As the *relaciones* suggest, the deities also were patrons of more mundane activities and reflected other aspects of social life. The *relaciones*, Córdova, and Burgoa permit reconstruction of some of these other functions. Additional data, particularly rich, pertain not to the Valley of Oaxaca but to the Southern Zapotec district of Sola (about eighty kilometers south-southwest of the present city of Oaxaca), as recorded in the seventeenth account of Gonzalo de Balzalobre and documents in the Ramo de Inquisición

Zapotec urn of the god Cocijo, Monte Albán IIIA; provenance, San Pedro el Alta, District of Tlaxiaco. (By permission of the Department of Anthropology, National Museum of Natural History, Smithsonian Institution; catalog no. 115,161.)

Zapotec urn of the god Cocijo, Monte Albán IIIA; exact Mexican provenance unknown. (By permission of the Department of Anthropology, National Museum of Natural History, Smithsonian Institution; catalog no. 215,067.)

of the Archivo General de la Nación, México, studied by Henrich Berlin.[127]

Balzalobre, who held the office of curate for the pueblo of San Miguel Sola (Sola de Vega) for over twenty years, found in 1653 that pre-Conquest pagan ceremonies still were being practiced by the natives of his area. Under the title of "Inquisitor Ordinario" given him by the Bishop of Oaxaca, the curate conducted an investigation of the indigenous ceremonies and published an account of his labors in 1656. This account contains a description of the major deities worshiped in Sola, the rites performed in connection with their worship, and data on the function of the deity in the native culture.

Numerous unpublished documents found by Henrich Berlin supplement Balzalobre's data on Sola. Most of the documents Berlin studied pertain to inquisitional processes against practitioners of native rites in Sola.

From these varied sources, a number of the major deities in the Zapotec pantheon can be identified. Of primary importance were the gods connected with agriculture and sustenance. In the Valley, Cocijo or Pitao Cocijo undoubtedly was the major deity; there is, in fact, evidence that Cocijo was the patron deity of all the Valley Zapotecs. Cocijo also presided over the cardinal directions, of which, among the Zapotecs, there were five: north, south, east, west, and the zenith.[128]

First on Balzalobre's list was Locucuy (in Sola) or Pitao Cozobi (in the Valley). Pitao Cozobi was the god of maize and all food, or simply the god of abundant sustenance. Concerning this deity, Balzalobre writes:

> on collecting the first ears of green maize from their fields, on the day indicated by the teacher of these rites, they sacrifice a black native hen, sprinkling with its blood thirteen pieces of copal in memory of their thirteen gods, and burning this copal, and with the rest of the blood sprinkling the patio of the house.
> This they offer to the god of maize and all food, called in their language Locucuy, in thanksgiving for the good harvest they have had; and on offering it they say certain words in a very low voice as they pray.[129]

Balzalobre informs us that in Sola they performed the same ceremony to Lociyo (Cocijo) on cutting the first chili plant as they did to Locucuy on collecting maize.[130]

Zapotec urn of goddess "2J" or Nohuichana. Monte Albán IIIB; provenance, Monte Albán. (By permission of the Peabody Museum, Harvard University; catalog no. 94,073.)

A third deity in Sola was Coqueelaa, the god of the cochineal harvest. Regarding this deity: "And on planting the nopal cactus, or on gathering the cochineal, they sacrifice a white native hen to the god whom they call Coqueelaa, and they say that he watches over it [the cochineal]."[131]

A number of deities were associated with hunting and fishing. Niyohua, Noçana, and Nohuichana were gods of the hunt and of fishing in Sola, while Pitao Cozaana and Huichana were the gods "of the animals to whom hunters and fishermen sacrificed for help" in the Valley.[132]

Noçana or Nosana Quiataa (in Sola) and Pitao Cozaana (in the Valley) also were deities associated with the "ancestors" or the "getting of life." Pitao Cozaana had a wife or female counterpart, Huechaana, Pitao Cochana, Nohuichana, or, as the *relación* of Chichicapa calls her, Pichanto. While the male deity was the creator of man and animals, Nohuichana was the goddess of childbirth and children, the goddess of creation. She also was associated with weaving and cotton; on Zapotec urns she is identified with the glyph 2 J, which is a representation of cotton.[133]

As already noted, the "begetter" also was associated with the sun god, Copichja, who had, as one of his refractions, the god of war, Cozichacozee (in Southern Zapotec).

The major god of death or the underworld was Leta Ahuila in Sola and Pitao Pezelao or Bezelao in other Zapotec regions. This deity apparently had both male and female refractions: Coqueehila, the lord of the underworld, and his wife Xonaxihuilia. Pezelao or Bezelao may have corresponded to the calendrical name 13 Monkey or 13 Vulture.[134]

Deities associated with major events in life were also found in the Zapotec pantheon. There was a god of earthquakes, Pitao Xee, who has always been quite literally active in Oaxaca. Gods of medicine and sickness were called Lera Acuece and Lera Acueca in Sola, while Pichana Gobeche was appealed to for relief in Chichicapa. A Valley Zapotec deity, Pixee Pecala, was the god of love, and Pitao Zicala was the god of dreams.[135]

Special groups of individuals also had patrons. Huiçana or Pitao Huichaana was the goddess of children in the Valley. In Sola, Laxee was the god of sorcerers; he was known as Pitao Pijzi in the Valley.

The miserable, lost, or unfortunate appealed to Pitao Zij or Pitao Tee. Merchants, wealthy individuals, and those involved in gaming or chance appealed to Pitao Peeze, Pitaoquille, or Pitooyage.[136] This list of deities, almost endlessly expandable,[137] while elucidating the functions of religion in Zapotec life, does not itself provide an understanding of the complexity of the Zapotec world view.

Zapotec religion appears from these lists to be little more than a complex, baffling, polytheism. To be certain, it was that. But on the other hand it also consisted of a world view that integrated the attributes of man, society, and the elements into a supernatural system.

This integration is suggested in the nature of the deities. All deities were but aspects, attributes, or refractions of a supreme force or principle, Coqui Xee or Coquixilla, He or "It" without "beginning or end, the unknowable one." Coqui was designated in Zapotec as "lord" or "prince," while Pitao was an ordinary name for "god."

Xee was an abstract concept suggesting "infinity," "unknowable," or simply "above." Sometimes He or "It" was also called Pijetao, the "great time," for Pije meant "time" and tao, "great." He also was designated as Pije Xoo, "the source of time," as he governed the "thirteen," the thirteen gods of the Zapotec sacred calendar.[138]

But this supreme force was not like ordinary gods or forces, for he had no image or material manifestation. Most gods could be represented in material forms or idols, and their image was the same as the deity. The "great source" was, however, like man in one respect; he was multifarious. As man was divided into various groupings and came in numerous varieties, so did gods. And gods who emanated from the "great source" did not all have the same power. Some were more powerful than others and evoked more awe, as did some men. The more powerful consequently could not be reached directly but could be approached only through intercessors or intermediaries, as could powerful men. Since many deities also had female counterparts, as men did, they could perhaps be reached through this source if others failed.

Men often operated on a *quid pro quo* principle; so did the gods. One owed one's lord tribute, so one owed tribute to the gods to receive favor; on the other hand, ignoring their demands would bring disfavor or punishment. To this extent, deities were but the ultimate projection of human society onto a larger cosmos.

Zapotec brazier with the figure of a young man displaying the mask of a butter-fly in his headdress; this mask may have represented his alter ego. Monte Albán IIIB; provenance, Zaachila. (By permission of the Department of Anthropology, National Museum of Natural History, Smithsonian Institution, catalog no. 115,151.)

Zapotec urn of a young man displaying the mask of a quetzal bird; this bird may have been his alter ego. Monte Albán IIIB; provenance, Pochutla. (By permission of the Department of Anthropology, National Museum of Natural History, Smithsonian Institution; catalog no. 115,158.)

This bewildering cosmos, which in its details was the province of the priests, was probably understood in principle by most Zapotecs, for it mirrored a common occurrence. In Zapotec society, every individual at birth received a calendrical name; connected with this name was an alter ego (*huechaa* or *huichaa*). This alter ego often took the form of an animal (such as a bat, lizard, or owl), or a plant, vegetable, or natural phenomenon (such as wind or rain). Thus, a common man knew that he himself took, or could take, various forms.

If men had alter egos, so must the gods. But gods were more powerful than even the most powerful men; therefore, their alter egos must also have alter egos. This principle explains why the Zapotec deities take such a diversity of forms.

The whole Zapotec cosmos was systemized in a sacred book, the book of the 260-day calendar. This calendar was used for a variety of purposes, including the prediction of numerous pheonomena. Periods of time, events, and happenings not only were thought to be controlled by deities but also were thought of as manifestations or attributes of gods. The sacred calendar was a device to order the Zapotec universe.

Córdova has given the most detailed account of this calendar in the Valley, and Alfonso Caso has succinctly summarized this material:

> Cordova tells us of the existence of the *tonalpohualli*, which they called *pije* or *piye* and consisted of 260 days divided into four periods of 65 days each, each one a "sign" or "planet" also called *pije* or *piye* "time" or "time duration," but Cordova also calls this 65-day-period *cocijo*. These 65 days were divided into five parts of 13 days each, which were called *cocij* or *tobicocij*, as if we were to say one "month," or a time period; each day had its name. The four planets, which presided over the main divisions and were the cause of everything, were called *cocijos* or *pitaos*, that is, gods; they were given offerings each one at their proper time, and blood was drawn in their honor. Each *piye* or *cocijo*, or 65-day period, was called by the same name of the day of the 13-day unit which began them.[139]

The *piye*, like the Mexican *tonalpohualli*, was extremely important in the lives of the Zapotecs and was managed by special priests, *huebee pijze* or *huechilla pijzi*.[140] It was consulted for prognostications to determine whether an event should be performed on a given day, for some days would bring good fortune while others were malevolent.

Table 3. Major Zapotec Deities*

Deity	Valley Zapotec	Sierra Zapotec	Southern Zapotec	Aztec
1. God of Infinity; and God of the Thirteen	Coquixee Pijetao		Leta Aquichino Liraaquitzino	Tloque-Nahuaque
2. God of Rain and Lightning	Cocijo	Gozio	Lociyo	Tlaloc
3. God of Maize and All Food; and God of Abundant Sustenance	Pitao Cozobi	Betao Yazobi	Locucuy	Centeotl
4. Creator God of Man and Animals; and God of the Ancestors	Pitao Cozaana Cozaana	Betahoxona	No͵ana Cosana Nosana	Tonacatecuhtli
5. Creator Goddess of Man and Animals; Goddess of Children; Mother Goddess; Goddess of Parts; and Goddess of Fishing	Pitao Huichaana Cochana Nohuiçana		Nohuichana	Tonacacihuatl
6. God of the Underworld; God of Death; and God of Earth	Pitao Pezelao Coqui Bezelao		Coqueelaa	Mictlantecuhtli
7. Goddess of the Underworld; and Goddess of Death	Xonaxi Quecuya	Xonaxi Gualapag	Xonaxihuilia Jonaji Belachina	Mictecihuatl
8. Sun God; and God of War	Copijcha Pitao Copijcha		Cozicha Cozee	Tonatiuh
9. God of Earthquakes	Pitao Xoo	Laxoo	Laxee	
10. God of Love, Dreams, and Excesses	Pitao Xicala Pecala			Xochipilli Macuilxochitl

* From José Alchina Franch, "Los dioses del panteón zapoteco," *Anales de Antropología*, Vol. 9 (1972).

Balzalobre indicates the importance of this forecasting in his account, and although he alludes to ceremonies with some Christian components, the Zapotec elements are clear:

> For offering alms in the church, they have good and bad days; and these are indicated to them by some counselor who judges of that, according to his computations from the book of their doctrine. If the day is good, although it be during the week, all or many of them come together to light candles or to bring other offerings, which, it is evident by their own declarations, they do in reverence of their thirteen gods. For example: if such a day is good for offering, and the counselor told them to perform it at the altar of the Virgin offering or lighting so many candles, they do it; and they offer them in reverence of the goddess *Nohuichana*; and if at all of the altars they perform this sacrifice, it is done in reverence of all the thirteen gods; and the other offerings are made in the same respect. They are accustomed to perform many other ceremonies and rites on burying the dead, upon getting married, on copulating with their wives, on building their houses, on sowing, and on gathering their harvests....[141]

However, there is some evidence that the Zapotec calendar was slightly different from other Mesoamerican ones. Features interpreted by Alfonso Caso and Eduard Seler seem to indicate that it has great antiquity and perhaps is the oldest calendar in Mesoamerica. It already has been mentioned that it is divided into *cocijos*, or sixty-five-day periods, which are not found elsewhere. Thirteen particles also were combined with the day-sign and number; presumably these particles represent the thirteen gods or lords of the days.[142]

Some information on the 260-day calendar from the Southern Zapotecs, as it survives in modern times, also amplifies current knowledge of Zapotec calendars.[143] There, among the Loxichas, all that survives is a system of nine day-names of deities, representing objects or natural forces, with numbers from one to thirteen running parallel with them. In this case, however, the numbers do not combine with the day-names to designate the day. Instead, the calendar consists of the union of five "periods" with four "times." "Times" (composed of thirteen numerals joined by a series of nine plus four day-names) are designated by a particular name. Four of these "times" make up a "period," which is named in accordance with its first "time." This will produce five "periods" of 52 days each, or 260 days.

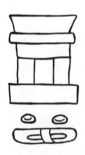

Examples of Zapotec day glyphs: *top*: *a*, Quiachina (Idol of Yogana, Frissell Museum, Mitla, Oaxaca); *b*, Pexoo (Tomb 104, Monte Albán); *c*, Calicij (*Lápida* 12 of Frissell Museum, Mitla, Oaxaca); *d*, Quiachina (Stela 4, Monte Albán). (Drawn by Sarah Whitecotton after Howard Leigh, "An Identification of Zapotec Day Names," *Boletín de estudios oaxaqueños*, No. 6 [1958].)

Alfonso Caso argued that this feature may represent but one component of the 260-day calendar, namely, that which corresponds to the so-called Lords of the Night of the Mexican *tonalpohualli*, which fit into this calendar in much the same way. Thus, while the Southern Zapotec calendar is somewhat aberrant, in principle it is the same as other Mesoamerican calendars, for "the numbers that intervene in the formation of this calendar are the same as those that intervene in the *piye* and the *tonalpohualli*: nine, thirteen, twenty, and two hundred sixty."[144] All were sacred numbers throughout Mesoamerica.

The Zapotecs also had a calendar of 365 days, called *yza*; this was the basic agricultural calendar. Like other Mesoamerican calendars, it probably consisted of eighteen "months" (*peo*, "moon" in Zapotec) of twenty days each; an additional period of five days was added at the end. Running in combination with the *piye*, the calendar would get back to the same combination of numeral, day-sign, and "month" after fifty-two years. Combined with thirteen numerals and four "year bearers," the same year would thus be repeated every fifty-two years. This constituted an "era" of history for most ancient Mesoamerican peoples, and, as among the Aztecs, the end of this cycle was fraught with fear, anguish, and uncertainty and was a time for special caution and obedience to the gods, lest the world, as the Aztecs knew it, be destroyed. In the post-Classic, periods of time longer than fifty-two years were not indicated calendrically.[145]

The Zapotecs also made astronomical observations of Mars, Venus, Mercury, and perhaps Jupiter and Saturn. According to Howard Leigh, the revolutions of these planets formed one basis for a Zapotec long count of time, especially in Classic times.[146] As with most other matters, these planets were deified and carried special religious significance.

5

Zapotec Elites and Peasants in New Spain

B Y THE TIME of the conquest of Mexico in 1519, Spain had
evolved from a land of independent kingdoms into a centralized empire. In 1492 it accomplished two feats that were
to shape its destiny: the discovery of America and the expulsion of the
Moors from Granada, their last stronghold on the European con-
tinent. As a nation, Spain achieved unity through conquest.

Spanish conquests and the colonial empire which ensued were justified on a religious basis, a rationale strengthened by the combined religious and secular authority of the state—a sovereignty which
prompted a holy quest to save the world for Christianity, specifically
Spanish Catholicism. The holy quest was to be led by a group of military warriors—knights errant from a feudal world—who sought a
Utopia in unexplored territory. They were to capture riches for Castile
and souls for the clergy and were to receive special tribute privileges
for themselves. Thus, service begot privilege, and privilege begot
wealth.

As in pre-Spanish Mexico, Spanish society was hierarchical with
three primary estates: nobles, priests, and commoners. Imbued with
the spirit of a Carolingian world, the crown stood at the summit of
this system—dispensing favors, titles, and offices to its servants. Sumptuary rules divided the empire between those who provided and those
who were provided for.

Accordingly, there were many similarities between Spanish society
and pre-Columbian Mexico of the post-Classic stage. Sovereignty was
based on the tutelage of favoring deities, status was determined by
favor and service as well as heredity, and the society was "directed" and
"protected" by a small group of power holders supported by a majority of tribute payers, mostly peasants.[1]

Peasants, or peasantries, constitute a generic social and cultural type which emerged as folk societies and tribesmen were engulfed by the centralization of power in the hands of the few and the mighty. In short, they came into being with the emergence of the state and have formed the vast majority in preindustrial and industrializing societies. Traditional and conventional histories frequently ignore them, giving precedence to more prominent men, although peasants have been an important ingredient in history as the prominent men have fought to control and subjugate them. Peasants have seen many conquerors, many lords, different religious ideas, poverty, disease, famine, war, and death as their toil in the fields has gone on.

Anthropologists think of peasants as displaying structural, economic, and social similarities regardless of time and place and have extended the meaning of the term *peasantry* beyond the confines of Europe and Asia in given historical periods. Peasantries generally are characterized as part-cultures and part-societies—a distinction that emphasizes that they are but a single segment of a complex society. They are further defined as rural cultivators existing in specific relationships to market towns and elites, practicing a simplified version of the Great Tradition of the elite class, producing for subsistence as well as to pay taxes or tribute to overlords, but rarely thinking of their way of life as a form of capitalistic enterprise or investment—a factor that differentiates them from farmers. While peasants are not necessarily isolated physically from nonpeasant sectors of the society (for some live in settlements which include nonpeasant inhabitants), they usually are separated both socially and culturally, and their isolation is generally fostered by sumptuary rules or legal mechanisms. Peasantries, then, largely although not exclusively, underwrite the existence of an elite class and form the backbone of preindustrial states.

However, these traditional anthropological views of peasantries require expansion. Their tradition, created by elite policies from above and economic necessities from within, constitutes more than a part-culture. Their social relationships, restricted to specific forms of interaction with others, are not simply "part-society" relationships. More properly, those relationships are *different* from the relationships of townsmen (or burghers) and elites. The societies and cultures of which they form parts are "dual" or "plural"—societies integrated through political power from above but with different cultures.[2]

Spanish society, like the societies of the pre-Spanish states of Meso-america, included the peasant as an important category in the social order. Most Indians in pre-Spanish Mexico had been peasants, and they remained so under Spanish colonial rule. To be sure, there would be changes that would affect the Indian peasant as the transition to Spanish rule took place. But, as with most peasants, the Indian peasant was to remain tied to the land and a "little tradition" that had much in common with the previous one.

But although Spanish society was oriented toward peasants and tribute, it also had a focus unfamiliar to the Indians of New Spain. Even though they sought to become aristocrats, the Spaniards who came to the New World were not all noblemen. Many were simple adventurers of humble stock. The New World offered them not only an opportunity for mobility and privilege, but also an opportunity for independence and wealth—a wealth fashioned on a capitalism forged from the heritage of the rich merchant cities of Catalonia.[3] To an extent this capitalistic trend sought to undermine the old order where privilege begot wealth and to substitute a new order where wealth begot privilege.

The clergy represented a third trend or tendency in Spanish society. Rejuvenated by the discovery of new primitive souls, the priests sought to forge yet another Utopia based on the protection and conversion of their new "children"—the Indians. Arguing against their abuse by those with strictly worldly motives, the clergy sought to undermine the notion that wealth and privilege could be obtained at their expense or, at least, at the expense of the Church. For them, the Indians were to form part of a different empire, one that was envisioned as a return to a kind of primitive Christianity directed and controlled by a sacred institution.

All of these trends emerged in New Spain and are found in various degrees throughout the long Colonial period ending in 1810. From the earliest period, Spaniards were to receive tribute payments, in the form of the *encomienda,* from the Indian peasantry. At the same time, not content to receive only tribute, Spaniards also sought to develop capitalistic enterprises, particularly mining and ranching. The friars argued against both systems, for to the extent that Indian labor was demanded and abused, Indian souls were destroyed and with them the power of the Church.

The crown sought to compromise all of these points of view while protecting to the utmost the central power of the empire. Abolishing or limiting the *encomienda*, a decentralizing element which granted virtual autonomy to New World aristocrats, a substitute system of crown control, called the *corregimiento*, was instituted. Attempting to limit the abuses of Indian labor, a strict set of controls was developed through the *repartimiento* system, in which Indians were to get a fair wage for their services. Capitalistic enterprises were heavily taxed and, in theory, strictly controlled and regulated by the Spanish bureaucracy.

However, the crown was but moderately successful in mediating all of these trends; instead, a society was formed which lacked integration through a common bond, a society held together only by political power from above and segmented into islands or worlds with contradictory foci. Further, by the middle of the seventeenth century Indian society had been totally decapitated in New Spain—the priests, nobles, and lords of pre-Columbian times had been eradicated, absorbed, or reduced to peasants residing in relatively homogeneous rural communities. Bureaucrats of the crown, called *corregidores*, replaced native *caciques* as intermediaries between the larger society and the local Indian communities. These Indian communities, although their populations had been decimated by epidemic disease, enjoyed a protected status as subjects of the crown and had been virtually cut off from the New World aristocracy.

By the eighteenth and nineteenth centuries, after a severe economic depression in the seventeenth century that virtually ruined their capitalistic endeavors, the New World nobility, isolated from their tribute-paying peasants, usurped the lands that had provided the tribute and sustenance of the peasant and turned him into a peon, or landless worker. The crown, now paralyzed, had lost the battle—parts of Mexico were virtual enclaves of autonomous feudal states where wealth begot privilege. The synthesis of capitalism and feudalism, then, never really achieved in Spain, came to fruition in the New World in the form of the hacienda.[4]

The processes of social and cultural development in the Valley of Oaxaca generally conform to this model of the evolution of the society of New Spain, although, as with all generalizations, it applies in varying degrees to any given area or region. In certain areas, the native

nobility persisted for a longer period than in other areas of Mexico, although in most parts of the Valley it was reduced to the status of a peasantry. Here also the Indian pueblo enjoyed protected status and became cut off from the society of New World entrepreneurs. Inability to obtain Indian labor through legal means ultimately forced the Oaxacan entrepreneur to seek such labor through extralegal means, although his lack of success helped to prevent the development of a pervasive hacienda complex in this region.[5]

CROPS, ANIMALS, AND MATERIAL CULTURE

As almost everywhere else in New Spain, Spaniards introduced new crops, domesticated animals, and items of material culture to the Indians of the Valley of Oaxaca almost immediately after the Conquest. Carrying his cultural preferences with him, however, did not mean that the Spaniard intended to become a primary producer himself. For even if he were of humble stock, the New World Spaniard aped an Old World aristocracy; he was determined to be a *gente de razón*, a gentleman, and he eschewed working with his hands.

New crops changed the face of the land. Wheat, preferred to Indian maize by the Spaniards, and chick-peas, desired over beans, were among the crops introduced. Other preferred foods included sugarcane, grapes, lettuce, cabbage, onions, garlic, radishes, apples, pomegranates, peaches, melons, figs, oranges, lemons, grapefruit, and pears.

While the Valley of Oaxaca was well suited to the cultivation of all these items, many were limited to specific locales within the Valley. For example, the Etla arm remained the major producer of wheat throughout the Spanish Colonial period. Peculiarities of geography and climate in other areas of the Valley limited wheat growing success elsewhere.

Sugarcane was grown mainly near Huitzo in the Etla arm and in the valley of Zimatlán, where its production was relatively slight until the nineteenth century. The valley of Tlacolula generally was unsuited for the growing of sugarcane, which caused discontent among Spanish *hacendados* there.[6] In other Zapotec areas, such as the Isthmus of Tehuantepec, the growing of sugarcane was much more lucrative.

Both wheat and sugarcane, however, largely were commercial crops, produced for sale to the Spanish residents of Antequera (Oaxaca City), Villa Alta, and Nejapa—the only Spanish communities in the region. Although they were cultivated by Indians, sometimes on Indian land, they did not become an important part of the Indian diet. Generally, the majority of the Indian population continued the pre-Spanish corn, beans, and squash diet with its associated tortillas, tamales, and sauces.[7]

The same was true of many other Spanish crops. While the *relaciones* of the 1580's indicate that Spanish crops were grown in sizable quantities in areas where environmental conditions were suitable, many complained that the Indians accepted them only slowly and clung tenaciously to their old food staples.[8] However, Spanish crops were grown largely for Spanish consumption, and to the extent that the Indian population cultivated them, they did so to meet tribute payments or demands for cash, not for subsistence.

Domesticated animals, largely absent in pre-Columbian Oaxaca, particularly *ganado mayor* (cattle, horses) and *ganado menor* (sheep, goats), also were introduced by the Spaniards. Livestock were put to graze on previously unused grassy areas; in some cases they strayed and damaged Indian crop lands. However, the Spanish bureaucracy moved early to limit the number of cattle in the region in an attempt to prevent such damage.

Ownership of cattle and horses almost exclusively was restricted to the Spanish entrepreneur nobleman and the native Indian nobility. The grazing of cattle carried with it prestige in Spanish society, a factor soon emulated by the Spanish-oriented Indian *caciques*. The largest cattle ranches were found in the southern part of the Valley of Oaxaca, in the Zimatlán branch. The discovery of mines in this region, near Chichicapa, created new markets for meat and tallow and led to a concentration of cattle there.

Although some cattle were grazed in the valley of Tlacolula, it primarily was devoted to raising *ganado menor*, and the Indians rapidly adopted sheep for the production of wool. The Etla arm had smaller numbers of livestock than either the Tlacolula or Zimatlán regions.[9]

As with many other Spanish items, meat from Spanish animals did not become an important part of the native peasant diet; hunting continued to provide most of their meat. An exception was Spanish chicken, which replaced the older pre-Spanish variety.

However, the Indians rapidly adopted the plow and the ox. The Roman *ard* (Latin *aratrum*), the only kind of plow transported to the New World, supplemented the Indian digging stick and was used in the cultivation of native crops, particularly maize.[10] It also was likely that an Indian family would own a team of oxen during the Colonial period in the Valley. Indeed, Burgoa notes that "in all of New Spain one cannot find Indians with so many teams of oxen" as in the Valley of Oaxaca.[11] Nevertheless, humans continued as the major beasts of burden, which for some became a specialization in a few Zapotec sierra towns, although at a later date the burro became extensively utilized for this purpose.

Other items of Spanish origin also had an impact on the Valley's native inhabitants. Metal was used for machetes (although daggers and swords were restricted to the Spanish and the Indian nobility), introduction of the wheel brought the ox cart, tile roofs sometimes replaced the older thatched roofs, and new pottery techniques (including glazing) were adopted in some communities. In general, however, crafts underwent a simplification instead of developing an increased complexity; many of the old techniques were lost as both Indian noblemen and Spaniards preferred clothing, house furnishings, and luxury items produced by Spanish craftsmen.

Native Indian dress shocked the Spanish friars, and very early both men and women were required to completely cover their bodies and limbs.[12] Male dress underwent more modifications than did the female. The characteristic male peasant attire, still worn in some areas of the Valley, probably took form during this period: the sombrero, a longsleeved cotton shirt, white trousers resembling pajamas tied at the waist and ankles, and *huaraches*. Women retained the *huipil*, although it might now be of wool, and the full-length wraparound skirt. A shawl was added to cover the head, although feet generally were bare.

Almost everywhere the Indian community underwent a change in physical appearance. The temples were destroyed, and Indian labor was employed to construct Spanish-style churches, although frequently stones (some carved) from old structures were incorporated into the new edifices, as at Teotitlán del Valle, Macuilxóchitl, and

The church at Teotitlán del Valle (above), displaying Spanish colonial style. Detail of one of the church towers (opposite), showing pre-Spanish stones incorporated in its construction.

Tlacochahuaya. The former palaces of the Indian nobility also were replaced by Spanish-style structures.

Some communities were moved to new locations, and in general the Spaniards favored a nucleated grid community with a concentrated civil-commercial and religious precinct (the plaza). Such an ideal was not attained everywhere, however, and variation on this pattern was found in many Indian communities.[13]

POPULATION

Indians remained in the large majority of the population of the Valley as well as of other Zapotec regions throughout the Spanish Colonial period; Spaniards and others always constituted a small minority in

Portion of the Hall of the Columns at Mitla, looking east; the Spanish Colonial basilica in the background is surrounded by post-Classic ruins.

the Colonial period, which accounts, in part, for the strong viability of the Indian community in this area.

There was some increase in the Nahuatl-speaking population during the early Colonial period, and the Mixtecs underwent some distributional shifts. By the end of the Spanish Colonial period, however, both Nahuatl and Mixtec had decreased in importance in the Valley, while Zapotec remained the predominant indigenous language.

Nahuatl-speaking soldiers, particularly the Tlaxcalans who had served as allies of Hernán Cortés in the conquest of the Mexicas, settled around Antequera, the Spanish capital of Oaxaca. Perhaps as many as four thousand resided in communities ringing the Spanish city. More Nahuatl speakers were brought in to work the mines southeast of Antequera. By the end of the Colonial period, however, because they underwent rapid acculturation, Nahuatl speakers had virtually disappeared in the Valley.[14]

The Mixtecs, who had been distributed in a number of places in the Valley in the late pre-Conquest period, were congregated by Hernán Cortés in and around Cuilapan.[15] In 1529 Cortés had taken the Valley as part of his vast *marquesado*, which also included part of the Valley of Mexico, much of the present state of Morelos, the area around Toluca, and later Tehuantepec.

Cortés held almost all of the Valley towns during the early part of the Conquest period, but by the 1540's his holdings had been restricted, for various political and economic reasons, to the Cuatro Villas (Etla, Cuilapan, Tlapacoya, and the Villa de Oaxaca).[16] With the exception of the Villa de Oaxaca, which was predominantly a Nahuatl-speaking community, these towns contained Mixtec speakers. Other Mixtecs were brought into the Valley, especially to the Etla region and to San Lorenzo Albarradas, near Mitla, from the Mixteca Alta.[17]

Documentary records describe the sizable, if concentrated, Mixtec-speaking population in the Valley during the Colonial period. For example, one source states that in 1570 there were 18,000 Zapotec tributaries in the entire Valley and some 6,000 tributaries in Cuilapan, primarily a Mixtec town and by this time the largest Indian settlement in the Valley, with about 20,000 inhabitants. At a slightly later date there were 12,100 Zapotec tributaries in the Valley and 5,000 tributaries in Cuilapan.[18] While Mixtec was spoken in the Valley throughout the Colonial period, there are few, if any, Mixtec speakers there today, even though communities such as Cuilapan, Atzompa, and Santa Cruz Etla claim a Mixtec heritage.[19]

A number of factors account for the disappearance of the Mixtec language. As minorities in Zapotec-speaking areas, the Mixtecs abandoned their native language and adopted Spanish, which became the *lingua franca* in the region. In other communities they intermarried with Zapotecs. In the Etla and Cuilapan areas, where native *cacique* and Spanish control and influence were particularly strong, they rapidly adopted Spanish.[20]

The Valley's indigenous population suffered a tremendous decrease during the early Colonial period, a phenomenon characteristic of most of New Spain. Although the conquest of the Valley was a relatively peaceful one and the inhabitants escaped the military combat losses suffered by the Mexicas of Tenochititlán,[21] they did not escape epidemic disease. Diseases brought by the Spaniards, against which the Indians had no resistance, reduced the native population of the Valley by half by 1568. The population fell even more in the early seventeenth century, dwindling perhaps to one-fourth of its size at Spanish contact.[22]

The native population recovered somewhat during the next hundred years, although there were cycles of decrease and increase; by 1740 there were about 70,000 inhabitants (including natives, mixed-bloods or mestizos, and Spaniards) in the Valley. By 1790 the Valley population had increased to some 110,000 inhabitants. In 1959, the population had grown to 290,000 inhabitants, perhaps equal to or slightly surpassing its population in aboriginal times.

The Spanish population of the Valley mostly was confined to Antequera. In 1526 Antequera had a population of 120, which increased to 3,000 by 1660. It then underwent a boom and grew to 19,000 by 1777, but declined to about 17,000 by the end of the Spanish Colonial period.

In the sixteenth century Antequera's population was almost exclusively Spanish. Later, however, it took on a more diverse character. For example, some nearby Indian communities, such as Villa de Oaxaca, gradually lost their lands, became infiltrated with mestizos and Negroes, and turned to more commercial enterprises. Additional migrants led to an increasing diversification of the city. Antequera thus developed a highly mixed population perhaps as early as the middle of the seventeenth century.

In the 1790's, when the population of Antequera reached 18,000, it included some 7,000 mulattoes and Indians, and about 11,000 Spaniards and mestizos.

Although the mestizo and Spanish population of Antequera was quite large, it remained small elsewhere in the Valley, as did the Negro and mulatto population. Spaniards and mestizos resided on some rural estates, and a few towns contained token populations.[23] By law, Spaniards (except *corregidores* and the clergy) and mestizos were forbidden to reside in Indian towns.

Negro slaves were imported into the Valley in the sixteenth century, particularly following the official abolition of Indian slavery by the New Laws of 1542. The dwindling native population, and strong legal pressures limiting access to its labor, also promoted the importation of Negro slaves. Most Negroes were employed as cowpunchers, laborers in sugar mills, and servants for both Spaniards and Indian *caciques*. However, the Negro population of the Valley always was relatively small; in the 1790's there were only 2,436 Negroes in the Valley.[24]

INDIAN CACIQUES

The Spaniards recognized the noble status of local Indians and, with certain reservations, permitted them to retain their favored positions. In the Valley of Oaxaca, having submitted peacefully to the conquistador Francisco de Orozco in 1521, native *caciques* were given special treatment; the Spaniards incorporated the Indian nobles as a special branch of their own nobility, according them *hidalgo* status. It was readily acknowledged that the prestigious native *caciques* would be helpful to the Spanish cause in collecting tribute, in serving as military leaders, and in converting commoners to Christianity.

Since *caciques* retained their traditional prerogatives, as did *principales*, they developed a loyalty to their Spanish overlords and rapidly became acculturated to Hispanic patterns: wearing Spanish clothing, carrying swords and daggers, riding horses, and using the appellation "Don" in front of their new Spanish names—prerogatives restricted to nobles.[25] They also rapidly learned Spanish, left their Indian communities to reside in the more prestigious Antequera, and became converts to Christianity. However, intermarriage between Indian nobles (whether male or female) and Spaniards was relatively rare in the Valley of Oaxaca.[26]

Caciques had to meet two criteria to maintain their positions. First, they had to convert openly to Christianity, denouncing the old gods for all to see, and undergo baptism. Second, they had to demonstrate their descent in a direct line from a native pre-Spanish lord. The same strictures applied to the *principal* or lesser nobility group; they also had to proclaim themselves Christian and be able to demonstrate their noble status.

Caciques, as well as *principales,* were entitled to exact tribute, in kind and in labor, from their subject populations. Many *caciques* also held grants of land and retained tenant farmers (*terrasgueros*) to work them. This practice especially was true in the valley of Etla and around Cuilapan, where even some *principales* enjoyed the prerogative of retaining *terrasgueros.*[27]

The size of noble landholdings also was increased. Following destruction of the temples and abolition of the native priesthood, the former temple lands frequently were assigned to native *caciques.*[28] Additional increases in noble landholdings sometimes came from the usurpation of pueblo or communal lands assigned to *macehuales.*

But Spaniards also brought with them a new concept of wealth, and *caciques* soon learned not to be content to simply exact tribute in the old manner; maize, cacao beans, feathers, and jade meant little in the new society. As a result, *caciques,* emulating the Spanish entrepreneurs, turned toward more capitalistic enterprises. Cattle and sheep ranches frequently were owned by Indian nobles. Others became involved in the cochineal industry, which became very important during the Colonial period, especially in the Zimatlán arm of the Valley. Some invested in stone quarries, salt deposits, and wheat mills, especially in the Etla wing of the Valley.[29]

Generally, after 1650 the native nobility, particularly in the Valley of Mexico and in Michoacán, hardly was distinguishable from *macehuales,* either by wealth or prestige,[30] but in parts of the Valley of Oaxaca they remained relatively prosperous throughout the Colonial period. A number of factors account for this: in addition to the relatively peaceful conquest of the Valley and the lack of a strong Spanish *encomendero* group there, the fact that many *caciques* were able to consolidate and maintain their estates (*cacicazcos*) intact is significant, for in other areas of Mexico the estates were usurped by Spanish landowners. The Indian *cacicazcos* of Cuilapan and Etla constituted the largest individual estates in the Valley of Oaxaca, whether Spanish or Indian, throughout the long period of Spanish rule.[31]

But in other areas of the Valley and Zapotec Oaxaca a more typical pattern ensued. Estates were fragmented and dispersed, and tensions between *macehuales* and nobles reduced the supply of Indian labor for *cacicazco* lands. Costly land disputes with *macehuales* and others, the squandering of money to emulate Spanish patterns of luxury, droughts, frosts, wheat blights, and an epidemic among cattle and sheep in the eighteenth century caused many *caciques* to go into debt —debt that could be repaid only by breaking up their estates.[32] In the valley arm of Tlacolula, in the Southern Zapotec region around Miahuatlán, in Tehuantepec, and in the Zapotec sierra, *caciques* hardly were distinguishable from *macehuales* by the middle of the Colonial period.[33] Since most *principales* never succeeded in crystallizing and entailing their estates, they suffered a similar fate. In fact, even Spaniards, particularly the Creoles, were unsuccessful in transmitting large landholdings and retaining labor for their estates in the Valley—a factor that distinguishes these Oaxacan areas from others in Mexico and helped to prevent the strong development of the hacienda there.[34]

While some *caciques* in the Valley were relatively wealthy, almost everywhere the Indian nobility suffered loss of prestige in their local Indian communities. Struggles with *macehuales* over land and labor led to an increasing gulf between the two groups and the partial undermining of the political power of the native nobility in Indian communities. As the Colonial period went on, *caciques* enjoyed prestige, and some enjoyed wealth, in the new Spanish society, but wealth was a guarantee neither of effective prestige nor of political influence in the local Indian community; conversely, prestige was not a guarantee of wealth. For while *caciques* and other nobles were favored by Spaniards, such favoritism, along with the pursuit of Spanish entrepreneurial activities, alienated them from the common Indian. Perhaps this was inevitable from the beginning of the Colonial period, for as Taylor writes: "The nobles' loyalty to their Spanish rulers was accompanied by a ready acceptance of Spanish ways. Caciques considered themselves aristocrats on the Spanish level. In many respects they had more in common with the Spanish society of Antequera than with the people of their own jurisdictions. This aloofness early became a matter of physical as well as psychological distance. . . ."[35]

In short, Indian nobles either were alienated from *macehuales*, becoming wealthy and prestigious in Spanish society, or were reduced to the level of *macehuales* in wealth, and also suffered a loss of prestige. In a social and cultural sense, then, although Indian *caciques* were recognized as distinct, they either became nonIndians or common Indians. This dual process, described by Charles Gibson as typical of the fate of the Indian nobility throughout the New World,[36] reflects the basic nature of the plural society of New Spain—one divided into isolated worlds with little allowance for groups intermediate between them.

THE INDIAN POLITICAL COMMUNITY

The Indian community, or pueblo, defined by law as a discrete entity in the Spanish system (the *república de los indios*), went through various stages of evolution after the Spanish conquest of Mexico. During the early part of the post-Conquest period, *caciques* and other Indian nobles continued to govern their communities, exact tribute, and supervise most activities—positions apportioned on the basis of pre-Conquest privileges. But beginning in the 1530's, the Indian community was organized, with some modification, in accordance with the basic institution of Spanish town government—the *cabildo*.

The Spanish envisioned the creation of an Indian community that was largely self-governing as well as economically self-supporting. This had been the model of municipal (*cabildo*) organization in Spain, where offices were elective and were rotated. The major offices were *alcaldes* (judges for minor crimes and civil suits) and *regidores* (councilors who legislated laws for local matters).

In the New World, these offices were continued, except that in Indian communities an additional office was added—that of *gobernador*, or governor. The *gobernador* was the highest elected political office and the most powerful and prestigious position in the Indian community. The origins of this position may have related to a position in the aboriginal town government, to some precedent in Spain, or, more probably, to a combination of both of these factors, an adaptation of Spanish and Indian forms of government to the specific conditions of the New World. It is known that in the early stages of *cabildo* government in the Indian community of New Spain, the highest positions were occupied by members of the Indian nobility, and the office of *gobernador* frequently was held by a *cacique*, the most prestigious individual in the community.[37]

Also during this early period, only Indian nobles could serve as electors, and only Indians could serve on Indian *cabildos*. These *cabildo* officers carried out a number of local functions: they guarded communal properties, collected local tribute, enacted local legislation not covered under Spanish law, and were responsible for maintaining peace, enforcing compliance to Spanish orders, and assuring attendance at religious functions.

In addition to the offices of *gobernador, alcalde* and *regidor* there were lesser offices, appendages to the *cabildo*. While these positions varied from town to town, most *pueblos* had *mayordomos* (supervisors) of communal lands, *escribanos* (scribes), *alguaciles* (police officers and custodial workers), and *cantores* (singers for masses and religious ceremonies). These positions generally were assigned through a system of rotation—a system that probably was responsible for development of what was to become the core of the Colonial Indian community, the civil-religious hierarchy or *cargo* system.

The domination of the Indian *cabildo* offices by the native nobility was but a transitional phase, however, for by the end of the sixteenth century their hold over *cabildo* posts had declined. A number of factors account for this development. First, the tremendous population decline that took place in the sixteenth century, coupled with Spanish legal restriction of *cabildo* posts to Indian nobles, created a lack of personnel that made enforcement of such restrictions difficult. Second, the rapid Spanish acculturation of Indian *caciques* turned their local populations against them. Finally, as the power of the Spanish bureaucracy increased, the prerogatives of the native nobility to *cabildo* posts decreased. Election to the main *cabildo* offices required approval of the viceregal arm of the Spanish government, enforced within the various levels of the Spanish Colonial bureaucracy, the *corregimiento*, the *audiencia*, and the Viceroy. Conflicts between Indian commoners, who soon gained access to Spanish legal channels, and their native nobility, along with the reduction of prerogatives to tribute and wealth for most Indian nobles in the 1560's, ultimately meant that the distinction between Indian noble and commoner became less clear. Thus, legal strictures could not be enforced, and common Indians gained access to *cabildo* posts even though the Viceroy continued to insist that voting rights should be restricted to Indian nobles.[38]

The evolution of *cabildo* government in the Valley of Oaxaca followed this general model, although the process was somewhat slower: "the *macehual* class gained more and more political control as the colonial period played out."[39]

Macehuales in the Valley of Oaxaca ultimately gained the right to vote, although in no Valley town was an entire *cabildo* elected by the whole community in the Colonial period. In some towns, such as Tlacochahuaya in the eighteenth century, *macehuales* could be elected to the posts of *alcalde* and *regidor* without having privileges as electors (*vocales*). In others, such as in Zimatlán, they gained the right to serve as electors for certain stipulated offices.

Legally and officially, *cabildo* offices were for a one-year term, and a person could not serve again in the same office for a period of three years. However, in the early years *caciques* and *principales* repeatedly were elected to the same office, some serving for as many as eleven to fifteen years.[40]

But continual abuse of these offices, plus the rising aspirations of certain *macehuales*, led to the decline of *cacique* rule. For example, only one *cacique* held the office of *gobernador* in the Valley after 1725.[41] The abuses of *caciques* frequently are mentioned in Spanish sources, and their character often is described in harsh terms. Burgoa, for example, describes seventeenth-century *caciques*:

> The caciques [of Huitzo] nowadays are half as intelligent and twice as wicked as their predecessors. All the old caciques have died, and with them have gone their esteemed reputation and courage, as well as the cattle estates they once possessed. Their heirs, more absentminded than vigilant, find themselves poverty-stricken. Their habits are corrupt; and when they lack outsiders with whom to quarrel, they stir up disputes and misunderstandings within the towns. . . . To sustain their petulant excesses they even usurp the *capellanías* [benefices] that were granted to the convent by former caciques.[42]

Another source speaks of the *cacique* of Matatlán in the 1720's: "He is a captious, bold, and shameless man whose only interest is in stirring up the rustic temperament of the natives of this town. He constantly arouses them against their priests and ministers, the *alcaldes mayores*, and the other representatives of justice."[43] In 1689, the *cacique* of Etla, who had given away community lands to the Church, declared: "The people of the Villa de Etla have declared themselves my enemies."[44]

Cacique disputes with their town populations were frequent in the seventeenth and eighteenth centuries. In some towns they were barred from holding any *cabildo* post. In others, such as Coyotepec, a *cacique* was elected to a lowly office and refused to serve because he felt it beneath his dignity. Some *caciques* attempted to usurp the office of *gobernador*, as in Zimatlán in the 1690's, and both the *principales* and the commoners united against him, taking the issue to a higher authority; the *cacique* ultimately was forbidden to hold office and had his estate confiscated.[45] Appeals by Indians to Spanish authorities were frequent in the Colonial period, a mechanism some have interpreted as a substitute for the warfare of pre-Spanish times as a means of resolving disputes.[46] Open violence also frequently erupted in towns over noble usurpations of office. The *macehuales* of Zaachila disrupted the elections of 1590, and in 1719 they ousted the *gobernador* of the town. At Macuilxóchitl in 1790 the townspeople removed the *gobernador* by force.[47]

Caciques ultimately disappeared from the local community political scene, although in some cases they attempted, mostly unsuccessfully, to reassert their influence. *Principales* also lost their hold over offices as their status and wealth declined. Finally, prestige based on community service instead of hereditary privilege became much more important as a criterion for serving in an important *cabildo* post.

By the end of the Spanish Colonial period, the Indian *cabildo* had taken a form that was neither distinctively Spanish nor like the government of pre-Conquest times. Instead, it represented an adaptation of Spanish town government to local conditions—conditions that made the holding of political office less a right that could bring wealth and power to a privileged nobility than a duty designed to preserve and protect a local Indian community of peasants. In this system, prestige became synonymous not with wealth and power but with their antithesis—poverty and service.

In other respects, the post-Conquest Indian community as a political entity had more in common with its pre-Spanish past—a commonality resulting more from the structural similarity between the political communities of ancient Oaxaca and Spain than from the survival of aboriginal institutions. The relationship between a *cabecera* and its *sujetos* was similar in both periods: the *cabecera* dominated the political life of the *sujetos,* as *sujetos* did not have *cabildos* of their own.

Throughout the Colonial period, however, there was shifting in the

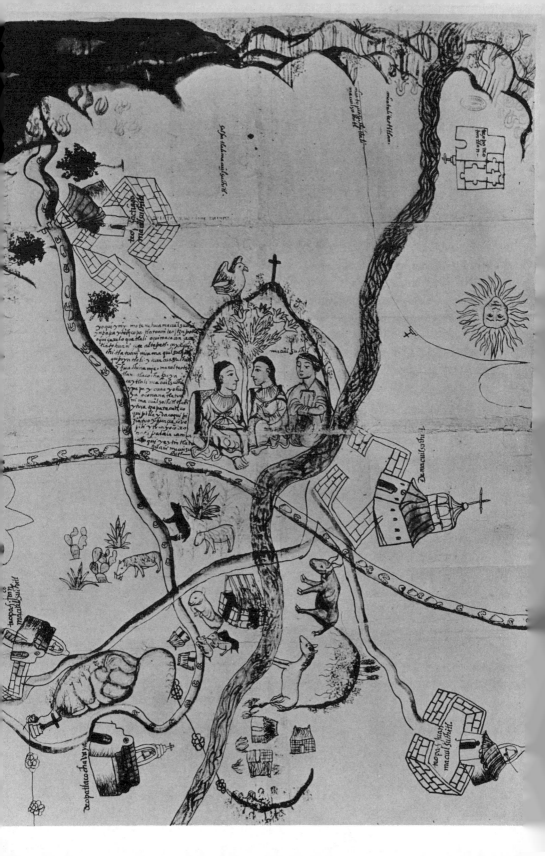

political status of Indian towns. Depopulation brought about the con-
solidation of many towns into single entities, brought about the ex-
tinction of some communities, and created towns which had no pre-
Spanish antecedents. In other cases, inhabitants abandoned whole
towns or *barrios* because of population pressures or attempts by authorities to subject them to a labor draft; some became squatters on
abandoned land. Bitter disputes, leading to violence and litigation,
also ensued over the political status of towns; some objected to the
rule of the *cabecera* and petitioned for *cabecera* status. In general,
there was a tendency for political units to increase in size in the early
Colonial period, while smaller units obtained independent political
status in the later years of Spanish rule.[48]

THE LANDED INDIAN PUEBLO

The Indian community in the Valley of Oaxaca was conceived, above
all, as a land-based entity. Grants of land, generally made to whole
communities, had the long-term effect of solidifying the identification of the Indian commoner with a place, of pitting community
against community and commoners against an Indian noble or
Spaniard who received a separate individual grant. The strong community tradition, characteristic of pre-Spanish times, was strengthened in the Colonial period; for Indian commoners the pueblo remained their major unit of identification.

A number of types of grants were given to Indian communities.
The first—and the only one really protected by colonial law—was the
fundo legal, or townsite. The size of this entity varied slightly during
various phases of the Colonial period, but in numerical terms each
town was entitled to a grant of five hundred squared *varas* (a *vara*
equaled approximately one meter) of land, which was divided into
houseplots. Technically, only Indian commoners could hold culti-

Colonial map of Macuilxóchitl, part of the 1580 *relación* of Macuilxóchitl, showing locations of its *sujetos* (by chapels), roads, footpaths, fields, grazing areas,
and important native nobles. Text in Nahuatl. (From Francisco del Paso y
Troncoso (ed.), *Papeles de Nueva España*, Vol. 4, p. 109; original in Real
Academia de la Historia, Madrid.)

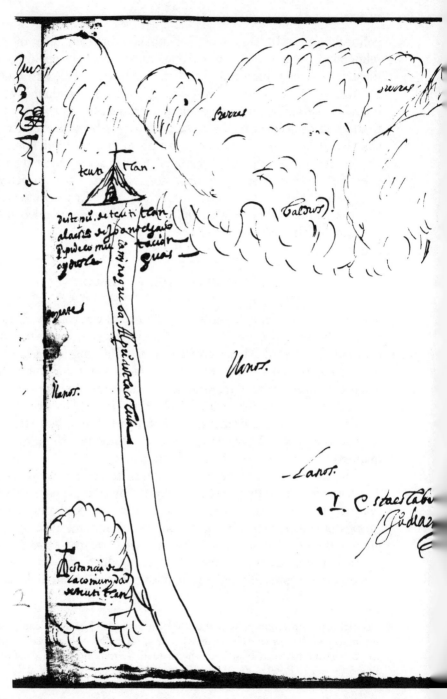

Colonial map of Teotitlán del Valle. Depicted are locations of Teotitlán del Valle (upper left) and an *estancia* (lower left); also included are vacant or public lands (*baldíos*) to the right of Teotitlán del Valle, level field areas (*llanos*) at the middle left and center, less productive field areas (*llanos con*

montes espessos) at the middle right, and surrounding mountains (*sierras*), at the top and right. Text in Spanish. (In Archivo General de la Nación, México, *Tierras*, Vol. 35, Exp. 7.)

vated fields within this area, and there were to be no ranches within one thousand *varas* of an Indian community.[49]

Second, there were four other types of communal lands: (a) communal lands for the support of religious festivals and similar community-wide expenses; (b) communal pasturelands and woods; (c) communal *barrio* lands, owned separately by the residents of a section of a community (which sometimes corresponded to a group of related individuals or a former community), divided into plots and worked by nuclear families; and (d) communal tracts given to otherwise landless individuals who entered into a *terrasguero* relationship with the community, often performing services for the town in exchange for the use of these plots.

Theoretically, all communal lands were inalienable—that is, they could not be sold except under very special conditions—and individuals within communities held only usufruct rights over them. But in the Valley of Oaxaca much land was sold, encroached upon, or usurped by other Indian communities, native nobles, or Spaniards. While some towns retained large areas of land, many others were reduced to their *fundo legal*.

There also were privately owned lands within Indian communities. At first, these were restricted to the Indian nobles, but eventually the notion of private, alienable holdings also was adopted by *macehuales*. *Macehuales* sometimes acquired lands by purchase from nobles or from communities needing funds to pay tribute or debts or by usurping communal lands in cases when the community could not demonstrate clear legal title to a plot of land, for boundaries often were vague and unclear. The *audiencia* usually automatically approved the sale of land valued at less than thirty pesos. The extent of private *macehual* holdings in the Colonial period cannot be ascertained, but, although it probably increased as the Colonial period neared its end, it undoubtedly represented the exception instead of the rule.

Indian communities soon learned to employ legal procedures to meet their land needs in the Valley, and Spanish colonial records attest to frequent litigations. Disputes between pueblos over lands were common,[50] and there was a tendency for larger communities to expand at the expense of smaller ones, a procedure almost always supported by the Spanish authorities. Frequently, threatened communities argued that lands were theirs in *primitivo patrimonio* (held in pre-Spanish times), a strong argument to the colonial authorities. Nevertheless, many communities lost those lands. However, since land varied greatly in quality throughout the Valley, the size of a community's holdings was not necessarily an index of its productive capacity.

For example, the Etla arm contained the most productive land.[51] But it also was in the Etla arm that the most serious erosion of Indian community lands occurred; few towns there held more than their *fundo legal* by the end of the colonial period, and some even held less. Such a phenomenon is partly explicable by the strength of the native *cacicazcos* in the Etla arm as well as by the expansion there of other private estates.

While the fertility of the land, coupled with irrigation, somewhat compensated for this situation, frequent squabbles over water rights reduced many communities to poverty. As a response to this situation, some Etla towns specialized in a commercial crop. For example, San Sebastián Xochimilco supplied onions for the Antequera market, San Andrés Ixtlahuaca specialized in tomatoes, and several communities supplemented their income by using nearby woodlands for charcoal, firewood, and other wood products.

Nevertheless, the communities of the Etla wing of the Valley had such reduced landholdings that they could not absorb—except in the community of Huitzo—any population growth. In the eighteenth century the Etla region was described as a land "of pestilence, hunger, shortage of water, continuous land usurpation, and other afflictions."[52]

The southern arm of the Valley displayed variation throughout the Colonial period.[53] Some communities, such as Cuilapan, Zimatlán, and Ocotlán, were relatively prosperous. In other communities, inadequate landholding generated problems in maintaining a food supply. There also were found large Spanish haciendas as well as large, expanding Indian communities, a situation which generated boundary disputes and reduced the landholdings of many communities. A sharply fluctuating population added to peasant misery in many communities in this region.

Cuilapan, the former Mixtec capital favored by Cortés, retained large landholdings throughout the Colonial period, encroached on nearby towns, and grew a great variety of marketable crops; in fact, Cuilapan often had an excess of land. Zaachila, however, continued to suffer a land shortage throughout the Colonial period, and the former Zapotec capital never really escaped the continuing expansion of the Mixtecs. Its lands were encroached upon by Cuilapan and later in the Colonial period by Spanish haciendas; many Zaachila men were forced to serve on haciendas to meet tribute demands. Much later, Zaachila was among the very few Valley towns that contained active *agraristas* during the Mexican Revolution of 1910—a phenomenon that supports the general reason often given for that conflict, chronic land shortage. Today it appears to be one of the most xenophobic towns in the Valley, understandable in view of its history.

Zimatlán had ample lands, and Ocotlán prospered through ranching, which supplied most of the meat for the important regional market there, but, as in Etla, other communities in this area turned to specialization to help alleviate land shortages. Atzompa specialized in a green-glazed pottery; Coyotepec first turned to maguey and later to black pottery. This strategy of specialization was attempted by a number of towns in the Valley—a strategy symptomatic of their inability to sustain themselves and meet tribute demands with their local land base.

Many towns in the valley of Zimatlán also produced cochineal, a product that required little productive land. The Bishopric of Oaxaca was the major producer of cochineal, which underwent a great boom in the eighteenth century and became a major source of dye in Europe. It stood third in export products from New Spain until aniline dyes brought about its demise in the latter part of the nineteenth century.[54]

Cochineal was not produced in the northwestern and southeastern arms of the Valley, although, in addition to Zimatlán, it also was produced in Tehuantepec, the Sierra de Juárez region at Ixtepeji, in the Mixteca Alta, and in the Southern Zapotec region around Miahuatlán, where it was reported to have been of superior quality. In many cases, communities became prosperous for short periods because of cochineal, and special Indian officials were appointed to handle it, although it always was under strict Spanish regulation and control.[55]

The valley of Tlacolula, generally lacking the development of large *cacicazcos* and Spanish haciendas, retained pueblos with large landholdings throughout the Colonial period; however, these larger holdings did not also imply a greater productive capacity. Sheep and maguey cultivation were also more important in the valley of Tlacolula than elsewhere, often leading to extensive, not intensive, use of the land.[56]

Community specialization and trading were more typical of the Tlacolula arm than of any other area in the Valley, as were highly developed local markets. Typical was a specialization in serapes, found only in the Tlacolula arm of the Valley, and the distillation of *pulque* or *mezcal*. Even today towns such as Teotitlán del Valle continue to specialize in weaving serapes. In the Colonial period, weavers were found also in Santo Domingo del Valle (now Díaz Ordaz), Tlacolula, Mitla, and Macuilxóchitl.

Besides *pulque* and weaving, towns in the eastern arm specialized in *petates* (palm-leaf mats), firewood, charcoal, wooden spoons, and other items. Such community specialization did not, however, mean the demise of subsistence agriculture—communities continued to protect their land base and to use specialization as supplementary income. As in most peasant societies, craft specialization was not a substitute for agriculture.

Disputes over land always were common in the Tlacolula wing of the Valley; violence, strong community xenophobia, and constant litigation between pueblos were characteristic of the area. While it remained heavily Zapotec, strong dialectical differences between communities probably developed during this period as Spanish became the *lingua franca* for intercommunity negotiations. The strong protective stance that most communities took toward their land base also encouraged community endogamy here as it did elsewhere in the Valley of Oaxaca.

One of the most prosperous towns in the Tlacolula arm was Tlalixtac, which constantly encroached on its smaller neighbors. Not only did it have an important maguey industry—it was the major producer in the area—but it also irrigated lands and had at least two sheep ranches. It was described as well kept and prosperous as late as the 1820's, when economic problems had reduced most Valley towns to utter poverty.

The expansion of some larger Indian towns at the expense of their neighbors represented a common phenomenon in the Valley and shows that Indian communities frequently lost lands to their nearby Indian neighbors, and not exclusively to predatory *caciques* and Spanish *hacendados*, the picture most often presented in works dealing with the Spanish Colonial period .

Of the many communities in the Tlacolula arm, only Mitla had serious disputes with Spanish haciendas, which bordered it on the east, north, northwest, and southwest. Mitla also lost communal lands when its *sujetos* were allowed to become independent entities. While Mitla probably retained enough land for subsistence purposes, it primarily became a town of itinerant merchants, a specialty it still enjoys along with its importance as a place of Zapotec religious pilgrimage.[57]

On the average, the Valley of Oaxaca was not characterized by a paucity of Indian land. It is estimated that during the seventeenth and eighteenth centuries the average Indian plot ranged from 2.26 to 3.43 hectares, or about twice the size of the present-day Indian plot. In addition, the average Indian family usually had at least two plots which, as in most peasant societies, were seldom contiguous, bringing the total family landholding to between 4.44 and 8.87 hectares.[58] The ideal, probably seldom met, was for all Indian families to have land of equal productive value and fertility—a value consistent with the egalitarian ethics of most peasant societies.

INDIAN TRIBUTE AND LABOR

The Indians of New Spain were peasants in the Spanish estate system, a fact well illustrated by examining the system of tribute and labor. Indian communities were given lands not only for subsistence but also to provide revenues for noblemen, the Spanish crown, and its subsidiary bureaucracy and to serve as a captive source of labor for various enterprises. Finally, Indian peasants were to underwrite the maintenance of their own local *cabildo* offices through a system of tribute assessment.

The earliest institution that recognized this fact was the *encomienda*—a grant of Indian towns to a Spaniard, giving him the right to exact tribute and recruit labor from them. But the *encomienda* was subject to much abuse, and the crown attempted early to abolish it, or to curtail its growth, not only in response to pressures from the Church, but also because so much autonomy was thereby given to Spanish noblemen that it threatened to undermine crown control.

The Spanish colony of New Spain was envisioned above all as a controlled society, economically, politically, spiritually, and culturally administered by the crown and its bureaucratic arm.

The *encomienda* was relatively insignificant in the Valley of Oaxaca, although it was somewhat important in the Zapotec sierra and south.[59] Oaxaca's first *encomendero* was Hernán Cortés—the Marqués del Valle—who had, as his title suggests, almost unlimited powers, a situation he created for himself after the conquest. As marqués, Cortés could grant *encomiendas* and lands within his jurisdiction, although he handed both out sparingly. But the history of the marquessate reflects the overall fate of such enclaves within crown territory: Cortés' power and jurisdiction were continually reduced. By the 1530's the marqués' jurisdiction in the Valley had been reduced to the Cuatro Villas (Cuilapan, Villa de Oaxaca, Etla, and Tlapacoya), even though he also retained possessions in Tehuantepec, Morelos, and Toluca. His heirs, however, were to lose much of this vast estate as the crown continually curtailed their prerogatives.[60]

While the Spanish authorities, with crown aid, moved rapidly to revoke or control *encomiendas*, they did not abandon the idea that the Indian community should be a source of revenue. *Corregimiento*, in a sense a crown *encomienda*, was in force throughout the Colonial period, and Indians were assessed royal tribute. Various bureaucratic salaries, including those of the *corregidores*, also came from these peasant revenues.

The tribute system in the Valley of Oaxaca underwent several stages of evolution. In the sixteenth and seventeenth centuries tribute was collected in various forms and was converted into a crown standard. Later, royal tribute was collected in specie or currency, a factor that continued throughout the Colonial period.

Tribute was levied according to a census of the adult male population; exemptions were made for the old and sickly, the extremely poor, and the nobility. After 1560, exemptions for the *principal* group were no longer in effect, although *caciques* continued to be exempt and legislation to remove their exemption was retracted.

A community tribute, in addition to the royal or *encomienda* tribute, was assessed to underwrite the salaries of community officials and to defray certain costs (such as the sustenances of priests and the costs of religious observances), and special lands were set aside for this purpose; this community tribute generally was in addition to Church tithes. In the Valley of Oaxaca, beginning in the 1550's, lands supplying community tribute were divisible into fields of about 0.028 hectares, each plot to be worked by a tributary male.[61] A married male represented one tributary, while a widow, widower, or unmarried male corresponded to one-half tributary in the assessment system.

Documents pertaining to Zapotec Valley towns provide an illustration of how the tribute system operated in crown communities.[62] In the southern arm of the Valley, Zimatlán and its associated towns (Tepezimatlán and La Magdalena), which were put in *corregimiento* in 1532, paid tribute valued at 266 pesos of gold each year in addition to crops from a designated field and one chicken every day, given to sustain their *corregidor*. In 1536, Zimatlán (not including its associated towns) paid tribute valued at 206 pesos of gold and also contributed crops valued at 48 pesos, bringing the total tribute to 254 pesos. Of this, 41 pesos went to the crown, while 178 pesos went to pay the salary of the *corregidor*. The Marqués del Valle, who had residual rights to tribute at this time over most of the Valley towns, received 35 pesos. According to the *Suma de visitas*, which probably dates from this period, Zimatlán paid its *cacique* 454 pesos and seven *tomines* of gold, and, of this, the *cacique* gave 57 pesos to the crown. This tribute was given every hundred days in equal proportions. The inhabitants of Zimatlán also contributed four hundred *fanegas* (a *fanega* equaled approximately ninety liters) of maize and gave one chicken every day.

The tribute lists for other towns in this period reveal a similar profile, although tribute varied depending on the size of the population. In 1531, when Mitla and Tlacolula in the eastern part of the Valley were put in *corregimiento*, these towns paid four tributes each year, valued at between 192 and 208 pesos, in addition to an unspecified amount from a small field. In 1536 they were assessed a total of 159 pesos, divided as 130 pesos of gold (paid in *tejuelos*, ingots) and 29 pesos for crops. Of these, the crown received 26 pesos while the *corregidor* got 133. According to the *Suma*, Mitla gave 7 pesos and six *tomines* of gold each eighty days and an additional 130 *fanegas* of maize each year. The author of the *Suma* adds that these people grew little maize because of their poor land but lived mostly by selling chickens and soap.

The author of the *Suma* also claimed that some of the Valley towns, such as Zimatlán, Tlalixtac, and Zaachila, paid too little tribute—the Indians there are described as rich and able to pay more. Such a phenomenon illustrates quite well the status of peasants in Spanish colonial society and helps account for observations that peasants had little desire to increase their productive capacities: the larger their production, the more the required tribute.

The *Suma* document for Zaachila also illustrates the variety of products paid as tribute during this early period. Zaachila paid to its *cacique* 325 pesos and four *tomines* of gold; the *cacique*, in turn, gave to the crown 28 pesos of gold dust each year. For six months of the year, Zaachila gave the *corregidor* one chicken, two hundred tortillas, five *cargas* (one *carga* equaled approximately two *fanegas*) of firewood, one hundred cacaos (cocoa beans), one-half *fanega* of maize, and the services of five Indians. The *corregidor* each year also reserved twenty-five *fanegas* of maize, three *fanegas* of beans, and ten *fardos* (bundles) of chilies. In 1531, when Zaachila and Iztepeque were combined into a *corregimiento*, they gave, each eighty days, four *tejuelos* of gold, and they had two fields producing one thousand *cargas* of maize. They also gave the *corregidor* a "moderate" amount of food. In 1536 these two towns paid a total valued at 275 pesos of gold, including 235 pesos in gold dust and 11 pesos in crops. Of these, 48 pesos went to the crown, 128 pesos and four *tomines* to the *corregidor*, and 33 pesos to the marqués.

Later documents for these same towns indicate that the crown moved to standardize procedures and also give some indication of the relationship between local Indian officials and the tribute they received.[63] In 1572 Zaachila gave 1,699 pesos and four *tomines*, paid in three installments, as well as 717 *fanegas* and three *almudes* (one *almud* equaled approximately one-twelfth of a *fanega*) of maize. The Zaachila document also states that after the 1,434 pesos and the maize were paid to the crown, the remaining pesos were deposited in the community strongbox or *caja*. This *caja* had three keys to it; one was in the possession of the *gobernador*, another was held by an *alcalde*, and a third by a *mayordomo*. This fund was to be used for whatever was deemed necessary by these officials to maintain the community (including, presumably, their own salaries), although they had to keep a strict accounting of their expenditures.

Also, according to the Zaachila document, each tributary in the community was assessed nine and one-half *reales* of silver and one-half *fanega* of maize; widows and widowers paid one-half of this assessment. The aged, very poor, and infirm were not assessed, nor could further tribute or services be demanded of them. The officials of the community should make sure, the document insists, that the Christian religion was maintained and that the priests had their needs satisfied.

Similar documents pertain to other Valley Zapotec communities, and the general tribute system is described similarly in all of them, although each total tribute, of course, varied depending on the number of tributaries in the community. For example, in 1574 Zimatlán gave 1,676 pesos, five *tomines* and six *granos* (there were approximately twelve *granos* per *tomín*) of gold (*oro común*), along with 297 *fanegas* and nine *almudes* of maize. Of this, the crown received 73 pesos and one *tomín* for the community. As in Zaachila, Mitla, Tlacolula, Tepezimatlán, and most other Valley communities, each tributary was assessed nine and one-half *reales* of silver and one-half *fanega* of maize. In Tlalixtac, however, they were assessed only eight *reales* of silver per full tributary, and in Ixtepec each full tributary paid only six *tomines*.

The crown and its legislative arm worked hard to standardize tribute schedules but found it almost impossible. One continuing problem was the fluctuation of the population. In response, tribute assessments periodically were revised, but the slowness of bureaucratic procedures and communications usually meant that the assessments were dated, usually excessive, and therefore could not be met by many Indian communities. There also were many opportunities for abuse. Since the salaries of *corregidores*, officials of the communities, and the funds for other privileged individuals came from the tribute quotas, excessive demands could not be controlled easily, nor could corruption be curtailed. Such abuses seem especially to have been characteristic of communities held in *encomienda*.

Excessive demands sometimes led to Indian violence; a serious rebellion took place in Oaxaca in the seventeenth century among the Zapotecs of the isthmus and the sierra. It started in Tehuantepec, where the Spanish *alcalde mayor* was stoned to death and an Indian mob sacked Spanish establishments, seizing muskets and other weapons. After establishing an Indian government in Tehuantepec, the revolt spread through Nejapa and finally to Ixtepeji and Villa Alta in the sierra. The Indian army ultimately grew to ten thousand men.

The Indian leaders of the revolt held out for a year, communicating with the viceroy and explaining that they were not in rebellion against the crown but against excessive tribute. However, in 1661 an envoy from the viceroy subdued the rebellion with an army. The Indian governor of Tehuantepec was dismembered and hung in quarters at the four entrances of the town of Tehuantepec. Others also were quartered and mutilated. A peace finally was proclaimed with a solemn mass.[64]

While such widespread peasant rebellions were not characteristic of Colonial Oaxaca (and especially the Valley region),[65] the economy of Spain in the seventeenth century and throughout the later Colonial period led to increased demands for tribute to be paid in specie instead of in kind. The increasing demand for currency generated a number of changes in Indian communities. In the sixteenth century and early part of the seventeenth century, communal lands for the purposes of filling tribute coffers were kept intact. But beginning in the seventeenth century, some communal lands were sold, rented, or diverted to cash crops to meet the new tribute quotas.[66] Increasingly, peasants turned to outside sources of revenue. Some peasants became heavily involved in commerce. Others acquired cash through wage labor or became involved in the prosperous cochineal industry. As a result, there was some "opening" of the peasant community during this period, and cash became more and more a crucial part of the peasant economy.

However, this situation did not continue for long. Yellow fever epidemics in 1739, 1766, and 1780, along with serious famines in 1779–80 and 1785–87, intensified the economic problems of the eighteenth century. The cochineal industry started its decline in the early eighteenth century and, although it recovered for short periods, went into permanent decay after 1783. Communities that had become overspecialized or almost totally dependent on this crop, such as Ixtepeji and Miahuatlán, had neglected their basic subsistence needs and were in such a dire situation that they applied for and were granted exemptions from royal tribute.[67]

Most other peasant communities, however, did not become over-specialized to this extent, nor did they so radically divert their tra-ditional land use patterns. Therefore, when the larger economy col-lapsed, they still could meet their subsistence needs. This ability to survive illustrates the dual adaptive nature of peasant communities: they can "open" or "close" depending on the economic environment of the larger society in which they find themselves embedded. The viability of the peasant eocnomy, however, depends on the retention of a subsistence land base. To the extent that it mitigates against such retention, "opening" cannot go too far. The Valley Zapotec communi-ties, on the whole, remained "closed" in that those lands which pro-vided their subsistence mainstay were not diverted. But those com-munities that did overspecialize were unable to "close" when eco-nomic conditions changed.

Tribute involved more than payment in kind or specie in New Spain and Oaxaca—it also involved labor. The early *encomendero* was entrusted not only with things but also with backs to produce things. The Spanish administration wrestled continuously with the problem of providing goods and labor for the Spanish colonists, their vanguard, and protection from abuse for the Indians, their wards. In the middle of the sixteenth century (1549) a compromise was reached for the labor issue; the administration of tribute was separated from the administration of the labor system, and the *repartimiento* was created to handle the latter. Under this system, Indians were subject to labor drafts to work for the Church, for the Spanish estates, and for mines and other enterprises.[68]

The history of the labor system in the Valley of Oaxaca, as in all of New Spain, is a grim one. Frequent protests, abuses, coercion, incon-sistency in policies, and misery for both Indians and dependent Creoles mark its pages. The Indians felt this system to be the most abusive of all, and in various ways they attempted to escape its wrath; the Spanish colonist felt that the *peninsulares* (Spanish bureaucrats born in Spain) had abandoned them with their policies. Labor issues brought pervasive conflict between Spaniard and Spaniard, Spaniard and Indian, and Indian and Indian.

When royal and *marquesado* tributes were paid partly in kind in the sixteenth century, the relatively small Spanish community in the Valley of Oaxaca was supplied with cereals. Spanish estates at that time were few, and they specialized mostly in livestock production, which required only a few Indian laborers supplemented by Negro slaves. A decline in population and the new cash tribute demands in the seventeenth century altered this situation. The Spanish estate now played a much more important role in supplying the Spanish community; consequently, more laborers were required.

The *repartimiento* had supplied most of the needs for labor in the sixteenth century both in the mines (which generally were closed by the seventeenth century) and on the Spanish estates. Generally, under this system, normal service for Valley Indians was for one week (with Sundays off) each year; 4 per cent of all tributary males were expected to be used at a single time. Each enterprise was assigned a fixed number of Indian workers who were to be paid a wage, a stipend that frequently was avoided in practice.[69]

But Indian labor did not meet demand as Spanish agricultural enterprises expanded. Further, the crown moved to limit labor demands on the Indian population. For example, in 1609 *repartimientos* for agricultural purposes were banned, even though reasons of "public utility" forced the *audiencia* to grant some immunities. Because of these and other factors, the *repartimiento* system went into decline throughout the Colonial period. While abuses were common, and Indians often were forced to serve illegally, the labor needs of the Spanish estates in the Valley never were adequately met.

One response to the decline of Indian tribute in kind, and the inadequacy of Indian labor through the *repartimiento* system, was the hacienda. This institution, "half capitalist, half feudal," as described by Eric Wolf,[70] represented both the entrepreneurial orientation of Spaniards and older feudal notions, but more than anything else it was a response to the economic dilemma inherent in the structural separation of the Indian population from the Spanish colonists.

Haciendas often are thought of simply as large landed estates. But although they generally were large, they most of all represented a type of social and economic organization, not simply an area of land. The hacienda combined both intensive and extensive patterns of agriculture and stock grazing. Further, it fostered close social relationships between masters and peons, providing most of the material and spiritual needs of the workers. Workers bound to *hacendados* were given advances of money, a subsistence plot, masses, and medical services as well as protection; basically, they received goods and services in exchange for loyalty, devotion, and hard work.[71] In the sense that it was an economic enterprise designed to feed cities and towns, the hacienda was entrepreneurial in orientation: in the sense that it represented an enclave or domain of a patron and his clients, it was feudal.

Only a few Spanish estates in the Valley of Oaxaca corresponded to the classic haciendas of northern or western Mexico, although haciendas were found in all three arms of the Valley during the Colonial period. Of the more than sixty haciendas of which there are records, the heaviest concentration was in the Zimatlán or southern arm of the Valley. Haciendas in the eastern part of the Valley were larger in size but fewer in number. Those in the Etla arm generally were smaller than elsewhere in the Valley, although they normally had proportionally more land under cultivation, as opposed to grazing land, than was found in other Valley regions.[72]

It also seems that these haciendas, in general, did not approach the size of those elsewhere in Mexico, many of which held land well in excess of 8,800 hectares.[73] In the Tlacolula arm, for example, haciendas held between 8,000 and 12,000 hectares; in the southern arm, between 3,200 and 1,160 hectares; and in the Etla arm, between 3,200 and 1,000 hectares.[74]

Only a few haciendas in the Valley of Oaxaca achieved political and economic autonomy, had large, luxurious *cascos* (buildings), and contained numerous resident peons—characteristics associated with the classic hacienda. The six Valley estates that were entailed (*mayorazgos*) seem to have most closely achieved these characteristics. A few others also achieved religious and political autonomy; for example, San José, in the Zimatlán arm, and Santo Domingo Buenavista, in the eastern arm, received licenses in the seventeenth century permitting masses to be held in their chapels. Such a license severed the last ties between Indians residing on the hacienda and their town of origin, as they then were no longer subject to the political and religious jurisdiction of their former *cabecera* and *doctrina*. After a period of expansion in the seventeenth century, however, the haciendas in the Valley suffered the effects of the economic decline of the early eighteenth century, and hacienda lands frequently were sold, rented, or mortgaged.[75]

One reason for the relative insignificance of the hacienda in the Valley of Oaxaca was that debt peonage, the institution that kept the hacienda viable, met with but limited success in the region.

To an extent, given the shortage of the labor supply, since most Indians had adequate lands and could not be pressed into service because they lacked the means to meet their royal tribute schedules, they were in a favorable negotiating position in the Valley. A shortage of adequate labor meant that Indians interested in working on haciendas could demand significant advances from the *hacendado*. The crown moved to limit such advances, however, imposing a five peso limit on *hacendados* which limited their ability to attract peons, an imposition that engendered bitter complaints from many *hacendados*.[76] The small size of the Negro and mestizo population did not make up for the shortage of Indian peons. For example, in 1777, when debt peonage was dominant elsewhere in Mexico, of the fifty-six Valley estates, twelve had no resident peons, thirty-three had from one to three, and only four had more than fifty. Of the 1,499 non-Spanish residents on Valley haciendas in the same year, 966 were Indians, 411 were mulattos, and 122 were mestizos.[77]

Debt peonage thus seems to have been relatively insignificant in the Valley, and by the middle of the eighteenth century, even though the Indian population had recovered from the drastic decline of the sixteenth century, haciendas still could not obtain adequate labor. Deterioration of the economy, plus unattractive working conditions on haciendas, meant that many Indians refused to work on haciendas at all, even as paid day-laborers. In exceptional cases, such as in Zaachila in the 1790's, Indians were forced to serve on haciendas by Spanish authorities because they could not meet their royal tribute payments.[78]

By the end of the Colonial period haciendas were not a pervasive force in southern Oaxaca; they never had been present in the sierra, for mining enterprises and other commercial ventures had been much more lucrative there, and in the Valley they failed to take hold and significantly expand. By the end of the eighteenth century many *hacendados* were forced to rent their lands to get some returns on their investment, and Spanish estates (the majority of which could not be classified as haciendas) held no more than one-third of the land in the Valley.[79]

INDIANS AND THE CHURCH

The Spanish Conquest was, above all else, a conquest of souls: the Spanish Church, in the guise of its friars, moved rapidly to eradicate the old religions. Native priests were deposed and native temples and idols destroyed. Catholicism was to become more than an appendage of Indian life; it also was to dominate its major focus of social life—the pueblo.

The Dominicans were entrusted with the conversion of souls in Oaxaca, although others, such as the Franciscan, Jesuit, Augustinian, Carmelite, and Mercedarian orders, founded houses in Oaxaca in the late sixteenth century. However, the influence of these latter orders was small: while the Franciscans and Augustinians established themselves in the core area of New Spain (the Valley of Mexico and its environs), the Dominicans concentrated most of their efforts in Oaxaca.

From the beginning Dominicans were few and Oaxaca was vast. Communication was a problem. They early friars worked both through intermediaries—native *caciques*—and through a *lingua franca*—Nahuatl. At a later date many learned the indigenous languages, but there were never enough friars who spoke them.

In the early period there were but four *doctrinas* (seats of ecclesiastical establishments) and many *visitas* (towns without resident friars or priests). *Doctrinas* were established at Etla, Cuilapan, and the Villa de Oaxaca by 1550. Huitzo and Ocotlán were added a few years later. By the end of the sixteenth century, many more were added: Zaachila, Santa Ana Zegache, Santa Cruz Mixtepec (Ixtepec), Santa Catarina Minas, Santa Marta Chichicapa, San Miguel Tlalixtac, San Gerónimo Tlacochahuaya, San Juan Teitipac, Teotitlán del Valle, and Tlacolula. These were administered by approximately seventy Dominicans.[80]

With that many souls, and only a few friars, they concentrated on the ritual nature of Catholicism—participation was the key—even though they tried to present more subtle understandings. The Indians were taught in large groups; many villages could be visited only rarely and others not at all. At least, however, every community was to have a church—and building by labor drafts soon accomplished this task for even small communities.

As with most peoples, the Zapotecs interpreted the new religion in

Two Spanish Colonial churches of Santiago Cuilapan; the earlier church (at left) remained unfinished.

terms of the old. There were many similarities between the two, and many of the differences were subtle. For example, while human sacrifice was strictly prohibited by Catholicism, sacrifice was a basic tenet. Both religions stressed man's subservience to the supernatural, and both had had important figures sacrifice themselves to this end. To this extent, the notion of Christ's sacrifice on the cross for man was comprehensible to the Zapotecs, as was the ritual communication with him through blood (wine) and flesh (bread).

In a general sense, anthropologists call what happened syncretism —a fusion of the two religions. Saints, strongly emphasized by the friars, could be interpreted in terms similar to those used to relate to the old deities. Saints were represented by figures which had human attributes and human needs; they must be clothed and given offerings; they bled, wept, and held miraculous powers of healing, or cur-

Lápida set in the rear wall of the early Spanish Colonial church of Santiago Cuilapan; the glyphic style is Mixteca-Puebla.

ing. As they were closer to man, they were intercessors for him with higher supernaturals. To a very real extent they were directly analogous with the old gods—saints were deities or deified men who were leaders of the faith.

Communities very early adopted Catholic patron saints who were substituted for the old ones. Etla became San Pedro y San Pablo Etla; towns in its jurisdiction adopted such names as San Agustín Etla, Santa Cruz Etla, and the like. Cuilapan became Santa María Cuilapan. Teitipac became San Juan, and Chichicapa became Santa Marta. Towns or villages within jurisdictions of *doctrinas* also adopted Spanish saints.

In many cases, these Christian saints were given attributes of the old gods: San Pedro assumed attributes of the old rain god Cocijo, a leading figure in the Zapotec sacred calendar as San Pedro was in the Catholic one. In Jalapa, Saint Catherine of Siena and Pinopiaa, a Zapotec heroine who was deified, were equated and worshiped at a common shrine.[81] The Virgin Mary became but another saint in the pantheon, an important intercessor, as a female counterpart to the major supernatural figures. Christ had various refractions, symbolized by a variety of images, and pilgrimages were made to special locations where these were housed.[82]

In addition to the many basic similarities in the religions—both used incense in their churches, both fasted and did penance, both went on pilgrimages, both believed in a supernatural mother, both were hierarchical in their conceptions of religion—were similarities that permeated the simplest levels. Both had a naming ceremony couched in mystery and guarding against evil; as the old priests divined, the new ones baptised. Both religions gave a special place and special exemptions to children who died; in the old days Zapotec children went to a special heaven, a kind of dwelling place for the innocent, as they now ascended directly to heaven as *angelitos*. Marriage (although now there would be no polygyny) and death in both religions were special times for religious celebrations. Burgoa, for example, discusses misunderstandings concerning death practices arising from similarities in the two religions and what for him became an unwanted equation of the offering of bread and wine in the mass with the offering of food to accompany the dead on their journey through the underworld in the old religion.[83]

While there were these similarities that eased the transition to Catholicism, the friars were not always happy with the outcome. For although they could turn their backs on simple errors and the worship of new saints in old disguises for the sake of participation, they could not tolerate idolatry or the worship of the old gods in old forms. Above all, they felt they had to eradicate the old priesthood, the guardians of the old gods. The Inquisition, especially as directed against Indian nobles, was an instrument to accomplish this task.

It has been argued that the Inquisition was not directed toward the Indians, but abundant documentation has refuted this contention. For example, it already has been mentioned that in Sola, native beliefs and practices continued into the seventeenth century, and native priests, called *letrares* (then not a formally constituted priesthood), were tried and sentenced for idolatry.

Another example comes from the Valley of Oaxaca and concerns the priesthood at Mitla and the last prince of Tehuantepec, Cosijopii. Although Cosijopii embraced the faith immediately and was baptised as Don Juan Cortés, this conversion did not end his important links with his pre-Spanish past.

When the Spanish discovered a strong Zapotec priesthood at Mitla, they moved rapidly to close the temples there. The Zapotec priests then appealed to Cosijopii, offering him the position of high priest of the old religion, thinking he would not be suspected by the Spaniards. But the plot to go underground was discovered, and the Inquisition was ordered to try Cosijopii. Cosijopii died of a cerebral hemorrhage before his fate could be sealed; the native priests who had appealed to him were executed in a solemn ceremony by the Inquisition.[84]

Nevertheless, on many levels old customs survived and have continued to the present, although by now aboriginal and Spanish notions have become so fused that it is almost impossible to separate them into their constituent components. Like the Spanish peasant, the Zapotec peasant practiced a folk religion far removed from the world of official, complicated theology. Belief in witches, in evil spirits, and appeals to special patrons for intercession became the most important religious elements in Zapotec life. As in the pre-Spanish past, the complex theogeny of official Catholicism was transformed into a mundane setting by the Zapotec peasant. Peasants have to live in a mundane world, and gods who have mundane powers have the most appeal to them.

In a strict sense, the effect of the Church on the Zapotecs was more than simply religious, for the Church was also a social and economic institution and had an important effect on the social organization of the Indian community. For example, the Dominicans, unlike the Franciscans, did not take vows of poverty and early became involved in economic enterprises. Receiving donations of land from Indian nobles and Indian communities, the Church became the largest non-Indian landholder in the Valley, and the Dominicans were the largest landholders among the Church groups. It is estimated that the Church held approximately one-fourth of the land in the Valley at

Facade of La Asunción Cathedral in Oaxaca City; this cathedral was the seat of
the Colonial bishopric of Oaxaca.

the end of the Colonial period, although Church groups did not, in general, turn to agriculture but concentrated instead on livestock and other enterprises.[85]

Nor was the Church a homogenous group oriented to a single set of principles. The Dominicans, for example, came into conflict with the secular clergy who generally followed the friars, constituting a sort of rear guard in the Christianization process; while the friars were to convert, the secular priests were to maintain. By 1760 the Dominicans had lost some of their most important, and most wealthy, parishes to the secular priests: Etla, Zimatlán, Tlalixtac, Zaachila, and Cuilapan.[86]

Further, the secular priests, unlike the Dominicans, derived many of their revenues from a system of tithes. Although the revenues from this source were smaller for Oaxaca than for bishoprics in highly populous areas of New Spain, Indians were nevertheless subjected to tithes on community treasuries (*cajas de communidad*) and on Old World crops, particularly wheat and livestock. The friars opposed the tithes, or *diezmos* as they were called, arguing that the Indians were too poor to pay them; the seculars argued that on the contrary, it was the Spaniards in Oaxaca that were poor, not the Indians.[87]

While the Indians also were subject to a Church labor draft for work on Church lands and for building and repair projects, the institution that most affected the local community was the *cofradía.*

Indian *cofradías* (brotherhoods) in the Valley of Oaxaca were responsible for staging various religious festivities and providing supplies for them. They were responsible for vespers, processions, masses, and sermons for Corpus Christi, Holy Week, Christmas, and the *fiestas* of the local patron saints, providing not only the organization but also salaries for the priests. Further, they supplied candles and wine for masses, oil for sacramental lamps, adornments for altars and saints' images, and other items involved in maintaining the cults as well as maintenance of the church itself.

Lands set aside for the maintenance of community *cofradías* were collectively owned and operated. They were supervised by *mayordomos,* a general term for supervisors of collective land in the Colonial period. In the Valley of Oaxaca, most communities used ranching, which required less of a community labor pool than did agricultural lands, or some other enterprises such as wheat mills to meet *cofradía* expenses. Of eleven eighteenth-century Indian *cofradías* in the Valley, only one worked arable land.

In some cases *cofradías* served as a cover for lands owned by the local priest, a practice strictly forbidden by law. *Cofradía* lands in Etla, Zimatlán, Santa María Tenexpan, Atzompa, and Zaachila were reported as being controlled and administered by clerics instead of the local hierarchy. This practice led to some conflicts. For example, complaints were made that the priest in Zaachila received an annual tribute of one hundred pesos from the community as well as his usual fees for marriage, burial ceremonies, and religious festivities, and that he sometimes charged twelve pesos instead of the normal seven for directing the religious holidays.[88]

Officeholding by indigenous inhabitants within the *cofradía* organization became intertwined with the *cabildo* organization, leading to a system that has been called the civil-religious hierarchy. This system eventually became the core of the colonial Indian community. While its exact development in the Valley of Oaxaca cannot be traced, indirect evidence suggests that its development there followed a process similar to that found in other areas of New Spain. Individuals would be pressed into service by the community, performing first menial jobs for *cofradías* (sweeping the church and so on), and then, after a lapse of a few years, moving to a more important post, ultimately reaching a post such as *mayordomo*. Civil posts would either follow the religious ones or would alternate with them. All men would be expected to serve and would be subject to harassment (if not physical abuse or expulsion from the community) if they did not do so. In addition to guaranteeing that individuals performed important community functions, this system served two additional functions: it allocated prestige to individuals in the society, for those that served the highest posts had the most prestige, and it served to undermine development of huge wealth differences among Indians, for outlays of some funds and time were required in fulfilling their duties.

This institution again illustrates the adaptive nature of the peasant way of life and provides yet another index of the peasant's plight. As excess wealth was siphoned from peasant communities by outside elements, so would excess wealth be siphoned off by internal elements. Wealth tended to threaten the peasant's existence on both fronts. It could lead to increased external demands as it could alter the power balance within, pitting peasant against peasant. Shared poverty thus became an adaptive strategy and a cultural tradition passed on through a characteristic form of social organization—the civil-religious hierarchy or *cargo* (literally, "burden") system. The peasant could survive only by controlling the forces of his undoing, internal and external, and poverty was his weapon.

Thus, the civil-religious hierarchy tended to create a homogeneous community in wealth and to reinforce the distinctiveness of the Indian community as a corporate institution in New Spanish society. As Pedro Carrasco has written, the civil-religious hierarchy "is a direct function of the peasantization of the Mesoamerican Indian—a fact that formerly independent stratified societies become unstratified peasant communities within a wider social system."[89]

Religion, to the extent that it provided yet another focus for strong Indian community solidarity in the face of pressures from within and without, also provided an important psychological function for the Indian. Fiestas, held in conjunction with the cult of the saints, became a time when Indians could escape the tensions of everyday life, of poverty, of alienation, and of strong pressures to become submerged in a tightly knit social unit as well as a time to dream of utopias. Alcoholic beverages constituted an important ingredient to achieve these ends as they became incorporated, often in a ritual context, into these major events. The native Indian in New Spain turned readily to drink; friars, priests, and others frequently criticized and lamented this development. But it was widespread—a survey of the drinking establishments for Indians in the Valley of Oaxaca in 1726 located 513 of them for only forty-six towns.[90]

6

The Zapotecs in Modern Mexico

By THE END of the Spanish Colonial period, the Zapotecs had been reduced to a peasantry, or, more properly, to communities of peasants. Little that was distinctively Zapotec remained of their culture and society; instead, the rural Indian peasant culture of central and southern Oaxaca was a conglomeration of things pre-Spanish and of things Spanish. While Zapotec languages continued to be spoken, rural Zapotecs identified mostly with a community and very little with a Zapotec ethnic group. As today, it is probable that one first was a member of a town (a Mitleño, Tehuano, Teotitleño, Yalalteco, or the like) and second a member of a region (*vallista*, *istmeño*, *serrano*, and so on).[1] Although the Spanish designation *zapotecos* may have entered into their vocabulary, Zapotec ethnicity, on a larger level, was of little consequence, as there were (and are) few, if any, social forms that gave it unity.

Further, the designation "Indian" was much more important than the designation "Zapotec" in the society of New Spain; Spanish policy made few ethnic distinctions among Indians, so their cultural and ethnic differences were of little consequence. Membership in a peasant estate and affiliation with an Indian community, as primary criteria for the assignment of status and identification, became much more important for the local Indian peasant.

Events in the nineteenth century, after independence from Spain, and during the first half of the twentieth century did little to alter this situation. To be sure, there were personnel changes among elites, legal changes in the society regarding the various ethnic strata (Indians and mestizos no longer were barred from certain positions), and changes in the conception of the role of the state. But these events, frequently turbulent and fast-changing, affected the upper and intermediate orders of the society much more than they did the Indian peasant.

219

There are three major periods of importance in modern Mexican history: the movement for independence from Spain, the Reforms (La Reforma) of the middle of the nineteenth century begun by Benito Juárez, and the Mexican Revolution which began with the overthrow of Porfirio Díaz in 1910 and continues, at least in the ideology of the Mexican government, until the present day.

The movement for independence, initiated with the famous *grito* of the priest Miguel Hidalgo y Costilla in 1810, ultimately was the wrenching culmination of Spanish economic and political dilemmas;[2] it climaxed in the coronation of Agustín de Iturbide as the first emperor of Mexico in 1822. Iturbide's reign was short-lived (only two years), after which Mexico was thrown into a political turmoil that lasted, with few peaceful interludes, for one hundred years. The major effect of Mexican independence, then, was the creation of a power vacuum that cast Mexico into an era of political instability, aptly characterized by Charles Cumberland as the age of "Marking Time."[3]

The Mexican independence movement, although for the most part a mere political struggle, also was fired with the anger of social reformers. Hidalgo had led what essentially was a peasant revolt aimed not against the Spanish crown but against the abuses of a Spanish bureaucracy. A compatriot, José María Morelos, also a priest, led a peasant army through the south, sacking haciendas and Spanish towns and confiscating lands belonging to the Church. His successes culminated in the capture of the city of Antequera in 1812, a bitter victory, for he was defeated and executed there as well. Vicente Guerrero, who fought under the commands of both Morelos and Iturbide, was president of Mexico for a nine-month period (April–December, 1829). However, his fate was as violent as that of Morelos; he was deposed by force, fled south, finally was captured, and was shot at Cuilapan, which added his martyred name to its own to become Cuilapan de Guerrero.

The struggles headed by Hidalgo, Morelos, and Guerrero all struck against the power of the *criollos* and the Church (both large landowners) and sought reforms for the Indian population. Perhaps above all they were opposed to the peasant's universal enemy, a strong, centralized state, as they sought virtual autonomy for the local Indian peasant community. But these hopes proved futile; Mexico was claimed by the *criollos* and the Church.

During the era that followed independence and the Reform movement of the Juaristas from the 1850's to the 1870's, the country was in turmoil as liberals and conservatives fought over the proper constitution and function of government. Few policies actually were implemented during this period; struggles for control of the government and power were the order of the day.

During most of the period of La Reforma, Benito Juárez struggled simply to control the country. By 1867, however, this Zapotec from Guelatao had gathered sufficient power to institute his program in full force, reforms hailed in Mexico as the triumph of liberalism over conservatism.[4]

La Reforma had a number of goals, including general constitutional reform, but, from the perspective of the Indian population, its most significant aspect probably was its attack on the power of corporate institutions. Specifically, Juárez and his cohorts sought to disamortize their lands, particularly those of the Church, and directed a frontal assault on such properties. It often is remarked that while anticlerical (against the secular power of the Church), La Reforma was not anti-Catholic (against the Church as a religious institution), a distinction often made when church-state conflicts occur in predominantly Catholic countries.

Institutions besides the Church also came under attack, including the corporate landholdings of Indian communities; Indian communal lands also were to be sold or, more properly, individualized. The Juaristas thought that communal properties were too vulnerable to usurpation by other entities; individual private property was to solve this ill.[5]

As La Reforma unfolded, the central district surrounding the city of Oaxaca, like much of Mexico, was economically depressed and lacked political stability.[6] There had been several cholera epidemics in 1833 and 1854 and serious virus epidemics in 1851 and 1852 which caused the death of 1,146 individuals. The important cochineal industry was largely defunct.

Zapotec still was the most important language in rural communities, although by 1850 Spanish also was widely spoken in the area. Agricultural practices had changed little since the Colonial period; the diet still was based primarily on maize and beans, and the number of livestock was very low in relation to population size.

Each pueblo had a weekly market and was part of a system which included the capital, where the market was held on Saturday. However, craft specialization, a characteristic of present-day Valley communities, apparently was of little importance in this period.

Political functions still were largely in the hands of local community officials, as they had been in Colonial times; even though a *municipio* type of government had replaced the Colonial *cabildo*, it functioned much the same as *cabildo* government on a local level. However, as a result of liberal legislation in 1858, the Valley was divided into a number of districts beyond the *municipio* level; a political official at the district level generally was appointed by the state governor and served as an intermediary between *municipio* officials and the state government.

However, political authority in the Valley during this period was quite weak. There was considerable fear of robbery, murder, and violence. For example, many towns which normally held annual saints' fiestas had to cancel them during this period for fear of brawls and riots. Vagabonds, who apparently were numerous during this period, were thought to be the major cause of such incidents.

Before La Reforma, most Indian communities in the central district of Oaxaca had retained their communal lands, a heritage from Colonial days. There were both communal lands, which were apportioned to nuclear families, and *municipio* lands cultivated in common for the support of community activities. In some cases, communal lands were rented or leased to acquire funds to support community enterprises or for fiestas in honor of a town's patron saint.

Nevertheless, it appears that communal lands generally were small in size, and existing data suggest that private ownership already had become the most important type of land tenure in Indian communities before La Reforma.

During 1856 and 1857, after the initial disamortization of lands brought about by the Juárez reforms, Indian communities surrounding the city of Oaxaca in the central district, those in the Etla district, and perhaps those in other districts of the Valley, sold most of their remaining communal lands to conform to the new laws. These lands seem to have been purchased mostly in small parcels by nuclear families already residing within the Indian community; in rare cases, some lands were bought by outsiders.

Traditionally, it has been argued that properties disamortized by Juárez and his cohorts fell into the hands of *hacendados,* land speculators, or corrupt politicians and that the Indian peasant received few benefits from the redistribution of land—in effect, that the poor became poorer as the rich became richer. It appears, however, that this process did not occur in the Valley of Oaxaca to the extent that it may have occurred elsewhere in Mexico. The reasons seem to be that the Church had comparatively little rural wealth in central Oaxaca— what wealth it had was invested mostly in urban real estate—and, as noted in Chapter 5, hacienda development was not as pervasive in Oaxaca as elsewhere.

While most communities in the Valley defended themselves against the sale of lands to outsiders, this defense did not necessarily mean that privatization of property favored the equitable distribution of land to all villagers as Juárez intended. Instead, in the Valley as elsewhere in Mexico, the privatization of land sometimes led to its acquisition by more prosperous local villagers. For example, in San Juan Guelevía,[7] in the Tlacolula arm, a small group of related village families by the name of López managed to gain control of over 92 per cent of the arable land within that village; the remaining 8 per cent was held by 354 villagers.

This situation developed as the cost of saints' fiestas was transferred from income from communal lands (worked by all through a draft system) to private sponsorship under the *mayordomía* system, which theoretically placed the burden of sponsorship on the wealthiest individuals within the community, thus economically "leveling" its various families.

However, sponsoring a fiesta in the *mayordomía* system also became a prerequisite for secular political offices within the community; further, the local political council designated which individuals would assume *mayordomía* obligations. Sponsoring a saint's fiesta in turn brought prestige in exchange for an outlay of funds, a commodity sought by most members of the community. Therefore, since the council appointed the *mayordomos* and those so appointed were bound by tradition to serve—a tradition backed up by considerable community pressure—control of the council meant control of the community's wealth.

One astute villager, a López, followed just such a strategy. He coerced the council, with the support of an area priest, into designating poorer villagers for *mayordomo* positions, then he gave them loans to defray their sponsoring costs and required them to put up their lands as collateral. Since most villagers could never repay the loan, López gained control of most of the land in the *municipio* by foreclosure. A similar process has been reported for other Valley villages, such as Díaz Ordaz,[8] also in the valley of Tlacolula.

In addition, it appears that there was some growth of the hacienda, especially in the Valley's Zimatlán arm, during the eighteenth and nineteenth centuries.[9] While detailed studies are lacking for this period, apparently some families managed to purchase haciendas and maintain them intact over generations (an inheritance pattern much rarer in the Colonial period)[10] and probably acquired lands in Indian communities through the process of advancing loans. In general, the privatization of all lands made this strategy much more feasible than it previously had been.

Although apparently not as disastrous for Indian landholders in the Valley of Oaxaca as it was elsewhere in Mexico, Juárez' land program did not accomplish its intended result; privatization did not protect Indian lands from usurpation. Nor was Juárez able to bring political stability, through constitutional rule, to Mexico.

Mexico was in a state of economic and political chaos throughout most of the nineteenth century. Political stability and economic solvency, at least in the eyes of those outside Mexico, were to come only with the dictatorship of Porfirio Díaz, former liberal ally of Juárez who turned into his conservative enemy; Díaz assumed the presidency in 1870 after the death of Juárez and remained the strong man in Mexico until 1910, although at times he followed constitutional convention to the extent that he ruled in the guise of puppet presidents.

Díaz developed a strongly centralized government and a federal police invested with the authority, and weapons, to keep peace in the country. He turned to and succeeded in attracting foreign investments to stabilize the Mexican economy. Internally, the trends of the nineteenth century reached their culmination: the hacienda continued its "creeping paralysis" over most areas, and the gulf between the rich and the poor widened to perhaps its maximum extent in Mexican history.

Lacking resources to attract foreign investors, and without a tradition of haciendas to attract a vigorous new breed of *hacendados*,[11] the Valley of Oaxaca remained isolated from major developments in Mexico. Díaz, although of Oaxacan birth, seems to have taken little interest in the region, ruling it the same as others through appointed governors loyal to his program.

However, the Isthmus of Tehuantepec, where Díaz had been active as a military *jefe*, constituted an exception in the Oaxacan scene, as this area was an important center of commercial activity and wealth, much of which was concentrated in the hands of Doña Juana C. Romero, *cacica* of Tehuantepec, whose favors Díaz, among others, enjoyed.[12]

It was against Díaz and his policies that the bloody Revolution of 1910 was directed. However, the Revolution cannot be characterized in simple terms.[13] It was more than simply a peasant revolt, a struggle for land—it also was a struggle for power by those denied a niche in the Porfirian structure—vagabonds, runners of contraband, day laborers, bandits, disenfranchised intellectuals, aspiring politicos, and others.

The main areas of the military phase of the Revolution were centered in the north and central areas of Mexico and were led by quite different figures. Pancho Villa was a bandit from the north, a former peon on the rampage with no social program but the destruction of those he despised; Emiliano Zapata was a peasant apologist from Morelos. Recent evidence suggests that even Zapata's cause, at least intially, was not as much a reaction against peasant disenfranchisement from their lands as it was a rebellion aimed at restoring their relationships to haciendas. In Morelos many peasants had been attached to haciendas and constituted the major labor force for the cultivation and refining of sugarcane, a major crop there. New techniques, developed by Germans, were introduced for the refining and processing of sugar in the late nineteenth century, and peasants in Morelos fell victim to industrial innovation. Many were released from the haciendas, and with no land of their own for support, they rebelled, at first not for land but for reinstatement. At a later time, when reinstatement became impossible, land for peasants and their communities became the issue.[14]

But both Zapata and Villa were incapable of controlling a government of or usurping power on any widespread level, and the Revolution, turbulent throughout the decades on both sides of 1920, became a struggle for political power, for caudillo rule. It was not until the 1930's that some programs, including programs of agrarian reform, were successfully implemented and the centralization and stabilization of power under a single political party—the Partido Revolucionario Institucional (PRI)—was effected.

In general, the Revolution was much more important in the sierra and isthmus regions of Oaxaca than in the Valley. Communities in the sierra rebelled, fought one another, or allied themselves with the changing currents of the struggle by reducing their neighboring communities to rubble.[15] The isthmus, too, became an area of strife as communities split over the issues of the Revolution and their allegiance to Díaz, who was a hero for some;[16] bandits, such as Nicanor Díaz (apparently not a relative of Porfirio), emerged to terrorize the rich and, allegedly, to undo their wrongs and distribute their wealth to the poor.[17] Similar phenomena, symptomatic of the chaos of the Revolution, also occurred in the Oaxacan south, especially around Miahuatlán.[18]

But as in previous periods of history, the Valley of Oaxaca seems to have played a less active part in the commotion. The *vallistas* had little interest in plundering, allegiance to changing causes, or agrarian reform. Developments of the military phase of the Revolution, as well as the social phase which followed, were much less important in the Valley region than have been developments of the last two decades, when Mexico entered what has been called the industrial phase of the Revolution, aimed primarily at economic growth.

SUBSISTENCE, LAND USE, AND MATERIAL CULTURE

Agriculture forms the basis of the economy of modern Zapotec Oaxaca. Maize and beans remain the staples, as they have since pre-Spanish times, and much of the arable Valley land is used for their cultivation. For example, between 30 and 50 per cent of the agricultural land in the Valley of Oaxaca is devoted to maize.[19]

Three general types of cultivation are in practice. On steeper slopes, the *coa* (digging stick) and the hoe are used, and the land is cleared,

Zapotec peasant plowing with oxen, Valley arm of Tlacolula (1957).

with the aid of the machete, by a slash-and-burn method. The ox and plow remain the major type of tillage on the Valley floor or on gently sloping land. In some parts of the Valley and of the isthmus tractors recently have been introduced, although their presence still remains conspicuous, not ubiquitous.[20]

Maize farming illustrates well the "dual" nature of the peasant economy, since maize is grown both as a subsistence crop (to feed humans and animals) and as a cash crop. However, the importance of maize as a cash crop varies depending on the availability of water. Since pre-Spanish times the Etla arm of the Valley has had the highest agricultural yields per hectare and the most extensive irrigation systems (although it has the smallest amount of cultivated land; Zimatlán is intermediate, while the eastern Tlacolula arm has the lowest yield per hectare).[21]

In addition, Zapotec peasants do not have a "farmer ethic"; that is, they make few attempts to increase agricultural yields beyond a "fixed" amount. For example, Valley *coa* farming often is more productive (given total costs) than is ox plowing. But villagers still prefer the latter since the amount of profit considered "satisfactory" for a given year relates to social considerations as well as to strictly "economic" ones.

In addition to corn and bean farming, a wide variety of other crops are cultivated, depending on the nature of the local environment and community traditions. In the isthmus, for example, while maize is both a subsistence and a cash crop, a number of other crops also are grown. In the past, sugarcane was important, but it declined after the first quarter of this century when prices fell on the international market. Today, mangoes, coconut palms, and bananas are cultivated in irrigated fields but are not particularly profitable. Other crops such as sesame and sorghum, both recently introduced, and tomatoes, sweet potatoes, and native flowers, are sold for cash.[22]

Chili is grown wherever suitable environments exist; peanuts are Valley crops, and coffee lands are in the sierra. Wheat is grown both in the Valley and in the district of Ixtlán in the sierra. Maguey is a special crop of the Valley, today used also for the production of *mezcal*, a distilled alcoholic beverage related to tequila.[23]

Most peasant families keep some domesticated animals. Pigs, chickens, and oxen are frequent possessions. Sheep raising represents a specialty for certain villages, and goats sometimes are herded. Cheese is produced in the Valley, while fishing is important in isthmus coastal Zapotec villages and in some sierra villages, where trout (*bovos*) are caught in nearby streams. Hunting and gathering also are still of some importance as supplements to the diet of some sierra villagers.[24]

The basic diet throughout Zapotec Oaxaca consists of maize and beans, although there is great variation in their preparation. Maize is used for tortillas, which vary in shape, size, and width from region to region and are an ever-present item at meals. In some areas of the Valley, wheat flour tortillas are available and sometimes are considered a higher-status food item than maize tortillas.

The Zapotec village usually is nucleated, although dispersed communities are found in the sierra and among the Southern Zapotec.[25] Generally, *milpas* (cornfields) or other agricultural plots are located on the outskirts of the village and are visited daily by the cultivators. Fields are demarcated and clearly separated from one another. A

Zapotec village, Valley arm of Tlacolula.

peasant commonly will have fields in numerous places in the *munici-pio* instead of in a large, contiguous block. Such a pattern often means that cultivators spend considerable time traveling to and from their *milpas*; in the sierra, peasants often camp or live in huts near their plots although they maintain a permanent dwelling in their town.[26] In general, however, Zapotecs are town dwellers.

Most Zapotec settlements contain about one thousand inhabitants, although there is considerable variation; some are small hamlets, while others, such as the isthmus towns of Tehuantepec and Juchitán, approach twenty thousand. However, although large in size, these settlements still retain a distinct rural atmosphere and are perhaps best characterized as semiurban instead of rural.[27]

Although densely populated, and contrary to some opinion, further population growth might not necessarily cause an intolerable land-man ratio in the central and southern parts of Oaxaca. For example,

a recent study concludes that the Valley is not overpopulated in relation to agricultural productivity and that agricultural productivity
could be increased by twenty to fifty percent with present technological and capital resources.[28]

Most communities show mixed types of land tenure; private holdings, municipal communal lands, and *ejidos* all are in evidence in
various Zapotec regions. However, there is great variation in the relative quantities of these lands. For example, in Ixtepeji,[29] located on
the edge of the sierra and Valley (although *serrano* in speech), title
to all land is legally vested in the community and is administered by
the elected officials of the *municipio*. Any adult member of the community has the right to individual use of this land, although plots are
assigned to individual families for as long as they exploit them. Land
cannot be sold or inherited, however, and use of this land is attained
only by birth or marriage into the community. Private property is
restricted to ownership of house plots. This land tenure pattern
emerged after the 1910 Revolution period when Ixtepeji was decimated and depopulated as a result of military activity from 1912 to
1924 and then resettled.

Private holdings of agricultural plots predominate in most Zapotec
settlements, especially in the larger towns of the Valley. In most, however, village authorities have some control over the sale of private land
and frequently prevent sales to outsiders, particularly to peasants from
other villages.[30]

Generally, where private land tenure prevails, partible inheritance
is practiced, a system which assures at least male heirs of parcels. However, this subdivision of lands has led to considerable fragmentation,
as it has in many areas of the world, particularly in Latin America
and the Mediterranean region.

In Valley villages, peasants usually own from one to twenty parcels
of land.[31] Characteristically, holdings in dry-farming areas are larger
than those where irrigation is practiced. A study of three towns,
Tlalixtac de Cabrera, San Juan de Estado, and San Agustín Etla,[32]
indicates that irrigated parcels generally range in size from one-fourth
to one-half hectare. It is estimated that most peasant holdings in the
Valley are from one and one-half to two and one-half hectares in total
size.[33]

Many towns and villages in the Valley also have some municipal

Zapotec dwelling with thatched roof, Valley arm of Zimatlán.

communal land controlled by local village authorities. This land consists of areas which can be used for grazing or cultivated by any member of the community, although generally they are of poor quality. Some very good lands also are often owned communally and are worked under a system of obligatory labor called the *tequio*, a retention from Colonial, or possibly even pre-Spanish, times. These parcels provide for general community expenses, particularly for the upkeep of the church, municipal buildings, and the school.

Ejidos are communities or portions of communities which hold land in common and which are controlled by a set of *ejidal* authorities, similar to civil ones in regular villages.[34] *Ejidos* were established as a result of the agrarian reforms of the Mexican Revolution. These lands theoretically are divided equally among *ejido* members, who hold usufruct rights. *Ejidos* vary in the ways in which they assign lands: in

Oxcart and house compound, Valley arm of Zimatlán.

some, members hold rights over parcels which pass from father to son; in others, the parcels periodically are rotated among *ejido* members.

Generally, there is only one *ejido* per village, although not all villages have *ejidos*. Nor was all of the land redistributed as a result of the agrarian reforms assigned to *ejidos*. *Ejido* lands generally are in great demand and scarce, although they vary in quality. *Ejidal* banks have been set up by the Mexican government so that *ejidos* may apply directly for improvements and loans.

Village architecture displays a mixture of pre-Spanish, Colonial, and modern features. The single-story, one-room adobe house is widespread, although tile roofs generally have replaced the highly pitched native thatch roof; two-storied houses also are found and, having more than one room and being whitewashed, are considered more

Plaza of a Zapotec village, Valley arm of Tlacolula; the municipal building (*ayuntamiento*) is at left.

prestigious. Houses may be surrounded by fenced areas or they may have little land around them, in which case they frequently have an inside patio. In some larger towns houses may be built adjoining one another along a street. These variable patterns indicate that there now are no distinctive Zapotec housing complexes.

Villages usually are arranged around a plaza, fronted by the municipal building, the church (it may be adjoining), and a school. Schools, a relatively recent innovation, are more apt to display "modern" architecture, that is, be of brick, contain many glass windows, and often have tin roofs. Public buildings follow a range from colonial to modern, sometimes in the same structure. Churches, most originally built in the Colonial period, display various building stages and remodelings.

Main street of a Zapotec village, Valley arm of Tlacolula.

Fiesta in the Isthmus of Tehuantepec; the *huipiles grandes* worn by the women are typical of the isthmus. (Courtesy Beverly Chiñas.)

Dress also is changing rapidly. The *calzón*, traditional *sombrero*, and *huarache* combination for men is being replaced by tailored trousers and shirts, shoes, and various styles of straw hats. Women's styles tend more to display regional variations, especially in types of *huipiles*, hair styles, shawls, and other apparel. These regional "costumes" rapidly are disappearing as factory-made dresses become standard for everyday use. Fiestas and public occasions remain the time when regional dress is most markedly expressed.

Other items associated with modern mass society and culture have made inroads into the most remote villages.[35] Plastic and metal containers rapidly are replacing pottery as Coca-Cola and beer become widely used drinks. Transistor radios also are common and are considered prestige items. Tourism, the major industry in Oaxaca, has brought increased exposure to elements of modern mass culture as well as more cash.

Government programs of education, health care, electrification, and water control have brought significant changes to Zapotec villagers. In general, however, peasant families lack "modern" conveniences and the income to purchase the major status symbols associated with mass society and culture. Television sets, automobiles, electric stove-refrigerator-dishwasher combinations, flush toilets, and elaborate bath facilities are well beyond the reach of most Zapotecs.

ECONOMICS AND THE MARKET SYSTEM

Peasant economies have been said to differ from capitalist economies in that peasants are influenced less by the level of market demand for products and the cost-accounting dimensions of labor than they are by subsistence considerations, social factors, and ceremonial obligations.[36]

While it is useful to view peasants in such a manner, thus emphasizing the differences between peasants and modern entrepreneurs, this conceptualization represents only part of the story.

In the first place, peasant economies differ not so much in kind from other economies as in degree.[37] Contrary to the ideas of some economic and anthropological thinkers, both modern entrepreneurs and peasants "economize," even though their standards of reference may be different. Modern entrepreneurs theoretically "economize" through "capital gains," a concept intimately tied to quantifiable currency, such as cash. Peasants also may be seen to "economize," but they do so with reference to what might be called social capital, that is, prestige and respect. In this kind of analysis, which broadens the traditional concept of economics, "economizing" does not refer exclusively to material things, including cash currency, but also to social contexts or cultural values, which are observable as processes, which can, with equal validity, be called "capital," "credit," "savings," and "investment," and which are found in *all* societies.

After all, Westerners, too, are rewarded for the accumulation of

Ocotlán market; note the plastic as well as the pottery containers (at the right).

capital in the narrow sense only to the extent that capital can be converted into "desired goods"; "desired goods," while desired in all societies, must be defined culturally—they are not given by nature.

This view does not, of course, imply that social capital does not involve material considerations basic for human survival. On the contrary, social capital, especially in economies of scarcity, that is, where basic material necessities are in short supply, involves substantial ma-

terial considerations. To understand the materialistic dimensions of social capital, however, the cultural context of "economic" processes must be clearly elucidated.

In the second place, traditional peasants and modern peasants are embedded in different kinds of external social systems. Traditional peasants, limited by formal sumptuary rules and controlled economies, could not penetrate the world of the entrepreneur. But traditional peasants are no more; older formal restrictions have disappeared as the societies in which peasants find themselves embedded have become part of a modern world economy. As modern currency and cash considerations permeate the peasant community, so do different attitudes defining "desired goods." Modern Zapotec peasants, accordingly, are becoming more involved, if only on a small scale, in phenomena familiar to Western economists.

These various dimensions of "economic" processes are illustrated by a traditional institution of Zapotec Oaxaca, the *guelaguetza* (also called *gozana* or *guzón* in the Zapotec sierra),[38] a type of highly formalized reciprocal giving.

One variety of *guelaguetza* involves reciprocal labor exchange for farm work and house construction. Formal invitations are made to individuals to help in such work, with the understanding that their labor will be repaid in equivalent amounts. The workers are fed, and, except for relatives, records of their labor contributions are kept.

This type of *guelaguetza*, while embedded in social relationships, primarily is a way of paying for needed assistance and a means of building up credit and savings, for one may count on *guelaguetza* being returned.

This type of *guelaguetza* is not strictly social, and that peasants economize in the strict sense of that term, is illustrated by the fact that the use of *guelaguetza* as a labor device largely has declined in the Valley as money has come into general use, for wage labor is deemed less costly in a materialistic sense; paid laborers need not be fed, and there is no obligation to return labor. As might be expected, then, the use of *guelaguetza* as general labor exchange today is most prevalent in the sierra, where money has made fewer inroads into the economy.

Guelaguetza in the Valley now occurs more generally within the context of ritual activities, particularly religious fiestas, marriage ceremonies, and birthday celebrations. Its use in this context emphasizes the social factors that influence definitions of "capital." In many villages in peasant Oaxaca strong pressures are put on individuals to participate in religious fiestas, to outlay expenditures so that goods may be distributed to others, and to perform tasks to gain "respect" or "acceptance" by other villagers.

Such activities require funds. Thus, on these ritual occasions the person sponsoring them may solicit *guelaguetza* gifts to help him meet his obligations in a socially acceptable manner. These gifts, like any loan, are recorded and appraised, generally by a friend or relative of the host of the event as well as by each person who contributes, for they must at some time be returned in a gift of equal value. This return may occur when the giver in turn solicits *guelaguetza* gifts, for at the same time he also may call for return of his previous contributions.[39]

Thus, in the absence of currency, and in a ritual context, *guelaguetza* becomes an investment, and its returns may be conceptualized in terms of savings and credit. For if a person "gives," he also "receives" when it is necessary for him to make expenditures. But instead of investing in banks, he invests in others.

There are yet other types of "savings," "credit," and "capital accumulation" in peasant Oaxaca. For example, there are a great number of exchanges between neighbors, friends, and relatives which take place outside of the context of formal reciprocal exchanges. So far, these aspects of the peasant economy have not been detailed, however, and their exact contributions to the total economy are difficult to quantify.[40]

As more currency penetrates into the villages of Oaxaca, Zapotecs are beginning to save for other things besides "prestige" or "respect" capital. They save for more land, for ox teams, for houses, lots, and equipment, or for crops for resale.[41]

Cash hoarding is relatively rare as a form of saving, apparently as much because it so easily can be used to meet short-term emergencies as because of its scarcity. Consequently, Zapotecs tend to buy and raise animals as a frequent form of investment. Raising small pigs seems to be the most common investment strategy of this type although they generally do not yield a substantial capital gain. But the "economizing" aspect is clear, for:

> Many pig raisers . . . recognize that the enterprise is unprofitable but consider it to be a form of forced savings; the pig is really a live piggy bank. Numerous informants in various villages state, in effect: If I had the cash I would spend it on day-to-day luxuries (and luxuries can be defined at a very low level here). If I have to feed the pig I can't get at the money and at the end it returns a sum large enough to make an investment or meet a critical emergency. In other words, if the choice is between buying new clothing or feeding the pig, the clothes can be patched and worn a little longer.[42]

Meat stall in an old area of Ocotlán market.

However, the Zapotec economy is not entirely "internal." Zapotec communities also are intimately involved in a wider system of market relationships; not only are they affected by fluctuations in the market economy, but in addition they are participants. The market system in the Valley of Oaxaca generally corresponds to what has been termed a sectional or cyclical market system. In this system, "a market links a set of communities which are scattered around it in radial fashion, like the planets of the solar system around the sun. Each of these communities may have its own economic speciality. Usually the mainstay of the majority of communities is some form of cultivation, and the speciality is carried on part-time. . . ."[43]

In the Valley of Oaxaca, as in some other areas of Mexico, markets are held periodically, and products for sale are brought from throughout the region.[44] Certain towns have been designated as sites for weekly markets, but the hub of the system is the market held in Oaxaca City (Oaxaca de Juárez) on Saturday. Other markets are held in Tlacolula (de Matamoros)[45] on Sundays, Miahuatlán (de Porfirio Díaz) on Mondays, Ayoquesco (Santa María Ayoquezco de Aldama) on Tuesdays, both Etla and Zimatlán on Wednesdays, Zaachila and Ejutla on Thursdays, and Ocotlán (de Morelos) on Fridays.

Towns traditionally have special products which are brought to the marketplace for sale. For example, Atzompa specializes in a green glazed pottery (also a red ware), Coyotepec in black pottery, Zapotec Teotitlán del Valle in serapes, and Teitipac specializes in *metates*. Some towns, such as Mitla, specialize in trading.[46]

On market day the town becomes a sprawling mass of people, stalls, street vendors, and *movimiento*. In Oaxaca City, the largest market, as many as thirty thousand people may attend.[47]

The marketplace generally fans out from a central public market building and occupies the streets radiating from and surrounding this area, which is closed to traffic for the day; in Oaxaca City it occupies some twelve square blocks.

There are a number of types of vendors in the market, ranging from small to large, from those who arrive with only their own produce to large-scale commission wholesalers. Most of the vendors, however, are retail intermediaries. This group includes city-dwelling retail vendors who operate permanent stalls in the public market buildings (*locatarios*), itinerants (*regatones*) who travel from market to market, and individuals who sell their produce while walking around in the streets of the market (*ambulantes*).

The capital invested in market activities varies widely. The largest operation may have as much as two hundred thousand pesos invested in it, while the smallest may have a capital investment of less than ten pesos. Everything from tortillas and other small treats to factory-produced clothing may be sold in the market.

There is little hawking in the market, but a great deal of haggling. Prices fluctuate rapidly, depending on a number of factors. In the past, commodities were exchanged in kind; today a combination of currency and kind is employed, depending on the item involved.

As Ronald Waterbury has pointed out: "the backbone of the tradi-

Pottery area of the Oaxaca City market.

tional market system is a high volume of low cost transactions by a multiplicity of small-scale economic units. The traditional market system—like peasant production—operates on a high ratio of labor to capital investment. Total mark-up from producer to consumer is low, which corresponds to the limited buying power of the peasant and lower class urban consumer. . . ."[48]

Many items which can be distributed on this high-volume, low-cost basis, such as yard goods, ready-made clothing, plastic containers, combs, detergent, and so on, have been incorporated into the traditional market.

But there also is a dual system of marketing that appeals to others. Supermarkets, international general merchandise chains, and other stores operating with fixed prices and advertised name brands are found in the larger towns and cities (especially Oaxaca City). These stores sell to the urban rich and seldom to the urban poor and the peasants.[49] Some small country stores sell to peasants and frequently extend credit to them,[50] but the traditional market remains the major system of exchange and selling.

There is little evidence that this system is weakening. Some urbanites would like to see it abolished, arguing that it is unsanitary and presents an unsightly spectacle for tourists who come to Oaxaca (but in fact, as Ronald Waterbury notes, many tourists come to Oaxaca for the atmosphere of its traditional market).[51] Also, unions sometimes clash with the marketeers.

But total abolition seems unlikely. The market system is adaptive in an area with a limited amount of capital for investment and with a clientele having limited buying power. It also reinforces, on another level, the strong community tradition in the Valley of Oaxaca for craft or economic specialization and signals the viability of peasant communities as distinct units in the larger social order.

COMMUNITY ORGANIZATION AND POLITICS

Communities are clearly demarcated political entities in modern Zapotec Oaxaca. Since the institution of the *municipio libre* following the Revolution of 1910,[52] most political matters are vested in local communities. The reforms of the Revolution, like Spanish policy in the Colonial period, have reinforced a strong community tradition.

Municipio organization is much like the *cabildo* system of earlier times. *Municipios* contain head towns (*cabeceras*) and a number of hamlets or smaller villages (called *agencias*), although, unlike the Colonial *cabecera-sujeto* relationship, larger *agencias* frequently are independent communities and have their own governing bodies. Often these bodies ignore the local *cabecera* and appeal directly to higher levels of political authority, underscoring the strong, recent tendency toward segmentary opposition, that is, communities struggling for political autonomy, which has led to the formation of smaller units of administration. For example, even the official population minimum of five thousand inhabitants necessary for *municipio* status is loosely enforced in the Valley of Oaxaca; *municipios* range between five hundred and five thousand inhabitants.[53]

Municipios are grouped into *distritos*, including six in the Valley of Oaxaca; they also have *cabeceras*, which generally are the larger towns having major regional markets. State and federal governments lie on yet a higher level.

But these last political units are much less important to the average Zapotec peasant than is his local government; local government is vested in an *ayuntamiento* (town council; also the name of the municipal building).

Ayuntamientos generally consist of a core of five men (in some villages called *principales* or *ancianos*),[54] who are elected by the local population for a term of three years and legally cannot be elected for two consecutive terms. The principal officials of the *ayuntamiento* are the *presidente municipal*, the *sindaco*, and three *regidores*. The *presidente* is the chief officer, the *sindaco* is second in command, and the *regidores* discharge various duties ranging from responsibility for finance, labor, and the school to administration of the local water supply.

Ayuntamiento members also have alternates, called *suplentes*, who serve in their absence and who also may be assigned additional duties. The *ayuntamiento* is further assisted by errand boys, secretaries, and police officers.

Communities also frequently have officers in addition to those of the *ayuntamiento*. *Alcaldes* (generally two) dispense local justice and deal with crimes not considered to be in the province of the state. A *comisarido de bienes communales* also is frequent; this office, which may include from one to several officers, deals with communal lands. *Ejidos* also have a separate set of officials.

While election to office officially follows a set of PRI guidelines, which include the criteria of literacy (minimally defined) and good character for the higher posts, these guidelines are loosely enforced. Instead, the municipal organization, like that of *ejidos* and *agencias*, is constituted on the basis of the *cargo* system. All male members of the community are expected to serve during their lifetimes in various posts and are expected to discharge their duties, with minor exceptions, without salary. Thus, election is intimately tied to forced community service, and although PRI representatives must approve the election of officials to municipal posts, they generally abide by local community decisions on such matters.

In the past, the *cargo* system was linked to the *mayordomía* system of religious sponsorship, that is, specific *mayordomo* posts were a prerequisite for specific municipal posts.[55] Today, however, there is great variability. In some communities the *mayordomía* system functions on a completely different level from the *cargo* system; in others it has lapsed altogether; in still others the two remain linked.[56] In general, however, the *mayordomía* system and the *cargo* system have tended to diverge from one another.

The civil-religious hierarchy of the past has been further modified. It no longer has an exclusively "leveling effect."[57] For example, in some communities men may enter the system at various points instead of "working their way up from the bottom." As wealth becomes the single most important criterion for serving, then, the majority of men can never expect to serve. A hierarchy is thus formed in which wealth and prestige become synonymous.[58]

As the structure and function of the *mayordomía* system has undergone considerable modification, so have attitudes toward the *cargo* system. In the past, *cargo* positions brought considerable prestige, and still, in some places, individuals who are overlooked for a *cargo* attempt to take positions by force.[59] Much more frequently, however, serving a *cargo* is considered a burden (as its name translates) almost despised, reluctantly accepted, and, if possible, avoided. In Ixtepeji, for example, "there is open and unconcealed attempt to avoid service and strongly voiced displeasure at having to serve. Pablo Martínez, who three years before finished a term as *suplente de primer regidor* and now faces the prospect of another assignment, is not an outspoken man, yet he says 'Nobody likes to fulfill cargos, we just don't like to do it. It is only by force that we are made to do it. The people who vote for a candidate are punishing us. It's a punishment.' "[60] But as in most Zapotec communities, individuals who refuse to serve in Ixtepeji will meet with ostracism, verbal abuse, perhaps even violent acts directed against them, or worse—banishment from the community.

One reason for the unwillingness of individuals to serve is the loss of time and funds involved. To Zapotec peasants, many of whom exist on the margins of poverty, the loss of time from agricultural or related pursuits while serving a *cargo* may produce debts that require a lifetime to escape.

Another reason, which perhaps influences the more wealthy and prestigious to escape serving on *cargos*, is that local political officials are afforded no real authority within the community and, in fact, are subject to considerable suspicion and potentially damaging corruption.[61] The municipal *presidente*, for example, is recognized by district, state, and federal governments as the official representative of the community. From the villagers' point of view, the *presidente* is expected to be able to deal with and influence these higher authorities and to act effectively on the community's behalf. But on the community level he must not exert his influence; he must act, instead, in accordance with the community's notion of consensus; he cannot enforce his will on the citizens. As a result, aggressive *presidentes*, along with other community officials, frequently are accused of overstepping their roles, of bribery, of dipping into the community treasury, or of using influence for personal gain. In some cases aggressive *presidentes* have been killed or banished from villages.

Presidentes, then, as are other political officials in Zapotec communities, immediately are placed in a dilemma which frequently is solved or dealt with effectively by skillful politicians but for most mitigates against the acceptance of a position of authority. Power corrupts in the peasant view; it brings suspicion, possible ruin, and is thus to be avoided if possible. The community, if it is to defend itself against outsiders and remain a viable unit, must avoid internal dissensions, and power can bring such dissensions.

But Zapotec peasants also think of themselves as fierce individualists, which perhaps is a reflection of their desire to escape the strong community pressures of consensus and cooperation. And, while many villages deny internal dissension, attributing it to villages other than their own, internal factionalism does occur.

However, the extent to which factionalism actually is disruptive of the community as a unit depends largely on external factors.[62] In past times, when there were active opposition parties or movements in Mexico, internal community factionalism was more crystallized. For example, in nineteenth-century Yalálag, a sierra community, there were factions associated with the "Greens" (progressives) and the "Reds" (conservatives). Later, during the early stages of the Revolution, there were *constitucionalistas* and *soberanos*. Still later, there were *agraristas* and anti-*agraristas*.[63] These local factions, of course, did not necessarily follow the ideology of the larger parties or movements whom they imitated, for local disputes constituted the primary rallying points. But the larger society provided a climate conducive to local factionalism.[64]

In another community, then Santo Domingo del Valle and now Díaz Ordaz (named after the grandfather of the recent Mexican president), there were two factions centered on the leadership of two strong political bosses.[65] In other areas, such as the isthmus, internal factionalism in the past caused communities to split into opposing segments which still today are associated with different ideological beliefs.[66] Yet while factionalism still is reported for most communities, today there is less of a tendency for it to center around large, crystallized groups and more of a tendency for it to take an individual or familial character.

The major reasons for this change seem to relate to the strength of the PRI as a centralizing force in Mexico as well as to increasing struggles between whole communities as competing entities. Strong internal factionalism weakens the ability of communities both to ward off government intervention and to preserve themselves against neighboring communities. Therefore, communities wish to present, at all costs, a united front against outside threats.

In some communities, the reasons for maintaining a united front relate to real historical circumstances. Ixtepeji, a town noted for its participation in rebellions, once was the major center of its region of the sierra.[67] However, at one point it took up arms against the revolution and supported the *soberanos*. Ultimately, as already noted, the town was attacked by its neighbors and completely destroyed, and its inhabitants fled. The town was not resettled until 1924, and it remains unimportant economically and politically, as political authority has shifted to nearby Ixtlán.

These events remain impressed on the minds of present-day Ixtepejanos. They now side with the government on all issues and attempt to present a united front; internal peace and tranquillity must be preserved above all else. They want no repeat of the events of the early part of this century.

In other places, such as Mitla, internal dissension is avoided for fear of humiliation by outside power figures or for fear that outside authorities will not understand their problems and deal unfairly with them. Thus, Mitleños turn their backs on disputes that might bring violence and ignore involvements which might bring about the crystallization of factions. Mitleños express this situation, in opposition to the old days when factionalism was rampant, by the epithet "Now we are civilized."[68] This attitude also relates to relationships with other pueblos, an attitude that might be explained because of the trading interests of Mitleños, interests which necessitate amiable external relationships.[69]

In communities which contain *ejidos*, a potential for crystallized factionalism exists and frequently erupts between *ejidatarios* and other members of the community, especially over the apportioning of political officials. This conflict generally is resolved, however; in one case both sides compromised by permitting half of the offices to be filled by *ejidatarios* and the other half by those from the non-*ejidal* part of the community.[70]

But while villages generally avoid massive internal disputes or are able to deny or repress them with strong appeals for community solidarity, disputes between communities are more common. In a sense, as Julio de la Fuente has characterized them, Zapotec peasant communities are like small sovereign states constantly at war with each other.[71]

Two Valley villages, for example, have been engaged in a land dispute that goes back at least as far as 1694. On several occasions this dispute has erupted into bloody conflict, which brings in outside and

higher-level political authorities. The violent conflict usually is followed by a period of peace and long litigation. Philip A. Dennis has
pointed out that such litigation serves to siphon surplus wealth from
the communities as revenue flows into the pockets of lawyers and government officials responsible for mediating such feuds.[72] But while
litigation between communities is much more common than violence
and bloodshed, disputes make communities vulnerable to higher authorities. Thus, as pointed out by Eric Wolf, even though peasant
communities attempt to defend themselves from intervention by outside authorities, they generally are not capable of the task.[73] In a sense,
by their presumed solidarity as units they make themselves easy prey
to outside intervention.

Perhaps the area in which the community has become most vulnerable to state intervention is in the area of canal irrigation and the
general control of water resources,[74] a key item affecting the productivity of agriculture in the Valley of Oaxaca. Although where
feasible canal irrigation has been practiced in the Valley for some
time, its control has been highly variable. In some communities it is
controlled by the *presidente*; in others, control is dispersed among
lower-ranking community officials. But until recently, wherever
found, the control of water resources has been much the same as the
regulation of other community resources; that is, it has been the
province of community officials and has been subject primarily to the
community.

Differences in communities with regard to access to water have in
the past generated a potential superordinate-subordinate relationship
between communities. Downstream villages are often at the mercy of
those upstream. On the whole, however, this situation has not brought
a restructuring of the formal political organization of such communities. In some cases it has been resolved through informal agreements
between community officials, agreements requiring renewal with
each new set of *ayuntamiento* officers; in other words, the subordinate
community has become resigned to its fate. Both of these consequences illustrate, given the strong tendency toward community sovereignty, that there are few formal internal organizational structures
which promote higher levels of political integration.

Since the 1930's and 1940's, however, a special federal government
agency has been created to improve the nature of the water supply in

villages and to develop the organization of such improvements. Control of new sources of water and the irrigation canals which are related to them is vested in a specialized body, the *junta de aguas*, organized much like the community government although often cutting across communities and completely separate from *municipio* or *agencia* government. This cross-sectioning creates a special body directly concerned with hydraulic interests which is responsible to a federal governmental agency, the Secretaría de Agricultura y Ganadería, not to the local community governments.

There have been few such projects, but where they have occurred the federal agency has influenced the organization of production and has undermined the autonomy of the community in a crucial area, promoting not only new levels of political integration but also altering the nature and means of agricultural production. As Susan Lees has stated: ". . . through developmental programs the state can alter community structure more than has any historical event, law, or decree in the past 450 years. By making the community look outside itself for solutions to internal problems, these programs begin to eliminate the functions of the traditional organization, and thus undermine its effectiveness."[75] Although it is difficult to predict the exact effects of government developmental programs on local community organization, it should be expected that community autonomy, and the forms of social and political organization which promote it, will suffer as the countryside is bombarded in future years with an increased bureaucratization emanating from the federal level.

HOUSEHOLD, FAMILY, AND SOCIAL ORGANIZATION

Regardless of recent changes, modern Zapotec peasant communities generally remain as corporate entities—clearly defined social entities with enduring social roles. A number of features demarcate this entity: a local political body acting on behalf of community members; a land base wherein even private lands are reluctantly sold to outsiders; a strong identification with the community as a place; and a tendency toward community endogamy which perpetuates the continuity of the group. Thus, one basic building block of Zapotec society is the community; another is the household. These two entities constitute the major structural units of the Zapotec peasant social order.

To be certain, some communities have units other than the household and the community. Not including *ejidos* and *juntas de aguas*, which are of recent formation, perhaps the most important of these are sections of communities called *barrios*. But *barrios* are less enduring, less structurally consistent, and less socially important than are communities and households. In some places, *barrios* have patron saints. Where such *barrios* are found, however, the saint's fiesta may be sponsored by a non-*barrio* member and may be participated in by the whole community.[76] In other places, *barrios* are simply residential sections with no ceremonial functions, a kind of locus for the identification of a member within the larger community.[77] In other communities, *barrios* refer to non-localized savings and loan associations.[78] In rare cases, as at Zaachila, they may represent vestiges of distinct ethnic groups.[79]

In larger towns, where *barrios* might be expected to constitute more significant groupings, there also is no uniformity. For example, at Tehuantepec *barrios* are ceremonial entities, but at Juchitán, also a large isthmus Zapotec town with perhaps twenty thousand inhabitants, there are no *barrios* of this type.[80] In many larger towns *barrios* have disappeared altogether.[81] Thus, even though *barrios* may have had their origins in Spanish patterns of resettlement during the Colonial period and in some cases may represent vestiges of older communities, their importance today clearly has diminished and has taken on various meanings. Certainly there is no form of *barrio* organization that is typical of all Zapotec communities.

To the Zapotec peasant it is his community and his household that provide primary bases of identification as well as the contexts in which most social relationships take place. Most households consist of single nuclear families, considered the ideal throughout the Zapotec area. However, households are not necessarily synonymous with nuclear families. Economic pressures sometimes lead to extended family households, even though each nuclear family maintains a separate kitchen as a focus of identity.[82] Residence patterns also bring about modifications of the household structure during various phases in the domestic cycle.

Residence patterns after marriage display some variation throughout the area, but the general pattern is for the bride to move into the household of the husband (patrilocal residence) until the birth of the first child, at which point a new household is set up (neolocal residence).[83]

Marriage generally is negotiated through intermediaries, in some cases by the families involved, in others by close relatives or fictive (ritual) kin, and in still others by specialists in arranging marriages. Marriage usually is thought of as an economic arrangement between families or households; "love" generally is considered unimportant and not a basic criterion for marriage. However, in some areas a pattern called *robo* permits couples to choose their mates. Usually with her consent, a boy and his close friends will abduct a girl—literally steal her from her parents. The couple remains *incognito* for at least one night, which, to their parents and to the community, symbolizes sexual consummation of their union, whether or not it actually occurred. The "reputation" of the girl's family thus has been stained. A generally formalized period of negotiations follows, usually initiated by an intermediary acting on behalf of the male, and after some restitution is assured to the injured parents the marriage is allowed to take place and is accepted by the community.

Under modern Mexican law, all marriages must be legitimated by a civil ceremony; most families also desire them to be consecrated in a religious ceremony as well. However, there is great variation in this respect, and the full cycle of civil and religious sanction often is not achieved. In many communities, a religious ceremony coupled with the ritual and festival events is deemed most important.

Relationships within the nuclear family follow a strict division of labor. There are clear-cut male and female roles. Heads of households are expected to be domineering and authoritarian; as a result, a male displays few outward signs of affection toward his wife and children— such affections are deemed most appropriate for women and children.

The nuclear family household regularly "segments" at various stages in its cycle.[84] Marriage of the children attached to a household ultimately brings its demise. The pattern of patrilocal-neolocal residence continues until all children are married, the last of which inherits the family housesite. After this event, the elderly parents live for periods of time in the households of each of their married children.

As a result of the segmentation of the household, sibling relationships may not carry with them strong bonds of attachment between neolocal households. Brothers, in particular, frequently become bitter enemies, especially over matters of inheritance. But parent-child relationships generally remain strong. Violation of this bond constitutes an immoral act in most Zapotec communities.

As the community constitutes a type of sanctuary from the outside society, so the household is a kind of sanctuary within the community. The family household is a place where a man, particularly, can feel secure against the accusations and abuses of others. There is physical as well as social distance reflected in the structure of Zapotec households. Households often are separated from one another by a high fence to prevent neighbors or others from spying on family activities.

Allegiance to one's household or nuclear family is strongly enforced, for it is this unit that is the reference point for individuals within the community. An individual's reputation, prestige, and wealth are measured in terms of his household or nuclear family and whole households or families are given reputations on the basis of the behavior of each member; therefore, the actions of one member may bring disgrace to the whole unit.

In the *cargo* system, and traditionally in the *mayordomía* system as well, appointments are made with reference to households. Only one adult male of the household is required to serve at any one time. Community taxes are assessed on and collected from households. Communal lands are alloted on the basis of households. Obligations, such as *guelaguetza* and *tequio*, are household or nuclear family obligations, not individual ones. According to the Zapotec system of inheritance, debts and obligations are inherited by the male members of a household upon the death of the household head. Thus, there are strong social and economic pressures to maintain a tight nuclear family or household unit, as community membership is dependent upon family or household, as are "reputations" and "acceptance." And, since continuing social reciprocities as well as the formation of new beneficial relationships, both of which include the exchange of material goods, require good "reputations" and "acceptance," survival in a Zapotec peasant community depends largely on these qualities.

Besides the family and the community at large, there are few other formal social groupings in Zapotec communities. Outside of families, group cooperation centers mostly around religious activities. It already has been noted that special-interest associations are sparse and, to the extent that they undermine community consensus and bring potential suspicion to their members, are to be avoided.

Lacking a varied associational life, Zapotec communities thus appear structurally incomplete. But in Zapotec society, as in most others in Mesoamerica, there is another order of social relationship, one belonging to a more "private" realm and one favoring "individual" instead of "group" interests.[85]

The principle on which such relationships are based is reciprocity—an agreement of mutual aid. The relationships so formed are generally dyadic—that is, they unite two individuals, not groups. They are thus "particularizing" and not "generalizing," they underlie "all formal ties, cross-cutting them at every point," and they "serve as the glue that holds society together and the grease that smooths its running."[86]

These "dyadic contracts," as George M. Foster calls them,[87] may take place within the context of formal institutions. *Compadrazgo* (ritual co-parenthood) is extremely important in Zapotec society. *Compadres* are individuals who agree to sponsor important life crisis events—baptisms, confirmation, marriage, and death.

Agreeing to be sponsors, they enter into an obligation to their godchild's well-being and security and agree to give aid to his parents; they receive respect and some aid in return. *Compadrazgo* thus creates a bond between pairs of individuals and implies respect, aid, and closeness, signaled by the reciprocal use of the term *compadre* or *comadre* (between parents and sponsors), *padrino* or *padrina* (between sponsored child and godparents), and *ahijado* or *ahijada* (between godparents and sponsored child).

In Zapotec communities *compadres* generally are nonkinsmen; *compadrazgo*, as in many other societies which practice this Latin godparenthood pattern, thus extends relationships instead of reinforcing already existing ones. In a real sense, *compadrazgo* makes kinsmen out of nonkinsmen, and, within the context of the community, *compadres* are second in importance only to real kinsmen.[88]

But this is only the formal aspect of the relationship, and, as with any formal relationship, reciprocal behavior must accrue and continue for the relationship to be viable. Actual behavior must approximate the expectations of formal roles no matter how a relationship may be constituted. It is in this sense that the dyadic contract operates. It is only when *compadres*, *padrinos*, or *ahijados* actually engage in reciprocal behavior that a viable social relationship is formed. In most cases, *compadrazgo* relationships are validated in Zapotec communities.

There also are many other relationships formed on the basis of dyadic contracts, although the majority of these are formed on a non-ritual, nonformal basis; that is, there may be no ritual validation, no institution, no initiation, and no ceremony, as in *compadrazgo*. Contracts of this type quite frequently take place between neighbors, friends, and others within the community as well as linking individuals from different communities.

Such relationships permeate the society and unite equals as well as unequals. More wealthy or prestigious individuals may enter into patron-client relationships with the less wealthy or prestigious, offering favors, loans, influence, and other aid in exchange for support of various kinds. It is these patron-client relationships that have served as the basis for political power in traditional Mexican society, as a strong *jefe* largely depends on the continued reciprocity of his clients.

Moreover, patron-client relationships are not restricted to humans. Saints are often offered *promesas*—new clothes, candles, or special sacrifices such as pilgrimages—in exchange for special favors. Individuals often form enduring relationships with saints as a result of favorable responses and adopt specific saints as their special patrons.

In general, dyadic contracts, especially those of the colleague type which unite individuals of equal status and wealth, do not form permanent groups, for each individual has a unique set of such contracts. For them to continue to function, principles of cost accounting cannot apply to dyadic contracts, for equal payment implies the termination of the relationship. In fact, the relationship continues because equalization of exchange is never really met and debts or "favors" are never totally paid, since they cannot usually be assessed in explicit terms.

But, conversely, dyadic contracts also can lead to interpersonal conflict, since ambiguous cost-accounting easily can turn to accusations or suspicions of noncompliance; "friends" can be accused of turning to others and abandoning the "good will" of their former colleagues. Thus, dyadic contracts often end abruptly and with considerable bitterness and antagonism; friends can become enemies as easily as they became friends.

All societies have formal and informal spheres, as all societies, even highly bureaucratic ones, have formal social structures and informal dyadic contracts. But in societies permeated with bureaucratic ideologies, where rules ideally are enforced impersonally by anonymous bureaucrats, relationships antithetical to these ideologies are deemed "corrupt" or "unfair." Further, as bureaucratic procedures permeate more areas of social life, previously personal relationships become increasingly subject to "corrupting" influences. In a sense, then, society is integrated from above, not from below.

Zapotec society also can be viewed as composed of these two arenas of social life. But these two realms intermesh to a greater extent than they do in large-scale bureaucratic nation-states, for in Zapotec society the body of formal rules which composes the community and the individuals who relate to each other on a face-to-face basis are largely synonymous. This intermeshing breeds a particular kind of ideology.

In this ideology, personal relationships and what they can accomplish, are stressed over impersonal rules, because security, if only fleeting, comes from a personal relationship in which "quid pro quo" applies. Consequently, one does not aid a stranger, for one cannot know his motives. In a similar manner, impersonal bureaucracies are to be avoided or dealt with only to the extent that their rules can be transformed into a personal relationship.

Therefore, instead of accepting more rules, men must attempt to escape those binding them, for impersonal rules undermine personal morality and make all vulnerable to accusations of "corruption," as damaging in Zapotec society as in others.

Escaping rules, although to be preferred over following them, does not bring human perfection, however, for the Zapotecs, hardened by an economy of scarcity, view "unfairness" as a basic fact of human nature; individuals are fundamentally self-serving regardless of their relationships. Perhaps the Zapotecs, like the anthropologist Paul Stirling, would agree that: "The problem is not why 'corruption' exists; it is a perfectly reasonable institution and precisely what one would expect. The problem is why on earth there are some relatively non-corrupt systems."[89]

WORLD VIEW AND RELIGION

The Zapotecs view their world, as do most modern peasants in Mexico and elsewhere, as a place filled with danger, uncertainty, and potential catastrophe. The Zapotec world, composed of supernatural beings, the elements, and human nature, is fundamentally deceitful and aggressive. In their view, the individual faces this hostile world alone; generally, he cannot count on others, who will take advantage of any situation if given the opportunity. Zapotec society thus is permeated with widespread distrust (*desconfianza*). As a result, even "good" things that happen are thought of as deceptive illusions (*ilusiones*).[90]

This pervasive world view, which approaches cultural paranoia, is called "a culture of insecurity" by Beverly Chiñas,[91] and it may be accounted for by a number of factors.

George M. Foster, who recognizes this view as characteristic of a wide variety of peasant societies, has argued that such a view arises from a situation of economic scarcity in part brought about by the nature of peasant agriculture. Given the nature of peasant technology, a general lack of economic resources for improvements, and an existence clearly tied to crops which may be ruined or destroyed at any time by the uncontrollable elements of rain, drought, frost, or hail, production clearly cannot be expanded beyond a certain limit without also expanding landholdings—thus at the expense of others.[92] Additional factors, not detailed by Foster, also seem to contribute to a culture of insecurity. Given the ubiquitousness of raw political power which controls their lives, and their lack of influence in decision making at higher levels, peasants always are at the mercy of higher authorities; further, given the prevalence of disease, and a lack of means to control it, men may be struck down, incapacitated, or disabled at any moment without warning; finally, given the extreme fluctuations of the external market, peasants do not count on getting a "fair" or even "adequate" price for commodities or work accomplished.

Years of exposure to such situations builds what originally was an adaptive strategy for survival into a cultural tradition, a way of life passed on from generation to generation. This cultural tradition, or way of viewing the world, not only relates to material wants but also extends into other realms. The Zapotecs thus see nonmaterial items as governed by the same forces and subject to the same limitations as are material wants; an older child loses love as a new one appears to be cared for; a mother loses the love of a son when another woman marries him; as one advances in age, one's health decreases, for it, too, cannot be expanded beyond a certain limit—newborn individuals acquire as you expire; social relations, like man's relationship to economic necessities, are governed by definite availabilities, and as the elements may strike one down without warning, so may a friend. An Ixtepejano proverb relates, "The best friend is the worst traitor."[93]

Foster has characterized this general outlook as the "Image of Limited Good,"[94] a concept derived from his study of Tzintzuntzan, a mestizo village in Michoacán, but equally applicable to most Zapotec communities.

The Image of Limited Good is a notion that peasants act *as if* they were following the rule that all goods (material and nonmaterial) exist in finite quantities and cannot be expanded beyond a certain limit. Therefore, the only way one individual can acquire additional resources (be they land, love, health, political power, or other needs or desires) is at the expense of another. Specifically, since most necessities and desirables are available in limited supply (and this supply generally is below a minimum that all could enjoy), all are in competition, and, given the situation of scarcity, losing is much more characteristic than winning. Only "respect" seems to constitute the exception to this rule, for within the context of the traditional community its supply is unlimited.[95]

In such a generally desperate world defense is a more viable strategy than offense, as regularity and continuity are more secure than frightening change and aggressive individuality. Change cannot but be for the worst, for given the limitations of the universe an individual can only receive less, not more. Further, aggressive individualism breeds contempt and threatens others, who may be provoked to strike back— thus it is better to be like all others, or at the very least to let all others think you are like them.

A defensive strategy seems to demand a society of passive individualists who must not let down their guard with others. Thus, Zapotec peasants, as do those from Tzintzuntzan, do not reply to inquiries such as "How are you?" with the response, "Fine."[96] A more likely response would be, "I am managing to defend myself." Similarly, they do not share knowledge with others or ostentatiously dis-

play wealth or accomplishments (except in socially sanctioned situations such as *mayordomías*) for fear of creating envy on the part of
others which in turn could lead to verbal abuse or attacks of witchcraft. Much Zapotec conversation thus takes the form of what could
be called gossip—bickering and backbiting designed to prevent others
from taking the offensive.[97]

An example serves to illustrate the fear involved in letting down
one's defenses against others. Beverly Chiñas relates an incident involving her move from one house to another in an Isthmus Zapotec
peasant community. She had made arrangements to move into the
household of a Zapotec family, a shift in residence that involved trans-
ferring some furniture and other items from one location to another;
the items were not numerous, and the move, by most criteria, could
have been accomplished in a short time. Her new hosts, however, refused to move the goods during the day or at one time. Instead, they
wanted to move her articles item by item at night when others could
not see them, and over an extended period, fearing that an open addition of goods to the household would generate jealousy, and damaging envy.[98]

This anecdote illustrates the Zapotec peasant's way of coping with
the world—it could be characterized as one in which individuals attempt to achieve a balance of conformity, or a pretense of uniformity,
instead of attempting to control or change fundamentally malevolent
forces.

Another facet of the attempt to maintain a balance of conformity
can be seen in formalized male drinking behavior. For example,
Ixtepeji, like most Zapotec communities, is an "alcohol culture."[99] In
most activities where men come together, heavy drinking (of *mezcal*,
tepache, or beer) ensues; such hard drinking may last for three or
four days, during which time the men may become intoxicated to
the point of passing out many times. Such drinking rarely leads to
alcoholism in the sense of physical addiction or social anomie, but
Ixtepejeños recognize both negative and positive effects of alcohol;
thus, as with other things in their culture, attitudes toward drinking
are ambivalent.

On a positive level, drinking serves as a way to resolve a paradox
in Zapotec culture. As already noted, their society is tense and anxiety
ridden, and physical and emotional closeness are to be avoided, pro-

ducing a kind of subdued isolation of individuals. On the other hand, solidarity and closeness with others must be stressed if the community is to be united against all possible threats to its existence. Clearly, drinking permits the transformation from a society of defensive individualists to one of united community brothers. From drinking, in most cases carefully ritualized, themes of brotherhood, happiness, and general well-being begin to emerge—ideas contradictory to everyday mundane struggles between man and man, and man and the universe. Men become physically closer, something that in normal activities only women and children do. Spontaneous orations break out in which themes such as "we all are brothers" or "we are all sons of the pueblo" are emphasized. Men "open up," expressing their emotions and experiencing "happiness." As one Ixtepejano put it, "After a few cups I feel very happy and gay and talk better; I feel stronger and almost invincible."[100]

But drinking in Zapotec culture also becomes more than a means of escaping "sadness" or of achieving "happiness," and it is more than a means of "escape" from the real world, an idea negatively valued in the culture. It is also a way to conform to or come to terms with a malevolent social universe, a way to reassert a balance with other human beings and particularly with the community. "Everyone Must Drink," as Michael Kearney, who studied Ixtepeji, has put it,[101] or, as put by the Ixtepejanos themselves, "You can't escape the cups."[102] Excessive drinking is not really an individual act—if it becomes so it is negatively valued—but instead it is a group performance.

For example, all men who assume office in the pueblo must drink during the town fiesta. One man, who had become converted to a Protestant sect (active in some villages in Oaxaca) held the position of *primer regidor* but refused to drink during the preliminaries of the town fiesta. Reaction against his behavior became so strong that the sponsors threatened to cancel the fiesta, blaming him for its potential failure. With repeated pressure, the *regidor* finally started drinking, got very drunk, denounced his Protestant religion, and continued drinking for days. Thus, in Ixtepeji, "one must adapt to and obey the town's wishes."[103]

Diseases, undesirable psychological states, or psychosocial disorders also are attributed to imbalance by the Zapotecs. The Hippocratic system of medicine, introduced by the Spanish, although it may have had analogies in pre-Spanish times, probably has generally influenced Zapotec notions of etiology.[104]

In the Hippocratic system, the body is governed by humors—hot, temperate, and cold (the exact number of these humors varies from region to region and community to community). Diseases result from an improper balance of these humors. Foods, psychological states, natural elements, and the universe as a whole are classified according to this system. However, the assignment to a humor does not correspond to contemporary Western notions of temperature but instead according to its effect; ice, for example, is hot, not cold, for it "burns" vegetation and produces a "burning" sensation when swallowed.

The system also is not easily divisible into internal and external elements. Any combination of internal physiological or psychological imbalance plus external forms beyond the control of individuals may produce an undesirable result. As in the Hippocratic system, the Zapotec world is not readily segmentable into physiological, psychological, social, and cosmic phenomena, an ordering which is a product of fairly recent Western thinking.

Among the Zapotecs, envy (*envidía*) or anger may cause *muina*, or, in children, *chípil*. These are psychogenic ailments which poison the blood, cause the heart to swell, and, if not checked, eventually result in permanent physical disabilities, such as paralysis. A person with *muina* turns red and has a feeling of "hotness" in his head. The usual direct symptom of *muina* is loss of appetite, and it is thought that intake of food or drink while the condition persists can raise the concentration of blood poisoning to a fatal level. *Muina*, while it is sometimes associated physiologically with the stomach or appendix as well as the heart and blood, can be cured only by *curanderos* (native healers); medical doctors are thought to be ineffective against it.[105]

Muina presents a dilemma to the Zapotecs, for, while it is considered a serious ailment, it also is *prima facie* evidence that the individual suffering from it was angry or envious; therefore, he constitutes a threat to others. The others, in turn, may counterattack by witchcraft. Therefore, one must eat and drink to hide *muina* symptoms and hope for a cure. According to local opinion, however, *muina* is difficult, if not impossible, to conceal.

Soul loss (*susto* or *espanto*) is another common condition among the Zapotecs.[106] This disease, as are most others, is part of a much wider complex and may be caused by a variety of factors. Basically, however, it comes about as a result of a sudden, frightening encounter of some kind—either with other human beings, animals, objects, or spirits. *Susto* causes the soul or spirit to leave the body, making it susceptible to malevolent forces; in short, the body loses one of its defense mechanisms, and the individual is rendered vulnerable.

A number of symptoms are attributed to *susto*: listlessness, depression, timidity, loss of appetite and strength, restlessness in sleep (due to troublesome dreams), fever, muscular pain, complexion changes, nausea, stomach or intestinal upsets, vertigo, intense thirst, and rectal bleeding.

Zapotecs believe that medical doctors may be helpful in treating some of the symptoms of *susto*, but that only a *curandero* or *curandera* may cure it. Unless cured, *susto* is believed to culminate in death.

While *susto* may occur in both males and females, it is more commonly a female disease. For this reason, it has been hypothesized that *susto* is a mechanism of escape and rehabilitation for individuals suffering from sex-role stress; women are most vulnerable to sex stress in Zapotec culture and, in fact, have fewer outlets for aggression and the release of anxiety.

The potential for greater anxiety on the part of women begins early in the socialization process. As infants, boys are thought to be more delicate than girls and are given more liberties. Both young boys and young girls are given explicit duties, but girls more frequently are punished and reprimanded for failure to perform them than are boys. Boys are allowed some aggressive behavior, such as teasing animals and other children, while girls are not permitted such habits. Boys more frequently are permitted to play in the streets and to stray throughout the village, while girls are kept close to home.

As adolescents, girls are expected to learn and master tasks and assume responsibilities which males assume only much later in life. Marriage and its responsibilities generally come earlier for girls (as early as fourteen years) than for males.

At marriage, the change is more abrupt for females than for males, for girls move into a new family setting or household. A bride is subject to the authority of her husband, her new father- and mother-in-law, and her husband's brothers. Men continue to work with their fathers and brothers after marriage.

Men, married or unmarried, are given considerable freedom of movement and leisure; women have practically none. A new bride, for example, is under the constant watch of her mother-in-law, a surveillance that permits no disrespect or disobedience. Generally, mothers-in-law are stricter than mothers, and beating, tongue-lashing, and other disciplinary measures are within her rights and duties to "control" or "train" her son's bride.

There are other situations in which female stress can develop. Children are highly valued in Zapotec society, and the inability to produce offspring because of sterility generally is attributed to the female. Women are often held responsible for infant mortality, which is extremely high among young children. While malevolent forces invade both men and women, only women are held responsible for those that affect them.

As adults, after setting up a new household, women are expected to work constantly, caring for their husbands, children, and household duties. Men may rest periodically, escape to the cornfield, and take trips, but "woman's work never ends." To be accused of idleness is, except for infidelity, the worst thing that can happen to a woman in a Zapotec community.

A woman must always be submissive to her husband; she has no freedom of sexual expression. Until she becomes a mother-in-law, she must remain in the background of the fiesta and may not drink alcohol (although even at that point women do not participate as fully as males). Above all, she must remain sexually faithful to her husband. While men may exploit women other than their wives, the slightest suspicion of infidelity, and such suspicions are frequently expressed, gives a man license to beat his wife. For this reason, unaccompanied women do not move about freely, or in cases where they do, as among the Isthmus Zapotecs, they develop effective defensive postures to ward off expected male provocations.[107] In general, however, Zapotec "women do not go out in the streets so that there will be no suspicion of vice."[108]

Thus, there are few, if any, standardized means of reducing female anxieties. *Susto* provides one such mechanism, for its possession gives one license to escape one's normal role and, at least for a time, "provides a channel of escape for the relief of psychological stress engendered within the cultural framework."[109]

Zapotec religion, like most rural folk Catholicism, stresses, or has become adapted to, the exigencies of peasant life. It seems to retain little that is distinctively Zapotec. In the sierra the Zapotec rain god was worshiped until recently,[110] and when Elsie Clews Parsons studied Mitla in the 1930's, *Gusi* (Cocijo) also lived on in Mitla life,[111] but these gods clearly were secondary to the cult of the saints and have today been reduced to remote memory and folktale. Pilgrims still come to Mitla, but now they "visit" with the souls of departed kinsmen on All Souls Day, celebrated throughout Mexico. The Danza de las Plumas, frequently described as Zapotec in tourist literature, takes as its theme the conquest of Moctezuma by Hernán Cortés.

Indigenous concepts have been thoroughly fused with notions emanating from Roman Catholicism; it would thus be difficult, if not unrewarding and impossible, to divide all modern Zapotec beliefs into those elements that are pre-Spanish and those Spanish in origin.

Zapotec religion and beliefs are perhaps best viewed on a level different from a simple list of traits and trait complexes, for most of all they amplify themes which are expressed in other realms of the social and cultural order, providing a kind of map of the role of man in the constant struggle between the forces of good and evil.

As with most Mexican rural Catholicism, great emphasis is given in Zapotec culture to death and suffering. In fact, in her study of the belief system of a Zapotec village in the eastern arm of the Valley of Oaxaca, Fadwa El Guinde remarked that "the only live thing in it was death itself."[112] In this village, there appear to be two primary categories of death: those of "people" and those of "nonpeople." Nonpeople are those who die unbaptized, are murdered, or die by accident or suicide, for in Zapotec peasant belief such deaths are caused by evil acts. There is no ritual activity associated with the death of nonpeople, and they are buried in a different cemetery (the old cemetery) from people.

People who die also are divisible into two categories: *angelitos* and *difuntos*. While most ethnologists have maintained that child or adult status differentiates *angelitos* from *difuntos*, in the community studied by Fadwa El Guinde the distinction is one of *inocente* (innocence) or *pecador* (sin). Marriage is the act that brings about this distinction.

Angelitos (unmarried persons, either children or adults) and *difuntos* (married persons) have different fates and roles in death as they do in life. An *angelito* goes directly to heaven, to peace and serenity, while a *difunto* must struggle in death and achieves peace dependent on the acts of the living. The ritual associated with *angelitos* and *difuntos* is different. Ritual activities for *angelitos* are happy, with dancing, drinking, and joyful activities; those for *difuntos* are sad and morose. While both *angelitos* and *difuntos* are buried in the new cemetery, *angelitos* are interred in the center of the cemetery, undifferentiated as to sex; *difuntos* are placed on the peripheries of the cemetery according to sex distinctions—males to the north, females to the south.

The conception of God or Christ (or more properly Christs, that is, *Cristos*) also has a dual aspect. God or Jesus takes two forms: as a child, he evokes happiness, joy, and life (one year the Christ child is represented as a boy, the next as a girl); and as an adult (or as adults, for he has more than one image in the village), he evokes sadness, suffering, and death. Adult *Cristos* are always male.

The notion of Christ in most Zapotec villages has a similar association with death and suffering, one that frequently does not include the joyful side of the adult Christ complex in Christian thought. For example, Ixtepejanos "identify with a Christ that embodies only certain attributes of the complete Christian myth. The Christ of Ixtepeji suffered martyrdom, agony, and death without the benefits of divine ecstasy, wisdom, and triumph over death by ascension to heaven. All of the numerous images of Christ portray him, in realistic and gory detail, in some part of the Passion. Christ in Ixtepeji never has a halo; he is a Christ of Good Friday, but not Easter Sunday."[113]

In the village studied by Fadwa El Guinde, Christ is opposed by the devil. The devil, like Christ, also takes two forms: a *matlacigua* (woman) and the *diablo* (male). While Christ in his various manifestations is both superhuman and human, devils are superhuman but, unlike Christ, deceptively human; they use their supernatural powers to transform themselves into human forms which tempt, exploit, and bring evil to man—the opposite of Christ. As a female, the devil (known also as María Sánchez and elsewhere in Oaxaca as La Llorona) appears as a beautiful woman who seduces men and takes away their penises. As the *diablo*, he appears as a wealthy *catrín* (mestizo) who tempts people with money. Thus, as a female, sex is the evil peddled by the devil; as a male, money is used to tempt man to do evil.

Belief in witchcraft is pervasive in Zapotec villages, and in a symbolic sense witches (*brujas*) typify all the forces acting on man.[114] Witches may be male or female in sex, but, at least in the village studied by Fadwa El Guinde, could more frequently be associated with women of the village.

But in the minds of these Zapotec villagers there was ambiguity about the sex of witches; frequently they were thought of as combining both male and female characteristics. They might have both male and female sets of breasts (one on top of the other) or the body of a woman and the head of a man. When transformed into their evil state, *brujas* appear to humans as a black or white dog or cat, as a headless donkey, or, more frequently, as a buzzard. In these forms, *brujas*, who otherwise have no special powers, possess the power of killing children and leading adults astray by supernatural means.

Humans generally undergo the transformation into a *bruja* in the cemetery (generally the old cemetery). There, a woman who is a potential witch will remove her head, the process of which will make her into a buzzard. She will then leave the cemetery, kidnap a child, and flee to the *campo* (a field in the countryside) to practice her evil on the child. The witch will then return to the cemetery, where she puts her head back on and thus resumes human form before returning to her home.

The symbolism here appears significant; witches operate in and out of cemeteries, homes, and the *campo*—all of which evoke special feelings in Zapotec peasants. The cemetery is a neutral place, neither bad nor good; the house, on the other hand, is a sacred place without danger where edible food may be found along with drinkable water and where legitimate sex may be practiced—in short, a place favored by Jesus and the saints. The *campo*, however, is a place of distrust and evil, a place of danger, a place where illicit sex is practiced, a place with undrinkable water and inedible food (food and water from the *campo* must be blessed by Christ, who descends each day at noon to do so, before it can be consumed), a place associated with the animal part of a person (*tono* or *nagual*), and a place of the devil. Only evil ritual is practiced in the *campo*, and it is there that witches meet for black masses and play with children as if they were balls, after which time the child falls ill and dies.

Witches usually appear during the "heavy" hours (*horas pesados*) of the day (noon to midnight), hours they share with Jesus, who descends to bless the fields; the places where they are encountered most are at "heavy" intersections (*esquinas pesados*) where two roads cross—a place where devils also are most frequently encountered. *Brujas* thus share the "heavy" hours with Jesus (goodness) and "heavy" intersections with devils (evil).

In short, the belief system surrounding *brujas* embodies those phenomena most intimately associated with modern Zapotec peasant life —households, fields, cemeteries, males, females, children, deception, good, evil, life, and death—and contains a kind of summary of the major beliefs that permeate the emotional life of modern Zapotec peasants.

Epilogue
Zapotecs, Indians, and Peasants

THE DESIGNATION *Zapotec* has varying utility in tracing the long history of the people and the area with which this book has been concerned. Generally, it has been more of an artifact of external observers than a meaningful unit for the people to whom it has been applied.

In pre-Spanish times, for which archeological remains give only hints of ethnic proclivities, Zapotec perhaps was synonymous with an elite speaking a distinct language, presiding over the Classic Monte Albán empire, and with a distinctive art style or culture. In post-Classic times this identification continued, although elites with different ethnic associations influenced the values of the Zapotec nobility to the extent that its cultural distinctiveness was seriously undermined. At the Conquest, probably to both indigenous as well as Spanish observers, the Zapotecs primarily were speakers of a distinct language (or group of languages)—a designation continued until the present; the relationship between this linguistic tag and cultural distinctiveness must have been problematical then as it is today.

Part of this separation between language and culture, or the breakdown of a pervasive ethnicity, must have arisen as Mesoamerican elites intermarried with one another, were conquered by one another, and adopted common values and languages. This process began when power and access to privileged resources became the province of the few, and an increased isolation of elites from commoners must have contributed to it. It is not known to what extent commoners owing allegiance to Zapotec elites were distinctive from commoners owing allegiance to other native Mesoamerican nobilities. Presumably, in the Classic the commoners of the Zapotec empire also spoke Zapotec and shared, if only in a marginal way, in the Zapotec Great Tradition. However, in the post-Classic, when changes in the elite portion of the society were rapid, the extent of this participation probably was much different from earlier Classic times.

In the Colonial period the designation *Zapotec* certainly was secondary to the designation *Indian*. Arising from a misnomer and Columbus' uncertainties of his whereabouts, the latter appellation marked the great mass of "they" as opposed to "we," the Spanish. Relegated to a specific niche in the Spanish Colonial social order, Indians became synonymous with an estate, an estate of commoners. For a while Indian elites lived on, but they, too, lived on primarily as Indians in relationship to the larger society, not as Zapotecs or Mixtecs. Although they may in theory have been separate from others, the processes of the Colonial period ultimately forced them to conform to the mold of a rigid colonial social structure; they either became absorbed into the Spanish Colonial "upper crust" or were reduced to the status of other common Indians.

To the inhabitants of colonial New Spain the term *Indian* became largely synonymous with that great mass of humanity who anthropologists have called peasants. European Spanish society had had long familiarity both with groups of different ethnic persuasions and with peasants. While the two were quite distinct in Spain, in the New World they tended to merge. For Indians were to assume the former role of Spanish peasants; Spaniards, whether peasant in origin or not, sought to abandon the ignobled masses for a station among the ennobled few. And as Spanish society had made few distinctions among Spanish peasants, so Spanish colonial society ultimately was to make few distinctions among Mesoamerican Indians. Further, a similar policy toward Mixtecs, Zapotecs, and others, and the similar manner in which they were embedded in the plural society of New Spain, fostered a common adaptation which tended to undermine their cultural distinctiveness.

While the Indian peasant's way of life has displayed continuities from the colonial past, it has nevertheless undergone changes in the modern period. The Indian in modern Mexico might still be called a peasant, as he is by many anthropologists, but he clearly is a peasant in a different sense than he was in the Colonial period. Independence, the reforms of Juárez, and the Mexican Revolution of 1910 removed the external legal baggage which affiliated Indian peasants with an estate. Furthermore, the increased presence of a cash economy, tourism, and mass media has put the Indian peasants in contact with modern world culture even though their involvement in it remains only peripheral. But the presence of modern mass culture, with its emphasis on material accomplishments and accoutrements, has served primarily to amplify the lowly station of Indian peasants and has made them part of a social class which includes other *campesinos*, whether or not they speak an indigenous language. This social class is defined primarily by its poverty, backwardness, illiteracy, traditionalism, and xenophobia. In short, it is a category, primarily economic, defined by the absence of those things associated with the modern world instead of the presence of a set of legal, social, linguistic, or "racial" attributes used to define the estates or *castas* (mestizos and other "mixed bloods") of the old colonial social order. As such, it may include individuals with all kinds of ethnic, cultural, or linguistic proclivities.

This class also may include the urban poor, for they, too, occupy the bottom of the social order. City dwellers, however, always have elicited more prestige than *campesinos* in Mexican society; when coupled with the alleged benefits of modern mass culture available in the city, this supposed opportunity for greater prestige is bringing *campesinos*, Indians and non-Indians alike, to the swelling urban centers of Mexico. Oaxaca City is exhibiting a similar profile as droves of people are leaving their rural communities and homes to squat on its peripheries or to inhabit its older sections. There, the Indian peasant, formerly the "wretched of the earth," will perhaps become absorbed into an equally old but more rapidly spreading mass of humanity, "the wretched of the city." To have been Zapotec, Indian, or peasant makes little difference in this context.

Appendix

Zapotec Kin Terms: Ancient and Modern

I

HERBERT R. HARVEY has reconstructed the kinship terminology of proto-Zapotec based on a study of terms from Mitla, Tehuantepec, Tlacochahuaya, San Pablo, "Valle," Mixtepec, Teotitlán del Valle, the *Vocabulario* of Córdova, San Agustín Loxicha, Miahuatlán, S.M. Coatlán, Comaltepec, Choapan, Ocotlán, Yalálag, Yatzachi, Arenal Grande, San Juan del Río, Jalahui, and Tres Arroyos.[1] His general conclusions are as follows:

A. Descriptive terms of the bifurcate collateral type were employed for brothers and sisters of parents.

B. The cousin terms were of Hawaiian type.

C. The criterion of sex of speaker was acknowledged in one's own generation and in the first generation above ego for collateral kinsmen as well as affines.

D. There were three terms for children and grandchildren, one of which did not recognize the criterion of sex.

E. Terms for children were extended to include the grandchildren group, although a diminutive form was used for the latter.

F. Distinct terms were employed for mother, father, brother (male speaking), sister (female speaking), sibling of opposite sex, son and grandson (without distinction as to sex), son, daughter, grandson, and granddaughter.

G. Derived terms were employed for grandfather, grandmother and possibly for father-in-law and mother-in-law.

Harvey reconstructs the following terms (numbers to the left are keyed to those in part A, page 276):

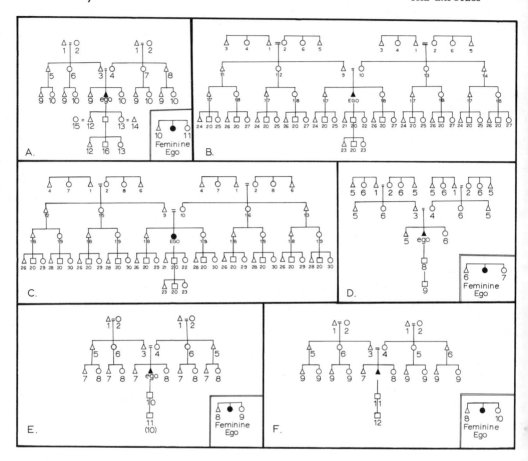

Zapotec kinship terminologies: *a*, Proto-Zapotec; *b*, Córdova, male ego; *c*, Córdova, female ego; *d*, Modern Juquila; *e*, Modern Mitla; *f*, Modern Talea. (Drawn by Terry Prewitt.)

1 *pissosekola	5 *pečˇapiṣṣose	9 *pečˇa
*takola	*pečˇetata	10 *pisaʔna
2 *ṣinakola	6 *pisaʔnapiṣṣose	11 *pelaʔ
*nakola	*pisaʔnatata	12 *ṣinekana
3 *pissose	7 *pisaʔnaṣinaʔ	13 *ṣinesupaʔ
*tata	*pisaʔnanana	14 *suʔčˇa
4 *ṣinaʔa	8 *pečˇeṣinaʔ	15 *suʔliṣṣa
*nana	*peccenana	16 *ṣiyaʔka

Further, Harvey concludes that proto-Zapotec conformed to the general Otomanguean pattern, which contains implications for features of social organization. These features are:

A. A general tendency for bilateral descent

B. The presence of polygyny (although of low frequency)

C. Neolocal or patrilocal residence

D. Patrilocal residence probably was prevalent at the time of the Spanish Conquest, and the tendency toward neolocal residence seems more recent.

Overall, Harvey's reconstruction supports the hypothesis that proto-Zapotec social organization generally conformed to Murdock's Hawaiian type of social organization.

Data from the Córdova and the *Junta Colombina* dictionaries, while extremely difficult to interpret until a complete morphemic analysis of ancient Zapotec has been accomplished, lend further support to the hypothesis that Zapotec social organization at the time of Spanish contact was ambilineal and stressed lineality of descent. The following hypothesis can be made on the basis of data contained in these sources:

A. The avuncular-aunt terms were bifurcate collateral and all terms for consanguineals one generation above ego were descriptive as the terms for MB, MZ, FB, and FZ were derived from combinations of F, M, B, and Z.

B. Parents were distinguished from all others as lineals.

C. Lineal kinsmen two generations above ego were distinguished by generation and sex, and the evidence suggests that FF and MF were brothers while FM and MM were sisters.

D. The cousin terms were Hawaiian.

E. Sons, daughters, and grandchildren were distinguished as direct lineals of ego.

F. For most purposes, consanguineals were distinguished from affinals.

The terms for consanguineal relatives one generation above ego were probably the following (the numbers on the left are keyed to those in parts B and C, page 276) :[2]

Male Ego	Female Ego
Male Ego	*Female Ego*
9 pixoze, tatitia	9 pixoze, tatitia
10 naaya, xinaa	10 naaya, xinaa
11 pechepixoze, pechetitia	12 pizaanapixoze, pizaana titia
12 pizaana pixozea, pizaana titia	15 pela pixoze, pela titia
13 pizaana naaya	13 pizaana naaya
14 peche naaya	16 pela naaya

This is one of the most difficult areas of the terminology to interpret, for both Córdova and the *Junta Colombina* give various entries without noting the sex of speaker. It has been my assumption that a male would apply the sibling designations in the same way that he would for his own generation; that is, MB would be called *peche naaya* instead of *pizaana naaya* (the term given by Córdova for MB); this latter term would presumably be the term used by a female speaker.

Harvey has used the term *xinaacoxana* or *xizanaya* as the descriptive rendering for M and *naaya* as the vocative rendering. Likewise, he has given *pixoze* as descriptive for F and *tatitia* as the vocative. The reasons for such an interpretation are not clear to me. For example, if *xinaacoxana* (from *xinaa*, meaning "kinsman's woman," and *coxana*, meaning "begetter," or "engenderer") was used as the descriptive for mother, then *pixocecoxana* (*bixocegoxana* is recorded in the *Junta Colombina*) must have been the descriptive for F. The meaning of *xizanaya* remains unclear; Córdova also gives it as an alternate for "my father."

I had thought earlier that Córdova also registered a bifurcate merging avuncular terminology and a generational aunt terminology—that is, F, *pixoze*; FB, *pixoze*; M, *naaya*; MB, *pixioa*; MZ, *naaya*; FZ, *naaya*. This now seems unlikely; *pixioa*, for example, is clearly suspect and closely resembles the lexeme for affine, *pixioni*. Many other entries recorded by Córdova also remain unclear.

With reference to the grandparent group (consanguineals two generations above ego), the following terms seem to have been used (the numbers on the left are keyed to those in parts B and C, page 276) :[3]

Male Ego	*Female Ego*
1 pixoze gola, tatitia gola	1 pixoze gola, tatitia gola
2 xoce gola	2 xoce gola
3 pechepixozecolaya, pechetitigolaya	4 pizaanapixocecolaya,
4 pizaanapixocecolaya,	pizaanatitigolaya
pizaanatitigolaya	7 pelapixocecolaya
5 pechexocea	6 pizaanaxocea
6 pizaanaxocea	8 pelaxocea

These data seem to indicate that FF and MF were brothers and FM and MM were sisters as they are equated; note also that FFB is equated with MFB, FFZ with MFZ, FMB with MMB, and FMZ with MMZ. This arrangement seems to suggest that the Zapotecs practiced sister exchange, a practice that would tend to reinforce the ranked status of a ramage and promote ramage endogamy.

The dictionaries clearly indicate that Hawaiian terms were used for all consanguineals within ego's generation.[4] The terms are as follows (numbers on the left are keyed to those in parts B and C, page 276):

Male Ego	*Female Ego*
17 peche	18 pizaana
18 pizaana	19 pela

Other terms recorded by Córdova and the *Junta Colombina* have various analyses. It seems clear, for example, that some are descriptive and single out specific individuals, for example, *xinipizaanatitia*, literally "son of my father's sister." Others, also descriptive, seem to be reciprocal terms between two sons whose mothers were sisters, for example, *xinipelanaaya*, literally, "son of mother's sister." Many other terms for siblings and cousins are found in Córdova which could be analyzed in a similar manner as these other descriptive terms; whether Córdova generated these terms from Zapotec morphemes without there actually being a Zapotec term (always a distinct possibility) cannot be known at present.

The dictionaries also indicate that siblings were divided into categories on the basis of a seniority principle; for example, two terms separated an "ermano mayor" from all other brothers. Within the "ermano menor" category there were four terms distinguishing the age or status of brothers. A similar phenomenon is recorded for female siblings, although only three terms seem to have been employed in this case.

Regarding the child-grandchild-nephew-niece group, the following terms seem to have been employed (numbers on the left are keyed to those in parts B and C, page 276):[5]

Male Ego		*Female Ego*	
20	xini	20	xini
21	xinigana	21	xinigana
22	xinichapa	22	xinichapa
23	xinigagaya	23	xinigagaya
24	xini peche	26	xini pizaana
25	xini chapa peche	29	xini chapa pizaana
26	xini tazanaya, xini pizaana	28	xini chapa pela
27	xini chapa tazanaya, xini chapa pizaana	30	xini chapa pela

This set of terms uses sex distinctions just as the sibling-cousin group does except for S and D, where the distinction is sex of child, not of speaker, and the GS and GD, where no distinction is made as to sex. A general term (*xini*) was employed for all sons, daughters, grandchilden, nephews, and nieces, along with derived descriptive terms for the various categories.

The dictionaries also indicate that distinct terms were used to refer to the relative ages or statuses of children; nine terms are given for male children, for example, while six are recorded for females.

The data in the dictionaries also indicate that all affinals were distinguished from all consanguineals.[6] Derived descriptive terms were employed for father-in-law and mother-in-law; that is, *bixoceguehui* and *xinaaguehui* clearly distinguishing them as affines. Exceptions to the consanguineal-affine distinction may be ZH, called *pechea*, although BW is clearly distinguished as *xinaa pechea* or *chilonaya*. *Peche* was also used to refer to any other Zapotec, as they were all thought to have been descendants from a common source.

Another exception to the affine-consanguineal distinction might be *xocea*, which is used for WBW; this stem, of course, was used in the construction of the terms for MMB, FMB, MMZ, and FMZ. The implication would be that WBW is a "sister" of MM or FM. Given sister exchange, then, she would be a consanguineal to ego.

II

The modern Zapotec kin terminology displays considerable variation, depending on the specific village or region. In general, there have been considerable changes, especially in the areas of the avuncular-aunt group and the cousin-sibling group.

One of the most interesting is the terminology found in the sierra town of Juquila. The terms recorded for that place are as follows (the numbers on the left are keyed to those in part B, page 276) :[7]

1 šoʷzaʔgul	4 šnaʔa	7 rjilaʔ
2 šnaʔagul	5 bulča?	8 rjiʔnaʔ
3 šoʷza?	6 zana?	9 rsua?

Here the descriptive bifurcate collateral character of the terminology for the avuncular-aunt group (one generation above ego) has been lost, although the sex-of-speaker feature has been retained. It is also noteworthy that the generational distinctions of earlier times have broken down, as only F, M, FF-MF, and FM-MM are distinguished. All other consanguineals are equated with B and Z.

A similar classificatory phenomenon is also noted for Yalálag,[8] where brothers, sisters, aunts, uncles, and cousins are equated, distinguished only by the sex of speaker.

Romney has interpreted this phenomenon as a "conservatism" in the kinship terminology of these Zapotec towns.[9] However, the "conservatism" would seem to relate only to the retention of sex-of-speaker criterion. The other features would seem best explained by a tendency toward bilaterality, community endogamy, and a greater nuclear family emphasis since the Spanish Conquest.

Among most modern Zapotec groups, the avuncular-aunt terminology has undergone considerable modification. Consanguineal kinsmen of F and M generation are undistinguished in Mitla, Yatzachi el Bajo, among the Isthmus Zapotecs, in Talea, and in Yalálag.[10] Among most of these groups, Spanish or Spanish-derived terms have been substituted for the Zapotec ones. For example, the following terms are recorded for Mitla and Talea (the numbers on the left are keyed to those in parts E and F, page 276) :[11]

Mitla	Talea
1 statʔgōle (D)	1 šozaʔgul
Datgōl (V)	2 šnaʔagul
2 shmaʔme (D)	3 šoza?
mam (V)	4 šna?
3 shtade (D)	5 tio
dat (V)	6 tia

4 shnana (D)
 nan (V)
5 sti ʔwa (D)
 ti ʔwǎ (V)
 tiwu
6 shnantiwa (D)
 nantiwa (V)
7 be ʔtse
8 Bisiana
9 be ʔle
10 shi ʔne (D and V)
11 sha·ge (D)

7 buľča ʔ
8 zana ʔ
9 primo kiu ʔ
10 řila ʔ
11 ři ʔna ʔ
12 rsna ʔ

The cousin-sibling terms display considerable variation through the area. In Mitla and Yalálag the Hawaiian system remains intact (see Fig. 16 E); in Talea, Yatzachi el Bajo, and the isthmus, Eskimo terms are in evidence. Either type can support a bilateral system, although Eskimo terms are more typical of strong nuclear family systems. Hawaiian terms are, of course, found in all types of kinship terminological systems.[12]

Almost all Zapotec groups continue to employ three terms for B-Z, two denoting sex of sibling and the other as a B-Z reciprocal.

In the child-grandchild terms, simplification also has occurred. Child and grandchild seem almost universally to be distinguished, but sex and other distinctions have by and large disappeared, as they are not reported for most sierra, isthmus, or Valley towns; they still seem to be used among the Southern Zapotec, however.[13]

In many places, Spanish terms are rapidly replacing, or have already replaced, Zapotec ones. Consanguineals are still distinguished from all affinals in some villages, although for "aunts" and "uncles" this tendency is rapidly being undermined. Reciprocal terms of respect, such as *compadre*, *primo*, or *hermano* (and their female equivalents) are replacing much of the old kinship terminology as first names replace kin terms for siblings and others.

Generally, these changes reflect the increased emphasis on bilaterality as opposed to ambilineality, the predominance of nuclear families over wider kin groups, and the increased emphasis on dyadic contracts over consanguineal and affinal ties of kinship. While kin terms are unique in that they reflect linguistic, historical, and perhaps psychological processes, they nevertheless reflect changing emphases in areas of social organization.

Notes

ABBREVIATIONS IN THE NOTES

AA: *American Anthropologist.*

A de A: *Anales de antropología,* Universidad Nacional Autónoma de México.

A del INAH: *Anales del Instituto National de Antropología e Historia,* México.

AGI: Archivo General de Indias, Seville, Spain.

AGN: Archivo General de la Nación, México.

BEO: *Boletín de estudios oaxaqueños,* Mitla, Oaxaca.

B-INAH: *Boletín* Instituto Nacional de Antropología e Historia, México.

Blanton, "Valley of Oaxaca": Richard E. Blanton, "The Valley of Oaxaca Settlement Project: 1971–1972," Progress Report to the National Science Foundation and the Instituto Nacional de Antropología e Historia, unpublished manuscript, 1973.

Burgoa, *GD*: Fray Francisco de Burgoa, *Geográfica descripción,* 2 vols. (Mexico, 1934; Orig. 1674).

Butterworth, "Relaciones": Douglas Butterworth (trans. and ed.), "Relaciones of Oaxaca of the 16th and 17th Centuries," *Boletín de estudios oaxaqueños,* no. 23 (1962).

Córdova, *Arte*: Fray Juan de Córdova, *Arte del idioma zapoteca* (Morelia, Michoacán, 1886; Orig., *Arte en lengua zapoteca,* México, 1578).

Córdova, *Vocabulario*: Fray Juan de Córdova, *Vocabulario castellano-zapoteco* (México, 1942; Orig., *Vocabulario en lengua zapoteca,* México 1578).

DII: *Colección de documentos inéditos relativos al descubrimiento, conquista, y organización de las antiguas posesiones españolas de América y Oceania, sacados de los archivos del reino, y muy especialmente del de Indias,* 42 vols. (Madrid, 1864-84).

ENE: Francisco del Paso y Troncoso (ed.), *Epistolario de Nueva España,* 16 vols. (México, 1932-42).

Flannery, "Farming Eystems": Kent V. Flannery, Anne V. T. Kirkby, Michael J. Kirkby, and Aubrey W. Williams, "Farming Systems and Political Growth in Ancient Oaxaca," *Science,* Vol. 158, no. 3800 (October 27, 1967), 445-54.

Flannery, "Village": Kent V. Flannery, "The Origins of the Village as a Settlement Type in Mesoamerica and the Near East," in Peter J. Ucko, Ruth Tringham, and G. W. Dimbleby (eds.), *Man, Settlement and Urbanism* (London and Cambridge, Mass., 1972), 23-53. Also a *Warner Modular Publication,* Reprint No. 1, Andover, Mass., 1972.

HAHR: *Hispanic American Historical Review.*

HBMAI: Robert Wauchope (gen. ed.), *Handbook of Middle American Indians,* 13 vols. (Austin, Texas, 1964-74).

Horcasitas and George, "Relación": Fernando Horcasitas and Richard George (trans.

and eds.), "The Relación de Tlacolula y Mitla," *Mesoamerican Notes*, Vol. 4 (México, 1955), 13–24.

IJAL: *International Journal of American Linguistics.*

Junta Colombina: *Vocabulario castellano-zapoteco* (México, 1893).

Kirkby, *Land and Water*: Anne V. T. Kirkby, *The Use of Land and Water Resources in the Past and Present Valley of Oaxaca, Mexico. Memoirs of the Museum of Anthropology, University of Michigan*, No. 5 (Kent V. Flannery [gen. ed.], *Prehistory and Human Ecology of the Valley of Oaxaca*, Vol. 1), Ann Arbor, 1973.

Lees, *Irrigation*: Susan H. Lees, *Sociopolitical Aspects of Canal Irrigation in the Valley of Oaxaca. Memoirs of the Museum of Anthropology, University of Michigan*, No. 6 (Kent V. Flannery [gen. ed.], *Prehistory and Human Ecology of the Valley of Oaxaca*, Vol. 2), Ann Arbor, 1973.

Mendieta, *Zapotecos*: Lucio Mendieta y Núñez, *Los zapotecos: monografía histórica, etnográfica y económica* (México, 1949).

Paddock, *AO*: John Paddock (ed.), *Ancient Oaxaca: Discoveries in Mexican Archeology and History* (Stanford, Calif., 1966).

PNE: Francisco del Paso y Troncoso (ed.), *Papeles de Nueva España*, 9 vols. (Madrid and México, 1905–1908).

RMEA: *Revista mexicana de estudios antropológicos.*

RMEH: *Revista mexicana de estudios históricos.*

Spores, *Mixtec*: Ronald Spores, *The Mixtec Kings and Their People* (Norman, Okla., 1967).

SWJA: *Southwestern Journal of Anthropology.*

Taylor, *CO*: William B. Taylor, *Landlord and Peasant in Colonial Oaxaca* (Stanford, Calif., 1972).

1. OAXACA AND THE ZAPOTECS

1. Various attempts to define an Indian in Mexico are reviewed by Anselmo Marino Flores, "Indian Population and Its Identification," *HBMAI*, Vol. 6 (1967), 12–25.

2. May N. Diaz, *Tonalá* (Berkeley and Los Angeles, 1966), 37–38, 43.

3. These data are contained in the 1970 Mexican census: Estados Unidos Mexicanos, Secretaría de Industria y Comercio, Dirección General de Estadística, *IX Censo general de población, 1970* (México, 1971), Vol. 1, 259–66; see especially 265. Vol. 20 (Pts. I and II) deals specifically with Oaxaca.

Table 4. Indigenous Languages in the Republic
of Mexico with the Largest Numbers of Speakers

	1950			1970	
1.	Nahuatl	641,334	1.	Nahuatl	799,394
2.	Maya	328,255	2.	Maya	454,675
3.	*Zapotec*	226,995	3.	*Zapotec*	285,345
4.	Otomí	185,656	4.	Mixtec	233,235
5.	Mixtec	185,470	5.	Otomí	221,062
6.	Totonac	106,696	6.	Totonac	124,840
7.	Mazahua	84,125	7.	Mazahua	104,729
8.	Mazatec	77,530	8.	Mazatec	101,541
9.	Tzotzil	74,827	9.	Tzeltal	99,412
10.	Huastec	66,646	10.	Tzotzil	95,383

Additional data on indigenous languages are presented in tables 4, 5, and 6. The 1950 data are from Flores, "Indian Population and Its Identification," *HBMAI*, Vol. 6 (1967), 20–23. All data on indigenous speakers refer to members of the population five years of age and older.

Table 5. Indigenous Languages in the Republic of
Mexico with Largest Numbers of Monolingual Speakers

	1950			1970	
1.	Nahuatl	212,813	1.	Nahuatl	227,757
2.	Mixtec	76,946	2.	Mixtec	79,332
3.	*Zapotec*	60,680	3.	Maya	68,459
4.	Otomí	57,559	4.	Tzeltal	57,314
5.	Totonac	54,333	5.	Mazatec	54,282
6.	Maya	50,912	6.	Tzotzil	50,329
7.	Mazatec	47,167	7.	*Zapotec*	49,652
8.	Tzotzil	44,103	8.	Totonac	42,262
9.	Tzeltal	31,856	9.	Otomí	37,701
10.	Mixe	21,005	10.	Chol	30,434

Table 6. Percentage of Monolinguals among Those Speaking Indigenous Languages
in the Republic of Mexico

	1950			1970	
1.	Tlapanec	67.4		Amuzgo	63.9
2.	Tzeltal	66.0		Tzeltal	57.7
3.	Chatino	61.4		Tlapanec	56.2
4.	Mazatec	60.8		Mazatec	53.5
5.	Chol	60.7		Tzotzil	52.8
6.	Tzotzil	58.9		Chatino	48.3
7.	Totonac	50.9		Chol	41.5
8.	Mixtec	45.6		Mixe	38.0
9.	Amuzgo	45.5		Cora	37.6
10.	Tarascan	44.3		Huave	37.4
11.	Chinantec	44.0		Huichol	34.8
12.	Mixe	41.5		Mixtec	34.0
13.	Tepehuan	33.8		Totonac	33.9
14.	Otomí	31.0		Tarahumara	31.7
15.	Nahuatl	30.1		Nahuatl	28.5
16.	Huichol	30.0		Zoque	27.9
17.	*Zapotec*	26.7		Chinantec	25.7
18.	Zoque	26.7		Tepehuan	18.7
19.	Kickapoo	26.4		Huastec	18.0
20.	Huastec	25.9		*Zapotec*	*17.5*
21.	Tarahumara	22.2		Tarascan	17.5
22.	Mazahua	19.3		Popoloca	17.1
23.	Maya	15.5		Otomí	17.1
24.	Popoloca	9.1		Maya	15.1
25.	Mayo	8.1		Cuicatec	12.0

4. This phylum also has been called Macro-Manguean or Macro-Otomanguean. The Otomanguean designation was proposed in 1936 by Miguel Othón de Mendizábal and Wigberto Jiménez Moreno, *Mapa lingüístico de Norte- y Centro-América* (México, 1936); for a more formal demonstration of the unity of Otomanguean, see María Teresa Fernández de Miranda and R. J. Weitlaner, "Sobre algunas relaciones de la familia mangue," *Anthropological Linguistics*, Vol. 3, No. 7 (1961).

Morris Swadesh has denied the relationship of Zapotecan and Mixtecan to the Manguean languages although he accepts the relationship among Zapotecan, Mixtecan, and Otomian; he posits instead an Oto-Huavean, Oto-Zapotecan, or Macro-Mixtecan phylum; see his *Estudios de lengua y cultura* (México, 1959); "The Otomanguean Hypothesis and Macro-Mixtecan," *IJAL*, Vol. 26 (1960), 79–111; and "Lexicostatistic Classification," *HBMAI*, Vol. 5 (1967), 79–115. See also R. J. Weitlaner, Morris Swadesh, and María Teresa Fernández de Miranda, "Some Findings on Oaxaca Language Classification and Cultural Terms," *IJAL*, Vol. 25 (1959), 54–58.

Robert E. Longacre, "Swadesh's Macro-Mixtecan Hypothesis," *IJAL*, Vol. 27 (1961), 9–29; "Systemic Comparison and Reconstruction," *HBMAI*, Vol. 5 (1967), 117–59; and D. L. Olmstead, "Lexicostatistics as Proof of Genetic Relationship: The Case of Macro-Manguean," *Anthropological Linguistics*, Vol. 3, No. 6 (1961), 9–15, have been critical of Swadesh's classifications, in particular his use of lexicostatistics as a method for determining the genetic relationships of languages.

For a more extensive bibliography on Otomanguean, see María Teresa Fernández de Miranda, "Inventory of Classificatory Materials," *HBMAI*, Vol. 6 (1967), 67–72.

My designation of the branches of Otomanguean has been considerably simplified. Otomian, for example, often is referred to as Oto-Pamean. Also, I here have used the term Mixtecan for the branch instead of Popotecan (a coined word combining Popolocan and Mixtecan). The term Mixtecan has been used more frequently by linguists to designate the family which includes Mixtec, Trique, and Cuicatec.

Sarah C. Gudschinsky has demonstrated the unity of Popotecan (my Mixtecan) in her *Proto-Popotecan: A Comparative Study of Popolocan and Mixtecan, Indiana University Publications in Anthropology and Linguistics*, No. 15 (1959), and has defined the Mazatec family in "Proto-Mazatec Structure," Ph.D. diss., University of Pennsylvania, 1956; María Teresa Fernández de Miranda has defined the Popoloca family (Popoloca, Ixcatec, and Chocho) in "Reconstrucción de protopopoloca," *RMEA*, Vol. 12 (1951), 61–93; in "Resumen sobre la reconstrucción del protopopoloca," in Ignacio Bernal and E. Dávalos (eds.), *Huastecos y Totonacos*, (México, 1953), 115–17; and in *Glotocronología de la familia popoloca, Museo Nacional de Antropología, Serie Científica*, No. 4 (México, 1956).

Robert E. Longacre in *Proto-Mixtecan, Indiana University Research Center in Anthropology and Linguistics*, Publication No. 5 (1957), has shown the unity of Mixtec, Trique, ad Cuicatec as a separate family. He also has argued that Amuzgo reconstructs on an earlier horizon than the other languages of the Mixtec family in "On the Linguistic Affinities of Amuzgo," *IJAL*, Vol. 32 (1966), 46–49. For the potential value of linguistic reconstructions for cultural history, see Robert E. Longacre and René Millon, "Proto-Mixtecan and Proto-Amuzgo Vocabularies: A Preliminary Cultural Analysis," *Anthropological Linguistics*, Vol. 3 (1961), 1–44.

Swadesh, "Lexicostatistic Classification," *HBMAI*, Vol. 5 (1967), 96–98, has placed Huave in his Oaxacan branch of languages and thus related it to Zapotecan and Popotecan (Mixtecan); since the affinities of Huave remain unclear (others relate it to Maya-Zoque), I have not included it here.

On Chinantec, see R. J. Weitlaner and Pablo Smith, *Notas sobre la fonología del idioma proto-chinanteco* (México, 1957); on the Mangue family, which reconstructs on an earlier level than other families of Otomanguean, see Fernández de Miranda and Weitlaner, "Sobre algunas relaciones de la familia mangue," *Anthropological Linguistics*, Vol. 3, No. 7 (1961).

5. The relationship of Chatino to the Zapotec languages proper has long been posited; an early demonstration was by Morris Swadesh, "The Phonemic Structure of Proto-Zapotec," *IJAL*, Vol. 13 (1947), 220–30. Juan José Rendón has added an additional language to the Zapotecan branch—Papabuco, spoken in the southern part of Oaxaca—see *Boletín bibliográfico de antropología americana*, Vol. 35 (1972), 25. Juan José Rendón, "Relaciones internas de las lenguas de la familia zapoteco-chatino," *A de A*, Vol. 4 (1967), 187–90, also claims Chatino is related to the other Zapotec languages but at a somewhat greater distance, with nineteen or more centuries of separation from them, and, therefore, forms a separate division within Zapotecan. However, Gabriel De Cicco, "The Chatino," *HBMAI*, Vol. 7 (1969), 360, states that Chatino is closer to the neighboring Zapotec dialects (Southern Zapotec) than to Valley Zapotec.

6. This reconstruction is based on Eric R. Wolf, *Sons of the Shaking Earth*, 35–42,

288   THE ZAPOTECS

and Ralph L. Beals, "Southern Mexican Highlands and Adjacent Coastal Regions: Introduction," *HBMAI*, Vol. 7 (1969), 322–26.

7. Archeological evidence, based on excavations by Kent V. Flannery (see Chapter 2) indicates that the Zapotecs possibly were present in the Valley of Oaxaca by 1450 B.C.

On the basis of linguistic evidence, Beals has argued that the point of divergence of the Otomanguean languages, and thus the homeland of the Zapotecs, was in the highland valleys and tributaries of the Balsas and Papaloapan rivers, "Southern Mexican Highlands and Adjacent Coastal Regions: Introduction," *HBMAI*, Vol. 7 (1969), 323. Herbert R. Harvey, "Cultural Continuity in Central Mexico: A Case for Otomangue," *Actas y memorias del XXXV Congreso Internacional de Americanistas*, Vol. 2 (México, 1964), 525–32, posits that northeastern Oaxaca was the most probable center where the Otomanguean languages dispersed; Swadesh, "The Phonemic Structure of Proto-Zapotec," *IJAL*, Vol. 13 (1947), 220–30, sees the homeland of the Zapotecs as north of the Sierra de Villa Alta and northeast of the Sierra de Juárez; Wolf, *Sons of the Shaking Earth*, 40, also postulates a northerly place of origin for the Zapotecs, although his location is more westerly than that of most investigators.

8. Some descriptive works on the Zapotec languages include: Morris Swadesh, "El idioma de los zapotecos," in Mendieta, *Zapotecos*, (415–49), on which my depiction is largely based; Paul Radin, "A Preliminary Sketch of the Zapotec Language," *Language*, Vol. 6 (1930), 64–85; Jaime de Angulo, "Tone Patterns and Verb Forms in a Dialect of Zapotec," *Language*, Vol. 2 (1926), 238–50; Eleanor Briggs, *Mitla Zapotec Grammar* (México, 1961); V. B. Pickett, *Dialecto del zapoteco del istmo* (México, 1959); *The Grammatical Hierarchy of Isthmus Zapotec* (Baltimore, 1960); and "Type Linguistic Descriptions: Isthmus Zapotec," *HBMAI*, Vol. 5 (1967), 291–310; Eunice V. Pike, "Problems in Zapotec Tone Analysis," *IJAL*, Vol. 14 (1948), 161–70; and Juan José Rendón, "Notas fonológicas del zapoteco de Tlacochahuaya," *A de A*, Vol. 7 (1970), 247–62.

9. For studies of the influence of Spanish on Zapotec, see Andrés Henestrosa, *Los hispanismos en el idioma zapateco* (México, 1965), and María Teresa Fernández de Miranda, "Los préstamos españoles en el zapoteco de Mitla," *A del INAH*, Vol. 17 (1965), 259–73. Studies of the influence of Zapotec on Spanish remain to be undertaken.

10. For studies of the Zapotec language, folklore, customs, songs, poetry, and dances by *istmeños*, see *Neza: Órgano mensual de la sociedad nueva de estudios Juchitecos* (1935–?); for the numerous works dealing with such matters, see Jorge Martínez Rios, *Bibliografía antropológica y sociológica del Estado de Oaxaca* (México, 1961).

11. For amplification of this point, see Laura Nader, "The Zapotec of Oaxaca," *HBMAI*, Vol. 7 (1969), 331.

12. This classification was proposed in 1905 by F. Belmar, *Lenguas indígenas de México* (México, 1905). It has been followed with minor modifications by Paul Radin, "The Distribution and Phonetics of the Zapotec Dialects," *Journal de la société des Américanistes*, Vol. 17 (1925), 27–76; Swadesh, "El idioma de los zapotecos," in Mendieta, *Zapotecos*, 415–48; and Jaime de Angulo and S. L. Freeland, "The Zapotecan Linguistic Group," *IJAL*, Vol. 8 (1933-1934), 71–83, 111–30. Rendón, "Relaciones internas de las lenguas de la familia zapoteco-chatino," *A de A*, Vol. 4 (1967) 187–90, proposes four subdivisions for the Zapotecan branch: (1) Mitla, Juchitán and Tejalapan, which has an interval divergence of six and five-tenths to eight and five-

tenths centuries; (2) Loxicha and Miahuatlán, with at least seven centuries of divergence; (3) northern Zapotec languages (Atepec, Comaltepec, and Yatzachi) with nine and five-tenths to twelve centuries of divergence; and (4) Chatino, with a divergence of nineteen or more centuries. This study, based on the collection of word lists and on glottochronological considerations, is part of a larger study projected by Rendón of all the Zapotecan languages.

13. As proposed by Laura Nader and R. J. Weitlaner; see Nader, "The Zapotec of Oaxaca," *HBMAI*, Vol. 7 (1969), 331.

14. Environmental aspects of the Valley of Oaxaca are discussed in Flannery, "Farming Systems"; José L. Lorenzo, "Aspectos físicos del valle de Oaxaca," *RMEA*, Vol. 16 (1960), 49–64; and Kirkby, "Land and Water," 7–25. A more extensive geographical study of the Valley by Michael J. Kirkby soon will be published by the Museum of Anthropology of the University of Michigan.

15. Beverly Chiñas, *The Isthmus Zapotecs: Women's Roles in Cultural Context*; for the traditional view, see Miguel Covarrubias, *Mexico South: The Isthmus of Tehuantepec*.

16. For a historical, geographical, and ethnographic description of the isthmus, see Covarrubias, *Mexico South*.

17. For a bibliography on the Southern Zapotec, see Nader, "The Zapotec of Oaxaca," *HBMAI*, Vol. 7 (1969), 329–59.

2. THE GROWTH OF THE ZAPOTEC GREAT TRADITION

1. The information on the etymology of the words *Zapotec* and *Mixtec* follows John Paddock, "Oaxaca in Ancient Mesoamerica," in Paddock, *AO*, 238–39. Paddock bases his reconstruction of the Zapotec *Ben 'Zaa* on Howard Leigh, "The Zapotec Name for the Zapotecs," *BEO*, No. 18 (1960). The modern Zapotecs of the isthmus refer to "the ancients" as *Binii Gula'sa'*; see Beverly Chiñas, *The Isthmus Zapotecs*, 10. Earlier scholars had surmised that the Zapotecs called themselves *Didjazaa*, from *didja*, "tongue or speech" and *zaa*, "cloud or sky." But this interpretation is probably in error, for the Zapotec word for "people" is *bene*, *pene*, or some similar rendering; for the earlier interpretation, see Manuel Martínez Gracida, *El rey Cocijoeza y su familia* (México, 1888), 163–64.

2. For citations to the sources of these legends, see Philip Dark, "Speculations on the Course of Mixtec History Prior to the Conquest," *BEO*, No. 10 (1958), and Spores, *Mixtec*, 61–62.

3. The Zapotec legends can be found in Burgoa, *GD*, Vol. 2, 117, and in Juan de Torquemada, *Los viente i un libros rituales y monarchía indiana* (México, 1943), 117; see also Paddock, "Oaxaca in Ancient Mesoamerica," in Paddock, *AO*, 239.

4. Alfonso Caso established the basic Monte Albán sequence during excavations in the 1930's and concluded, on the basis of cultural continuities to Spanish Conquest times, that the Monte Albán III and IV inhabitants of the Valley of Oaxaca were Zapotec. However, he did not project this identification onto earlier periods. Subsequently, most investigators have followed Caso's suggestion; see Paddock, "Oaxaca in Ancient Mesoamerica," in Paddock, *AO*, 126, and Ignacio Bernal, "Archaeological Synthesis of Oaxaca," *HBMAI*, Vol. 3 (1965), 802. Recently, however, Kent V. Flannery and Richard E. Blanton (personal communications, 1974), currently conducting archeological studies of the Valley, contend that cultural continuities persist

from at least 1400 B.C. and thus suggest that the earlier inhabitants also should be identified as Zapotecs.

5. The dating of the Monte Albán sequence is being continually revised through new radiocarbon dates, changing interpretations of the old dates, and additional archeological evidence. Therefore, these dates are to be considered tentative. The dates for Monte Albán I and II are those currently being employed by Kent V. Flannery and are based on recent radiocarbon determinations (Flannery, personal communications, 1974). Those for Monte Albán III, IV, and V are the more traditional dates and follow, with minor modification, Bernal, "Archaeological Synthesis of Oaxaca," *HBMAI*, Vol. 3 (1965), 789.

6. The earlier excavations at Monte Albán are discussed in Alfonso Caso, *Las exploraciones en Monte Albán, Temporada, 1934–1935* (México, 1935); *Exploraciones en Oaxaca, quinta y sexta temporadas 1936–1937* (México, 1938); and "Resumen del informe de las exploraciones en Oaxaca, durante la 7a y la 8a temporadas, 1937–1938 y 1938–1939," *Actas del XXVII Congreso Internacional de Americanistas*, Vol. 2 (México, 1939), 159–87. An archeological survey of the Valley of Oaxaca which determined the basic chronological and geographical extension of the Monte Albán periods is reported in Ignacio Bernal, "Distribución geográfica de las culturas de Monta Albán," *El México Antiguo*, Vol. 7 (1949), 209–16.

7. Both Paddock, "Oaxaca in Ancient Mesoamerica," in Paddock, *AO*, 127, and Bernal, "Archaeological Synthesis of Oaxaca," *HBMAI*, Vol. 3 (1965), 801–803, single out these "transitions."

8. This sequence has been worked out by Kent V. Flannery and his associates and forms a long-term project entitled "Prehistory and Human Ecology of the Valley of Oaxaca, Mexico." Two volumes have so far appeared in connection with the project: Kirkby, *Land and Water*, and Lees, *Irrigation*. Other publications dealing with the early sequence include Flannery, "Farming Systems," Flannery, "Village," and Kent V. Flannery, "The Olmec and the Valley of Oaxaca," in E. P. Benson (ed.), *Dumbarton Oaks Conference on the Olmec* (Washington, D.C., 1968), 79–117. The Rosario phase is not discussed in the above publications, but recently has been defined (Kent V. Flannery, personal communications, 1974).

9. Julian H. Steward, "Cultural Causality and Law: A Trial Formulation of the Development of Early Civilizations," *AA*, Vol. 51 (1949), 1–27, and Eric R. Wolf, *Sons of the Shaking Earth*, 48–151, have also emphasized the sociopolitical or sociocultural aspects of the Mesoamerican stages; Gordon R. Willey and Philip Phillips, *Method and Theory in American Archaeology* (Chicago, 1958), were among the first archeologists to point out that developmental stages and chronological periods should be treated as separate concepts.

10. The two most recent syntheses of Oaxacan archeology are those of Paddock, "Oaxaca in Ancient Mesoamerica," in Paddock, *AO*, 83–243, and Bernal, "Archaeological Synthesis of Oaxaca," *HBMAI*, Vol. 3 (1965), 788–813. For the pre–Monte Albán sequence, see note 8 above. For good general summaries of Mesoamerican prehistory, see Wolf, *Sons of the Shaking Earth*, 48–151; William T. Sanders and Barbara J. Price, *Mesoamerica*, and Murial Porter Weaver, *The Aztecs, Maya and Their Predecessors* (New York and London, 1972).

11. V. Gordon Childe, in *Man Makes Himself* (London, 1956) and *What Happened in History* (Baltimore, 1957), is perhaps the single most important author who has influenced anthropological conceptions of civilization, drawing heavily on the much earlier work of Lewis Henry Morgan. The problems with Childe's formulations, as

well as with those of more recent anthropologists, have been extensively critiqued by Paul Wheatley, *The Pivot of the Four Quarters* (Chicago, 1971) and "The Concept of Urbanism," *A Warner Modular Publication*, Reprint No. 12 (Andover, Mass., 1972).

12. The problem is, of course, much more complex than I have formulated it here. A civilization is not easily defined: For example, should reference be made to Greek civilization, Hellenic civilization, or Western civilization? Is Byzantine civilization a new one or simply a fusion of the Hellenic and Western Roman traditions, which is also a fusion? I am inclined to believe that the term *civilization*, like the culture area concept, has very limited utility when it cannot be related to societal forms, such as states. It may be that the crystallization of any civilization requires political unification at some point in its history, or at the very least, a common elite united by ties of marriage and kinship. However, much more investigation is needed into the topic that Robert Redfield referred to as "the social organization of tradition"; for Redfield's works, see *Peasant Society and Culture, The Primitive World and Its Transformations* (Ithaca, N.Y., 1956), and *Human Nature and the Study of Society* (Chicago, 1962), in which he explicates his notions on civilization, the "Great Tradition," and the "little tradition."

13. For the food-collecting phase, see Flannery, "Farming Systems," 450.

14. For a discussion of Early Formative sites, see Flannery, "Farming Systems," 450–51, and Kirkby, *Land and Water*, 129–33; a discussion of well-pot irrigation may be found in Flannery, "Farming Systems," 50, and Kirkby, *Land and Water*, 41–45.

15. Flannery, "Village," 22–23, stated that Tierras Largas by 1300 b.c. had some six to twelve households and by 900 b.c. contained twelve to twenty households; but these data recently have been "revised on the basis of finer chronology" (Kent V. Flannery, personal communications, 1974). The new data seem to indicate that roughly eight to ten households was the "modal size for early hamlets in Oaxaca." The Tierras Largas phase is defined and extensively described in Marcus Winter, "Tierras Largas: A Formative Community in the Valley of Oaxaca," Ph.D. Diss., University of Arizona, 1972.

16. Kirkby, *Land and Water*, 141–46.

17. Information on houses and households at San José Mogote is found in Flannery, "Village," 22–24, and Flannery, "Farming Systems," 450–51.

18. Traits associated with the Olmec style are the *danzantes* of Monte Albán I times and the stone carvings of Dainzú, along with some influences in ceramics; these traits also are thought to persist into Monte Albán II times although their influence is not as pervasive there. See Bernal, "Archaeological Synthesis of Oaxaca," *HBMAL*, Vol. 3, 798–99, "Excavaciones en Dainzú," *B*-INAH, No. 27 (1967), 7–13, and "The Ball Players of Dainzú," *Archeology*, Vol. 21, No. 4 (1968), 246–51; for speculations on the possible existence of an "Olmec empire," see Alfonso Caso, "¿Existió un imperio olmeca?" *Memorias de El Colegio Nacional*, Vol. 5, No. 3 (1965). Good summaries of the Olmec materials in general, along with discussions of Olmec manifestations in Oaxaca, may be found in Ignacio Bernal, *The Olmec World* and Charles R. Wicke, *Olmec* (Tucson, Ariz., 1971).

19. Flannery, "The Olmec and the Valley of Oaxaca," 79–117.

20. Data on the number of sites in the Valley of Oaxaca during various periods may be found in Bernal, "Distribución geográfica de las culturas de Monte Albán," *El México Antiguo*, Vol. 7 (1949), 209–16; Kirkby, *Land and Water*, 129–37; and Blanton, "Valley of Oaxaca," 12. Blanton's data are based on a survey by Marcus Winter, a co-investigator on the Monte Albán project.

21. Flannery, "Farming Systems," 451–52; see also James A. Neely, "Organización hidráulica y sistemas de irrigación prehistóricos en el Valle de Oaxaca," *B*-INAH, No. 27 (1967), 15–17.

22. Blanton, "Valley of Oaxaca," 19.

23. For Dainzú, see note 14.

24. This phrase is borrowed from Flannery, "Farming Systems," 452.

25. The hydraulic theory is associated with Karl A. Wittfogel, *Oriental Despotism* (New Haven, 1957), and Julian H. Steward, *Theory of Culture Change* (Urbana, Ill., 1955).

26. Wheatley, *The Pivot of the Four Quarters*, 289–98, reviews the recent evidence on irrigation; Robert McC. Adams, *The Evolution of Urban Society* (Chicago, 1966), presents the evidence for Mesoamerica and Mesopotamia.

27. Flannery, "Village," 24, has pointed out that agriculture no longer necessarily correlates with sedentary life and nucleated settlements. The quote also is from Flannery, "Village," 48, originally in Marshall D. Sahlins, "Essays in Stone Age Economics," unpublished manuscript.

Evidence that hunters and gatherers are underproductive is presented in R. B. Lee and I. De Vore (eds.), *Man the Hunter* (Chicago, 1968). Of the many studies of extensive agriculture and its implications, perhaps the best are Robert Carneiro, "Slash-and-Burn Agriculture," in A.F.C. Wallace (ed.), *Men and Cultures* (Philadelphia, 1960), 229–34, and "Slash-and-Burn Cultivation among the Kuikuru and Its Implications for Cultural Development in the Amazon Basin," in Yehudi A. Cohen (ed.), *Man in Adaptation: The Cultural Present* (Chicago, 1968), 131–45.

28. The literature dealing with this topic is vast, and all authors would not necessarily agree with my contention. Wheatley, *The Pivot of the Four Quarters*, supports the notion that no single causal factor can explain the origin of the state. Don E. Dumond, "Population Growth and Political Centralization," in Brian Spooner (ed.), *Population Growth* (Cambridge, Mass., 1972), 286–310, sees population growth as a necessary but not sufficient cause of political centralization. William T. Sanders, "Population, Agricultural History, and Societal Evolution in Mesoamerica," also in Spooner, *Population Growth*, 147, questions the "unidirectional cause-and-effect relationship between population growth and agricultural systems" but still seems to favor some variation of the hydraulic theory. Robert L. Carneiro, "A Theory of the Origin of the State," *Science*, Vol. 169 (1970), 733–38, would seem to favor a unicausal theory linked to population pressure. Kent V. Flannery, "The Cultural Evolution of Civilizations," in Richard F. Johnson, Peter W. Frank, and Charles D. Michener (eds.), *Annual Review of Ecology and Systematics* (Palo Alto, Calif., 1972), 399–425, not only rejects a unicausal or prime mover theory, but also provides one of the first attempts toward the systematization of alternative factors or processes which could give rise to the state. Flannery also has pointed out, based on Lees, *Irrigation*, that water control is one likely resource around which the state can promote greater centralization. However, this likelihood would not seem to imply that irrigation is either a necessary or a sufficient cause of political centralization.

29. Wheatley, *The Pivot of the Four Quarters*, advocates the position that religion was an important force in the development of the state and that the ceremonial center was the earliest form in which increased power was expressed. Robert McC. Netting, "Sacred Power and Centralization," in Spooner, *Population Growth*, 219–44, constitutes an important essay on the role of the religious practitioner in the centralization of power.

Ideology or religion as a mechanism for the legitimation of power has a large literature. In addition to the above, I have been particularly influenced, as has Paul Wheatley, by Numa Denis de Fustel de Coulanges, *The Ancient City* (Garden City, N.Y., n.d. [original 1864]), and the writings of Max Weber, Vilfredo Pareto, and Gaetano Mosca—the classic sociological authorities on power relationships.

30. Blanton, "Valley of Oaxaca," 21.

31. *Ibid.*, 35; the investigation of the irrigation system at Monte Albán was conducted by James A. Neely of the University of Texas, co-investigator in the Blanton project.

32. See Wilfrido Cruz, *Oaxaca recóndita* (México, 1946); for another discussion, see José María Bradomín, *Toponimia de Oaxaca* (México, 1955), 18–19.

33. This was first suggested by Leopoldo Batres, who excavated Monte Albán toward the turn of the century; it later was expanded by Paul Van de Velde. See George Russell Steininger and Paul Van de Velde, *Three Dollars a Year* (New York, 1935), 110. Van de Velde claims that the Zapotecs called Monte Albán "Danni Dipaa," which means "fortified hill."

34. The first two suggestions are traditional ones and go back many years; the latter suggestion is that of Michael D. Coe, *Mexico* (New York, 1962), 95–96.

35. See Bernal, "The Ball Players of Dainzú," *Archaeology*, Vol. 21, No. 4 (1968), 246–51.

36. Bernal, "Archaeological Synthesis of Oaxaca," *HBMAI*, Vol. 3 (1965), 798.

37. A similar structure, although smaller, has been found at Caballito Blanco in the Valley arm of Tlacolula.

38. Alfonso Caso, "Calendario y escritura de las antiguas culturas de Monte Albán," in *Obras completas de Miguel Othón de Mendizábal* (México, 1947), Vol. 1, 113–44; Joyce Marcus is conducting a study of Zapotec epigraphy in which she has identified a number of these place glyphs (Kent V. Flannery, personal communication, 1974).

39. Bernal, "Archaeological Synthesis of Oaxaca," *HBMAI*, Vol. 3 (1965), 800–801.

40. Blanton, "Valley of Oaxaca," 11, 20–21; Bernal, "Archaeological Synthesis of Oaxaca, *HBMAI*, Vol. 3 (1965), 801.

41. See René Millon, "Urna de Monte Albán IIIA encontrada en Teotihuacán," *B-INAH*, No. 27 (1967), 42–44.

42. For Classic Monte Albán influences in the Isthmus of Tehuantepec, see Agustín Delgado, "La secuencia arqueológica en el Istmo de Tehuantepec," in *Los mayas del sur y sus relaciones con los nahuas meridionales* (México, 1961), 93–104; James R. Forster, "Notas sobre la arqueología de Tehuantepec," *A del INAH*, Vol. 7 (1953), 77–100; and Matthew Wallrath, *Excavations in the Tehuantepec Region, Mexico* (Philadelphia, 1967). For the Pacific Coast, see Donald L. Brockington, "Investigaciones arqueológicas en la Costa de Oaxaca," *B-INAH*, No. 38 (1969), 33–39; for Monte Albán influence on the Mixteca Alta, see Ronald Spores, "Exploraciones arqueológicas en el Valle de Nochixtlan," *B-INAH*, No. 37 (1969), 35–42, and Ronald Spores, *An Archaeological Settlement Survey at the Nochixtlan Valley, Vanderbilt University Publications in Anthropology*, No. 1 (1972). Ignacio Bernal, "Urna Mixteca," *B-INAH*, No. 32 (1968), 33, has also published a photograph of a multicolored urn of Classic Zapotec style found in the Mixteca Alta; additional Zapotec influences on the Mixtec regions are treated in Bernal, "Archaeological Synthesis of Oaxaca," *HBMAI*, Vol. 3 (1965), 802.

43. Although no contents have been discovered in the Zapotec urns, John Paddock

has found an urn of Ñuiñe style in the Mixteca Baja which contained a fine ash; see Paddock, "Oaxaca in Ancient Mesoamerica," in Paddock, *AO*, 193.

44. Alfonso Caso and Ignacio Bernal, *Urnas de Oaxaca* (México, 1952), is the standard source on the urns of the Valley of Oaxaca. Extensive photographs of known urns, with some commentary, have been assembled by Frank H. Boos, *Ceramic Sculptures of Ancient Oaxaca* (South Brunswick, N.J., New York, and London, 1966), *Las urnas zapotecas en el Real Museo de Ontario* (México, 1964), and *Las urnas zapotecas de las colleciones Frissell y Leigh* (México, 1968); an earlier work is Sigvald Linné, *Zapotecan Antiquities* (Stockholm, 1938).

45. These "Tlaloc" urns are discussed by Stephen Kowalewski and Marcia Truel, " 'Tlaloc' in the Valley of Oaxaca," *BEO*, No. 31 (1970).

46. Boos, *Ceramic Sculptures of Ancient Oaxaca*, 21–22.

47. Alfonso Caso, "The Mixtec and Zapotec Cultures: The Zapotecs," *BEO*, No. 21 (1962), 11; Fray Esteban Arroyo, *Los dominicos, forjadores de la civilizacíon oajaqueña* (Oaxaca, 1958), xxvi, notes that when an important person such as a priest, lord, or warrior died, he was buried with persons and food to accompany him in the underworld.

48. Boos, *Ceramic Sculptures of Ancient Oaxaca*, 22, 249–50.

49. The standard work on the ceramics of the Valley of Oaxaca and Monte Albán is Alfonso Caso, Ignacio Bernal, and Jorge R. Acosta, *La cerámica de Monte Albán* (México, 1967); for a shorter summary, on which I have drawn, see Alfonso Caso and Ignacio Bernal, "Ceramics of Oaxaca," *HBMAI*, Vol. 3 (1965), 871–95.

50. Lapidary work is discussed by Alfonso Caso, "Lapidary Work, Goldwork, and Copperwork from Oaxaca," *HBMAI*, Vol. 3 (1965), 896–930.

51. The murals of Monte Albán tombs are described by Alfonso Caso, "Sculpture and Mural Painting of Oaxaca," *HBMAI*, Vol. 3 (1965), 849–70.

52. *Ibid.*, 856.

53. Jorge R. Acosta, "Exploraciones arqueológicas en Monte Albán, XVIIIa, Temporada, 1958," *RMEA*, Vol. 15 (1958), 14–20.

54. Zapotec writing is described in Alfonso Caso, "Zapotec Writing and Calendar," *HBMAI*, Vol. 3 (1965), 931–47. Caso also had dealt with this topic in an earlier work, *Las estelas zapotecas* (México, 1928). Howard Leigh, "An Identification of Zapotec Day Signs," *BEO*, No. 6 (1958); "Zapotec Glyphs," *BEO*, No. 2 (1958); and "The Evolution of the Zapotec Glyph 'C,' " in Paddock, *AO*, 256–69, has covered the same topic, frequently with different points of view from Caso's.

55. I have relied on Jorge R. Acosta, "Preclassic and Classic Architecture of Oaxaca," *HBMAI*, Vol. 3 (1965), 814–36, who summarizes Monte Albán architecture.

56. Munro S. Edmundson, "Play: Games, Gossip and Humor," *HBMAI*, Vol. 6 (1967), 200; Córdova, *Vocabulario*, 308v.

57. Blanton, "Valley of Oaxaca," 22.

58. *Ibid.*, 22.

59. *Ibid.*, 30–31, 35.

60. *Ibid.*, 30.

61. The manner in which "elite-oriented" societies tend to perpetuate themselves is discussed by Vilfredo Pareto; see Joseph Lopreato, *Vilfredo Pareto, Selections from His Treatise* (New York, 1965), 109–16. Pareto believed that elites always will serve as the main source of value influence in societies. Even if an elite is removed from power by a subordinate group, the new group would become an elite and subsequently embrace elite values. This theory, sometimes called "the circulation of elites," was a

response to and criticism of Karl Marx's notions concerning the "revolution of the proletariat" and the development of a "classless society."

62. Blanton, "Valley of Oaxaca," 32–33.

63. *Ibid.*, 33.

64. *Ibid.*, 34.

65. For an earlier discussion of the possibility of Monte Albán being the seat of an empire, see John Paddock, "Monte Albán ¿Sede de Imperio?" *RMEA*, Vol. 20 (1966), 117–46; for possible extensions outside of the Valley of Oaxaca, see note 38 above; see also Flannery, "Farming Systems," 454.

66. Blanton, "Valley of Oaxaca," 12.

67. *Ibid.*, 36.

68. As based on a preliminary study by Joyce Marcus of Harvard University, cited in *ibid.*, 37.

69. The traditional interpretation may be seen in Miguel Covarrubias, *Indian Art of Mexico and Central America* (New York, 1957); in Frederick A. Peterson, *Ancient Mexico* (New York, 1959); and, to an extent, in Wolf, *Sons of the Shaking Earth*.

70. Michael D. Coe, *The Jaguar's Children* (New York, 1965), 122; Coe has been the leading advocate of this position, especially with regard to the Olmec and Maya cultures.

71. William T. Sanders, "Review of Michael Coe's *Mexico*," *AA*, Vol. 65 (1963), 952–74, has pointed out the inadequacies of the theocratic-militaristic dichotomy; see also William T. Sanders and Barbara J. Price, *Mesoamerica*, 67. A study containing comparative data and propositions on a wide variety of preindustrial states and empires is S. N. Eisenstadt, *The Political Systems of Empires* (New York, 1963); one of the best anthropological studies of the relationship between priests and warriors in state systems is Fred Gearing, *Priests and Warriors: Social Structures for Cherokee Politics in the 18th Century*, American Anthropological Association, Memoir 93 (Menasha, Wisconsin, 1962).

3. CYCLES OF CONQUEST

1. This is an approximate date for the abandonment of Monte Albán; see Ignacio Bernal, "Archaeological Synthesis of Oaxaca," *HBMAI*, Vol. 3 (1965), 789; John Paddock, "Oaxaca in Ancient Mesoamerica," in Paddock, *AO*, 90, 174. Recent radiocarbon dates suggest that this date may have to be pushed back in time; see this chapter, note 4.

2. Paddock, "Oaxaca in Ancient Mesoamerica," in Paddock, *AO*, 149–52. Kirkby, "Land and Water," 153, has countered this proposal with the argument that the Valley of Oaxaca was not overpopulated and, in fact, could have supported a much denser and larger population without significant changes in technology. However, it does not appear that Kirkby totally negates Paddock's argument; societies can become overspecialized to the extent that they cannot adapt to new crises—whether they be crises of population pressure, technology, or other phenomena such as religious movements or the rise of militarism.

In a recent unpublished paper, "Pristine Urbanism in Mesoamerica," presented to the Society for American Archaeology in May, 1973, Paddock suggested that disease (specifically, amebiasis) might have played a part in bringing about the demise of the Classic cities.

3. The original finds from Tomb 7 were reported in Alfonso Caso, "Monte Albán,

Richest Archaeological Find in America," *National Geographic Magazine,* Vol. 62 (1932), 487–512; "Reading the Riddle of Ancient Jewels," *Natural History,* Vol. 32 (1932), 464–80; and "La tumba 7 de Monte Albán es mixteca," *Universidad de México,* Vol. 4, No. 20 (1932), 117–50. A more recent account is Alfonso Caso, *El tesoro de Monte Albán* (México, 1969).

4. The radiocarbon dates from Lambityeco, where Monte Albán IV has been most clearly delineated, range from A.D. 690–1055 and seem to cluster around A.D. 750. See Emily Rabin, "The Lambityeco Friezes: Notes on Their Content," *BEO,* No. 33 (1970), 15. However, the implications of these dates are not clear. Possibly Period IV began earlier than has been believed, or it began earlier elsewhere in the Valley than at Monte Albán.

5. The name of Zaachila probably was *Zaachila-Yoo,* meaning "palace or fortress of the dynasty of Zaachila." The Nahuatl word for the place, Teozapotlán, means "divine *zapote*"; the Zapotec name probably comes from *zaa,* meaning "cloud," and *chila,* meaning "lizard"; the cloud lizard apparently was the first sign in the Zapotec calendar and was depicted as an alligator—see *BEO,* No. 21 (1962), 12. Alfonso Caso, "The Mixtec and Zapotec Cultures: The Zapotec," *BEO,* No. 21 (1962), 5, contends that Zaachila also means "divine *zapote*" and that it is symbolized by this glyph in the *Lienzo de Guevea.* Cosihuesa, a prominent figure in the Zaachila dynasty, is associated with "cloud," "lightning," "thunder," and "movement," and thus with Cocijo, the Zapotec patron deity, who also was patron of the Zapotec calendar and was probably associated with the alligator; Cosihuesa, on the other hand, also may be associated with the "willow"—thus, the two interpretations may be linked. For citations, see this chapter, note 115.

While *Zaachila-Yoo* almost certainly was a post-Classic Zapotec capital, Burgoa, *GD,* Vol. 2, 117–28, discusses a legend claiming that Teotitlán del Valle was the first Zapotec capital. This claim never has been demonstrated to have any historical basis, although Caso, "The Mixtec and Zapotec Cultures: The Zapotec," *BEO,* No. 21 (1962), 4–5, contends that it may have been the Zapotec capital before Monte Albán.

Zaachila is one of the few Zapotec towns, as is Huitzo, that has reclaimed its Zapotec name in modern times. While the Zapotec names of most towns, as well as many Mixtec ones, could be reconstructed, Hispanicized Nahuatl names are given for most Zapotec towns in the following pages, for these were the ones collected by the Spanish in the sixteenth century which continue in current usage. For the etymologies and histories of various Oaxaca towns, see Peter Gerhard, *A Guide to the Historical Geography of New Spain,* and José María Bradomín, *Toponomia de Oaxaca* (México, 1955).

6. Many of these sources can be consulted in published editions which contain extensive commentaries. Noteworthy among these are: Alfonso Caso, "El mapa de Teozacoalco," *Cuadernos Americanos,* Vol. 8 (1949), 145–81; Alfonso Caso, "Explicación del reverso del Codex Vindobonensis," *Memoria de El Colegio Nacional,* Vol. 5 (1951), 46–70; Alfonso Caso, "Los lienzos mixtecos de Ihuitlán y Antonio de León," in *Homenaje a Pablo Martínez del Río* (México, 1961), 237–74; Alfonso Caso, *Interpretación del Codice Bodley 2858* (México, 1960); Alfonso Caso, *Interpretation of the Codex Selden 3135* (México, 1964); Alfonso Caso and Mary Elizabeth Smith, *Codex Colombino* (México, 1966); Mary Elizabeth Smith, *Picture Writing from Ancient Southern Mexico: Mixtec Place Signs and Names;* Zelia Nuttall, *Codex Nuttall* (Cambridge, Mass., 1902); C. A. Burland, *Codex Egerton 2895* (Graz, Austria, 1965); C. A. Burland and Gerdt Kutscher, *The Selden Roll* (Berlin, 1955); Karl Nowotny,

Codices Becker I/II (Graz, Austria, 1961); and Otto Adelhofer, *Codex Vindobonensis Mexicanus I* (Graz, Austria, 1961). Alfonso Caso also has contributed two general articles on Mixtec writing in "Mixtec Writing and Calendar," *HBMAI*, Vol. 3 (1965), 948–61, and "Historical Value of the Mixtec Codices," *BEO*, No. 16 (1960); Caso's major writings are scheduled to be published in two volumes by the Instituto Nacional de Anthropología e Historia, México, under the title, *Reyes y reinos de la Mixteca*.

7. Caso, "El mapa de Teozacoalco," *Cuadernos Americanos*, Vol. 8 (1949), 145–81.

8. J. C. Clark (ed.), *Codex Mendoza* (London, 1938), three volumes, is an incomplete copy, ordered by th efirst viceroy of New Spain, Francisco de Mendoza, of the *Matrícula de los tributos*. The *Matrícula de los tributos*, apparently pre-Spanish, is preserved in the Museo Nacional de Antropología in Mexico City; it remains unpublished in complete form. For its partial publications, see the bibliography in R. H. Barlow, *The Extent of the Empire of the Culhua-Mexica, Ibero-Americana*, No. 28, which is a study of the *Matrícula*; additional codical sources, of post-Conquest origin, which contain materials on the Mexica conquest of Oaxaca, are the *Codex Telleriano-Remensis* and the *Codex Vaticanus A*.

9. The *relaciones* are cataloged, analyzed, and given extensive discussion in *HBMAI*, Vol. 12 (1973). See also H. F. Cline, "The Relaciones Geográficas of the Spanish Indies," *HAHR*, Vol. 44 (1964), 341–74.

Most of the *relaciones* on Oaxaca are found in *PNE*, Vol. 4. Additional ones have been published by R. H. Barlow, "Dos relaciones antiguas del pueblo de Cuilapan, estado de Oaxaca," *Tlalocan*, Vol. 2 (1945), 18–28, and "Relación de Antequera," *Tlalocan*, Vol. 2 (1946), 134–37. The *relaciones* of Teocuicuilco, Atepec, Coquiapa, Xaltianguez, Tehuantepec, and Santa Crux Ixtepec are found in *RMEH*, Vol. 2. Horcasitas and George, "Relación," of the Tlacolula and Mitla document, is an English translation, as is Butterworth, "Relaciones," of the Cuilapan and Antequera documents. Some of the Oaxaca *relaciones* remain partly unpublished; others are lost.

10. Alonso de Molina, *Vocabulario en lengua castellana y mexicana* (México, 1944; facsimile edition of 1571 edition); A. de Olmos, *Arte para aprender la lengua mexicana* (México, 1904).

11. Antonio de los Reyes, *Arte en lengua mixteca* (Paris, 1890); Antonio de Alvarado, *Vocabulario en lengua mixteca* (México, 1962), introduction by Wigberto Jiménez Moreno.

12. Córdova's works are *Vocabulario*, and *Arte*. For information on Córdova's life, see the introduction by Wigberto Jiménez Moreno to Córdova, *Vocabulario*, and Fray Esteban Arroyo, *Los dominicos, forjadores de la civilización oajaqueña* (Oaxaca, 1958). The relationship of Córdova, *Vocabulario*, to the dialect of Teotitlán del Valle, along with additional analysis, may be seen in Juan José Rendón, "Nuevos datos sobre el origen del Vocabulario en lengua zapoteca del Padre Córdova," *A de A*, Vol. 6 (1969), 115–30.

13. *Junta Colombina*. This work at one time was presumed to be the property of the Dominicans of Oaxaca and was presented to Porfirio Díaz, in whose honor it was published by the Junta Colombina de México. It may be the same as a dictionary reportedly compiled in the seventeenth century by Fray Cristóbal Aguero.

14. For a list which indicates the potential volume of these sources, which may number in the hundreds, see Antonio Peñafiel, *Gramática de la lengua zapoteca por un autor anónimo* (México, 1887), and Arroyo, *Los dominicos, forjadores de la civilización oajaqueña*. Important unpublished Zapotec language materials are housed in the John Carter Brown Library at Brown University, Providence, Rhode Island, and in

the Latin American Collection of the University of Texas Library, Austin, Texas.

15. Bernardino de Sahagún, *Historia general de las cosas de Nueva España* (México, 1955), three volumes; see also Arthur J. O. Anderson and Charles E. Dibble (eds.), *General History of the Things of New Spain* (Santa Fe, N.M., 1950–69), twelve volumes, which contain the Nahuatl texts collected by Sahagún along with English translations; Alonso de Zorita, *Life and Labor in Ancient Mexico* (New Brunswick, N.J., 1963), trans. and with an introduction by Benjamin Keen.

16. Francisco de Burgoa, *Palestral historial de virtudes, y exemplares apostólicos* (México, 1934; reprint of the 1670 edition) and Burgoa, *GD*.

17. Juan de Torquemada, *Los viente i un libros rituales y monarchía indiana* (México, 1943), three volumes; Antonio de Herrera y Tordesillas, *Historia general de los hechos de los castellanos en las islas y tierrafirme del mar océano* (Madrid, 1947), fifteen volumes; Domingo Chimalpahin Cuauhtlehuanitzin, *Die Relationen Chimalpahin's zur Geschichte Mexiko's*, in Gunter Zimmermann (ed.), *Abhandlungen aus dem Gebiet des Auslandsckund*, Vols. 38–39, (Hamburg, 1963, 1965); Fernando de Alva Ixtlilxóchitl, *Obras históricas*, two volumes (México, 1952); Diego de Durán, *Historia de las indias de Nueva España y islas de Tierra Firme* (México, 1951), two volumes and atlas—for an English translation see Fray Diego Duran, *The Aztecs*, trans. with notes by Doris Heyden and Fernando Horcasitas (New York, 1964), and *Books of the Gods and Rites of the Ancient Calendar*, trans. and ed. by Fernando Horcasitas and Doris Heyden (Norman, Okla., 1971); Fernando Alvarado Tezozómoc, *Crónica mexicana* (México, 1944); for Sahagún, see note 15.

18. The most important documents from AGN are found in the sections *Hospital de Jesús* (documents from the Cortés marquessate), *Indios, Tierras, Mercedes, Civil, Vínculos, Inquisición*, and *General de Parte*; documents from Spain in published form are in collections such as the *DII, PNE*, and *ENE*; the most important sections in AGI for Oaxaca seem to be *Audiencia de México, Indiferente General*, and *Patronato*.

19. Such as Córdova, *Arte*, Burgoa, *GD*, and Gonzalo de Balzalobre, "Relación auténtica de las idolatrías, supersticiones, vanas observaciones de los indios del Obispado de Oaxaca," *Anales del Museo Nacional de México*, primera época, Vol. 6 (1892), 225–60.

20. The *Lienzo de Guevea* has been published with extensive analysis by Eduard Seler, "Das Dorfbuch von Santiago Guevea," in *Gesammelte Abhandlungen*, Vol. 3 (Berlin, 1908), 157–93; for a color reproduction of the same source, see Mendieta, *Zapotecos*, insert 38–39. Blas Pablo Reko, *Mitobotánica zapoteca* (Tacubaya, México, 1945) also has provided a partial analysis of the *Lienzo de Guevea*; for the *Mapa de Huilotepec*, see R. H. Barlow, "The Mapa de Huilotepec," *Tlalocan*, Vol. 1 (1944), 155–57; additional pictorial materials, largely unpublished, dealing with the genealogies of the Zapotec lords, are the *Árbol genealógico de los reyes zapotecas*, held by the Hispanic Society of New York, in New York City, and the *Genealogía Oaxaqueña*, held by the Museo Nacional de Anthropología, México; for a description of the latter source, plus additional materials, see John B. Glass, *Catálogo de la colección de códices* (México, 1964).

21. Much of this material remains unpublished in accessible form; for comments on these materials see Glass, *Catálogo de la colección de códices*; for the *Lienzo de Analco*, see Franz Bloom, "El lienzo de Analco, Oaxaca," *Cuadernos Americanos*, Vol. IV, No. 6 (1945), 125–36.

22. The Codex Sánchez Solís is the same as Codex Egerton 2895—see this chapter, note 6; for Baranda, see Alfonso Caso, "Comentario al Códice Baranda," *Miscellanea*

Paul Rivet Octogenario Dicata, Vol. 1 (México, 1958), 373–89; for a color reproduction of Baranda, see Mendieta, *Zapotecos*, insert 62–63.

23. John Paddock, "Oaxaca in Ancient Mesoamerica," in Paddock, *AO*, 200.

24. The Mixteca-Puebla concept was discussed by George C. Vaillant, *The Aztecs of Mexico* (New York, 1944); more recent discussions include Miguel Covarrubias, *Indian Art of Mexico and Central America* (New York, 1957), and H. B. Nicholson, "The Mixteca-Puebla Concept in Mesoamerican Archeology: A Re-Examination," in Anthony F. C. Wallace (ed.), *Men and Cultures: Selected Papers of the Fifth International Congress of Anthropological and Ethnological Sciences* (Philadelphia, 1956), 612–17.

25. Alfonso Caso and Ignacio Bernal, "Ceramics of Oaxaca," *HBMAI*, Vol. 3 (1965), 894.

26. *Ibid.*, 893.

27. Alfonso Caso, "Lapidary Work, Goldwork, and Copperwork from Oaxaca," *HBMAI*, Vol. 3 (1965), 917.

28. Covarrubias, *Indian Art of Mexico and Central America*, 311.

29. For a discussion of this point, see Philip Dark, "Speculations on the Course of Mixtec History," *BEO*, No. 10 (1958), 2–6; the dating is based on Caso—see this chapter, note 7.

30. For discussions of Mixtec culture and society, see Alfonso Caso, "The Mixtec and Zapotec Cultures: The Mixtecs," *BEO*, No. 22 (1962); Ronald Spores, "The Zapotec and Mixtec at Spanish Contact," *HBMAI*, Vol. 3 (1965), 977–85; *Mixtec*; and *An Archaeological Settlement Survey of the Nochixtlan Valley, Oaxaca, Vanderbilt University Publications in Anthropology*, No. 1 (Nashville, 1972); and Barbro Dahlgren de Jordán, *La Mixteca* (México, 1954). For evidence of the centralization of the Tututepec "empire" see Mary Elizabeth Smith, *Picture Writing from Ancient Southern Mexico*, 179–81.

31. For an interesting discussion of Eight Deer and his possible exploits, see Robert Chadwick, "Native Pre-Aztec History of Central Mexico," *HBMAI*, Vol. 11 (1971), 474–504.

32. *PNE*, Vol. 4, 190; Barlow, "Dos relaciones antiguas del pueblo de Cuilapan, estado de Oaxaca," *Tlalocan*, Vol. 2 (1945), 23.

33. Burgoa, *GD*, Vol. 1, 387.

34. Alfonso Caso, "The Lords of Yanhuitlan," in Paddock, *AO*, 313–35.

35. R. H. Barlow, "Dos relaciones antiguas del pueblo de Cuilapan," *Tlalocan*, Vol. 2 (1945), 23. The hill referred to undoubtedly is Monte Albán; for discussions of the hill of Monte Albán and the various names of Cuilapan and their significance in Mixtec documents, see Smith, *Picture Writing of Ancient Southern Mexico*, 64–65, 69, 158, 202–206.

36. Burgoa, *GD*, Vol. 1, 395–96; translated by Butterworth, "Relaciones," 37.

37. Burgoa, *GD*, Vol. 1, 395; translated by Butterworth, "Relaciones," 37.

38. *PNE*, Vol. 4, 116–17.

39. Butterworth, "Relaciones," 41.

40. Burgoa, *GD*, Vol. 1, 394–95.

41. *Ibid.*, 348, 395; translated by John Paddock, "Mixtec Ethnohistory and Monte Albán V," in Paddock, *AO*, 371.

42. Burgoa, *GD*, Vol. 2, 59–60; translated by Paddock, "Mixtec Ethnohistory and Monte Albán V," in Paddock, *AO*, 383–84.

43. Barlow, "Dos relaciones antiguas del pueblo de Cuilapan," *Tlalocan*, Vol. 2

(1945), 24; AGN, Tierras, T. 129, *exp.* 4; Smith, *Picture Writing from Ancient Southern Mexico*, 161.

44. Huitzo is called Guaxolotitlán in numerous Spanish Colonial documents; Huitzo comes from the Zapotec *Uizo, Uiya-zoo,* or *Huijazoo,* meaning "place of the warriors," denoting the last outpost on the frontier of the Valley of Oaxaca. The Nahuatl name, Guaxolotitlán, or Cuauhxolotitlan, probably means "place of the *guajalotes,* "turkeys"—this name also is rendered in some of the documents as Huexolotitlán. Eduard Seler, "The Wall Paintings of Mitla," *Bureau of American Ethnology,* Bulletin No. 28 (1904), 260, and the *relación* of the town, *PNE,* Vol. 4, 196, state that the Nahuatl name was Guaxilotitlán, "place of the *guaxilotes*" (the *guaxilote* is a tree which bears an edible fruit); the name Guaxolotitlán probably resulted from an error in pronunciation; see also José María Bradomín, *Toponimia de Oaxaca,* 49; the data concerning *barrios* in Huitzo may be found in Burgoa, *GD,* Vol. 2, 18; see also *PNE,* Vol. 4, 197.

45. *PNE,* Vol. 4, 199.

46. Barlow, "Dos relaciones antiguas del pueblo de Cuilapan," *Tlalocan,* Vol. 2 (1945), 25; see also Burgoa, *GD,* Vol. 1, 395, who also implies that the Mixtecs had taken over the entire Valley.

47. *PNE,* Vol. 4, 111.

48. *Ibid.,* 105.

49. See the *relación* of Macuilxóchitl, *PNE,* Vol. 4, 102; Paddock, "Mixtec Ethnohistory and Monte Albán V," in Paddock, *AO,* 375, interprets this document to mean that the Mixtecs had conquered Mitla; the datum that Mitla had war with Tututepec is found in *PNE,* Vol. 4, 149; Zaachila also waged war with Tututepec—see *PNE,* Vol. 4, 193–94.

50. For citations of sources concerning Tomb 7, see this chapter, note 3; see also Caso, "Lapidary Work, Goldwork, and Copperwork from Oaxaca," *HBMAI,* Vol. 3 (1965), 908–14.

51. Ignacio Bernal, "The Mixtecs in Valley Archeology," in Paddock, *AO,* 360.

52. The excavations at Zaachila are reported in Roberto Gallegos, "Exploraciones en Zaachila, Oaxaca," *B-INAH,* No. 8 (1962), 6–8, and "Zaachila: The First Season's Work," *Archaeology,* Vol. 16 (1963), 226–33; the most recent discoveries are discussed in Jorge R. Acosta, "Nuevos descubrimientos en Zaachila (1971)," *B-INAH, época* 2, No. 3 (1972), 27–34.

53. Alfonso Caso, "The Lords of Yanhuitlan," in Paddock, *AO,* 319–30; recently, Mary Elizabeth Smith has questioned Caso's interpretation of the wall figures at Zaachila, arguing that there is no concrete evidence linking these individuals to Cuilapan nor to known rulers of either Cuilapan or Yanhuitlán. Her main criticism is that Caso's identification of the place signs of Cuilapan and Yanhuitlán in the Mixtec codices, while "provocative and intriguing . . . cannot as yet be substantiated"; see Smith, *Picture Writing from Ancient Southern Mexico,* 64–65.

54. Caso, "Zapotec Writing and Calendar," *HBMAI,* Vol. 3 (1965), 942; Bernal, "The Mixtecs in Valley Archeology," in Paddock, *AO,* 365, suggests that the earlier "Mixtec" influences be designated as Monte Albán Va while the later ones should be called Vb.

55. Chris L. Moser, "La tumba 1 del barrio del Rosario, Huitzo, Oaxaca," *B-INAH,* No. 36 (1969), 41–47.

56. Ignacio Bernal, "Architecture in Oaxaca After the End of Monte Alban," *HBMAI,* Vol. 3 (1965), 838.

57. *Ibid.*, 847; Bernal, "Archaeological Synthesis of Oaxaca," *HBMAI*, Vol. 3 (1965), 810–11.

58. Bernal, "Architecture in Oaxaca After the End of Monte Alban," *HBMAI*, Vol. 3 (1965), 838–39.

59. Gold beads, copper objects, and polychromes were found in tombs at Mitla; see Alfonso Caso and D. F. Rubín de la Borbolla, *Exploraciones en Mitla, 1934–1935* (México, 1936).

60. Alfonso Caso, "The Mixtec and Zapotec Cultures: The Zapotecs," *BEO*, No. 21 (1962), 16.

61. This is the interpretation of Ignacio Bernal, "The Mixtecs in Valley Archeology," in Paddock, *AO*, 350–51; however, identification of the stone mosaics and miniature vessels as Mixteca-Puebla is open to question.

62. *PNE*, Vol. 4, 152; Burgoa, *GD*, Vol. 2, 121–25, 165–75, 338–59. The Zapotec name of Mitla, *Liobaa*, *Lyobaa*, or *Yoopaa*, means "place of rest," "burial place," or "place of the dead," a connotation also implied by its Nahuatl name, Mictlan; Mitla still carries this connotation in modern times as a resting place for souls of the dead; for example, see Elsie Clews Parsons, *Mitla*: 1–2; Mitla also is referred to as Mictla or Miquitla in the Spanish documents. Teitipac was called *Zeetoba*, "second burial place," in Zapotec, or sometimes *Queuiquijezaa*, "the palace on the rock"; its Nahuatl name, Teticpac, sometimes rendered as Titicapa, Tectipac, or Teticpaque in Spanish Colonial documents, also means "the palace on the rock"; Teitipac is not to be confused with Tetiquipa, or Titiquipa, which was located near Miahuatlán; for Teitipac, see Seler, "The Wall Paintings of Mitla," *Bureau of American Ethnology*, Bulletin No. 28 (1904), 248; Burgoa, *GD*, Vol. 2, 64–65; *PNE*, Vol. 4, 110–11; and Peter Gerhard, *A Guide to the Historical Geography of New Spain*, 73.

63. Burgoa, *GD*, Vol. 2, 121–26.

64. *PNE*, Vol. 4, 149.

65. The excavations at Yagul are discussed in John Paddock, "The First Three Seasons at Yagul," *Mesoamerican Notes*, Vol. 4 (1955), 25–47; "The 1956 Season at Yagul," *Mesoamerican Notes*, Vol. 5 (1957), 13–36; "MCC Field Workers Have Busiest Season Ever at 1958 Yagul Dig," *BEO*, No. 5 (1958); "Exploración en Yagul, Oaxaca," *RMEA*, Vol. 16 (1960), 91–96; "Oaxaca in Ancient Mesoamerica," in Paddock, *AO*, 210–26; and Bernal, "The Mixtecs in the Archeology of the Valley of Oaxaca," in Paddock, *AO*, 346–59; a monograph on Yagul by Ignacio Bernal soon will be published by the Universidad Nacional Autónoma de México. James P. Oliver, "Architectural Similarities between Yagul and Mitla," *Mesoamerican Notes*, Vol. 4 (1955), 49–67, includes detailed reconstruction drawings of the structures at these sites.

66. Ignacio Bernal, "The Mixtecs in Valley Archeology," in Paddock, *AO*, 351–56.

67. Charles Wicke, "Tomb 30 at Yagul and the Zaachila Tombs," in Paddock, *AO*, 336–44; Bernal, "The Mixtecs in Valley Archeology," in Paddock, *AO*, 356.

68. For Lambityeco, see John Paddock, Joseph R. Mogor, and Michael D. Lind, "Lambityeco Tomb 2: A Preliminary Report," *BEO*, No. 25 (1968); Horst Hartung, "Notes on the Oaxaca Tablero," *BEO*, No. 27 (1970); Rabin, "The Lambityeco Friezes: Notes on Their Content," *BEO*, No. 33 (1970); and William O. Payne, "A Potter's Analysis of the Pottery from Lambityeco Tomb 2," *BEO*, No. 29 (1970). For excavations at other Monte Albán IV sites in the Valley, see Ignacio Bernal, "Exploraciones arqueológicas en Noriega, Oaxaca," in *Homenaje a Rafael García Granados* (México, 1960), 83–88.

69. Paddock, Mogor, and Lind, "Lambityeco Tomb 2: A Preliminary Report," *BEO*, No. 25 (1968), 21–22.

70. An analysis of the plaster sculptures of Lambityeco and their implications can be found in Rabin, "The Lambityeco Friezes: Notes on Their Content," *BEO*, No. 33 (1970); my comments are based on her analysis.

71. John Paddock, "Oaxaca in Ancient Mesoamerica," in Paddock, *AO*, 212–13, for the shift from Lambityeco to Yagul; for the Etla sites, see Blanton, "Valley of Oaxaca," 13.

72. On this point, see Rosemary Sharp, "Early Architectural Grecas in the Valley of Oaxaca," *BEO*, No. 32 (1970); the Lambityeco grecas and those at Uxmal seem to date from about the same time even though the Uxmal buildings are assigned to the late Classic stage; grecas continue in the post-Classic in both the Yucatán Maya area and in Oaxaca.

73. On the Ñuiñe style, see Paddock, "Oaxaca in Ancient Mesoamerica," in Paddock, *AO*, 176–200; "Una tumba en Ñuyoo, Huajuapan de León, Oaxaca," *B*-INAH, No. 33 (1968), 51–54; "A Beginning in the Ñuiñe: Salvage Excavations at Ñuyoo, Huajuapan," *BEO*, No. 26 (1970); and "More Ñuiñe Materials," *BEO*, No. 28 (1970).

74. Ronald Spores, "Exploraciones arqueológicas en el Valle de Nochixtlán," *B*-INAH, No. 37 (1969), 35–43, "Settlement, Farming Technology, and Environment in the Nochixtlan Valley, Oaxaca: 700 B.C. to A.D. 1600," *Science*, Vol. 166 (1969), 557–569; and *An Archaeological Settlement Survey of the Nochixtlan Valley, Oaxaca. Vanderbilt University Publications in Anthropology*, No. 1 (1972).

75. Donald L. Brockington, *Archaeological Investigations at Miahuatlan, Oaxaca. Vanderbilt University Publications in Anthropology*, No. 7 (1973); for the Coixtlahuaca excavations, see Bernal, "Exploraciones en Coixtlahuaca," *RMEA*, Vol. 10 (1949), 5–76.

76. Paddock, "Mixtec Ethnohistory and Monte Albán V," in Paddock, *AO*, 377.

77. Careful attention should be given to distinguishing between elite and peasant cultures in archeological studies, for the relationship between the two certainly is not unidimensional. Too little attention has been given to determining such relationships in the Oaxaca Valley cultures; specifically, the ways in which peasants were affected by changing elite styles is a topic that needs considerable research in archeology, ethnohistory, and social anthropology. Because of their subordinate relationship, peasants do not seem to change as rapidly as elites do, and, while they may emulate elites, this emulation may "lag" behind current fashions of elite culture. For an interesting discussion of this phenomenon in a modern Greek village, see Ernestine Friedl, "Lagging Emulation in Post-Peasant Society," *AA*, Vol. 66 (1964), 569–86.

78. Similar interpretations are suggested by Paddock, "Mixtec Ethnohistory and Monte Albán V," in Paddock, *AO*, 367–85; Bernal, "The Mixtecs in Valley Archeology," in Paddock, *AO*, 345–66; and Jorge Fernando Iturribarría, "Yagul: Mestizo Product of Mixtecs and Zapotecs," *BEO*, No. 17 (1960), even though these authors favor a "Mixtec invasion" hypothesis.

79. Bernal, "The Mixtecs in Valley Archeology," in Paddock, *AO*, 361–64.

80. The best general account of Mexica society and culture is Jacques Soustelle, *Daily Life of the Aztecs*; perceptive analytical essays are those of J. C. Padden, *The Hummingbird and the Hawk: Conquest and Sovereignty in the Valley of Mexico, 1503–1541*; F. Katz, *Situación social e económica de los aztecas durante los siglos XV y XVI* (México, 1966); Pedro Carrasco, "Social Organization of Ancient Mexico," *HBMAI*, Vol. 10 (1971), 349–75; and Charles Gibson, "The Struc-

ture of the Aztec Empire," *HBMAI*, Vol. 10 (1971), 376–94. Burr Cartwright Brundage, *Rain of Darts* (Austin, Tex., 1972), is an exciting narrative history of the Mexica, while Benjamin Keen, *The Aztec Image* (New Brunswick, N.J., 1972), summarizes the major views that have been propounded about the Aztecs since their first contact with Europeans.

81. Fernando Alvarado Tezozómoc, *Crónica mexicana*, Chap. 39, cited in Seler, "The Wall Paintings of Mitla," *Bureau of American Ethnology*, Bulletin No. 28 (1904), 259.

82. Tezozómoc, *Crónica mexicana*, Chap. 39, and Codex Mendoza, 16, cited in Seler, "The Wall Paintings of Mitla," *Bureau of American Ethnology*, Bulletin No. 28 (1904), 259.

83. Sahagún, *Historia de las cosas de Nueva España*, Vol. 2, 105–106; Seler, "The Wall Paintings of Mitla," *Bureau of American Ethnology*, Bulletin No. 28 (1904), 263.

84. These events are summarized in Seler, "The Wall Paintings of Mitla," *Bureau of American Ethnology*, Bulletin No. 28 (1904), 260–65; the sources of Seler's information were *Histoire de la Nation Mexicaine depuis le départ d'Aztlan* (Paris, 1893), 76; *Codex Telleriano-Remensis*, Part 4; *Codex Vaticanus A*, 127; Tezozómoc, *Crónica mexicana*, chaps. 75–76; and *Anales de Domingo Francisco San Anton Muñon Chimalpahin Quauhtlehuanitzin* (Paris, 1889), 10, 167. Much the same information also is covered in Carlos María de Bustamante, *Historia antigua de Oaxaca* (México, 1968), and Jorge Fernando Iturribarría, *Las viejas culturas de Oaxaca* (México, 1952), 97–136; see also this chapter, note 17.

85. Barlow, *The Extent of the Empire of the Culhua-Mexica, Ibero-Americana*, No. 28, 118.

86. *Ibid.*, 118–22, includes these towns in the Mexica province; their *relaciones*, however, mention going to war with the Mexica but not being conquered by them; see *PNE*, Vol. 4, 106, 149, 194. In fact, the *relación* of Teozapotlán specifically states that this town did not pay tribute to the Mexica (*PNE*, Vol. 4, 194). There also are discrepancies between the Aztec sources and the *relaciones*; for example, the *relación* of Macuilxóchitl makes no mention of the Aztecs (*PNE*, Vol. 4, 101–102), even though Teitipac and Guaxilotitlán, which figure in the official Aztec sources as subject towns, acknowledged the Mexica hegemony in their *relaciones* (*PNE*, Vol. 4, 111, 197–98). In a similar manner, the sierra Zapotec towns of Ixtepeji, Teocuicuilco, Atepec, Coquiapa, and Xaltianguez acknowledged paying tribute to the Mexica ruler (*PNE*, Vol. 4, 16; *RMEH*, Vol. 2, 123–24).

87. Barlow, *The Extent of the Empire of the Culhua-Mexica, Ibero-Americana*, No. 28, 118–22; and *PNE*, Vol. 4, 127, 133, 138. These towns probably all were subject at one time to Tututepec, as their *relaciones* may imply, before being subject to the Mexica. Tututepec also seems to have conquered some of the Zapotec sierra towns; these numerous conquests and changing tribute subjugations illustrate the fluid and ephemeral nature of post-Classic political entities.

88. Butterworth, "Relaciones," 45, 52–53; *PNE*, Vol. 4, 194.

89. *PNE*, Vol. 4, 197–98.

90. *Ibid.*, 4, 111, on Teitipac; for other towns, see Barlow, *The Extent of the Empire of the Culhua-Mexica, Ibero-Americana*, No. 28, 124–25.

91. Barlow, *The Extent of the Empire of the Culhua-Mexica, Ibero-Americana*, No. 28, 123.

92. See *PNE*, Vol. 4, 196–205, on the relationship of Huitzo to the Mexica rule.

93. This battle and its consequences are outlined, in various versions, in numerous sources; see particularly Burgoa, *GD*, Vol. 2, 341–45; Seler, "The Wall Paintings of Mitla," *Bureau of American Ethnology*, Bulletin No. 28, 261, and Paul Radin, *An Historical Legend of the Zapotecs, Ibero-Americana*, No. 9 (1935).

94. Jacques Soustelle, *Daily Life of the Aztecs*, xxii.

95. Pedro Carrasco, *Los Otomíes* (México, 1950), S. W. Miles, *The Sixteenth-Century Pokam-Maya. Transactions of the American Philosophical Society*, Vol. 47, Part 4 (Philadelphia, 1957).

96. Jacques Soustelle, *Daily Life of the Aztecs*, xxii.

97. *PNE*, Vol. 4, 17.

98. *Ibid.*, 101, 105, 111, 116, 145, 148, 179.

99. *Ibid.*, 149.

100. *Ibid.*, 145.

101. *Ibid.*, 179.

102. *Ibid.*, 106.

103. *Ibid.*, 101.

104. *Ibid.*, 111.

105. *RMEH*, Vol. 2, 180–84.

106. *PNE*, Vol. 4, 119–43.

107. Burgoa, *GD*, Vol. 2, 2.

108. *PNE*, Vol. 4, 199.

109. *Ibid.*, 16.

110. *Ibid.*, 102.

111. *Ibid.*, 111.

112. Burgoa, *GD*, Vol. 2, 121–27.

113. Michael D. Coe, *Mexico* (New York, 1967), 147.

114. My distinction here follows the contrast between cumulative evolution and involution made by a number of anthropologists; see particularly Charles J. Erasmus, *Man Takes Control* (Minneapolis, 1961); Eric R. Wolf, "The Study of Cultural Evolution," in Sol Tax (ed.), *Horizons of Anthropology* (Chicago, 1964), 108–19; and Clifford Geertz, *Agricultural Involution* (Berkeley and Los Angeles, 1968).

115. This history, in various forms, was originally reported and is scattered throughout Burgoa, *GD*, and has undergone various modifications, along with legendary additions. For other accounts and interpretations, see Caso, "The Mixtec and Zapotec Cultures: The Zapotecs," *BEO*, No. 21 (1962), 5–6; Francisco Rojas Gonzáles, "Los zapotecos en la época prehispánica," in Mendieta, *Zapotecos*, 55–65; and Manuel Martínez Gracida, *El rey Cosijoeza y su familia* (México, 1888).

An account by Gilberto Orozco, *Tradiciones y leyendas del Istmo de Tehuantepec* (México, 1946), equates Mitla and Zaachila, stating that Zaachila was the dynastic name of the ruling family of Mitla, a unique interpretation.

The name Cosihuesa often is rendered as Cosijoeza; Martínez Gracida, *El rey Cosijoeza y su familia*, 160, claims that the name comes from the Zapotec *coxi* or *cosi*, meaning "ray of light" or "thunderbolt," *xoo*, meaning "movement," *e* from *bezo*, meaning "wind," and *zaa*, meaning "cloud"; thus, the name would be Cosixoezaa and clearly linked to Cocijo, the Zapotec patron deity. However, other Zapotec scholars, such as Gabriel López Chiñas, *El concepto de la muerte entre los zapotecas* (México, 1969), 64–65, and Orozco, *Tradiciones y leyendas del Istmo de Tehuantepec*, 13, argue that the name also might have different roots: both Orozco and Lopez think it might derive from the Zapotec *casigueza* or *zicasigueeza*, meaning "like tobacco" (*casi*, "like"; *gueza*, "tobacco"). Orozco adds that if this is the case, Cosihuesa would be adorned in the leaves of the tobacco; López contends that *queza* might also be the root which implies "valor" or "bravery." He also adds that the morpheme *guesa*, another possible derivative, means "willow."

116. For accounts of Cosijopii and Pelaxilla and their marriage, see this chapter, notes 93 and 115; for Donaji, see also Alfonso Francisco Ramírez, *Por los caminos de Oaxaca* (México, 1954), 41–44.

117. This is the version given in most Zapotec legends and histories; some accounts, however, state that the last ruler of the Zapotec inhabitants of Zaachila was a Mixtec prince by the name of Nuhucano (Diego de Aguilar), who was the lover of Donaji, daughter of Cosihuesa. According to this version, Donaji and Nuhucano are buried in the convent of Cuilapan; see G. R. Steininger and Paul Van de Velde, *Three Dollars a Year* (New York, 1935), 110.

118. Eduard Seler, "Das dorfbuch von Santiago Guevea," in *Gesammelte Abhandlungen zur amerikanischen Sprach und Altersthumskunde*, Vol. 3 (1908), 157–93; for another isthmus pictographic document, containing information on the rulers of Tehuantepec, see Barlow, "The Mapa de Huilotepec," *Tlalocan*, Vol. 1 (1943), 155–57.

119. Burgoa, *GD*, Vol. 1, 328; Vol. 2, 330.

120. *RMEH*, Vol. 2, 168–75.

121. Paddock, "Oaxaca in Ancient Mesoamerica," in Paddock, *AO*, 210; Juan José Rendón, "Relaciones internas de la familia zapoteco-chatino," *A de A*, Vol. 4, 188–89.

122. Paddock, "Oaxaca in Ancient Mesoamerica," in Paddock, *AO*, 223–25.

4. PRINCES, PRIESTS, AND PEASANTS

1. The *relación* of Cuilapan, a Mixtec-biased document, claims that the Mixtecs were more lordly: "The Indians of the Zapotec region [where this town is] are very different from the Mixtecs. One reason for the difference is that the Mixtecs are new-comers. Another reason is that they are more lordly in their behavior and dress, as well as in the way they treat their women, because even though the Zapotec lady may be of the nobility, she does her grinding in the same manner as the *macehuales*" (Butterworth, "Relaciones," 39).

2. Traditionally, the Toltecs were associated with Teotihuacán, thought to be Tollan. In 1942 the anthropologist Wigberto Jiménez Moreno associated the Toltecs with the site of Tula, Hidalgo—this is the identification now found in most standard textbooks on Mesoamerican archeology. It now appears that both associations may be correct, for Toltec and Tollan are associated with a number of places; for this reason I have interpreted them primarily as ideas or concepts and not as a specific people or a specific place. For further discussion, see Robert Chadwick, "Native Pre-Aztec History of Central Mexico," *HBMAI*, Vol. 11 (1971), 474–504.

3. Córdova, *Vocabulario*, 58v, 97r, 253v, 254r, 267v, 383v, 393v, 426v; *Junta Colombina*, 27, 110, 196, 217.

4. See *PNE*, Vol. 4, 102, 106, 112, 149–50, 191, 200.

5. Horcasitas and George, "Relación," 21; see also *PNE*, Vol. 1, 149.

6. For entries concerning beans and squash, see Córdova, *Vocabulario*, 67r, 200v, 201r; *Junta Colombina*, 16, 77.

7. The *relaciones* of Teozapotlán, Huitzo, Macuilxóchitl, Teotitlán del Valle, and

Tlalixtac mention the use of chili in the Valley; see *PNE*, Vol. 4, 102.

8. For the presence of the tomato, see Córdova, *Vocabulario*, 405v; for maguey, see Córdova, *Vocabulario*, 252r, 253v, 253r, 426v; *Junta Colombina*, 110, 217; and *PNE*, Vol. 4, 102.

9. Córdova, *Vocabulario*, 64v; Burgoa, *GD*, Vol. 2, 101.

10. *RMEH*, Vol. 2 (1928), 130.

11. For the use of copper axes as currency, see Dudley Easby, Jr., Earle R. Caley, and Khorsrow Moazed, "Axe-Money: Facts and Speculation," *RMEA*, Vol. 21 (1967), 107–48.

12. For agricultural practices in general, see Córdova, *Vocabulario*, 175r, 402r, and *Junta Colombina*, 185; for irrigation, see *PNE*, Vol. 4, 102, 112, 180, 191, 201–202, 314; *PNE*, Vol. 1, 144, 314–15; Burgoa, *GD*, Vol. 2, 2, 21, 36, 46, 51, 61, 100–101, 105, 119; and Barlow, "Dos relaciones antiguas del pueblo de Cuilapan, estado de Oaxaca," *Tlalocan*, Vol. 2 (1945), 25.

13. Córdova, *Vocabulario*, 78r; *Junta Colombina*, 35.

14. Kirkby, *Land and Water*, 135–42.

15. Horcasitas and George, "Relación," 17.

16. *Ibid.*, 21; *PNE*, Vol. 4, 102, 107, 112.

17. Burgoa, *GD*, Vol. 2, 21.

18. *PNE*, Vol. 4, 103, 106, 113, 150.

19. *Ibid.*, 194.

20. Burgoa, *GD*, Vol. 2, 28.

21. *Ibid.*, 51; Horcasitas and George, "Relación," 21; John Paddock, "Oaxaca in Ancient Mesoamerica," in Paddock, *AO*, 241.

22. Ronald Spores, "The Zapotec and Mixtec at Spanish Contact," *HBMAI*, Vol. 3 (1965), 967; Horcasitas and George, "Relación," 18.

23. Burgoa, *GD*, Vol. 2, 8; Córdova, *Vocabulario*, 195v, 195r.

24. Burgoa, *GD*, Vol. 2, 119–20; *PNE*, Vol. 4, 107–108; Horcasitas and George, "Relación," 22; *PNE*, Vol. 1, 315.

25. *PNE*, Vol. 4, 106.

26. *Ibid.*, 102, 103; Horcasitas and George, "Relación," 18; *RMEH*, Vol. 2 (1928), 184.

27. Horcasitas and George, "Relación," 22.

28. Paddock, "Oaxaca in Ancient Mesoamerica," in Paddock, *AO*, 241.

29. Spores, "The Zapotec and Mixtec at Spanish Contact," *HBMAI*, Vol. 3 (1965), 968; *PNE*, Vol. 4, 103, 107, 113; Horcasitas and George, "Relación," 18.

30. *RMEH*, Vol. 2 (1928), 184; *PNE*, Vol. 4, 204.

31. Spores, "The Zapotec and Mixtec at Spanish Contact," *HBMAI*, Vol. 3 (1965), 968; for the use of tobacco, see *PNE*, Vol. 4, 130.

32. Ignacio Bernal, "Distribución geográfica de las culturas de Monte Albán," *El México Antiguo*, Vol. 7 (1949), 209–16; William T. Sanders, "Population, Agricultural History, and Societal Evolution in Mesoamerica," in Brian Spooner (ed.), *Population Growth* (Cambridge, Mass., 1972), 143–45.

33. Kirkby, *Land and Water*, 137; I have used the figures in the text instead of those in Table 22 since there are discrepancies between them.

34. Woodrow Borah and Sherburne F. Cook, *The Aboriginal Population of Central Mexico on the Eve of Spanish Conquest, Ibero-Americana*, No. 45 (1963); Taylor, *CO*, 231, based on the Borah and Cook formula, has estimated the population at 367,038 inhabitants.

35. Kirkby, *Land and Water*, 137.

36. My projections are based on the *Suma de visitas* and not the *Matrícula de los tributos*, since those based on the latter document involve estimating the number of tributaries from tribute payments, while the *Suma* gives tributaries. The *Suma* data were collected between 1547 and 1551; this document is found in *PNE*, Vol. 1. It also has been extensively studied by Woodrow Borah and Sherburne F. Cook, *The Population of Central Mexico in 1548, Ibero-Americana*, No. 43 (1960).

My estimates generally are lower than those of Borah and Cook, for I project a smaller percentage of nontributaries (nobles, priests, *mayeques*, slaves, and so on). Others also have argued that their estimates are too high, even for the Valley of Mexico, a more socially complex and densely populated area than the Valley of Oaxaca. For example, Charles Gibson, "The Aztec Aristocracy in Colonial Mexico," *Comparative Studies in Society and History*, Vol. 2 (1959–60), 184, found, based on colonial documents, that the nobility constituted a much lower percentage of the population in many central Mexican towns than Borah and Cook have contended. William T. Sanders, "Review of Borah and Cook's 'The Aboriginal Population of Central Mexico,'" *AA*, Vol. 68 (1966), 1299, has written: "The present reviewer has conducted extensive studies of modern agricultural practices and land use, recent population growth, Aztec settlement patterns, and sixteenth century data for the Valley of Mexico, and to him the population estimates of Cook and Simpson and Borah and Cook seem wholly unrealistic. For the Valley of Mexico their population estimate for 1519 is approximately 3,000,000 (2,000,000 in the provinces of Texcoco and Mexico-Tlatelolco alone), or approximately six times the rural population in 1950. Even allowing for loss of land through erosion and for more intensive land use in 1519, the figure seems much too high."

Robert McC. Adams, *The Evolution of Urban Society* (Chicago, 1966), 71, also is extremely skeptical: "Systematic and detailed studies of Sherburne F. Cook, Woodrow Borah, and their co-workers, largely based on inferences in tribute roles in the light of Post-Conquest sources, have been interpreted as suggesting levels significantly higher even than those obtaining under modern conditions of industrialization and rapidly improving public health. . . . Some of the assumptions are clearly debatable, and a recent review by R. J. Russell seems to indicate that they are excessively high in comparison not only with Mesopotamia but with preindustrial societies generally." For a more recent methodological discussion, see Sherburne F. Cook and Woodrow Borah, *Essays in Population History* (Berkeley and Los Angeles, 1970).

37. Córdova, *Vocabulario*, 327, gives the Zapotec gloss "*quelacoqui*" for *principado*; "*xitaoqueche*" is the gloss given for "cabecera del pueblo el afsiéto principal," while "barrio o estancia" is rendered as "*quijñaqueche*." See Córdova, *Vocabulario*, 64r, 52r, and 188v (Córdova also placed accents, or possibly tone indicators, on Zapotec glosses in his *Vocabulario*. However, since the meaning and significance of these remain unclear, they have not been reproduced here or on the Zapotec items which follow); Huitzo, Teocuicuilco, Macuilxóchitl, and Teotitlán del Valle apparently all had ceremonial centers located on nearby *cerros*: *PNE*, Vol. 4, 101, 105, 198; *RMEH*, Vol. 2 (1928), 125. On the other hand, judging from the archeological remains, Yagul, Mitla, and perhaps Zaachila had centralized precincts; for evidence of dispersed communities in the Valley, see Taylor, *CO*, 26–27.

38. Both Córdova, *Vocabulario*, 327v, and *Junta Colombina*, 156, have entries under "prince" ("*principe*"): Cordova gives "*coquihalao*," while the *Junta Colombina* gives "*goquihualoo*." Analyzed, these glosses mean "first or primary lord," from *coqui* or

goqui, meaning "lord or señor," and *halao* or *hualoo*, which means "first, primary, or principal." An alternate rendering might be *"coquitelao"* or *"goquireloo"*—see Córdova, *Vocabulario*, 327v; *Junta Colombina*, 154. That the above gloss for *prince* did not refer to the son of the ruler (sometimes referred to as prince in European parlance) is confirmed by Córdova, *Vocabulario*, 327v, in which an additional entry is found for "Principe, hijo del Rey o del Señor." Córdova, *Vocabulario*, 357r, also contains the entry *"Coquitao huezaquiqueche"* for "Señor muy grande como emperador o rey"; this term may be an alternate for prince or first lord, may refer to a very powerful lord, such as that of Zaachila, or the emperor of the Mexica-Culhua, or, more probably, may have been generated by Córdova from Zapotec components to find an equivalent for the Spanish terms *rey* or *emperador*, for example, Charles V. The Zapotec is unclear; *Coquitao* means "greatest lord," while *queche* is the word for "town(s)" or "pueblo(s)"; the *Junta Colombina*, 186, contains a similar entry—"Señor grande, como emperador, goquiroohuezaquigueche." My hypothesis that there was no Zapotec concept comparable to the Spanish notion of *king* or *emperor* is based on the following glosses given in Córdova, *Vocabulario*, 95r, and *Junta Colombina*, 26: "Corte del rey o papa la gente. *Xicoego rey, nititopa xiquelahuexija rey, peniyootoa natij rey.* Corte del rey, el lugar donde efta. *Quechequehui chiñaa rey, xipe cogo rey.* Corte del rey. *xicoego rey; niritopaxiguelahuexiia rey.* Corte en que reside del rey. *guecheguehuichiña rey; xibecogo rey."* Note that *rey* is included in the Zapotec glosses, apparently indicating that there was no Zapotec equivalent. For additional corroborating evidence see Córdova, *Vocabulario*, 349r, under *"Rey," "Reina,"* and *"Reino,"* where the Spanish term *rey* also is incorporated into the Zapotec glosses; and *Junta Colombina*, 169.

"Señor natural" in the Spanish Colonial documents refers to an Indian ruler who held his status because he was descended through heredity in a direct line from a pre-Conquest native ruler—see Robert S. Chamberlain, "The Concept of Señor Natural as Revealed by Castillian Law and Administrative Documents," *HAHR*, Vol. 19 (1939), 130–37. The term *cacique* is of Arawakan origin; in the Antilles it designated a local chieftain and was subsequently used by the Spaniards to refer to a local chieftain in Mesoamerica—see R. E. Alegría, "Origin and Diffusion of the Term 'Cacique,' " in Sol Tax (ed.), *Acculturation in the Americas* (Chicago, 1952), 313–15.

39. Horcasitas and George, "Relación," 20.

40. *Ibid.*, 16.

41. *RMEH*, Vol. 2 (1928), 181.

42. *PNE*, Vol. 4, 199.

43. I have not been able to find a gloss for *tequitlato* in Cordóva or the *Junta Colombina*; the work of D. Antonio Peñafiel, *Gramática de la lengua zapoteca por un autor anónimo* (México, 1877), 111, contains the gloss *"colaabachiña"* for *tequitlato*. Data in this same source also seem to support the contention of Spores, *Mixtec*, 124, that *gobernador, regidor,* and *alcalde* had no pre-Spanish equivalents. Questions pertaining to confessions are given in both Spanish and Zapotec in the "Conffesonario de Zapoteco del Valle," published in Peñafiel, 97–116. It is noteworthy that the Spanish question, "¿Eres ó has sido Gobernador, Alcalde, Tiquitlaco ó Topil?" Peñafiel, 111, has the Zapotec translation, "Huanacalo, laa cocalo Gobernador, Alcalde, Colaabachiña laa Guixyaga?" Thus, the terms *gobernador* and *alcalde* are rendered in Spanish, while *tiquitlaco* (*sic*; *tequitlato*) is rendered in Zapotec, suggesting that there were no Zapotec equivalents for the concepts of governor or judge. *Tequitlato*, a Nahuatl term referring to a tax or tribute collector or procurer of labor, clearly is renderable

into Zapotec; in fact, since there was no Spanish equivalent for this term, a Nahuatl one was employed.

Data from Córdova, *Vocabulario*, 207r, supplement other material on the positions and functions of pre-Spanish officials even though they are difficult to interpret. Córdova, *Vocabulario*, 348r, gives, for example, the following glosses for governor: "*Huezaalao ticha*," "*huetocoticha*," "*coquiche pea*," "*cobee pea*," "*napani*," "*nal lani queche*." The glosses for *regidor* are identical to those for governor, while the glosses for *rey* and *alcalde* all can be derived from governor. This may suggest that *alcalde* and *regidor* were not Zapotec concepts and that the Zapotecs had no distinct terms for them. I suspect that Córdova tried to force the Zapotec terms into Spanish categories and, in some cases, to generate Zapotec terms for the Spanish glosses. In summary, all available data seem to support the contention that a prince and his officials (*tequitlatos*) comprised the entire system of native government in pre-Spanish times, as the *relaciones* assert.

44. *RMEH*, Vol. 2 (1928), 125–28.

45. *Ibid.*, 181; *PNE*, Vol. 4, 101, 106, 111, 145.

46. *PNE*, Vol. 4, 106, 179.

47. *Ibid.*, 17; AGN, *General de Parte*, T. 2, *exp.* 51v and *exp.* 148r.

48. See Chapter 3, notes 3, 93, and 115; for Teocuicuilco, see *RMEH*, Vol. 2 (1928), 129.

49. *PNE*, Vol. 4, 146.

50. *Ibid.*, Vol. 1, 179; Vol. 4, 117, 199.

51. *RMEH*, Vol. 2 (1928), 128–29; Spores, "The Zapotec and Mixtec at Spanish Contact," *HBMAI*, Vol. 3 (1965), 968.

52. *Tija* in Zapotec means "lineage or tribe"; *coqui* simply "lord" or "prince," and *tao* means "great or greatest"; thus, the lineage of the greatest lords would be rendered *tijacoquitao*. One might also interpret Córdova to mean, as does John K. Chance in *Race and Class in a Colonial Mexican City*, (Ph.D. diss., University of Illinois, Urbana-Champaign, 1974), 58, that there were three ranks of the Zapotec nobility, for he gives two entries: "Cavallero mediano o Hidalgo. joana lahuiti" and "Señor como cavallero o hidalgo. joana lahuiti"; the first entry implies that a *joana lahuiti* was a middle (*mediano*) noble. However, when Córdova lists the lineages of the lords, he presents only two categories, and, lacking any additional evidence, this seems the most likely interpretation at present.

Xonaxi seems to be a feminine indicator; *xini* means "son or daughter" but would here seem best interpreted in a figurative rather than a literal sense. Other terms also could be generated—a prince's head wife would be called *coquixonaxi*. For these data, see Córdova, *Vocabulario*, 76v, 219v, 246r, 252r, 327v, and 377r; see also *Junta Colombina*, 104, 154, and 186.

Following scholarly precedent, I have utilized the Spanish terms *caciques* and *principales* for the ranks of pre-Spanish nobles; the Spanish term *principal* actually is two lexemes, however, for it refers to both "the general nobility" and to the specific group of nobles below *caciques* in rank; I am employing it here only in the second sense.

53. Córdova, *Vocabulario*, 377r; *Junta Colombina*, 104.

54. For the Zapotec term see Córdova, *Vocabulario*, 246r, and *Junta Colombina*, 104.

55. *PNE*, Vol. 4, 199–200.

56. *Ibid.*, 149.

57. *Ibid.*, 179.

58. *Ibid.*, 112.

59. *RMEH*, Vol. 2 (1928), 129–30.

60. *PNE*, Vol. 4, 18, 140.

61. Córdova, *Arte*, 34, 55.

62. Barbro Dahlgren de Jordán, *La Mixteca* (México, 1954), 145–46.

63. *RMEH*, Vol. 2 (1928), 127, 169; *PNE*, Vol. 4, 198–99.

64. On Huitzo, see *PNE*, Vol. 4, 198–99. Both Córdova, *Vocabulario*, 52v, 219v, and *Junta Colombina*, 88, provide data indicating that the offspring between a noble man and a plebian woman was considered illegitimate; see also *RMEH*, Vol. 2 (1928), 127, 169.

65. *PNE*, Vol. 4, 198–99; *RMEH*, Vol. 2 (1928), 127.

66. On Huitzo, see *PNE*, Vol. 4, 198–99; on Ixtepeji, *PNE*, Vol. 4, 17.

67. Córdova, *Arte*, 217.

68. *Ibid.*

69. *RMEH*, Vol. 2 (1928), 125–26.

70. *Ibid.*, 127.

71. Burgoa, *GD*, Vol. 2, 350.

72. This probably is a more correct rendering than Burgoa's, at least if one follows Córdova. "Copa Vitoo" also could be rendered as "Copa Pitao"—"Pitao" being the general word for god or gods; see Córdova, *Vocabulario*, 140r, 299r. Some of the *relaciones* give the term *vigaña* or *bigaña* for priest. In fact, this is the term given by the *relación* of Mitla for the high priest or pontif of the Zapotec religion; *PNE*, Vol. 4, 152. It is doubtful that this was his correct name: "Coquihuiatao" would be preferable; Córdova, *Vocabulario*, 299v. *Vigaña* or *bigaña* probably was the result of an attempt to render the Zapotec *pizana*.

73. Eduard Seler, "The Wall Paintings of Mitla," *Bureau of American Ethnology*, Bulletin No. 28 (1904), 275–76.

74. Burgoa, *GD*, Vol. 2, 125.

75. *Ibid.*, 121–25.

76. *PNE*, Vol. 4, 198.

77. Burgoa, *GD*, Vol. 2, 121–25, 165–75, and 338–59.

78. Sahagún claims that this was true among the Aztecs, but not all chroniclers agree; this is mentioned in some *relaciones* from Oaxaca but may relate to practitioners of native rites in post-Conquest times who had no formally constituted authority or to diviners who were commoners and therefore did not belong to the priestly estate.

79. Córdova, *Vocabulario*, 252r, 321v; *Junta Colombina*, 109, 149.

80. Córdova, *Vocabulario*, 419v.

81. Oscar Schmieder, *The Settlements of the Tzapotec and Mije Indians, State of Oaxaca, Mexico, University of California Publications in Geography*, No. 4 (1930), 76–77; Spores, "The Zapotec and Mixtec at Spanish Contact," *HBMAI*, Vol. 3 (1965), 968.

82. These occupations have been reconstructed from data contained in Córdova, *Vocabulario*, 103r, 111v, 183v, 236r, 265v, 265r, 278v, 310r, 315v, 316v, 378r, 395r, and *Junta Colombina*, 30, 117, 130, 143, 146, 187, 197; day laborers (Zapotec: *penicopaci, colaneche*), free servants (*penihueyaana*), musicians (*penihuijlla chahui*), sculptors (*huecaa, huechiñe*), metalworkers (*copeecjepigaa pichichi*), painters (*huezee, huezeelohuaa*), interpreters (*penicoñij*), diviners (*peni colanij*), curers (*penihuizabi*),

merchants (*penicoonija*), peddlers (*conija xiohui*), and weavers (*copeeche cobee pizijña yoo*). Many of these remain unanalyzed.

83. Gideon Sjoberg, *The Preindustrial City* (New York, 1960), 120. .

84. Borah and Cook, *The Population of Central Mexico in 1548, Ibero-Americana*, No. 43 (1960), 54–74.

85. *RMEH*, Vol. 2 (1928), 127.

86. *PNE*, Vol. 4, 102, 129, 141.

87. Córdova, *Arte*, 216–17.

88. *PNE*, Vol. 4, 17.

89. Spores, *Mixtec*, 235–36.

90. Córdova, *Vocabulario*, 52r, 188v.

91. Pedro Carrasco, "Social Organization of Ancient Mexico," *HBMAI*, Vol. 10 (1971), 355.

92. See for example, Francisco Rojas Gonzáles, "Los zapotecos en la época prehispánica," in Mendieta, *Zapotecos*, 77–78.

93. Taylor, *CO*, 41–43.

94. Córdova, *Vocabulario*, 412r, gives the gloss "*copaci*" for "tributario," which is identical to one given for vassal; see this chapter, note 80.

95. *PNE*, Vol. 4, 111, 128, 198; *RMEH*, Vol. 2 (1928), 271.

96. Córdova, *Vocabulario*, 292r.

97. *Ibid.*

98. *Ibid.*, 181r, 79v; *Junta Colombina*, 67, 187.

99. *PNE*, Vol. 4, 127.

100. Carrasco, "Social Organization of Ancient Mexico," *HBMAI*, Vol. 10 (1971), 356.

101. Adolf F. Bandelier, "On the Social Organization and Mode of Government of the Ancient Mexicans," *Twelfth Annual Report of the Trustees of the Peabody Museum of American Archaeology and Ethnology*, Vol. 2 (1880), 557–669, and *Report of an Archaeological Tour in Mexico, 1881, Papers of the Archaeological Institute of America*, Vol. 2 (1884). Paul Radin, *Mexican Kinship Terms, University of California Publications in American Archaeology and Ethnology*, No. 31 (1931), 2, also concluded that the Zapotecs had unilineal kinship groups, specifically clans.

102. George P. Murdock, *Social Structure* (New York, 1949), 228–31.

103. For discussions of ambilineal and cognatic systems see: George P. Murdock, "Cognatic Forms of Social Organization," in George P. Murdock (ed.), *Social Structure in Southeast Asia* (Chicago, 1960), 1–14; William Davenport, "Nonunilinear Descent and Descent Groups," *AA*, Vol. 61 (1959), 557–72; Ward H. Goodenough, "A Problem in Malayo-Polynesian Social Organization," *AA*, Vol. 57 (1955), 71–83; Raymond Firth, "A Note on Descent Groups in Polynesia," *Man*, Vol. 57 (1957), 4–8; and Robin Fox, *Kinship and Marriage* (Baltimore, 1967), 146–74. On the kindred, see also D. Freeman, "The Concept of the Kindred," *Journal of the Royal Anthropological Institute*, Vol. 91 (1961), 192–220.

104. Murdock, *Social Structure*, 158–61.

105. Spores, *Mixtec*, 9–14; on the *calpulli*, see Carrasco, "Social Organization of Ancient Mexico," *HBMAI*, Vol. 10 (1971), 349–75.

106. For citations, see this chapter, note 52; *casta linaje* is glossed as "*tija*" or "*quelatija*"—Córdova, *Vocabulario*, 75r.

107. *RMEH*, Vol. 2 (1928), 127; for comparable Mixtec data, see Spores, *Mixtec*, 13.

108. Paul Kirchhoff, "The Principles of Clanship in Human Society," in Morton H.

Fried (ed.), *Readings in Anthropoolgy*, Vol. 2 (New York, 1959), 259–70; for additional discussion, see Marshall D. Sahlins, *Tribesmen* (Englewood Cliffs, N.J.), 48–73.

109. On the use of the term *ramage*, see this chapter, note 103.

110. For glosses dealing with inheritance, see Córdova, *Vocabulario*, 305r; for primogeniture, see *ibid.*, 327v.

111. *RMEH*, Vol. 2 (1928), 127ff.; Spores, "The Zapotec and Mixtec at Spanish Contact," *HBMAI*, Vol. 3 (1965), 969.

112. Taylor, *CO*, 35–66.

113. Alfonso Caso, "The Lords of Yanhuitlan," in Paddock, *AO*, 315.

114. See particularly *RMEH*, Vol. 2 (1928), 125.

115. Córdova, *Arte*, 16–17, states that the individuals of a place felt a particular affinity to an animal or element with which they were associated; it also is possible that a community revered a deity who governed their particular calendar, which could mean that each important community started their calendar with a different day or cycle sign corresponding to their patron deity. Communities also worshiped deified *caciques* or nobles (perhaps the origin of the patron deities?) as mentioned for Ocelotepec, *PNE*, Vol. 4, 139. A similar and related possibility is that they worshiped the patron of their *cacique*, who, in most cases, would have been the fictive ancestor of the ruling dynasty.

Other evidence seems to support a hypothesis that deities at one time were prominent men. For example, José María Bradomín, *Oaxaca en la tradición* (México, 1960), Chap. 4, cites a legend that claims that Cocijo once was a prominent lord who was buried at Monte Albán and that the months of the Zapotec calendar were named to perpetuate the memory of his greatness. Elsie Clews Parsons, *Mitla*, 214, footnote 57, cites the following passage from Burgoa, *GD*, Vol. 2, 319: "On the top of a mountain four leagues beyond Nexapa was buried the cousin of the king of Tehuantepec, son of the king of Zaachila. The deceased had been a valiant captain and they had ordered him to be buried with great accoutrement on that height so that he might be lord over the cardinal directions, east, west, north, and south and guard the vassals and lands of his uncle." Parsons adds: "A war chief become a war god! With a hint why a mountain tomb is of cruciform construction!" Prominent men frequently were deified throughout Mesoamerica.

116. *PNE*, Vol. 4, 179; Tlalixtac was called *Yatiqui* in Zapotec, which probably comes from *yati* meaning "white"; see Alfonso Caso and Ignacio Bernal, *Urnas de Oaxaca*, 365.

117. *PNE*, Vol. 4, 101–102; Caso and Bernal, *Urnas de Oaxaca*, 363.

118. Caso, "The Mixtec and Zapotec Cultures: The Zapotecs," *BEO*, No. 21 (1962), 4–5; Burgoa, *GD*, Vol. 2, 118–19; Seler, "The Wall Paintings of Mitla," *Bureau of American Ethnology*, Bulletin No. 28 (1904), 228–300.

119. *PNE*, Vol. 4, 117; Caso and Bernal, *Urnas de Oaxaca*, 363–64.

120. *PNE*, Vol. 4, 149; Spores, "The Zapotec and Mixtec at Spanish Contact," *HBMAI*, Vol. 3 (1965), 970; Alfonso Caso, "The Mixtec and Zapotec Cultures: The Zapotecs," *BEO*, No. 21 (1962), 10.

121. *PNE*, Vol. 4, 139; Spores, "The Zapotec and Mixtec at Spanish Contact, *HBMAI*, Vol. 3 (1965), 973.

122. *PNE*, Vol. 4, 127; this also might mean that the devil was universally worshiped by the Indians, thus reflecting Spanish ethnocentrism.

123. *PNE*, Vol. 4, 139; Caso and Bernal, *Urnas de Oaxaca*, 364.

124. *PNE*, Vol. 4, 134.

125. *RMEH*, Vol. 2 (1928), 125.

126. *Ibid.*, 121–32; Caso and Bernal, *Urnas de Oaxaca*, 363; Spores, "The Zapotec and Mixtec at Spanish Contact," *HBMAI*, Vol. 3 (1965), 977.

127. Gonzalo de Balzalobre, "Relación autentica de las idolatrias, supersticiones, vanas observaciones de los indios de Oaxaca," *Anales del Museo Nacional de México*, primera época, Vol. 6 (1892), 225–60; James H. Carmichael (ed. and trans.), "Balzalobre on Idolatry in Oaxaca," *BEO*, No. 13 (1959); Henrich Berlin, *Las antiguas creencias en San Miguel Sola, Oaxaca, México*, (Hamburg, 1957). Berlin used *tomos* 431, 437–38, 442, 445–57, 458, 571–73, 575, and 584 of the *Ramo de Inquisición* of the AGN; on Indians and the Inquisition, see Richard E. Greenleaf, "The Inquisition and the Indians of New Spain," *The Americas*, Vol. 22 (1965), 138–66.

128. For Cocijo, see Chapter 3, notes 5 and 115, and this chapter, note 115; see also Frank H. Boos, *Ceramic Sculptures of Ancient Oaxaca*, 27–28, 58; and Caso and Bernal, *Urnas de Oaxaca*, 17–64.

129. Carmichael, "Balsalobre on Idolatry in Oaxaca," *BEO*, No. 13 (1959), 7, for translation of the Balzalobre passage; data on the Valley deities are from Córdova, *Vocabulario*, 141r. Berlin, *Las antiguas creencias en San Miguel Sola, Oaxaca, México*, gives alternate spellings for many of the deities in Sola.

130. Carmichael, "Balsalobre on Idolatry in Oaxaca," *BEO*, No. 13 (1959), 7.

131. *Ibid.*

132. Córdova, *Vocabulario*, 141r.

133. Laurette Sejourné, "Identificación de una diosa zapoteca," *A de INAH*, Vol. 7 (1953), 111–15.

134. Caso and Bernal, *Urnas de Oaxaca*, 360.

135. Córdova, *Vocabulario*, 141r; Carmichael, "Balsalobre on Idolatry in Oaxaca," *BEO*, No. 13 (1959), 7.

136. Córdova, *Vocabulario*, 141r.

137. For a fairly complete list of all the gods in the Zapotec pantheon, including additions from the sierra and Southern Zapotec regions, see José Alcina Franch, "Los dioses del panteón zapoteco," *A de A*, Vol. 9 (1972), 9–40; see also Adelo Ramón *Dioses zapotecas* (México, 1972).

138. Córdova, *Vocabulario*, 141r; Caso and Bernal, *Urnas de Oaxaca*, 359.

139. Córdova, *Arte*, 201–12; Caso, "Zapotec Writing and Calendar," *HBMAI*, Vol. 3 (1965), 943–44.

140. Alfonso Caso, "Zapotec Writing and Calendar," *HBMAI*, Vol. 3 (1965), 944, refers to these priests as the *colanij* or *peni colanij*. While Córdova, *Vocabulario*, 13v, does give these glosses, *huebee pijze* and *huechilla pijzi*, probably refer to those that divined from the *piye*, which I have used as the names of these special priests. The glosses *colanij* or *peni colanij* probably refer to commoners who also divined in various matters. Córdova, *Arte*, 214–16, also gives a list of divination procedures besides those used in connection with the *piye*.

141. Carmichael, "Balsalobre on Idolatry in Oaxaca," *BEO*, No. 13 (1959), 9–10; Balzalobre has also provided the most detailed account available of Zapotec burial customs; see *ibid.*, 8–9.

142. Caso, "Zapotec Writing and Calendar," *HBMAI*, Vol. 3 (1965), 944–45; Eduard Seler, "The Mexican Chronology with Special Reference to the Zapotec Calendar," *Bureau of American Ethnology*, Bulletin No. 28 (1904), 55.

143. R. J. Weitlaner, "Un calendario de los zapotecos del sur," in *Proceedings of the Thirty-Second International Congress of Americanists* (Copenhagen, 1958), 296–

99; also summarized in Caso, "Zapotec Writing and Calendar," *HBMAI*, Vol. 3 (1965), 945–46. For a survival of indigenous deities among the Southern Zapotec, see also R. J. Weitlaner and Gabriel De Cicco, "La jeraquía de los dioses zapotecos del sur," in *Proceedings of the Thirty-Fourth International Congress of Americanists* (1962), 695–710.

144. Caso, "Zapotec Writing and Calendar," *HBMAI*, Vol. 3 (1965), 946.

145. For further information on Zapotec calendars, see José Alcina Franch, "Calendarios zapotecos prehispanicos según documentos de los siglos XVI y XVII," *Estudios de Cultura Nahuatl*, Vol. 6 (1966), 119–33; this article deals particularly with sierra Zapotec calendars.

146. Howard Leigh, "Zapotec Glyphs," *BEO*, No. 2 (1958), 3.

5. ZAPOTEC ELITES AND PEASANTS IN NEW SPAIN

1. I have made more detailed comparisons between Spanish and ancient Oaxacan society in my "Estamento y clase en el Valle de Oaxaca durante el periodo colonial," *América Indígena*, Vol. 30 (1970), 375–86. For other discussions of the estate system in Colonial New Spain, see L. N. McAlister, "Social Structure and Social Change in New Spain," *HAHR*, Vol. 43 (1963), 349–70, and D. A. Brading, "Government and Elite in Late Colonial Mexico," *HAHR*, Vol. 53 (1973), 389–91; for a view emphasizing social classes instead of estates in an urban environment, see John K. Chance, "Race and Class in a Colonial Mexican City: A Social History of Antequera, 1521–1800," Ph.D. diss., University of Illinois, Urbana-Champaign, 1974.

2. The anthropological literature on peasant societies is vast. For good introductions, see Robert Redfield, *Peasant Society and Culture: An Anthropological Approach to Civilization*; Eric R. Wolf, *Peasants*; and Frederick Gamst, *Peasants in Complex Societies* (New York, 1973). Robert Anderson, *Traditional Europe* (Belmont, Calif., 1971) has emphasized that peasants, elites, and townsmen have distinct cultures and that a part-culture characterization is inadequate.

3. Eric R. Wolf, *Sons of the Shaking Earth*, 152–75, has emphasized the importance of looking at various trends or tendencies in Spanish society to understand the New World situation.

4. The above synthesis of the history of the Indian community in New Spain depends heavily on Wolf, *Sons of the Shaking Earth*, François Chevalier, *Land and Society in Colonial Mexico: The Great Hacienda*, and Charles Gibson, "The Transformation of the Indian Community in New Spain, 1500–1810," *Cahiers D'Histoire Mundial*, Vol. 2 (1955), 581–607.

5. Many of the data which follow are found in Taylor, *CO*, an excellent study based on extensive examination of primary source materials. Therefore, in many of the following notes the reader simply is directed to appropriate pages in Taylor's work, which in turn will direct him to the appropriate primary documentation.

On an interpretative level, however, Taylor believes that the model developed by Chevalier, Wolf, and others does not apply to the Valley of Oaxaca, particularly because of the persistence of the native nobility and the lack of pervasiveness of the hacienda. These observations lead him to state that a different model of social development is necessary for the Valley and, further, that other areas of New Spain each may need separate models.

This use of the term *model* seems to restrict it to description. However, as a heuristic device, the *general* model does appear to apply to the Valley. It is true that the native nobility persisted for a longer period there than elsewhere, but eventually, throughout the Valley as in the rest of New Spain, they were reduced to *macehual* status, or were absorbed culturally and socially into the Spanish estate and thus cut off from the Indian community. It also is true that the hacienda was not as pervasive in the Valley as it was elsewhere in New Spain, but eventually it did develop here in response to the same kinds of pressures that created it elsewhere, that is, to feed Spanish cities in response to shortages of tribute in kind and in response to an unstable labor supply. The difference, then, between the Valley of Oaxaca and other areas in New Spain seems to be one of degree and not of kind.

6. Taylor, *CO*, 13–14.

7. Francisco Rojas González, "Los zapotecos en la época colonial," in Mendieta, *Zapotecos*, 175.

8. See especially *PNE*, Vol. 4, and "Relación de Bartolomé de Zárate . . . ," *ENE*, Vol. 4, 141–48.

9. The above data on domesticated animals are found in Taylor, *CO*, 15–16.

10. González, "Los zapotecos en la época colonial," 132; George Foster, *Culture and Conquest: America's Spanish Heritage* (Chicago, 1960).

11. Taylor, *CO*, 81; Burgoa, *GD*, Vol. 1, 272.

12. González, "Los zapotecos en la época colonial," 128–29; for additional information on Colonial dress, see A. H. Gayton, "Textiles and Costume," *HBMAI*, Vol. 6 (1967), 138–57.

13. Mitla was a notable exception; although initially the Spaniards attempted to combine the administrative-religious precincts into a single entity, the Church ultimately was built among pre-Spanish ruins to facilitate association of the new religion with a familiar place. See Oscar Schmieder, *The Settlements of the Tzapotec and Mije Indians, State of Oaxaca, Mexico, University of California Publications in Geography*, No. 4 (Berkeley, 1930), 41.

14. Taylor, *CO*, 20, 23.

15. John Paddock, "Mixtec Ethnohistory and Monte Albán V," in Paddock, *AO*, 374–75; *PNE*, Vol. 4, 117.

16. For the possessions of Cortés in 1533–37, see N. Cuevas (ed.), *Cartas y otros documentos de Hernán Cortés* (Seville, 1915), 101–256; see also this chapter, note 52.

17. Taylor, *CO*, 23.

18. Paddock, "Mixtec Ethnohistory and Monte Albán V," in Paddock, *AO*, 370–71.

19. Jean Clare Hendry, "Atzompa: A Pottery Producing Village of Southern Mexico," Ph.D. diss., Cornell University, 1957; Helen Miller Bailey, *Santa Cruz of the Etla Hills* (Gainesville, Florida, 1958). Xoxocotlán, a town near Cuilapan, still had Mixtec speakers in the eighteenth century; see Mary Elizabeth Smith, *Picture Writing from Ancient Southern Mexico*: 202–10.

20. Taylor, *CO*, 33–34.

21. For details of the Spanish conquest of the Valley of Oaxaca, see Jorge Fernando Iturribarría, *Oaxaca en la conquista* (Oaxaca, 1956), and *Oaxaca en la historia: de la época procolombina a los tiempos actuales*, 53–62.

22. My population data on the Valley come from Taylor, *CO*, 18–21. However, Taylor estimates that the population of the Valley in 1959 was smaller than it was at the time of Spanish contact. I feel this Conquest figure is too high (see chapter 4).

23. Taylor, *CO*, 19.

24. *Ibid.*, 21.

25. See my "Estamento y clase en el Valle de Oaxaca durante el periodo colonial," *American Indígena*, Vol. 30 (1970), 380, for citations of documents dealing with the privileges of the Indian nobility.

26. Taylor, *CO*, 39.

27. *Ibid.*, 46.

28. *Ibid.*, 43; Chevalier, *Land and Society in Colonial Mexico*, 52.

29. Taylor, *CO*, 47–48.

30. On these areas, see Charles Gibson, *The Aztecs under Spanish Rule: A History of the Indians of the Valley of Mexico, 1519–1810*, and Delfina Esmeraldo López Sarrelangue, *La nobeleza indígena de Pátzcuaro en la época virreinal*, (México, 1965).

31. Taylor, *CO*, 65–66.

32. *Ibid.*, 16; Brian R. Hamnett, "Dye Production, Food Supply, and the Laboring Population of Oaxaca, 1750–1820," *HAHR*, Vol. 51 (1971), 51–78.

33. For Tlacolula, see Taylor, *CO*, 63–65; for the Miahuatlán region, see *PNE*, Vol. 4, "Suplemento," and *DII*, Vol. 9, 210–393; for Tehuantepec, see *RMEH*, Vol. 2, 164–75; for the sierra, see *RMEH*, Vol. 2, 113–31.

34. Taylor, *CO*, 140–43.

35. *Ibid.*, 38.

36. Charles Gibson, *Spain in America*, 150.

37. Both Gibson, *Aztecs under Spanish Rule*, 163–93, and Spores, *Mixtec*, 119–22, discuss the *cabildo* and its various offices. As these scholars correctly point out, *gobernador* and *cacique* clearly were distinct concepts, although they had some similarities which have caused confusion:

A. While the *gobernador* often was a different individual from the *cacique*, one criterion for filling these two positions was the same, for both had to belong to the Indian nobility. A study of various documents pertaining to the Valley of Oaxaca confirms this statement; AGN, *Indios*, T. 2, no. 197, on Guaxolotitlán; *Indios*, T. 3, no. 623, on Tlacochahuaya; *Indios*, T. 6, 2a parte, no. 311, on Teozapotlán; *Mercedes*, T. 3, f. 143r–144r, on Tehuantepec; *Mercedes*, T. 8, f. 62r, on Ixtepec; *Mercedes*, T. 2, *Exp.* 410, on Tlalixtac; *Mercedes*, T. 3, f. 32r, on Tlalixtac; *Mercedes*, T. 2, f. 2r, on Tlacochahuaya; and *Mercedes*, T. 3, f. 151v, on Ocotlán.

B. They were different, however, in other respects. *Caciques* received their titles by heredity and succession—*gobernadores* by estate and election; see Spores, *Mixtec*, 110–30, and Gibson, *Aztecs under Spanish Rule*, 166–93.

C. *Caciques* and *gobernadores* often were the same individuals. Many individuals are referred to as "*cacique* and *gobernador* of ——"; see AGN, *Indios*, T. 2, no. 627, on Ocotlán; T. 4, on Teozapotlán; Vol. 5, no. 51, on Etla; and Vol. 6, 1a *parte*, no. 567, on Tlacolula. See also AGN, *Mercedes*, T. 3, f. 143r–144r, on Tehuantepec; and T. 3, f. 92r–92v, on Tlalixtac.

D. Many towns which received governorships apparently were often identical to those which were pre-Spanish *cabeceras* or seats of lordships; see *ENE*, Vol. 16, 68.

38. Gibson, *Aztecs Under Spanish Rule*, 166–93.

39. Taylor, *CO*, 49.

40. *Ibid.*, 51.

41. *Ibid.*

42. *Ibid.*, 51–52, translating Burgoa, *GD*, Vol. 2, 14.

43. Taylor, *CO*, 52.

44. *Ibid.*, 53.

45. *Ibid.*, 51–53.

46. Spores, *Mixtec*, 120–21.

47. Taylor, *CO*, 53.

48. *Ibid.*, 29.

49. Data in this section on Indian lands in the Valley are based on *ibid.*, 67–107.

50. For a history of long-standing disputes between two Valley towns, see Philip A. Dennis, "An Inter-Village Land Dispute in the Valley of Oaxaca, Mexico," Ph.D. diss., Cornell University, 1973.

51. Data on the Etla region are found in Taylor, *CO*, 90–94.

52. *Ibid.*, 90.

53. On the Zimatlán arm, see *ibid.*, 102–107.

54. For information on the cochineal industry, see Raymond L. Lee, "Cochineal Production in New Spain to 1600," *The Americas*, Vol. 4 (1947–48), 449–73; "American Cochineal in European Commerce," *The Journal of Modern History*, Vol. 23 (1951), 205–24; Barbro Dahlgren de Jordán, *La grana cochinilla* (México, 1963); and Brian R. Hamnett, *Politics and Trade in Southern Mexico, 1750–1821*.

55. Martin Diskin, "Market and Society in Tlacolula, Oaxaca," Ph.D. diss., University of California, Los Angeles, 1967, 41–44.

56. On the Tlacolula arm, see Taylor, *CO*, 102–107.

57. See Elsie Clews Parsons, *Mitla*, 10.

58. Taylor, *CO*, 77; all figures have been converted to the metric system.

59. *Ibid.*, 143; for listings of *encomiendas* in the sierra and south for the year 1560, see *ENE*, Vol. 9, 2–43; for a recent general statement on the *encomienda*, see Robert G. Keith, "Encomienda, Hacienda, and Corregimiento: A Structural Analysis," *HAHR*, Vol. 51 (1971), 431–46.

60. Immediately after the Spanish Conquest, the Marqués del Valle held most of the Valley towns, see *DII*, Vol. 12, 561. Later, although he maintained residual rights to many towns, in most cases there was no tribute left for him after crown and *corregidor* tribute was exacted—see *DII*, Vol. 12, 330–38; for a brief history of the marquisate in the Valley of Oaxaca, see Chevalier, *Land and Society in Colonial Mexico*, 127–34.

61. Taylor, *CO*, 71.

62. Documents on the early period are found in *El libro de las tasaciones de pueblos de la Nueva España* (México, 1952); for Zimatlán, see 636–38; for Mitla and Tlacolula, 245–46; for Teozapotlán, 477–78; for Tlalixtac, 506–507. For 1536, see "Tributos de los indios de la Nueva España," *Boletín: Archivo General de la Nación*, Vol. 7 (1936), 185–225; this represents a reproduction of a document from AGI, paleographed by France V. Scholes. For the *Suma de Visitas*, see *PNE*, Vol. 1; the item relating to Zimatlán is no. 230, 101–102; Mitla is no. 361, 149; Teozapotlán, no. 763, 287; and Tlalixtac, no. 846, 315.

63. These documents also are found in *El libro de las tasaciones de pueblos de la Nueva España*; Teozapotlán is discussed on 477–78. For weights and measures in the Colonial period, see Manuel Carrera Stampa, "The Evolution of Weights and Measures in New Spain," *HAHR*, Vol. 29 (1949), 2–24.

64. Documents pertaining to this rebellion are in Genaro García (ed.), *Documentos inéditos o muy raros para la historia de México* (México, 1907), Vol. 10, 77–109. It also is summarized in most histories of Oaxaca; for an English version, see Miguel Covarrubias, *Mexico South: The Isthmus of Tehuantepec*, 209–11; for a monographic study, see Basilio Rojas, *La rebelión de Tehuantepec* (México, 1964).

65. Most rebellions involving Zapotecs took place in the sierra, Isthmus, and

Southern Zapotec regions outside of the Valley of Oaxaca. For example, Ixtepeji had been involved in a rebellion before the larger one of 1660. There also was a rebellion at Titiquipa, a town near Miahuatlán, in the 1540's; in this outbreak the Indians refused to pay crown tribute, stating that they would pay tribute only to native lords, not to *corregidores*—see *ENE*, Vol. 5, 36–41.

66. Taylor, *CO*, 71, 132.

67. Hamnett, "Dye Production, Food Supply, and the Laboring Population of Oaxaca, 1750–1820," *HAHR*, Vol. 51 (1971), 61–62; for the history of Miahuatlán, see Basilio Rojas, *Miahuatlán*, 2 vols. (México, 1963).

68. Documents pertaining to labor and the *repartimiento* in Oaxaca may be found in Silvio Zavala and María Castelo (eds.), *Fuentes para la historia del trabajo en Nueva España* (México, 1939–46), 8 volumes.

69. Data on the *repartimiento* in the Valley of Oaxaca are drawn from Taylor, *CO*, 143–52.

70. Wolf, *Sons of the Shaking Earth*, 204.

71. Chevalier, *Land and Society in Colonial Mexico*, is the classic study of the Colonial hacienda; for a summary of recent research on the hacienda, see Magnus Mörner, "The Spanish-American Hacienda: A Survey of Recent Research and Debate," *HAHR*, Vol. 53 (1973), 183–216.

72. Taylor, *CO*, 134.

73. Some authors define the hacienda as having a minimum of 22,000 acres; see Taylor, *CO*, 122, 248.

74. *Ibid.*, 134–35.

75. *Ibid.*, 123–26, 140–42, 152–58.

76. My information on the hacienda, labor, and debt peonage in the Valley comes from *ibid.*, 143–52.

77. *Ibid.*, 148.

78. *Ibid.*, 152.

79. *Ibid.*, 163.

80. *Ibid.*, 165.

81. For Cocijo, see González, "Los zapotecos en la época colonial," in Mendieta, *Zapotecos*, 151–53; for Pinopiaa and Xalapa, see Burgoa, *GD*, Vol. 2, 330–31.

82. Burgoa, *GD*, Vol. 2, 330–31.

83. *Ibid.*, Vol. 2, 70.

84. González, "Los zapotecos en la época colonial," in Mendieta, *Zapotecos*, 152.

85. Taylor, *CO*, 171, 193.

86. *Ibid.*, 166.

87. For the history of tithes (*diezmos*) in Oaxaca, see Woodrow Borah, "The Collection of Tithes in the Bishopric of Oaxaca during the Sixteenth Century," *HAHR*, Vol. 21 (1941), 386–409, and "Tithe Collection in the Bishopric of Oaxaca, 1601–1867," *HAHR*, Vol. 29 (1949), 489–517; one document from AGI consists of a letter from twelve Indian governors from the "Province of the Zapotecs of the Valley of Oaxaca" to the King of Spain, pleading that *diezmos* not be imposed upon them; this letter, dated 1560, had the support of Fray Juan de Córdova—*ENE*, Vol. 16, 66–68.

88. Taylor, *CO*, 71, 169, provides data on the Valley's *cofradías*; for priestly abuses, see Taylor, *CO*, 193.

89. Pedro Carrasco, "The Civil-Religious Hierarchy in Mesoamerican Communities," *AA*, Vol. 63 (1961), 495; my interpretation of the function of the *cargo* system in the Colonial Indian community also depends on Wolf, *Sons of the Shaking Earth*,

214–18, and "Closed Corporate Peasant Communities in Mesoamerica and Central Java," *SWJA*, Vol. 13 (1957), 1–18.

90. Taylor, *CO*, 82.

6. THE ZAPOTECS IN MODERN MEXICO

1. Laura Nader, "The Zapotec of Oaxaca," *HBMAI*, Vol. 7 (1969), 349.

2. The Mexican war of independence was not an isolated case; works which summarize various points of view concerning the causes of the wars of Spanish-American independence are Charles W. Arnade, Arthur P. Whitaker, and Bailey W. Diffie, "Causes of the Spanish-American Wars of Independence," *Journal of Inter-American Studies*, Vol. 2 (1960), 125–45, and Charles C. Griffin, "Economics and Social Aspects of the Era of Spanish-American Independence," *HAHR*, Vol. 29 (1949), 170–87; the Mexican movement is well summarized in Charles C. Cumberland, *Mexico* (London, Oxford, and New York), 113–40.

3. Cumberland, *Mexico*, 141.

4. The politics of the Juárez era are discussed in Walter V. Scholes, *Mexican Politics during the Juárez Regime, 1855–1872* (Columbia, Mo., 1957); social developments and their consequences may best be seen in Daniel Cosío Villegas (ed.), *Historia moderna de México*, Vols. 1–4 (México, 1955–60). I also am indebted to the short discussion of the Juárez era in Eric R. Wolf, *Peasant Wars of the Twentieth Century* (New York, 1969), 11–18.

5. This may seem a strange program for an individual coming from a peasant background, for peasant utopias generally envision communal holdings vested in the peasant community and not in private property. While Juárez's deviation from this idea might be explained as a result of "enlightened" education, the explanation also might be sought in the particular characteristics of the region from which he came.

The sierra Zapotec region, unlike the Zapotec Valley of Oaxaca, had been at the mercy of a precarious land base; developments in the Colonial period had forced the inhabitants of some settlements in the region to turn to commercial enterprises, mining, and activities other than agriculture to meet their tribute schedules. Thus, communities became overspecialized and dependent on an international economy more than on an internal marketing system such as the one prevalent in the Valley. As a result, periods of economic depression, like the decline of the cochineal industry in the nineteenth century, hit the sierra towns particularly hard. Further, because of overspecialization, lands which had been devoted to subsistence activities were largely ignored or lost.

Juárez thus came from a land-hungry environment instead of the relatively stable peasant communities of the Valley, and from an area that long had been known for its tradition of rebellions. Thus, like many leaders with reformist ideas, he came not from a core conservative area but from a peripheral "liberal" one which was specialized in an important way.

6. My discussion of the central district of the Valley of Oaxaca immediately preceding and following La Reforma is based on Charles R. Berry, "La ciudad de Oaxaca en vísperas de La Reforma," *Historia Mexicana*, Vol. 19 (1969), 23–61, and "The Fact and Fiction of the Reform: The Case of the Central District of Oaxaca, 1856–1867," *The Americas*, Vol. 26 (1970), 277–90.

7. Data on historical events transpiring in San Juan Guelavía are found in Jorge

Martínez Ríos and Gustavo M. de Luna Méndez, "Efectos sociales de la reforma agraria en el Ejido de San Juan Guelavía, Estado de Oaxaca," in Lucio Mendieta y Núñez (ed.), *Efectos sociales de la reforma agraria en tres comunidades ejidales de la República Mexicana* (México, 1960), 207–324; these data also are summarized in Kent V. Flannery, "The Cultural Evolution of Civilizations," in Richard F. Johnson, Peter W. Frank, and Charles D. Michener (eds.), *Annual Review of Ecology and Systematics* (Palo Alto, Calif., 1972), 415–16.

8. For historical data on developments in Díaz Ordaz, see Antonio Ugalde, "Contemporary Mexico: From Hacienda to PRI, Political Leadership in a Zapotec Village," in Robert Kern (ed.), *The Caciques* (Albuquerque, N.M., 1973), 119–35.

9. A careful study still remains to be made of the development of the hacienda in Oaxaca during the nineteenth and early twentieth centuries. My contention that the hacienda underwent some growth during this period thus is based on scanty data; for a list of the haciendas, and the sizes of their landholdings in the early twentieth century, see Francisco Rojas González, "Los zapotecos en la época independiente," in Mendieta, *Zapotecos*, 179–84.

10. Taylor, *CO*, 200.

11. The city of Oaxaca did attract some foreign investors, although they seem to have been fewer there than elsewhere. At the end of the nineteenth century, for example, a group of foreign investors rejuvenated the mining industry and built a Mexico City–Oaxaca City railroad; see Ronald Waterbury, "Urbanization and a Traditional Market System," in Walter Goldschmidt and Harry Hoijer (eds.), *The Social Anthropology of Latin America*, 127; and Jorge Fernando Iturribarría, *Oaxaca en la historia*, 240–41.

12. For a history of Tehuantepec in the nineteenth century and Doña Juana C. Romera's role in it, see Miguel Covarrubias, *Mexico South*, 222–39.

13. One of the better accounts of the Mexican Revolution can be found in Wolf, *Peasant Wars of the Twentieth Century*, 1–48.

14. For a discussion of the Zapatista phase of the Revolution, see John Womack, Jr., *Zapata and the Mexican Revolution* (New York, 1969); Ronald Waterbury is currently preparing a comparative study of the respective roles of the peasants of Morelos and Oaxaca in the Mexican Revolution of 1910. This study will appear in *Comparative Studies in Society and History*.

15. See Michael Kearney, *The Winds of Ixtepeji*, 30–42.

16. See Beverly Chiñas, *The Isthmus Zapotecs*, 12–14, and Covarrubias, *Mexico South*, 232–42.

17. For the exploits of Nicanor Díaz, see Covarrubias, *Mexico South*, 237–38.

18. For data on the Miahuatlán region, see Basilio Rojas, *Miahuatlán*; additional accounts of the revolution in Oaxaca include Carlos Tamayo, *Oaxaca en la Revolución* (México, 1956); Alfonso Francisco Ramírez, *Historia de la Revolución Mexicana en Oaxaca* (México, 1970); and Angel Bustillo Bernal, *La Revolución en el itsmo* [*sic*, *istmo*] *de Tehuantepec* (México, 1968).

19. Kirkby, *Land and Water*, 53.

20. Concerning the use of tractors in the Valley, Kirkby, *Land and Water*, 74, has written: "Although tractors cost a little less than ox-ploughs per hectare if the land is in large enough units, they are not a feasible alternative for most peasants for several reasons.

1) Many landholdings are in parcels which are widely separated, and each parcel is too small to be practical enough to plow with a tractor.

2) A tractor is commonly hired by the day and can plough about 3.5 hectares so

that the landholding must be at least this size to be worth the cost of a day's hire charge.

3) The cost of buying a tractor is prohibitive for small peasant landowners so they must hire one by the day, and tractors available for hire are scarce."

21. Kirkby, *Land and Water*, 95–122.

22. Chiñas, *The Isthmus Zapotecs*, 24.

23. Nader, "The Zapotec of Oaxaca," *HBMAI*, Vol. 7 (1969), 338; Julio de la Fuente, "La cultura zapoteca," *RMEA*, Vol. 16 (1960), 236.

24. Nader, "The Zapotec of Oaxaca," *HBMAI*, Vol. 7 (1969), 339; Fuente, "La cultura zapoteca," *RMEA*, Vol. 16 (1960), 236.

25. For a study of two sierra towns or villages, one dispersed, one nucleated, and the effects of these different settlement patterns on social organization, see Laura Nader, *Talea and Juquila, University of California Publications in American Archaeology and Ethnology*, Vol. 48, No. 3 (Berkeley and Los Angeles, 1964).

26. Nader, "The Zapotec of Oaxaca," *HBMAI*, Vol. 7 (1969), 340.

27. The Isthmus Zapotec settlements often are described as cities, but as Chiñas, *The Isthmus Zapotecs*, 15, has pointed out, they should not be thought of as cities in the same sense as that term is used in the United States. The Isthmus Zapotecs, however, conceptualize them as urban and do so with considerable pride.

28. Kirkby, *Land and Water*, 146.

29. Kearney, *The Winds of Ixtepeji*, 5, 30–37.

30. Kirkby, *Land and Water*, 28; Theodore Edmond Downing, "A Report on the Social Consequences of Zapotec Inheritance," paper presented at the 72nd Annual Meeting of the American Anthropological Association, New Orleans, Nov., 1973, 3.

31. Kirkby, *Land and Water*, 28.

32. Lees, *Irrigation*, 45–81.

33. Kirkby, *Land and Water*, 28.

34. Discussions of *ejidos* in the Valley may be found in Kirkby, *Land and Water*, 30; Lees, *Irrigation*, 11; Antonio Ugalde, "Contemporary Mexico: From Hacienda to PRI, Political Leadership in a Zapotec Village," in Robert Kern (ed.), *The Caciques* (Albuquerque, N.M., 1973), 119–35, and Ríos and Luna Méndez, "Efectos sociales de la reforma agraria," 207–324.

35. For a study focusing on the effects of mass culture and society on a Zapotec village, see Manuel Avila, *Tradition and Growth* (Chicago, 1969), which deals with Mitla as well as villages elsewhere in Mexico; most recent village studies on Oaxaca deal with changes in material culture. For two studies dealing with the village of Teotitlán del Valle and its changing material culture, see Robert B. Taylor, "Conservative Factors in the Changing Culture of a Zapotec Town," *Human Organization*, Vol. 25 (1966), 116–21, and Pedro Yescas Peralta, "Teotitlán del Valle, muestra en el proceso de aculturación," *Revista Mexicana de Sociología*, Vol. 16 (1954), 397–408.

36. This is the view espoused by the so-called substantivists in economic anthropology as well as that put forth by a number of scholars who have studied peasant societies. For an example of the substantivist approach, see George P. Dalton, *Economic Anthropology and Development* (New York, 1971). Similar views of the nature of peasant economics may be seen in S. F. Franklin, *The European Peasantry* (London, 1969), and A. V. Chayanov, *The Theory of the Peasant Economy* (Homewood, Ill., 1966); a review of the various approaches to peasant economics may be found in Theodor Shanin, "The Nature and Logic of the Peasant Economy," *The Journal of Peasant Studies*, Vol. 1 (1973) 63–80.

37. A number of anthropologists, representing the so-called formalists, have at-

tempted to extend the methods of economics to the study of primitive and peasant societies; see particularly Edward E. Le Clair, Jr., and Harold K. Schneider (eds.), *Economic Anthropology* (New York, 1968), which includes reprints of articles explicating the "formalist" position.

38. The classic study of *guelaguetza* is that of Jorge Martínez Ríos, "Análisis funcional de la 'Guelaguetza Agricola,'" *Revista Mexicana de Sociología*, Vol. 26 (1964), 79–126; my discussion draws on Ralph L. Beals, "Gifting, Reciprocity, Savings, and Credit in Peasant Oaxaca," *SWJA*, Vol. 26 (1970), 234–37.

39. According to Beals, "Gifting, Reciprocity, Savings, and Credit in Peasant Oaxaca," *SWJA*, Vol. 26 (1970), 235, *guelaguetza* requests usually are solicited from relatives, *compadres*, neighbors, and friends (that is, individuals with whom one has close social ties); however, in some cases voluntary *guelaguetza* contributions may be made by others, a factor which illustrates the purely credit side of *guelaguetza*.

40. One of the problems that has faced economic anthropologists in their studies of peasant economics is development of a method to quantify the value of goods in semicash economies; for an attempt at quantification of a Valley Zapotec economy, see Antonio Ugalde, "Measuring Wealth in a Semi-Cash Economy," *Rural Sociology*, Vol. 35 (1970), 512–22.

41. Beals, "Gifting, Reciprocity, Savings, and Credit in Peasant Oaxaca," *SWJA*, Vol. 26 (1970), 237.

42. *Ibid.*, 238.

43. Eric R. Wolf, *Peasants*, 40.

44. The Valley of Oaxaca market system was studied by Bronislaw Malinowski and Julio de la Fuente, *La economía de un sistema de mercados en México*, Acta Anthropológica, época 2, Vol. 1, No. 2 (México, 1957). A more recent project under the direction of Ralph L. Beals has added greatly to knowledge of this market system; see particularly Ralph L. Beals, "Un sistema tradicional de mercado," *América Indígena*, Vol. 27 (1967), 566–80; "The Structure of the Oaxaca Market System," *RMEA*, Vol. 21 (1967), 333–42; and Ronald Waterbury, "The Traditional Market System of the Valley of Oaxaca," Ph.D. diss., University of California at Los Angeles, 1968. Two books dealing with studies of the Oaxaca market system will soon appear: Ralph L. Beals, *The Peasant Marketing System of Oaxaca, Mexico* (Berkeley and Los Angeles); and Scott Cook and Martin Diskin (eds.), *Market in Oaxaca* (Austin, Tex., forthcoming). Ronald Waterbury also is preparing a study based on the field notes of Bronislaw Malinowski.

The market system in the sierra is dealt with in Ralph L. Beals, "Estudio de poblados en la sierra zapoteca de Oaxaca, México," *América Indígena*, Vol. 31 (1971), 671–91, and Richard Lewis Berg, Jr. "The Impact of Modern Economy on the Traditional Economy in Zoogocho, Oaxaca, Mexico," Ph.D. diss., University of California at Los Angeles, 1968. Beverly Chiñas, "Zapotec 'Viajeras,'" in Cook and Diskin (eds.), *Markets in Oaxaca*, constitutes an important essay on isthmus markets and points out significant contrasts between this region and the Valley of Oaxaca.

45. Tlacolula and its market system have been the subject of a study by Martin Diskin, "Market and Society in Tlacolula, Oaxaca, México," Ph.D. diss., University of California at Los Angeles, 1967; see also his "Estudio estructural del sistema de plaza en el valle de Oaxaca," *América Indígena*, Vol. 29 (1969), 1077–99.

46. For Atzompa, see Jean Clare Hendry, "Atzompa," Ph.D. diss., Cornell University, 1957, and Charlotte Stolmaker, "Cultural, Social and Economic Change in Santa María Atzompa," Ph.D. diss., University of California at Los Angeles, 1973;

pottery making in Coyotepec is dealt with by Paul Van de Velde, and Henriette Van de Velde, *The Black Pottery of Coyotepec, Southwest Museum Papers*, No. 13 (Los Angeles, 1939); the weaving industries of Teotitlán del Valle, Diaz Ordaz, and Santa Ana are discussed in Emily Ann Vargas-Baron, "Development and Change of Rural Artisanry," Ph.D. diss., Stanford University, 1968; Teitipac and its *metateros* have been the subject of studies by Scott Cook, "Teitipac and Its Metateros," Ph.D. diss., University of Pittsburgh, 1968; "Price and Output Variability in a Peasant-Artisan Stone-Working Industry in Oaxaca," *AA*, Vol. 72 (1970), 776–801; "Stone Tools for Steel Age Mexicans? Aspects of Production in a Zapotec Stone Working Industry," *AA*, Vol. 75 (1973), 1485–1503. A full-length monograph on Teitipac by Scott Cook is now in progress; for Mitla, see Elsie Clews Parsons, *Mitla*, and Charles M. Leslie, *Now We Are Civilized*.

Not all Valley towns specialize in crafts, although most tend to have some kind of specialization. For example, San Antonio Ocotlán specializes in vegetables and flowers, Magdalena Ocotlán in maize and metates, San Lázaro Etla in dairying, and Tlalixtac de Cabrera in maize and alfalfa.

Crafts in the Zapotec sierra village of Yalálag are discussed in Carol F. Jopling, "Women Weavers of Yalálag," Ph.D. diss., University of Massachusetts at Amherst, 1973.

47. My discussion of the Oaxaca City market is based on Waterbury, "Urbanization and a Traditional Market System," 126–53.

48. *Ibid.*, 149.

49. *Ibid.*, 150.

50. Beals, "Gifting, Reciprocity, Savings, and Credit in Peasant Oaxaca," *SWJA*, Vol. 26 (1970), 240.

51. Waterbury, "Urbanization and a Traditional Market System," 152.

52. For the *municipio libre* system see Pérez Jiménez, Gustavo, *La institución del municipio libre en el Estado de Oaxaca y su reforma constitucional* (México, 1955).

53. Lees, *Irrigation*, 17.

54. My discussion of the *ayuntamiento* and its offices is based on Lees, *Irrigation*, 18–20; Jack Corbett of Vanderbilt University has also recently conducted a study of the nature of politics in Valley communities.

55. Lees, *Irrigation*, 10, 49; Fuente, "La cultura zapoteca," *RMEH*, Vol. 16 (1960), 240. In some areas of Mexico, such as Chiapas, the term *cargo* is applied exclusively to the religious posts; in Oaxaca, the term *mayordomo* is used.

56. For example: in Tlalixtac, *mayordomía* sponsorship still is considered a pre-requisite for political office, but specific *mayordomo* posts are not prerequisites for specific civil *cargos*—see Lees, *Irrigation*, 48–49. *Mayordomías* seem to have lapsed altogether in San Agustín Etla, and Díaz Ordaz—see Lees, *Irrigation*, 79, and Ugalde, "Contemporary Mexico: From Hacienda to PRI, Political Leadership in a Zapotec Village," 126–27. In Mitla *mayordomías* have increased in importance as commerce has developed—see Leslie, *Now We Are Civilized*, 9–10.

57. The traditional interpretation of the civil-religious hierarchy, as remarked in Chapter 5, was that it was a redistributive mechanism which selected in favor of poverty since the burden of office supposedly fell on the wealthiest individuals of the community, thus dispersing their "excess wealth."

58. For this interpretation, see Lees, *Irrigation*, 13.

59. Nader, "The Zapotec of Oaxaca," *HBMAI*, Vol. 7 (1969), 349; Julio de la Fuente, *Yalálag, Museo Nacional de Antropología, Serie Científica*, 215.

60. Kearney, *The Winds of Ixtepeji*, 91.

61. My discussion of the expected roles of political officials in Zapotec communities, particularly the *presidente*, is based on Philip A. Dennis, "The Oaxacan Village President as Political Middleman," *Ethnology*, Vol. 12 (1973), 419–27; see also Lees, *Irrigation*, 19.

62. For an excellent discussion of this point, see Eric R. Wolf, "Levels of Communal Relations," *HBMAI*, Vol. 6 (1967), 304–306.

63. *Ibid.*, 304; Fuente, *Yalálag*, 20–25, 239–49.

64. Wolf, "Levels of Communal Relations," *HBMAI*, Vol. 6 (1967), 304.

65. Ugalde, "Contemporary Mexico: From Hacienda to PRI, Political Leadership in a Zapotec Village," 124–29.

66. Chiñas, *The Isthmus Zapotecs*, 15.

67. Kearney, *The Winds of Ixtepeji*, 30–41.

68. Leslie, *Now We Are Civilized*.

69. According to Leslie, *Now We Are Civilized*, the increased interest of Mitleños in commerce was the major criterion for their insistence that they were now more "civilized"; that is, concern with monetary matters to them was synonomous with "civilization."

70. Lees, *Irrigation*, 19.

71. Julio de la Fuente, "Relaciones interétnicas," *Instituto Nacional Indigenista, Colección de Antropología Social* (México, 1965), 31–32, as cited in Philip A. Dennis, "Inter-Village Feuding," paper presented at the annual meeting of the American Anthropological Association, New Orleans, 1973, 2.

72. Dennis, "Inter-Village Feuding," 8; for a more extended discussion of feuding between Valley villages see Dennis, "An Inter-Village Land Feud in the Valley of Oaxaca, Mexico," Ph.D. diss., Cornell University, 1973.

73. Eric R. Wolf, "Closed Corporate Peasant Communities in Mesoamerica and Central Java," *SWJA*, Vol. 13 (1957), 13.

74. My account of the effects and nature of government-sponsored hydraulic projects in the Valley of Oaxaca is based on Lees, *Irrigation*, 83–87.

75. *Ibid.*, 21.

76. In Ixtepeji, *barrios* retain some semblance of religious functions; see Kearney, *The Winds of Ixtepeji*, 22–23; while in Tlalixtac de Cabrera, *barrio* patron saints may be sponsored by non-*barrio* members—see Lees, *Irrigation*, 46.

77. Many Zapotec communities have geographical divisions, such as upper and lower sections, some of which are called *barrios*.

78. Nader, "The Zapotec of Oaxaca," *HBMAI*, Vol. 7 (1969), 341; interests on loans apparently are used in Talea and Juquila to celebrate the *barrio* saint's fiesta and to pay taxes to the local town government—Laura Nader, *Talea and Juquila, University of California Publications in American Archaeology and Ethnology*, Vol. 48, No. 3 (1964), 237.

79. John Paddock, "Mixtec Ethnohistory and Monte Albán V," in Paddock, *AO*, 379.

80. Nader, "The Zapotec of Oaxaca," *HBMAI*, Vol. 7 (1969), 340–41.

81. *Barrios*, formerly important in Mitla, apparently disappeared by the 1930's, see Parsons, *Mitla*, 7.

82. Nader, "The Zapotec of Oaxaca," *HBMAI*, Vol. 7 (1969), 347–48.

83. My discussion of the household structure, residence patterns, and Zapotec inheritance is based on Theodore E. Downing, "A Report on the Social Consequences of

Zapotec Inheritance," paper presented at the annual meeting of the American Anthropological Association, New Orleans, 1973.

84. For data on the family cycle and inheritance, see this chapter, note 83; for further data, see Theodore E. Downing, "Zapotec Inheritance," Ph.D. diss., Stanford University, 1973.

85. Both Lees, *Irrigation*, and Chiñas, *The Isthmus Zapotecs*, have emphasized the importance of distinguishing between "public" and "private" spheres in understanding Zapotec peasant communities.

86. George M. Foster, "The Dyadic Contract: A Model for the Social Structure of a Mexican Peasant Village," in Jack M. Potter, May N. Diaz, and George M. Foster (eds.), *Peasant Society* (Boston, 1967), 214.

87. *Ibid.*, 213–30. My discussion of the "dyadic contract" generally follows Foster's conceptualization.

88. For a good discussion of *compadrazgo* in the Zapotec community of Zaachila, see María Eugenia V. de Stavenhagen, "El compadrazgo en una communidad zapoteca," *Ciencias Political y Sociales*, Año 4, No. 17 (México, 1959), 364–402; for a general treatment of *compadrazgo* in Mesoamerica, see Robert Ravicz, "Compadrinazgo," *HBMAI*, Vol. 6 (1967), 238–51.

89. Paul Stirling, "Impartiality and Personal Morality (Italy), in J. G. Peristiany, (ed.), *Contributions to Mediterranean Sociology* (Paris and The Hague, 1968), 64.

90. Kearney, *The Winds of Ixtepeji*, 44–45, 59–60, 65–69.

91. Chiñas, *The Isthmus Zapotecs*, 81.

92. George M. Foster, "Peasant Society and the Image of Limited Good," *AA*, Vol. 67 (1965), 297–98.

93. Kearney, *The Winds of Ixtepeji*, 60.

94. Foster, "Peasant Society and the Image of Limited Good," *AA*, Vol. 67, 293–315.

95. In reconsidering his model of "Image of Limited Good," Foster admits that not all "goods" are in limited supply; one of these is "prestige" or, perhaps more properly, "respect"—see George M. Foster, "A Second Look at Limited Good," *Anthropological Quarterly*, Vol. 45 (1972), 57–64. Michael Kearney, "An Exception to the 'Image of Limited Good,'" *AA*, Vol. 71 (1969), 888–90, has argued that emotional experiences at fiestas also are infinite rather than finite in conception.

96. George M. Foster, *Tzintzuntzan*, 135.

97. For illustrations of gossip in a Zapotec community, see Parsons, *Mitla*, 386–478.

98. Chiñas, *The Isthmus Zapotecs*, 82.

99. Kearney, *The Winds of Ixtepeji*, 97–99.

100. Kearney, *The Winds of Ixtepeji*, 102.

101. *Ibid.*, 96.

102. *Ibid.*, 99.

103. *Ibid.*, 108–109.

104. The hot-cold classification of foods, related to the Hippocratic system, has been reported, with considerable variation, for the Southern Zapotecs, the sierra Zapotecs, and the Isthmus Zapotecs; it apparently is more weakly developed among the Valley Zapotecs; see Nader, "The Zapotec of Oaxaca," *HBMAI*, Vol. 7 (1969), 340.

105. My discussion of *muina* is based on Kearney, *The Winds of Ixtepeji*, 70–74.

106. My discussion of *susto* and its relationship to sex-role stress is based on Carl W. O'Nell and Henry A. Selby, "Sex Differences in the Incidence of Susto in Two Zapotec Pueblos: An Analysis of the Relationships between Sex Role Expectations and a Folk Illness," *Ethnology*, Vol. 7 (1968), 95–105.

107. Chiñas, *The Isthmus Zapotecs*, 110; isthmus women do most of the buying and selling in the market and are thus in contact with outsiders and others more frequently than are Valley Zapotec women.

108. O'Nell and Selby, "Sex Differences in the Incidence of Susto in Two Zapotec Pueblos," *Ethnology*, Vol. 7 (1968), 99.

109. *Ibid.*, 97. Carl O'Nell has conducted additional studies concerning the relationship between stress and the sexes in Zapotec culture; see his "Human Development in a Zapotec Community with Emphasis on Aggression Control and Its Study in Dreams," Ph.D. diss., University of Chicago, 1969, and "Aging in a Zapotec Community," *Human Development*, Vol. 15 (1972), 294–309.

110. Julio de la Fuente, "Las ceremonias de la lluvia entre los zapotecos de hoy," in *Proceedings of the 27th Annual Congress of Americanists*, Vol. 2 (México, 1947), 479–84.

111. Parsons, *Mitla*, 324ff.

112. Fadwa El Guinde, "The Nature of Belief Systems: A Structural Analysis of Zapotec Ritual," Ph.D. diss., University of Texas at Austin, 1972; my discussion of death, Christ, and the devil is based on this source.

113. Kearney, *The Winds of Ixtepeji*.

114. My discussion of witchcraft also is based on El Guinde, "The Nature of Belief Systems"; a forthcoming book by Henry A. Selby, *Zapotec Deviance* (Austin, Texas), will discuss witches as well as other deviants in another Zapotec community in the Valley of Oaxaca.

APPENDIX. ZAPOTEC KIN TERMS

1. Herbert R. Harvey, *Terminos de parentesco en el Otomangue, Departmento de Investigaciones Antropológicas*, Publication 13, Instituto Nacional de Antropología e Historia (México, 1963).

2. The entries for these terms may be found in Córdova, *Vocabulario*, 178r, 252v, 297r, 400v, and 402r. See also *Junta Colombina*, 66, 109, 135, and 200.

3. For these terms, see Córdova, *Vocabulario*, 4v, 178r, 400v, 402r; *Junta Colombina*, 138.

4. See Córdova, *Vocabulario*, 178r, 327v; *Junta Colombina*, 66, 138.

5. For these terms, see Córdova, *Vocabulario*, 219v, 282r, 382v; *Junta Colombina*, 88–89, 127, 138, 189.

6. Distinctions between consanguineals and affinals may be found in Córdova, *Vocabulario*, 102v, 103r, 301v; *Junta Colombina*, 29, 138.

7. The Juquila terms may be found in A. Kimball Romney, "Kinship and Family," *HBMAI*, Vol. 6 (1967), 235; the kin terms were collected by Laura Nader.

8. Julio de la Fuente, *Yalálag*, 166.

9. Romney, "Kinship and Family," *HBMAI*, Vol. 6 (1967), 217.

10. For Mitla and the Isthmus Zapotecs, see Elsie Clews Parsons, *Mitla*, 545; for Yatzachi el Bajo and Talea, see Romney, "Kinship and Family," *HMBAI*, Vol. 6 (1967), 235–36; and for Yalálag, see Fuente, *Yalálag*, 166.

11. For the Mitla terms, see Parsons, *Mitla*, 545–46; for Talea, see Romney, "Kinship and Family," *HBMAI*, Vol. 6 (1967), 235. The Talea terms were collected by Laura Nader.

12. For a good discussion of cousin terms and their possible correlations, see Jack Goody, "Cousin Terms," *SWJA*, Vol. 26 (1970), 125–42.

13. Harvey, *Terminos de parentesco en el Otomangue*.

Bibliography

References to all the literature used in the preparation of this book are given in the notes; bibliographic commentaries pertaining to specialized topics also may be found there. Below are listed only selected basic works on Oaxaca, some of which contain substantial bibliographies (marked *) and some of which treat in a general manner topics discussed in this book (marked †).

Acosta, Jorge R. "Preclassic and Classic Architecture of Oaxaca." In *Handbook of Middle American Indians,* Vol. 3. Ed. Robert Wauchope and Gordon R. Willey. Austin, University of Texas Press, 1965, pp. 814–36.

Alcina Franch, José. "Los dioses del panteón zapoteco," *Anales de Antropología,* Vol. 9 (1972), 9–40.

†Aldrich, Richard. *Style in Mexican Architecture.* Coral Gables, University of Miami Press, 1968.

†Barlow, R. H. *The Extent of the Empire of the Culhua-Mexica. Ibero-Americana,* No. 28. Berkeley and Los Angeles, University of California Press, 1949.

Beals, Ralph L. "Southern Mexican Highlands and Adjacent Coastal Regions: Introduction." In *Handbook of Middle American Indians,* Vol. 7. Ed. Robert Wauchope and Evon Z. Vogt. Austin, University of Texas Press, 1969, pp. 315–28.

———. "The Structure of the Oaxaca Market System," *Revista mexicana de estudios antropológicos,* Vol. 21 (1967), 333–42.

———. "Gifting, Reciprocity, Savings, and Credit in Peasant Oaxaca," *Southwestern Journal of Anthropology,* Vol. 26 (1970), 231–41.

———. *The Peasant Market System of Oaxaca, Mexico.* Los Angeles, University of California Press, forthcoming.

*Bernal, Ignacio. *Bibliografía de arqueología y etnografía: Mesoamerica y Norte de Mexico, 1514–1960.* México, Instituto Nacional de Antropología e Historia, 1962.

———. "Archaeological Synthesis of Oaxaca." In *Handbook of Middle American Indians,* Vol. 3. Ed. Robert Wauchope and Gordon R. Willey. Austin, University of Texas Press, 1965, pp. 788–813.

———. "Architecture in Oaxaca after the End of Monte Albán." In *Handbook of Middle American Indians,* Vol. 3. Ed. Robert Wauchope and Gordon R. Willey. Austin, University of Texas Press, 1965, pp. 837–48.

————. "The Mixtecs in Valley Archeology." In *Ancient Oaxaca: Discoveries in Mexican Archeology and History.* Ed. John Paddock. Stanford, Calif., Stanford University Press, 1966, pp. 345–66.

†————. *The Olmec World.* Berkeley and Los Angeles, University of California Press, 1969.

————. *The Ball Players of Dainzú.* Graz, Austria, forthcoming.

Berry, Charles R. "The Fiction and Fact of the Reform: The Case of the Central District of Oaxaca, 1856–1867," *The Americas,* Vol. 26 (1970), 277–90.

Boos, Frank H. *Ceramic Sculptures of Ancient Oaxaca.* South Brunswick, N.J., New York, and London, A. S. Barnes and Co., Inc., 1966.

*Bright, William. "Inventory of Descriptive Materials." In *Handbook of Middle American Indians,* Vol. 5. Ed. Robert Wauchope and Norman A. McQuown. Austin, University of Texas Press, 1967, pp. 9–62.

Burgoa, Fray Francisco de. *Geográfica descripción.* 2 Vols., México, Archivo General de la Nación, 1934 (original edition, 1674).

Butterworth, Douglas, ed. " 'Relaciones' of Oaxaca in the 16th and 18th Centuries," *Boletín de Estudios Oaxaqueños,* No. 23 (1963).

Cámara Barbachano, Fernando. "Mixtecos y zapotecos: antiguos y modernos." In *Homenaje a Pablo Martínez Del Río en el vigesimoseptimo aniversario de la primera edición de los Orígines Americanos.* México, 1961, pp. 373–85.

Carmichael, James H., ed. and trans. "Balsalobre on Idolatry in Oaxaca," *Boletín de Estudios Oaxaqueños,* No. 13 (1959).

Carrasco, Pedro. "Las culturas indígenas de Oaxaca, México," *América Indígena,* Vol. 2 (1951), 99–114.

†————. "Social Organization of Ancient Mexico." In *Handbook of Middle American Indians,* Vol. 10. Ed. Robert Wauchope, Gordon F. Ekholm, and Ignacio Bernal. Austin, University of Texas Press, 1971, pp. 349–75.

Caso, Alfonso. "The Mixtec and Zapotec Cultures: The Zapotecs," *Boletín de Estudios Oaxaqueños,* No. 21 (1962).

————. "Mixtec Writing and Calendar." In *Handbook of Middle American Indians,* Vol. 3. Ed. Robert Wauchope and Gordon R. Willey. Austin, University of Texas Press, 1965, pp. 948–61.

————. "Zapotec Writing and Calendar." In *Handbook of Middle American Indians,* Vol. 3. Ed. Robert Wauchope and Gordon R. Willey. Austin, University of Texas Press, 1965, pp. 931–47.

————. "Sculpture and Mural Painting of Oaxaca." In *Handbook of Middle American Indians,* Vol. 3. Ed. Robert Wauchope and Gordon R. Willey. Austin, University of Texas Press, 1965, pp. 849–70.

————. "Lapidary Work, Goldwork, and Copperwork in Oaxaca." In *Handbook of Middle American Indians,* Vol. 3. Ed. Robert Wauchope and Gordon R. Willey. Austin, University of Texas Press, 1965, pp. 896–930.

*————, and Ignacio Bernal. *Urnas de Oaxaca.* México, Instituto Nacional de Antropología e Historia, 1952.

————, and ————. "Ceramics of Oaxaca." In *Handbook of Middle American*

Indians, Vol. 3. Ed. Robert Wauchope and Gordon R. Willey. Austin, University of Texas Press, 1965, pp. 871–95.

————, ———— and Jorge R. Acosta. *La cérámica de Monte Albán*. México, Instituto Nacional de Antropología e Historia, 1967.

†Chevalier, François. *Land and Society in Colonial Mexico: The Great Hacienda*. Berkeley and Los Angeles, University of California Press, 1966.

Chance, John K. "Parentesco y residencia urbana: grupo familiar y su organización en un surburbio de Oaxaca, México," *América Indígena*, Vol. 33 (1973), 187–212.

Chiñas, Beverly. *The Isthmus Zapotecs: Women's Roles in Cultural Context*. New York, Holt, Rinehart, and Winston, 1973.

†Cline, H. F. "The Relaciones Geográficas of the Spanish Indies," *Hispanic American Historical Review*, Vol. 44 (1964), 341–74.

*Cook, Scott, and Martin Diskin, eds. *Markets in Oaxaca: Essays on a Regional Peasant Economy of Mexico*. Austin, University of Texas Press, forthcoming.

Córdova, Fray Juan de. *Vocabulario castellano-zapoteco*. México, Instituto Nacional de Antropología e Historia, 1942 (original edition, *Vocabulario en lengua zapoteca*, México, 1578).

————. *Arte del idioma zapoteca*. Morelia, Michoacán, Imprenta del Gobierno, 1886 (original edition, *Arte en lengua zapoteca*, México, 1578).

*Covarrubias, Miguel. *Mexico South: The Isthmus of Tehuantepec*. New York, Alfred A. Knopf, 1954.

†Cumberland, Charles C. *Mexico: The Struggle for Modernity*. London, Oxford, and New York, Oxford University Press, 1968.

Dennis, Philip A. "The Oaxacan Village President as Political Middleman," *Ethnology*, Vol. 12 (1973), 419–27.

†Eisenstadt, S. N. *The Political Systems of Empires*. New York, The Free Press, 1963.

*Fernández de Miranda, María Teresa. "Inventory of Classificatory Materials." In *Handbook of Middle American Indians*, Vol. 5. Ed. Robert Wauchope and Norman N. McQuown. Austin, University of Texas Press, 1967, pp. 63–78.

†Flannery, Kent V. "The Origins of the Village as a Settlement Type in Mesoamerica and the Near East." In *Man, Settlement, and Urbanism*. Ed. Peter J. Ucko, Ruth Tringham, and G. W. Dimbleby. London and Cambridge, Mass., 1972, pp. 23–53. Also a Warner Modular Publication, Reprint No. 1, Andover, Mass., 1972.

————. "The Olmec and the Valley of Oaxaca." In *Dumbarton Oaks Conference on the Olmec*. Ed. E. P. Benson. Washington, D.C., 1968, pp. 79–117.

————, Anne V. T. Kirkby, Michael J. Kirkby, and Aubrey W. Williams. "Farming Systems and Political Growth in Ancient Oaxaca," *Science*, Vol. 158, No. 3800 (Oct. 27, 1967), 445–54.

†Foster, George. *Culture and Conquest: America's Spanish Heritage*. Chicago, Quadrangle Books, 1960.

†————. *Tzintzuntzan: Mexican Peasants in a Changing World*. Boston, Little, Brown, and Co., 1967.

Fuente, Julio de la. "La cultura zapoteca," *Revista mexicana de estudios antropológicos*, Vol. 16 (1960), 233–46.

———. *Yalálag: Una villa zapoteca serrana*. Museo Nacional de Antropología Serie Científica, No. 1. México, 1949.

†Gerhard, Peter. *A Guide to the Historical Geography of New Spain*. Cambridge, Eng., Cambridge University Press, 1972.

†Gibson, Charles. *Spain in America*. New York, Harper and Row, 1966.

†———. *The Aztecs Under Spanish Rule: A History of the Indians of the Valley of Mexico, 1519–1810*. Stanford, California, Stanford University Press, 1964.

Hamnett, Brian R. *Politics and Trade in Southern Mexico, 1750–1821*. New York and Cambridge, Eng., Cambridge University Press, 1971.

Harvey, Herbert H. *Terminos de Parentesco en el Otomangue*. Departmento de Investigaciones Antropológicas Pub. No. 13. México, Instituto Nacional de Antropología e Historia, 1963.

*Iturribarría, Jorge Fernando. *Oaxaca en la historia: de la época procolombina a los tiempos actuales*. México, Editorial Stylo, 1955.

Junta Colombina. *Vocabulario castellano-zapoteco*. México, Oficina Tipográfica de la Secretaría de Fomento, 1893.

Kearney, Michael. *The Winds of Ixtepeji: World View and Society in a Zapotec Town*. New York, Holt, Rinehart, and Winston, 1972.

†Keith, Robert G. "Encomienda, Hacienda, and Corregimiento: A Structural Analysis," *Hispanic American Historical Review*, Vol. 51 (1971), 431–46.

Kirkby, Anne V. T. *The Use of Land and Water Resources in the Past and Present Valley of Oaxaca, Mexico*. Memoirs of the Museum of Anthropology, University of Michigan, No. 5 (Kent V. Flannery, gen. ed., Prehistory and Human Ecology of the Valley of Oaxaca, Vol. 1), Ann Arbor, 1973.

Lees, Susan H. *Sociopolitical Aspects of Canal Irrigation in the Valley of Oaxaca*. Memoirs of The Museum of Anthropology, University of Michigan, No. 6 (Kent V. Flannery, gen. ed., Prehistory and Human Ecology of the Valley of Oaxaca, Vol. 2), Ann Arbor, 1973.

Leslie, Charles M. *Now We Are Civilized: A Study of the World View of the Zapotec Indians of Mitla, Oaxaca*. Detroit, Wayne State University Press, 1960.

†Marino Flores, Anselmo. "Indian Population and Its Identification." In *Handbook of Middle American Indians*, Vol. 6. Ed. Robert Wauchope and Manning Nash. Austin, University of Texas Press, 1967, pp. 12–25.

Martínez Gracida, Manuel. *El rey Cocijoeza y su familia*. Oaxaca, 1972 (original edition, México, Oficina Tipográfico de la Secretaría de Fomento, 1888).

*Martínez Rios, Jorge. *Bibliografía antropológica y sociológica del Estado de Oaxaca*. México, Instituto de Investigaciones Sociales de la Universidad Nacional, 1961.

†McAlister, L. N. "Social Structure and Social Change in New Spain," *Hispanic American Historical Review*, Vol. 43 (1963), 349–70.

Mendieta y Núñez, Lucio. *Los zapotecos: Monografía histórica, etnográfica y económica*. México, Imprenta Universitaria, 1949.

†Mörner, Magnus. "Spanish-American Hacienda: A Survey of Recent Research and Debate," *Hispanic American Historical Review*, Vol. 53 (1973), 183–216.

Nader, Laura. *Talea and Juquila: A Comparison of Zapotec Social Organization*. University of California Publications in American Archaeology and Ethnology, Vol. 48, No. 3. Berkeley and Los Angeles, University of California Press, 1964.

*———. "The Zapotec of Oaxaca." In *Handbook of Middle American Indians*, Vol. 7. Ed. Robert Wauchope and Evon Z. Vogt. Austin, Texas, University of Texas Press, 1969, pp. 329–59.

O'Nell, Carl W., and Henry A. Selby. "Sex Differences in the Incidence of Susto in Two Zapotec Pueblos," *Ethnology*, Vol. 7 (1968), 95–105.

†Padden, R. C. *The Hummingbird and the Hawk: Conquest and Sovereignty in the Valley of Mexico, 1503–1541*. Columbus, Ohio State University Press, 1967.

Paddock, John. "Oaxaca in Ancient Mesoamerica." In *Ancient Oaxaca*. Ed. John Paddock. Stanford, Calif., Stanford University Press, 1966.

———. "Mixtec Ethnohistory and Monte Albán V." In *Ancient Oaxaca*. Ed. John Paddock. Stanford, Calif., Stanford University Press, 1966, pp. 367–85.

———. ed. *Ancient Oaxaca: Discoveries in Mexican Archeology and History*. Stanford, Calif., Stanford University Press, 1966.

Parsons, Elsie Clews. *Mitla: Town of the Souls and Other Zapoteco-Speaking Pueblos of Oaxaca, Mexico*. Chicago, University of Chicago Press, 1936.

Paso y Troncoso, Francisco del, ed. *Papeles de Nueva España*. Segunda serie, 9 vols. Madrid, Sucesores de Rivadeneyra, 1905–48.

Pérez García, Rosendo. *La Sierra Juárez*. 2 vols. México, Comisión del Papaloapan, 1956.

Pickett, V. B. "Type Linguistic Descriptions: Isthmus Zapotec." In *Handbook of Middle American Indians*, Vol. 5. Ed. Robert Wauchope and Norman A. McQuown. Austin, University of Texas Press, 1967, pp. 63–78.

†Redfield, Robert. *Peasant Society and Culture: An Anthropological Approach to Civilization*. Chicago, University of Chicago Press, 1956.

Rendón, Juan José. "Relaciones internas de las lenguas de la familia zapoteco-chatino," *Anales de Antropología*, Vol. 4 (1967), 187–90.

†Ricard, Robert. *The Spiritual Conquest of Mexico: An Essay on the Apostolate and the Evangelizing Methods of the Mendicant Orders in New Spain, 1523–1572*. Berkeley and Los Angeles, University of California Press, 1966.

Rojas, Basilio. *Miahuatlán: Un Pueblo de México*. 2 vols. México, n.s., 1963.

†Sahlins, Marshall D. *Tribesmen*. Englewood Cliffs, N.J., Prentice-Hall, Inc., 1968.

†Sanders, William T., and Barbara J. Price. *Mesoamerica: The Evolution of a Civilization*. New York, Random House, 1968.

Selby, Henry A. *Zapotec Deviance: The Convergence of Folk and Modern Sociology*. Austin, University of Texas Press, forthcoming.

Seler, Eduard. "The Wall Paintings of Mitla." In Bureau of American Ethnology *Bulletin No. 28*. (Washington, D.C., 1904), pp. 243–324.

*Smith, Mȧry Elizabeth. *Picture Writing from Ancient Southern Mexico: Mixtec Place Signs and Names.* Norman, University of Oklahoma Press, 1973.

†Soustelle, Jacques. *Daily Life of the Aztecs: On the Eve of Spanish Conquest.* New York, The Macmillan Co., 1961.

Spores, Ronald. "The Zapotec and Mixtec at Spanish Contact." In *Handbook of Middle American Indians,* Vol. 3. Ed. Robert Wauchope and Gordon R. Willey. Austin, University of Texas Press, 1965, pp. 962–86.

*———. *The Mixtec Kings and Their People.* Norman, University of Oklahoma Press, 1967.

Swadesh, Morris. "El idioma de los zapotecos." In *Los zapotecos.* Ed. Lucio Mendieta y Núñez. México, Imprenta Universitaria, 1949, pp. 415–49.

*Taylor, William B. *Landlord and Peasant in Colonial Oaxaca.* Stanford, Calif., Stanford University Press, 1972.

Ugalde, Antonio. "Contemporary Mexico: From Hacienda to PRI, Political Leadership in a Zapotec Village." In *The Caciques.* Ed. Robert Kern. Albuquerque, University of New Mexico Press, 1973, pp. 119–35.

Waterbury, Ronald. "Urbanization and a Traditional Market System." In *The Social Anthropology of Latin America: Essays in Honor of Ralph Leon Beals.* Ed. Walter Goldschmidt and Harry Hoijer. Los Angeles, Latin American Center, University of California, 1970, pp. 126–53.

†*Wauchope, Robert, ed. *Handbook of Middle American Indians.* 13 vols. Austin, University of Texas Press, 1964–74.

†Weaver, Muriel Porter. *The Aztecs, Maya, and Their Predecessors: Archaeology of Mesoamerica.* New York and London, Seminar Press, 1972.

†Wolf, Eric R. *Sons of the Shaking Earth.* Chicago, University of Chicago Press, 1959.

†———. *Peasants.* Englewood Cliffs, N.J., Prentice-Hall, Inc., 1966.

†———. "Levels of Communal Relations." In *Handbook of Middle American Indians,* Vol. 10, Ed. Robert Wauchope and Manning Nash. Austin, University of Texas Press, 1967, pp. 299–316.

Index